Fundamentals of U.S. Foreign Trade Policy

FUNDAMENTALS OF U.S. FOREIGN TRADE POLICY

Economics, Politics, Laws, and Issues

Stephen D. Cohen
The American University

Joel R. Paul
University of Connecticut

Robert A. Blecker
The American University

 WestviewPress
A Division of HarperCollins*Publishers*

Copyright © 1996 by Westview Press, Inc., A Division of HarperCollins Publishers, Inc.

Published in 1996 in the United States of America by Westview Press, Inc., 5500 Central Avenue,
Boulder, Colorado 80301-2877, and in the United Kingdom by Westview Press, 12 Hid's Copse Road,
Cumnor Hill, Oxford OX2 9JJ

Library of Congress Cataloging-in-Publication Data
Cohen, Stephen D.
    Fundamentals of U.S. Foreign trade policy : economics, politics,
laws, and issues / Stephen D. Cohen, Joel R. Paul, Robert A.
Blecker.
      p.   cm.
Includes bibliographical references and index.
ISBN 0-8133-1746-0. — ISBN 0-8133-1747-9 (pbk.)
    1. United States—Commercial policy.   2. Free trade—United
States.   3. Foreign trade regulation—United States.   4. United
States—Foreign economic relations.   I. Paul, Joel R.   II. Blecker,
Robert A., 1956–.   III. Title.
HF1455.C5758   1996
382'.3'0973—dc20   95-37934
                                                                                          CIP

The paper used in this publication meets the requirements of the American National Standard for
Permanence of Paper for Printed Library Materials Z39.48-1984.

10   9   8   7   6   5   4   3   2   1

Contents

List of Tables, Boxes, and Figures ix

Preface and Acknowledgments xi

List of Acronyms xv

PART ONE: OVERVIEW

1   The Content and Context of Trade Policy   3

    A Narrow Definition of Trade Policy   5

    The Political-Economic Context of Trade Policy   7

    Why Countries Import, and Why They Do Not   10

    Why Countries Export, and Why They Do Not   12

    The Unique Aspects of U.S. Trade Policy   15

    A Case Study in the Political Economy of U.S. Trade Policy   19

    Conclusion   23

    For Further Reading   23

    Notes   24

2   Historical Survey of U.S. Trade Relations   25

    A Conceptual Blueprint   25

    The First Stage of U.S. Trade Policy, 1789–1929   27

    Going to Extremes: Revolutionary Changes in the 1930s   31

    The United States as Hegemon: Internationalism Prevails in the 1950s and 1960s   34

    The Agonizing Reappraisal of the 1970s   38

    The 1980s and Early 1990s: Is Free Trade Policy Obsolete?   41

    The Evolution of U.S. Export Policy, 1949–1994   44

    Conclusion   49

    For Further Reading   50

    Notes   50

PART TWO: ECONOMICS

3   Economic Theories of International Trade   55

    Mercantilism   56

    Classical Trade Theory and Comparative Advantage   56

    Neoclassical Trade Theory   60

    The Gains from Trade and the Costs of Protection   61

    The Distribution of the Gains and Losses from Trade   62

Exceptions to the Case for Free Trade 66
Problems with Traditional Theories of Trade 69
New Trade Theories 72
Economic Integration and Trading Blocs 77
Conclusion 79
For Further Reading 80
Notes 80

4   Economic Determinants of a Nation's Trade Performance   83
The Significance of a Trade Balance 83
Domestic Economic Determinants of a Trade Balance 85
International Commercial Determinants 89
International Monetary Determinants: Exchange Rates 93
Patterns of Foreign Direct Investment 97
Conclusion 99
For Further Reading 99
Notes 100

PART THREE: POLITICS AND ADMINISTRATION

5   The Formulation and Administration of U.S. Trade Policy:
    Who Does What   105
The Basic Principles of U.S. Organizational Dynamics 105
The Executive Branch 108
The Legislative Branch 114
The Private Sector: Special Interest Groups and Lobbying 116
Conclusion 119
For Further Reading 119
Notes 119

6   Decisionmaking Explained: The How and Why of
    Policymakers' Behavior   121
The Inevitable Diversity of Trade Policymaking 121
The Government as Reactive Decisionmaker 124
The Government as Active Decisionmaker 129
Conclusion 139
For Further Reading 139
Notes 140

7   Legislation Regulating Imports and Exports   141
Trade Liberalization Measures 141
Relief from Fairly Priced Imports 142
Unfairly Priced Imports: The Problem of Dumping 146
Export Promotion Laws 152
Market-Opening Laws 153

Export Restrictions 155
Conclusion 158
For Further Reading 158
Notes 159

8   **The International Legal Framework: The General Agreement
    on Tariffs and Trade**   162
    The GATT in Domestic U.S. Law   162
    The Substance of the GATT's Rules   163
    Conclusion   170
    For Further Reading   171
    Notes   171

PART FOUR: MAJOR CONTEMPORARY ISSUES

9   **Japan: America's Strongest Economic Competitor**   175
    Unique Aspects of U.S.-Japanese Trade Relations   176
    Is Japan the Innocent Victim of Overly Aggressive U.S. Trade Policies?   179
    Is the United States the Unwitting Victim of Overly Aggressive Japanese
        Trade Policies?   180
    The Domestic Foundations of Japan's Export Success   182
    The Goals and Strategy of U.S. Trade Policy
        Toward Japan   184
    Conclusions and Outlook   192
    For Further Reading   193
    Notes   194

10   **European Union–United States Trade Relations**   196
    Unique Aspects of U.S.-European Union Trade Relations   197
    The EU's Institutional Framework: Evolution and Operation   199
    Family Feuds   204
    Food Fights   209
    Completing the Common Market: The Europe 1992 Exercise   211
    Conclusions and Outlook   213
    For Further Reading   214
    Notes   215

11   **Trade Relations with the Nonindustrialized Countries**   217
    Unique Aspects of U.S.-LDC Trade Relations   218
    U.S. LDC Trade Policy Giveth and Taketh   220
    The Advanced Developing Countries of East Asia   227
    Countries in Economic Transition   229
    Conclusions and Outlook   235
    For Further Reading   236
    Notes   236

12   Regional Trade Liberalization: The North American
     Free Trade Agreement   238
     History, Content, and Objectives   239
     The Importance of Symbolism in the NAFTA Debate   244
     Economic Arguments and Counterarguments   247
     The Final Phase: Marketing NAFTA   250
     Conclusions and Outlook   257
     For Further Reading   258
     Notes   258

13   Multilateral Trade Liberalization: The Uruguay Round Agreement   260
     Historical Precedents   261
     The Political Economy of Successful Negotiations   263
     The Substance of the Agreement   267
     Conclusions and Outlook   273
     For Further Reading   274
     Notes   274

14   Trade Policy Options for the Future   275
     The First Task: Identifying Economic Reality   276
     Options for Pursuing an Optimal Import Policy   277
     Options for Restructuring Export Policy   283
     Conclusions and Outlook   285
     For Further Reading   286
     Notes   287

15   The Unfinished Agenda   288
     Emerging Issues   288
     Longer-term Issues   290
     A Concluding Outlook   292
     For Further Reading   293
     Notes   293

Appendix A: U.S. International Trade in Goods and Services:
  Balance of Payments Basis   297
Appendix B: U.S. International Trade in Goods: Balance of Payments Basis,
  1980–1993   298
Appendix C: Commodity Composition of U.S. Goods Trade with the World:
  Census Basis, 1993   299
Appendix D: Country Composition of U.S. Goods Trade with the World:
  Census Basis, 1993   300
Appendix E: U.S. Manufactures Trade, 1987 and 1993   301
About the Book and Authors   303
Index   305

Tables, Boxes, and Figures

Tables

1.1 Trade policy spectrum	5
1.2 The China MFN trade dilemma	21
3.1 Distributional effects of free trade	63
4.1 U.S. saving and investment disequilibrium, 1988–1994	87
4.2 U.S. merchandise exports to South America in the 1980s and early 1990s	93
9.1 Bilateral U.S.-Japanese trade balances	177
11.1 Top ten suppliers of petroleum products to the United States in 1993	220
11.2 U.S.-Chinese trade	231
12.1 Comparison of U.S. global trade in manufactured goods with U.S.-Mexican trade in manufactured goods	243
13.1 Multilateral trade negotiations in the GATT, 1947–1979	262
13.2 Uruguay Round negotiating structure	265

Boxes

3.1 An example of Ricardian comparative advantage	58
4.1 The political and economic allure of orderly marketing agreements	91
9.1 If the Japanese market is so tough to penetrate, why bother?	186
12.1 Some projected industry job winners and losers from NAFTA	252
12.2 Interest group attitudes toward NAFTA	254

Figures

4.1 Impact of exchange rate changes on the U.S. merchandise trade balance	95
11.1 U.S. net import reliance for selected raw materials, 1993	221
11.2 U.S.-Chinese trade	232

Preface and Acknowledgments

There is no shortage of good academic literature dealing with the foreign trade policy of the United States. Lack of time to read the thousands of books and articles written on this subject is the problem, not the lack of alternatives. Texts on trade theory are so plentiful that they are outnumbered only by the writings with a "policy attitude"—argumentative pieces advocating fewer restrictions on imports, more import restrictions, adoption or nonadoption of industrial policies, and so on. Legal scholars have written hundreds of articles on the meaning and implications of U.S. domestic trade laws and on the international obligations incurred from adherence to the General Agreement on Tariffs and Trade (GATT). Business specialists have written instructional books for would-be exporters and importers. Political scientists continue to write about their quest for a single, unified theory to explain decision-making in U.S. trade policy. Relatively new issues such as the escalation of Japanese-U.S. trade frictions, the North American Free Trade Agreement, declining U.S. industrial competitiveness, and the relationship between trade and the environment have quickly generated numerous studies whose authors argue all conceivable points of view.

Nevertheless, one important kind of trade study is still missing: a basic text that comprehensively explains the content, context, and agenda of U.S. trade policy in terms of the dilemmas inherent in making difficult choices among competing ideas. In this book we argue that trade policy is the result of the perpetual need for policymakers to select from among legitimate albeit competing objectives. Specifically, these objectives are spread among the four components of foreign trade policy: domestic and external economic and political priorities that often suggest diametrically different policy alternatives.

This thesis is found obliquely r not at all in the other writings on this subject. Amid the mountain of literature, we have yet to encounter an academic text that formally recognizes and integrates the three principal elements shaping and moving U.S. trade policy: *economic theory, political necessity, and federal legislation.* It is the ever-changing hierarchy of these three elements that guarantees evolution and nuance in the U.S. government's export and import actions. Appreciation of the interrelationship among economics, politics, and to a lesser extent statutes is the first step in fully understanding the performance, objectives, limitations, virtues, and failures of U.S. trade policy.

Most existing works view U.S. trade policy in an overly narrow context as essentially a struggle between champions of free trade and advocates of protectionism. Export policy often is completely ignored in the literature; import policy and trade policy often are implicitly but erroneously portrayed as being synonymous. A majority of these works are theoretical discourses or efforts either to offer and defend a recommended new course of action or to critique past policy measures.

This book is designed to fill an important but long ignored niche in trade policy analysis by providing a fully integrated explanation of the complementary and conflicting forces that create contemporary U.S. trade policy. Our book does not take positions on the debates about which theory should dominate and about the efficacy of and changes needed in trade policies. The objective here is neither to reshape the policy debate nor to offer value judgments. Rather, we seek to educate all interested parties about the subtleties and the multiple layers of reality in U.S. trade policy. Our book is designed to cover objectively all the major fundamentals and principal contemporary issues of U.S. trade policy at a level of detail appropriate to a one-semester university or law school course.

One practical explanation for the dearth of literature creating a seamless web among the three basic elements composing trade policy—economics, politics, and statutes—is that extremely few trade-oriented academics are adequately trained in all three disciplines. In order to reap the benefits of a division of labor, this book has been written by three academics, each of whom has extensive background in at least two of these three disciplines. This is a joint collaboration to the extent that we read and critiqued one another's drafts, and changes were made as the result of this review process. However, every chapter was entirely written by one person. In view of this "exclusiveness" and the fact that the three of us did not agree in every case on nuances and priorities, each of us wishes to be held personally responsible for the content and accuracy of only our "proprietary" chapters. Robert A. Blecker, a professor in The American University's Economics Department, is the author of Chapter 3, which deals with the evolution of international trade theory. Joel R. Paul, a professor at the University of Connecticut School of Law, wrote the chapter dealing with U.S. import and export laws and the chapter detailing the obligations associated with U.S. participation in the GATT. Stephen D. Cohen, a professor in The American University's School of International Service, conceived the book, fashioned its organization, and wrote all of the remaining chapters. Steve Cohen also prepared the appendixes, which document some of the key statistics associated with U.S. imports and exports.

The contents of the book were enormously enhanced by the valuable comments received on many of its chapters from several experienced, insightful outside readers who collectively possess specialized expertise on many aspects of U.S. trade policy. We extend our collective appreciation (in alphabetical order) to Ray Ahearn, Bill Cromwell, Geza Feketekuty, Renee Marlin-Bennett, Terry McKinley, Dick Nanto, Walter Park, and Robert Scott for their time and valuable advice. Needless to say, the authors take full responsibility for any factual errors and all conclusions to be found in their respective chapters.

A major expression of gratitude is also extended to six persons, all working as graduate assistants to Stephen D. Cohen, for their invaluable contributions to the preparation of this book. James Walsh and Jeffrey Miller provided excellent research and editing assistance and wrote portions of the European Union chapter. Final preparation of the manuscript was expedited and made more accurate because of the excellent editing help of James Lang, Kevin Opstrup, Russ Pennington, and Tara Rice. Finally, thanks are due to James Benseler and Robert O'Dair for their assistance in typing parts of the manuscript.

Stephen D. Cohen
Joel R. Paul
Robert A. Blecker
Washington, D.C.

Acronyms

AFL-CIO	American Federation of Labor and Congress of Industrial Organizations
APEC	Asia-Pacific Economic Cooperation
CAP	Common Agricultural Policy
CBI	Caribbean Basin Initiative
CBO	Congressional Budget Office
CEA	Council of Economic Advisers
COCOM	Coordinating Committee on Multilateral Export Controls
COMECON	Council for Mutual Economic Assistance
EAA	Export Administration Act
EAI	Enterprise for the Americas Initiative
EC	European Community
ECSC	European Coal and Steel Community
EEC	European Economic Community
EFTA	European Free Trade Association
EU	European Union
FCPA	Foreign Corrupt Practices Act
FDI	foreign direct investment
GATS	general agreement on trade in services
GATT	General Agreement on Tariffs and Trade
GDP	gross domestic product
GSP	Generalized System of Preferences
HDTV	high-definition television
H-O	Heckscher-Ohlin (trade model)
IEEPA	International Emergency Economic Powers Act
IMF	International Monetary Fund
ITA	International Trade Administration
ITC	International Trade Commission
ITO	International Trade Organization
LDCs	less developed countries
MFA	Multifiber Arrangement
MITI	Ministry of International Trade and Industry (Japan)
MFN	most favored nation
MNCs	multinational corporations
MOSS	market-oriented, sector-selective
MTNs	multilateral trade negotiations

NAFTA	North American Free Trade Agreement
NATO	North Atlantic Treaty Organization
NICs	newly industrialized countries
NSC	National Security Council
NTBs	nontariff barriers
OECD	Organization for Economic Cooperation and Development
OMAs	orderly marketing agreements
OMB	Office of Management and Budget
OPEC	Organization of Petroleum Exporting Countries
R&D	research and development
RTAA	Reciprocal Trade Agreements Act
SII	Structural Impediments Initiative
SPS	sanitary and phytosanitary measures
TRIMs	trade-related investment measures
TRIPs	trade-related intellectual property rights
TWEA	Trading with the Enemy Act
USTR	U.S. Trade Representative
VERs	voluntary export restraints
WTO	World Trade Organization

Fundamentals of U.S. Foreign Trade Policy

Part One

Overview

1 The Content and Context of Trade Policy

Foreign trade can be described as existing on two different levels. Outwardly, it consists of an economic transaction in which goods and services are exchanged for money (or other goods) by persons or entities in two different countries. Inwardly, it is a political process in which difficult choices must be made among competing values, priorities, and interest groups. Whatever the level of analysis, foreign trade is important. The international exchange of goods and services has increased in value and volume to the point at which it has become a pivotal factor in both the conduct of international relations and national economic performance.

Foreign trade policy is a convergence point. To understand trade policy in the broadest sense, it should be viewed as the end product of an official process involving decisions that need to reconcile economic and political substance at the same time that they need to advance governments' domestic and foreign concerns. These decisions are seldom taken independently of numerous trade statutes and international agreements that play a critical role in determining the content of trade policy's substance and process. In the United States, the trade laws passed by Congress set guidelines and boundaries for the executive branch's implementation of policy. Although laws are often a factor influencing specific trade policy decisions, trade statutes themselves emerge as outgrowths of a larger process: They are the manifestation of a political interpretation of what good economic policy should be.

The foreign trade policy of the United States consists of an infinite number of pressure points and is constrained by domestic laws and international obligations. It is filled with inconsistencies and shortcomings that baffle and annoy casual observers. These negative traits can best be explained by understanding the multiple forces that form the guiding principles of and the implementation of day-to-day actions in U.S. trade policy. The objective of this book is to provide that understanding by means of a detailed explanation of what this policy is and why it takes the forms that it does.

The economics and politics of U.S. foreign trade policy are two distinct phenomena shaped and guided by different forces. They do not necessarily move toward the same goals for the same reasons. The disconnect between politics and economics is observable in the dramatic 1934 shift in U.S. policy priorities from a historical embrace of protectionism to a forceful pursuit of global trade liberalization. This policy about-face did *not* occur and continue because the scholarly output of economists

3

succeeded in converting official Washington to the belief that a liberal trade policy was in the national interest. Rather, the change was sustained by emergence of a critical mass in the private sector's support for reducing U.S. trade barriers in return for enhanced opportunities to increase American exports.

In Hegelian terms, the economic thesis that a market-oriented global trading system was most compatible with U.S. economic interests grew increasingly dominant beginning in the mid-1930s. The political antithesis that politicians elected to national office should protect constituents from import competition suffered a relative decline. The result was a reorientation of the policy synthesis that continues through the present. The emphasis on escalating U.S. import barriers was abandoned. The new emphasis consists of an ongoing series of trade liberalization initiatives whose perceived economic virtues are partially constrained by legislated relief measures. The latter consist of relatively circumscribed, case-by-case provisions giving domestic interest groups the opportunity to petition for relief from alleged import-induced economic hardship or for the government's assistance in attacking foreign trade barriers.

Our study's integrating theme is that the task of formulating and conducting U.S. trade policy is an inherently difficult, inconsistent, and imprecise process. Trade policymaking involves both reconciliations and trade-offs among a variety of economic goals and political necessities. The executive and legislative branches of the government as well as the private sector usually must sort through numerous conflicting views in the effort to determine what constitutes "good policy."

U.S. trade policy exists on many planes of reality. The U.S. government (like its counterparts) professes to believe in free trade while increasing its trade barriers; it professes to believe in a global trade regime based on universal rules while negotiating exclusionary free trade agreements with other countries; and it professes to believe in export promotion while restricting exports to one country after another. There is method to the madness. The complexity and paradoxes of U.S. trade policy are due mainly to the existence of four principal factors, the first three of which are burdened by limited and often contradictory data:

1. the frequent conflict between economic logic and political necessity;
2. the conceptual disagreement among economists as to whether optimal trade policy is one that relies on free markets or one that incorporates repeated government intervention;
3. the intricate, ever-changing linkage between trade and other economic and political policy sectors, both domestic and foreign;
4. the diffusion of authority between the executive and legislative branches in formulating trade policy. Major limitations on presidential action are imposed by a voluminous, still-growing body of congressionally passed laws that affect all aspects of the conduct of U.S. trade relations.

In this chapter we review universal fundamentals of trade policy that influence its formulation and conduct, thereby establishing the rationale for the content of subsequent chapters. A concluding section deals with the unique characteristics of U.S. trade policy that differentiate it from worldwide concepts of trade policy.

A Narrow Definition of Trade Policy

Throughout history, trade policy—in a literal, narrow sense—has consisted of a constantly evolving series of official objectives, laws, and actions designed to influence the flow of imports and exports of goods and services in a manner different from what would otherwise occur in a free market. At any point in time, governments choose from among a wide spectrum of trade policy actions that fall between the two poles of total inaction and aggressive, comprehensive intervention. At one extreme, a government could adopt a completely *free* trade stance and consistently refuse to act for *any* reason to directly affect the flow of its exports and imports. Under this scenario, a country would totally avoid official import barriers and export controls or incentives. In addition, a country would dismiss the notion that the trade-restricting and -distorting policies maintained by its trading partners were on balance economically injurious to it. If a sovereign government ever chose this extreme course of policy action (none has), it would effectively have chosen to have no trade policy. At the other policy extreme, a government could essentially opt out of participating in the international economy by adopting pervasive, highly restrictive import barriers and by exporting little or nothing.

Defined in a narrow sense, trade policymaking in the United States (and in virtually every other country) is the act of determining how to find the optimal point along the policy continuum illustrated in Table 1.1. Calculations of the optimal trade-off between market orientation and interventionism must be made separately for imports and exports, the two core components of trade policy.

Import policy determines the relative openness of the home market to competition from foreign-produced goods and services. It does so mainly by judging where, at any given time, the most economically advantageous and politically comfortable location is on a spectrum that spans two poles:

TABLE 1.1 Trade Policy Spectrum

Intrusive Government Intervention	Moderate Government Intervention	Free Market Orientation
Extensive import protection; extensive export restraints; industrial policy supporting targeted industries	Ad hoc measures	Avoidance of import and export barriers; minimal governmental support of domestic industries

1. pursuit of "liberal" (or freer) trade based on an international division of labor. In this instance, market forces are emphasized; import barriers are reduced; all countries are encouraged to produce the goods that they can produce *relatively* efficiently and import those they cannot produce *relatively* cheaply; and the private sector is allowed to determine the amounts, kinds, and sources of foreign-made goods available to domestic consumers.

2. emphasis on "protectionist" measures. In this case, domestic production is given a maximum shield from fair foreign competition in order to retain existing production and jobs and in some cases to encourage the development of new industries. The desires to minimize hardships on domestic workers and companies or to support economic planning goals take preference over the alternative priorities of minimizing prices and maximizing consumption.

Erection of new import barriers under certain circumstances, however, can be in full conformity with internationally recognized trade standards. Retaliatory import duties imposed when exporters engage in the practice of recognized *un*fair foreign trade practices (described in this chapter) and injure domestic producers is considered legitimate self-defense, not protectionism.

Export policy has three basic dimensions: (1) use of governmental personnel and funds to promote foreign sales; (2) export controls that use domestic laws to restrict export of certain goods to unfriendly countries; and (3) export enhancement efforts through official pursuit of improved access to foreign markets. As with import policy, export policy for any given country at any given time is to be found on a continuum between a noninterventionist, free market approach and an aggressive, interventionist posture. The first approach allocates responsibility for export enhancement to private sector efforts and exchange rate realignments. The interventionist posture, in turn, can be tilted in one of two opposite directions. The first is an export-at-all-costs approach; in this instance, government officials adopt tunnel vision—to avoid being distracted by alternative strategies—and mount an extensive, expensive campaign to maximize overseas sales, presumably in an effort to achieve the largest possible trade surplus. A government tilted in the second direction is quick to embrace export restraints because of its willingness to subordinate the priority of export maximization to ethical and national security concerns. This approach condones the blockage of shipments abroad as the means of applying pressure on foreign governments to alter what are deemed to be their undesirable human rights, political, or military policies.

Trade policy also can be divided between proactive and reactive actions. The former are initiatives conceived to advance a country's perceived self-interests. For example, a trade policy decision to impose a new import barrier to enhance a favored domestic industry is proactive (but a possible violation of the theory and practice of liberal trade). A "passive" variant of proactive trade policy would be decisions *not* to act, for example rejecting pleas from a domestic industry for import protection. In other cases, trade decisions can be defined as being defensive in nature when they are taken in response to actions or policies originating in other countries.

Economists generally wish to maximize consumption, and virtually every one of them would agree that for maximizing efficiency and global welfare, an essentially open system that encourages trade flows is preferable to a tightly closed system that stifles trade. Nevertheless, the political leaders of the United States and those of every other sovereign country are, for a variety of reasons, unwilling to accept a totally hands-off approach to trade flows. The desire of politicians to seek favor with the electorate is incompatible with their placing complete trust in the invisible hand of the market to determine the composition, volume, and value of its imports and exports of goods and services. The result, simply stated, is that an interventionist, market-altering strategy dominates the conduct of all countries' trade policies. To achieve these ends, government officials—in accordance with the terms of foreign trade statutes—make a steady stream of specific decisions, conduct endless rounds of trade negotiations with other countries, and implement numerous operational programs to moderate imports, increase imports, promote exports, restrict exports, assist domestic producers to compete more effectively, and so on. Trade policy in one sense is the collective outcome of the twists and turns of these actions. Given constant changes in the political and economic environments, the import and export policies of the United States and most other countries are subject to constant evolution—and occasional revolution.

The Political-Economic Context of Trade Policy

If politics is about making important and difficult decisions affecting national welfare, then the trade policy process in the United States and elsewhere has been politicized. The foreign trade sector is an increasingly important variable in the performance of domestic economies, and the ability of national politicians to remain in office is closely linked to domestic economic performance, mainly the ability to deliver on promises of more jobs and less inflation. Conflicting opinions about optimal trade policies in response to an open-ended number of contingencies have assured a constant procession of difficult decisions.

Inspired by certain cherished economic principles, observing the need to be responsive to domestic and foreign political pressures, and operating within legislative constraints, U.S. trade policymakers are confronted by the need to make an endless series of value judgments in situations where the "correct" response is more a perception than an empirically demonstrable or self-evident truth. Virtually every significant trade issue will generate two or more rational alternatives as to which policy option will best serve the national interest. Political necessity and economic logic frequently are not congruent. In a sense, trade policy is the cumulative outgrowth of responses by usually well-intentioned policymakers to a barrage of intellectual and emotional stimuli and to a nonstop array of unique circumstances. Consistency, coherence, and wisdom are therefore frequently in short supply in a process involving so many difficult decisions.

Jobs, production, profits, and investment decisions at home and abroad are inevitably affected by what is and is not imported and exported. Ostensibly economic actions therefore closely dovetail with the classic definition of politics: the determination of who gets what, how, and when. Most trade policy decisions create winners and losers at home. The ability of consumers to enjoy inexpensive goods produced abroad comes at least partially at the expense of fellow citizens' jobs or salary levels. Conversely, import restrictions that prevent lower-cost foreign-made goods from disrupting favored domestic sectors often are tantamount to governmental subsidies bestowed on relatively inefficient producers, with consumers paying for them in the form of higher prices. In this case, foreign producers are penalized along with domestic consumers.[1]

Foreign trade also affects politics on the global level. Extensive commercial relations between countries create networks of interdependence, cooperation, and friendship. The exclusion of commercial relations between countries can create divisiveness and hostility.

In the absence of applicable universally accepted truths as to what constitutes economic logic, trade policy should be viewed as the end result of imperfect choices about economic options—a political process. Policymakers make decisions about relative importance and desirability offered by conflicting constituencies and policy options. Trade policy dilemmas abound because, more often than not, any given trade action involves contradictory rather than complementary effects on political and economic as well as domestic and external objectives; in short, the impact of a typical trade action is favorable to some, detrimental to others.

If one accepts the thesis that the "central feature of American politics is the fragmentation and dispersion of power and authority,"[2] it is obvious that the U.S. pursuit of a liberal trading system is perpetually saddled with policy compromises. Seldom explained in the traditional debate about freer trade versus protectionism is the U.S. government's political need to provide a sense of fair play, balance, and equity in its trade policy that is sufficient to prevent the formation of an overpowering anti-import coalition of aggrieved interest groups. The goal of maximizing economic efficiency is in constant tension with the political necessity of ensuring that the losers from increased imports are not too numerous, do not suffer too much, and are not displaced too rapidly. Since the end of World War II, Congress has consistently expanded and altered U.S. trade statutes to assure that there will be a minimum level of protection of the rights of domestic companies and workers to seek relief from import-induced injury, as well as opportunity to demand redress from foreign barriers against their exports. Within these same trade laws, Congress repeatedly has delegated power to the executive branch to pursue the long-term goal of a more liberal international economic order.

Trade policy decisions are not made in a vacuum. The full scope of trade relations is best described as a diverse, expanding agenda of issues that is the focal point for four critical policy spokes feeding into it:

- domestic politics
- international politics (foreign policy)

- domestic economic performance
- international economic efficiency

Linkage is an inescapable fact. Virtually every major foreign trade decision simultaneously affects the performance of the U.S. economy (in terms of employment, income, and price stability), other countries' economies, the welfare of domestic interest groups and factions, and political relations with foreign countries.

The demarcation line between trade policy and domestic economic policy management continues to blur. Trade policy now overlaps with an expanding cluster of economic issues that have traditionally been considered "domestic" in nature: monetary and fiscal (tax) policies; industrial policy measures such as corporate tax incentives and research subsidies; regulatory provisions covering environmental protection, safety, and health standards; agricultural subsidies; labor conditions and worker training programs; enforcement of antitrust laws; and so on. The old foreign policy adage that countries do not intrude into the internal affairs of other countries has been rendered obsolete. Whether deliberate or inadvertent, these ostensibly internal economic measures influence the cost structure of a country's products and therefore the value and product composition of its foreign trade flows.

Another line of demarcation that continues to blur is the one between national security ("high" foreign policy) objectives and international commercial ("low" foreign policy) objectives. There is a growing consensus that economic strength is now an integral part of the national security equation. Defense of domestic political values (e.g., opposition to human rights abuses) can lead to imposition of trade sanctions that could damage U.S. political and economic relations with other countries (see the China case study, later in this chapter). A hard-line defense of domestic U.S. industrial interests can push the United States on a collision course with a close overseas military ally.

The maxim that trade policy will be made in a manner consistent with the "national interest" is too vague to provide a sophisticated understanding of the subject. Government agencies seldom find it a simple task to agree on exactly which policy option in any given case would maximize the national interest, and they often have to adopt cumbersome compromises in charting a course of action. The attainment of a relatively open trading system that imposes few barriers to an efficient global allocation of resources while simultaneously inflicting minimum dislocations on domestic producers is a good all-encompassing definition of the national interest in trade policy. However, it is too general to provide a practical guideline for predicting or explaining individual policy decisions. In any event, economic efficiency must be viewed as only one possible priority in foreign trade. Social equity and national security are worthy contenders for the top priority position.

Definitions of "good" trade policy are shaped by the value judgments of individual observers. To some, the international flow of goods and services is mainly an inherent part of domestic social and political policies. To others, it is mainly a dimension of foreign policy. Domestic workers and business executives tend to view trade as a choice between opportunities for and threats to the generation and distribution of income, depending on which direction international commerce is flowing. Economists have traditionally viewed trade as a means of increasing efficiency by allocating the world's finite resources to their most productive use, thereby maximizing production and consumption.[3] Foreign affairs specialists would identify with the perspective of Cordell Hull, U.S. secretary of state from 1933 to 1944, that the trading system represents either support for or a threat to a peaceful international political system, depending on whether governments are moving toward a more open or a more restrictive flow of trade. In fact, trade policy is all of the above—and more. As already suggested, there are many layers of reality in international trade policy.

Why Countries Import, and Why They Do Not

All countries import goods and services from others because every country realizes that the practice of autarky (economic self-sufficiency) would render its national economy more underdeveloped and inefficient than if it avoided economic isolation. All governments engaging in trade do so, not because of altruism, but because they believe that being part of what is known as the international division of labor is cost-effective; that is, over time, more benefits are received than costs are incurred. Foreign competition is rightly seen as encouraging price discipline among domestic producers.

Nevertheless, bitter opposition inevitably arises among the political, business, and social leaders of all countries concerning the wisdom and equity of allowing the unlimited importing of goods made more cheaply in other countries. This explains the decision by all sovereign governments to impose some constraints on imports that compete with domestic production rather than to adopt the pure free trade policy option.

On one level, economically advanced countries do practice a largely hands-off approach. Import policy is seldom applicable in cases involving "noncompetitive" imports—goods that either are not available in the home market or are deemed by economic planners to be something that should not be made domestically. To the extent that they can afford them, countries usually are content to import whatever they need in terms of nonindigenously produced natural resources (e.g., petroleum) and manufactured goods like supercomputers and jumbo jet passenger planes. Purely economic considerations usually dominate as long as imported goods cause no harm to domestic producers. The United States imposes no trade barriers on such goods as bananas, coffee, or manganese because there is no domestic constituency to plead for import relief.

The public's desire to import begins with the simple economic decision of domestic consumers to favor foreign-produced goods over domestic equivalents. One of the most common reasons for such behavior is lower prices. Usually, lower prices reflect greater efficiency and lower production costs abroad, but sometimes they are due to unfair trade practices, such as sales at less than fair value, governmental subsidies, and violations of intellectual property rights. The motivation for importing can also be based on nonprice considerations, such as the desire to obtain higher-quality goods and the need to offset goods in short supply relative to domestic demand (the United States is the world's largest oil importer despite being among the three largest oil producers).

Importing goods, competitive or not, indirectly serves two international policy objectives. First, there is the old axiom in international economics that trade is a two-way street. If other countries are to be able and willing to buy your goods, they must be allowed to earn foreign exchange by exporting to your country. Second, the basic foreign policy goal of enhanced political friendships with other countries is served through expanding trade relationships.

The so-called dynamic benefits of trade provide yet another layer of encouragement for a country to import. When countries join together in a free trade area to phase out trade barriers, the result, other things being equal, may be a virtuous cycle that enhances production efficiency. Companies either sink or swim in an enlarged market that encourages the cycle of increased trade flows, stable or lower prices, increased real incomes, and increased domestic economic growth. Guesstimates of increases in GDP were regularly included in forecasts of the effects of creating the single European market and the North American free trade area.[4]

A government's desire to place limitations on imports of goods and services in direct competition with domestic producers begins with a fundamental political reality: Foreigners do not vote. Nothing in the theory of free trade says that *everyone* in a given country will benefit from it. In the short run, there are losers whenever imports increase fast enough relative to domestic production that they cause the loss of jobs, the bankruptcies of companies, or the decimation of entire industries.[5] No democratically elected government can continuously turn a deaf ear to any and all instances of pleas by workers and companies for protection from economic displacement by or income losses from imports. Nor can it totally ignore the social and economic costs involved in cases where a community is threatened with loss of its largest factory to import competition. It is therefore not surprising that international trade guidelines permit the imposition of *temporary* import restraints in the event that increased imports cause or threaten to cause "serious injury" to domestic producers. Countries therefore have a legal right under the General Agreement on Tariffs and Trade (GATT) to invoke the so-called safeguard mechanism (see Chapter 7). The presumption is made that import-impacted producers will use their temporary respite from intensifying import competition to restructure and modernize themselves and then will emerge strong enough to hold their own against foreign competition.

The international trade regime countenances three other major contingencies involving fair foreign competition in which imposition of temporary import restraints is legally justifiable:

- promotion of infant industries, whereby governments seek to foster the creation and maturation of a new industry that would otherwise have no chance to develop in the face of existing levels of import competition;
- preservation of industries that a country deems vital to its national security;
- limitations imposed by a deteriorating balance of payments position, in which declining earnings of foreign exchange inhibit a country's ability to pay for all of its import needs.

Contemporary international trade rules also accept as legitimate and appropriate the imposition of import barriers to negate three major *unfair* trading practices by other countries that injure or threaten to injure domestic producers:

- dumping, or the overseas sales of goods at less than fair value, either because export prices are set below domestic market prices in the exporting country or because export prices are below production costs;
- governmental subsidies that enable exporters to reduce prices from levels that would have prevailed in the absence of such subsidies;
- violations of intellectual property rights, or the unauthorized use (in this case by a foreign company) of a company's patents, trademarks, copyrights, business secrets, and so on. The United States retains a provision in its law that enables it to act unilaterally to bar imports of goods made by foreign firms that are violating U.S. companies' intellectual property rights.

Use of import barriers for retaliatory and political purposes constitutes a final category of acceptable trade-restrictive behavior. Import controls have the effect of denying foreign currency earnings to countries deemed to be guilty of such political transgressions as posing a military threat to others, violating human rights of their own citizens, and flouting international law (such as Iran's seizure of U.S. diplomats in 1979). Import sanctions may be imposed in a range extending from a unilateral basis up to collective action taken by all member countries of the United Nations (such as economic sanctions against South Africa). Import barriers also are imposed on a tit-for-tat basis for commercial reasons (sometimes in conformity with internationally accepted trade practices and sometimes not) as retaliation against countries (e.g., Japan) whose import barriers have been judged deleterious to the exports of others.

Why Countries Export, and Why They Do Not

A thriving export sector is a thing of absolute joy to political leaders. Although abandoned by most economists in the late eighteenth century, the theory of *mercantilism* (which equates a trade surplus with national wealth and power) still is embraced by almost everyone else.[6] Balance of payments surpluses no longer automatically trigger an offsetting inflow of shiny gold bars as they did under the gold standard, but the many positive economic trends associated with export growth explain why politicians (and workers) still have a love affair with exports. A sustained increase in the volume of exports will, in most cases, generate new jobs tending to pay above-average wages (because export workers usually have above-average productivity), increase corporate profits, increase tax revenues, encourage capital expenditures on new plant and capital equipment, and enhance the image of domestic economic vigor. Exports also add to foreign exchange earnings and support the strength of a country's currency in the foreign exchange market. Since exporters tend to be relatively large, efficient, and influential producers, politicians are happier (and, presumably, more re-electable) when these politically potent interests are happy.

In a world economy increasingly dominated by high-technology goods with high fixed costs (costly research and development [R&D] programs and expensive production facilities, for example), exports have another crucial economic role to play. High-tech companies must achieve *economies of scale* through maximum production and maximum sales. The greater the sales volume, the easier it is for a company to amortize (i.e., spread) high fixed costs and to reduce unit prices. To realize maximum sales volume, manufacturers cannot be limited to a single home market. The pursuit of economies of scale explains the move by all large industrial companies in all industrialized countries to global marketing strategies. The disappearance of national markets is epitomized by the hypothetical Belgian producer of machine tools that cannot possibly achieve optimal sales volume by selling only in its small home market. Even the $7 trillion U.S. economy is too confining to absorb efficiently the enormous fixed costs incurred by high-tech producers of such capital-intensive goods as jumbo jets and supercomputers. In sum, a successful global marketing effort is a necessity for high-tech manufacturers wishing to enjoy growth, profits, and longevity. The almost certain alternative to generating a large volume of international sales is to watch lower-cost, higher-volume, globally active competitors steadily decimate a stay-at-home company's market share.

The recognized advantages of exporting have spawned a standard menu of official export promotion programs maintained by all industrialized countries. They differ only in their magnitude and effectiveness, which are largely determined by budgetary resources and the competence in business matters of bureaucratic personnel, respectively. Perhaps the single most important export promotion program is officially subsidized export financing facilities (in the United States this function is rendered mainly by the Export-Import Bank). These programs provide foreign buyers of a country's goods with concessional, or below market, lending terms. If an export order runs in the tens of millions of dollars, such as is the case with jumbo jets and nuclear power plants, the ability of the buyer to obtain a loan with a relatively small down payment, low interest rate, and extended repayment period is frequently the determining factor as to which country gets the export order.

Governments also promote exports by sponsoring trade missions and trade fairs in foreign markets and by providing export awareness facilities at home to small companies that are new to exporting. Some countries provide direct funding or tax deductions to defray expenses incurred by companies in overseas market development efforts. Commercial attachés stationed overseas in embassies and consulates provide expertise in how foreign markets operate to potential exporters, conduct overseas marketing surveys, and ferret out and address foreign import barriers. On a macroeconomic basis, governments can indirectly promote exports by minimizing the costs of capital through low interest rates, providing favorable corporate tax treatment, and keeping their currency low in value relative to other currencies (hence the periodic efforts by U.S. officials to "talk down" the exchange rate of the dollar). Most of the pillars of industrial policy, such as subsidies and lax antitrust enforcement, also can contribute to export expansion.

On the other side of the coin are programs involving export restraints and embargoes, most of which are foreign policy measures designed to influence the political behavior of other countries. Except in very special circumstances, however, this option is a disdained aspect of ongoing export policy—in every country except the United States. The one purely economic reason found in U.S. law to restrain or prohibit export shipments occurs in cases of domestic shortages where large foreign sales would aggravate rapidly rising prices at home. In addition to wanting to contain domestic inflation, a government may wish to limit exports of nonreplenishable raw materials so as to delay their depletion. Exports (usually of primary products) may also be limited as part of an effort to maintain or boost the price of goods. This ploy is best exemplified by occasional efforts by major oil-producing countries to limit production and foreign sales.

Politicians and businesspeople are otherwise ecstatic about export maximization, but foreign policy practitioners, especially those in the United States, perceive a high-level national security need for a policy denying exports of goods capable of enhancing the military might of unfriendly countries. Whereas there is no disagreement among the industrialized countries about the need to restrict most weaponry, there has been no agreement about how far to extend export controls to so-called dual-use goods like computers, telecommunications equipment, and even trucks—all of which are commercial goods but can be adapted to military purposes. Export controls are also utilized as a middle-ground foreign policy strategy falling between inaction and military attack; as noted later, the United States has been the most frequent practitioner of this approach. In theory, disruption of trade can wreak sufficient havoc on the economy of a targeted country that it feels compelled to alter or cease certain domestic or external policies deemed by embargoing countries to be in violation of the norms of acceptable state behavior (e.g., human rights violations or state-sponsored terrorism).

Orderly marketing agreements are a final example of export restraints. In the early 1970s, the United States and what was then known as the European Community embraced the middle ground of negotiated protectionism as a politically attractive compromise between free trade and unilaterally imposed import barriers. This tactic takes the form of applying pressure on other countries, usually in East Asia, to agree "voluntarily" to restrain their exports of manufactured goods. In return for this concession, exporting countries get a voice in establishing annual export ceilings; the alternative is to face harsher, unilateral restrictions imposed by countries deeming it necessary to restrain rates of import growth for goods such as textiles, steel, and automobiles.

The Unique Aspects of U.S. Trade Policy

There are a number of economic and political idiosyncrasies in U.S. import and export policies that differentiate them in many ways from the trade policies of other industrialized countries. As a consequence, the basic principles of U.S. trade attitudes and actions discussed in subsequent chapters cannot always be extrapolated to provide an explanation of how and why other countries formulate trade policies as they do.

In the first place, shared political authority imposes a unique balancing act in the formulation and administration of U.S. trade policy. The constitutionally mandated separation of powers among branches of government assures that the joint roles of the executive and legislative branches (and occasionally the judicial branch), as well as the number of laws guiding executive branch behavior, are unlike anything found in any other country. One of the most common misperceptions about U.S. trade policy is that the president is fully in charge and does as he sees fit. As explained in Chapter 5, presidential trade power is formally limited to whatever authority Congress consents to transfer via trade legislation.

The strong political element of U.S. trade policy is reinforced by the divergent predilections that usually prevail in these two branches of government. On a purely informal, implicit basis, one branch places the burden of proof on interest groups advocating freer trade; the other branch places the burden of proof on interest groups advocating protectionist policies. The U.S. legislative branch tends to be relatively more sympathetic to responding to complaints of domestic constituents suffering from import competition than to pursuing global priorities. Most members of Congress are amenable to assuring that administrative procedures (described in Chapter 7) are readily available for addressing "justifiable" private sector demands for import relief. Conversely, the executive branch tends to favor the global priority of trade liberalization and to force groups seeking import barriers to make a convincing case before acting on their behalf. On the export side, Congress has placed the burden of proof on those who advocate limiting foreign sales, while the executive branch has leaned toward putting foreign policy priorities ahead of promoting export shipments.

A second differentiating factor contributing to a unique U.S. approach to trade policy is that exports and imports expressed as percentages of U.S. gross domestic product (GDP) are still relatively small. In fact, they remain the lowest of any major industrialized country and one of the lowest in the world. Despite their large absolute size, external economic transactions do not loom nearly as large as a variable in influencing total domestic economic activity in the United States as they do in Canada, Western Europe, and Japan. Whereas U.S. merchandise exports accounted for slightly more than 7 percent of GDP in the early 1990s, the comparable figures for Germany and Canada were about 25 and 22 percent, respectively.[7] U.S. lethargy toward the external sector may be dwindling. It was widely noted that a relatively strong U.S. export performance in the 1990–1991 period provided a significant statistical offset to weak domestic economic activity. In addition, many American companies in the services sector have been experiencing a boom in overseas sales.

Three unique aspects of U.S. *import policy* can be readily identified: relatively high receptivity to imports, the singular international role of the dollar, and the relative lack of U.S. domestic economic planning. Compared to most sovereign countries, the United States has both a high marginal propensity to import (the proportion of an increase in national income that is spent on foreign goods) and a relatively high tolerance for imports that inflict dislocations on domestic industries. The first explanation of this unusual import receptivity (and of the even more unusual U.S. priorities in the export sector described subsequently) is the influence of the residual status of the United States as an international economic superpower. In pursuit of what political scientists call "hegemonic stability," global superpowers in the nineteenth and twentieth centuries—the United Kingdom and the United States, respectively—demonstrated a high degree of willingness to make foreign trade sacrifices in the form of maintaining relatively low import barriers. Both hegemons used their influence to pursue a less restrictive trading system. The latter was viewed as very cost-effective because it enhanced global political stability and economic prosperity without generating a significant increase in imports into their own very strong domestic economies.

For more than half a century, U.S. tolerance of imported goods has been facilitated by an important international monetary phenomenon: the unique role of the dollar as the principal international reserve and transactions currency. Foreign citizens and governments have been willing to hold dollar-denominated assets and then either lend or invest portions of these assets in the United States. The result is that the United States has assumed a unique financial position since the end of World War II: *It is the only country that can pay for all of its imports by using its own currency.* The United States does not have to earn foreign currency to finance a current account (goods and services) deficit. The rest of the world must earn hard currency (mostly dollars) to pay for imports the old-fashioned way—by first exporting goods and services—or by borrowing foreign currency. However, the United States is unique in the relative ease with which it can finance the difference between its imports and exports of goods and services by attracting or borrowing back from overseas large amounts of financial assets denominated in its own currency, most of which had been previously sent abroad to pay for imports. Since President Richard Nixon closed the gold window in 1971, the country has not needed to fear loss of gold reserves—even in the face of what have been the world's most persistently large current account deficits.

The dominant economic question in this case is whether and if significant dollar depreciation and higher interest rates—both are economically undesirable trends—may become necessary to attract the net capital inflows from abroad required to finance the current account deficits that have dominated the U.S. balance of payments position since the mid-1980s. Because most other countries seem to be guided by a mercantilist philosophy that quietly welcomes the U.S. trade deficit's contribution to their trade surpluses, there has not been a protracted period of time between the late 1980s and 1994 when foreigners have been significantly reluctant to channel the needed volume of dollars to the United States. As long as this continues, the United States remains uniquely divorced from any urgent need to reduce or eliminate its large, continuous current account deficit.

Third, the United States also differs from other countries by doling out import relief only sporadically and usually only after domestic industries experience severe or unfair import competition. Relief almost always is provided in response to short-term problems and interest group pressures rather than as long-term visions of domestic economic development. This situation is perpetuated in part by the U.S. ideological predilection toward free market competition, consumer sovereignty, and maximum consumption.

The somewhat unique style of U.S. import relief tactics is also a reflection of a more specific economic policy rule of thumb: The priority accorded by a government to maintaining a cohesive, consistent import policy strategy is roughly proportional to the extent that the government is engaged in domestic economic planning and implementation of an industrial policy to achieve the domestic goals of a strong industrial sector, full employment, and so on. The fact that U.S. trade policies are less proactive and less comprehensive than those found in many other countries mirrors the relatively low-intensity approach taken by the U.S. government toward the larger issue of domestic economic policy planning and intervention. If a government is uncomfortable intervening to assist the growth of favored domestic industries, it is defensive about implementing policies providing import protection and export assistance to special interests.

Trade policies in countries like Japan are afforded greater importance because these countries have a domestic "vision" and trade flows have a direct effect on achieving the country's top policy priority—a strong domestic economic performance. Conversely, the United States has tended to respond to unacceptable import situations through statutory provisions and spasmodic, often poorly reasoned, politically induced protectionist measures. The latter do not reflect any integrating economic theme or strategic plan to maximize industrial competitiveness.

The unique nature of U.S. *export policy* centers on the unusually schizophrenic nature of U.S. government attitudes toward it. All administrations in the post–World War II era have paid lip service to the goal of increasing U.S. exports. But in terms of taking action, these same administrations have repeatedly refused to make export promotion a top policy priority. The zeal in virtually every other country to maximize exports is palpable. Most push exports close to the point of overt mercantilism; many countries seriously adhere to the slogan of "export or die." But the U.S. government has been in a league of its own in two respects: (1) its willingness to subordinate the goal of export maximization to restrictive export controls intended to advance foreign policy goals and (2) its reluctance to use government funds to provide subsidized export finance (i.e., generous loan terms) to potential foreign customers of U.S. goods. Much of the explanation for the uniquely relaxed U.S. government attitudes about the need to maximize exports comes from the same ideological, foreign policy, and international monetary reasons just mentioned as being responsible for the relatively high U.S. tolerance for imports.

Other countries have displayed a far greater skepticism than the United States about export controls being a cost-effective method to halt state actions that are deemed hostile or unacceptable by the international community. Western Europe and Japan have long been reluctant to use export sanctions because they abhor the concept of punishing their own exporting companies. Furthermore, they assume that a target country eventually will circumvent export sanctions by finding a means of obtaining needed goods from somewhere else, legally or otherwise.

For better or worse, trade sanctions built around export controls became the U.S. program of choice for attaining a wide range of foreign policy goals. Sanctions were employed to contain its former cold war adversaries, the Soviet Union and its communist bloc allies; to promote the protection of human rights (South Africa, China, etc.); to respond to what was branded state-sponsored terrorism (Libya, Iran, etc.); to retaliate against what was judged to be military aggression (Iraq, Serbia, and North Vietnam, e.g.); to demand restoration of a democratically elected government (Haiti, e.g.); and to try toppling political leaders deemed odious (Panama, Cuba, etc.). Government officials and businesspersons in the other industrialized countries frequently laugh all the way to the bank when thinking about lost American export sales stemming from what they surely see as excessive U.S. government morality in the rough-and-tumble international marketplace.

Yet another distinctive facet of U.S. export policy, at least since the late 1970s, has taken the form of export expansion through extraordinarily aggressive attacks on trade barriers restricting the access of specific U.S. goods to foreign markets. Ironically, almost all of these efforts have been directed at countries friendly to the United States but unappreciative of unilateral U.S. judgments as to what constitutes an appropriate degree of reciprocity (i.e., relative market openness in other countries). Since the mid-1980s, the executive branch has pursued the strategy of correcting the persistently large U.S. merchandise trade deficit through export expansion rather than import contraction. U.S. trade negotiators have used the leverage of specific language in U.S. trade statutes, mainly the Section 301 provision (see Chapter 7), as well as general allusions to congressional anger at unfair trade treatment for U.S. products to demand relentlessly and bluntly that major U.S. trading partners eliminate or reduce specified trade barriers or face U.S. retaliation.

A vivid but perhaps singular illustration of these "uniqueness traits" in practice is the admittedly extreme case of the Reagan administration's attitude in the early 1980s in the face of the U.S. trade deficit swelling to unprecedented heights. The deficit's upward spiral was due mainly to the overvalued exchange rate of the dollar, which made U.S. goods more expensive to foreign buyers and foreign goods relatively cheaper to U.S. consumers. The administration turned a blind eye to the ample evidence of deteriorating U.S. global competitiveness. It manifested little sympathy for the cries of American business being adversely affected by an import boom and stagnant exports induced by continued appreciation of the dollar. Instead, it told the private sector to live or die by the market mechanism and bragged that the strength of the dollar was a welcome reflection of U.S. economic strength. Congress eventually applied sufficiently intense pressure—in the form of inching closer to passing protectionist trade legislation—that the administration eventually was forced to respond in 1985 with remedial trade and international monetary policy initiatives.[8]

It is not hyperbole to argue that no parliamentary form of government—anywhere in the world—would have been able to survive the inflexible policy stance toward the economic consequences of an overvalued currency that the Reagan administration maintained with respect to the dollar between 1981 and 1984. European and Japanese prime ministers would not have had the political gall or ideological disposition to respond in the same way to a deteriorating trade balance of comparable relative magnitude as the one experienced by the United States. It would have been politically disastrous for them to display the same prolonged outpouring of free market rhetoric and overt indifference to legitimate private sector concerns about competitiveness. Congressional efforts to force the Reagan administration to take the foreign trade situation more seriously were a stunning, even if very rare, example of the beneficial aspects of a separation of powers between branches of government.

A Case Study in the Political Economy of U.S. Trade Policy

The agonizing debate held in the United States during the early 1990s about whether or not to attach specific conditions to the renewal of most-favored-nation (MFN) tariff treatment of China provides a classic case study of trade policy's four-dimensional character. The dynamics of trade policy can best be described as the meeting point of four quadrants: political and economic issues on one level and international and domestic concerns on another level. The China MFN issue was a multifaceted dilemma transversing all four of these sectors and mirroring executive branch concerns for both existing and potential legislation imposed by Congress. There was no theory, precedent, or econometric equation by which to make a definitive determination of the optimal means of changing Chinese behavior deemed to be repugnant. Instead, there were only conflicting priorities and value judgments that needed to be balanced in such a way as to lead the George Bush and Bill Clinton administrations to adopt policies that they calculated would best serve the "national interest."

The events producing this decisionmaking dilemma were numerous but straightforward. Because Congress took the initiative in drafting language in a section of the Trade Act of 1974, an annual review of renewing MFN treatment subsequently extended to China was (and still is) legally required. Despite the suggestion of favoritism in the term *most-favored-nation status,* no special treatment is involved. When a country receives MFN tariff treatment, its exported goods receive the same relatively low tariff schedule that the United States currently applies to imports coming in from virtually every other country. Failure to retain MFN status would bring discriminatory U.S. tariff treatment of imports from China, an action that by law would entail upward of a tenfold increase in average tariff rates on Chinese goods. This increase would be high enough to devastate most of that country's large, growing market in the United States for a number of products.

Opposition to unconditionally renewing MFN status was triggered by a number of actions by the Chinese government that were denounced as unacceptable behavior by every U.S. executive and legislative branch official publicly commenting on them. At the top of this list of perceived Chinese misdeeds was something in direct conflict with domestic U.S. political values: continuing human rights abuses since the Tiananmen Square massacre in 1989 and political repression in Tibet. Also chafing U.S. sensitivities were Chinese exports of chemical and advanced weapons technology to the Middle East and Libya, allegations of a number of trade transgressions (mainly the use of prison labor to make some exports and violations of U.S. intellectual property rights), and import barriers against U.S. goods that contributed to large bilateral trade surpluses with the United States. China agreed to a few limited concessions, though its immediate compliance was in dispute. However, the Chinese government summarily rejected full adherence to U.S. "behavior modification" demands and repeatedly promised retaliation against U.S. agricultural and manufactured goods exports if deprived of MFN status.

The bottom line was the absence of an easy answer to the policy question of whether the U.S. national interest would be served by having MFN unconditionally renewed or, as demanded by some, by making renewal contingent on substantial improvements in Chinese human rights practices. Table 1.2 illustrates the multiple conflicts inherent in this policy dilemma. In the international economics sector, there was an understandably inconclusive debate about the importance attached to the impending loss of MFN treatment by the Chinese leadership. Neither side of the argument could predict for sure whether the potential loss of China's lucrative U.S. export market ($39 billion of U.S. imports in 1994 made the United States the largest export market of China after Hong Kong) would trigger better human rights practices to avoid disruption to China's economy or an obstinate refusal so as to avoid being seen as capitulating to U.S. threats. In what was a link between domestic politics and international economics, some human rights advocates argued that even if the Chinese government refused to budge, the United States would register an important moral victory by demonstrating support for American values instead of turning a blind eye to secure monetary rewards.

Linkage between domestic politics and domestic economics was evident from the widespread support for continued MFN treatment that came from the U.S. business community. Exporters and investors were fearful that Chinese retaliation would marginalize them in one of the world's largest and fastest-growing markets. U.S. companies with major new export contracts feared losing them. American importers of low-cost Chinese goods, fearful of losing profitable business, made self-serving arguments that low-income Americans would be disproportionately penalized by higher prices for consumer goods no longer imported from China at low tariff duties.

TABLE 1.2 The China MFN Trade Dilemma

	Politics	Economics	Laws
Domestic	Ethical desirability of defending human rights and due process for all of mankind	Potential cost to U.S. consumers from loss of inexpensive, labor-intensive Chinese goods	Potential for Congress to pass new legislation forcing administration to make MFN renewal contingent on improved Chinese human rights practices
	Desire of export-oriented U.S. workers to expand job opportunities	Potential loss of U.S. corporate profits	Existing statute requiring annual renewal of China's MFN status
International	Desirability of maintaining harmonious, cooperative relations with a great power	Threat of doors being shut to U.S. exports to world's fastest growing market	Chinese government might bow to threat of passage of more restrictive U.S. MFN legislation
	Desirability of demonstrating U.S. commitment to protecting human rights on global basis	Possibility of China acceding to U.S. demands to avoid jeopardizing its biggest overseas market	Chinese government might put sovereignty issues before commercial interests reject any accommodating responses to U.S. legislative moves to suspend its MFN treatment

Advocates of avoiding risk of loss of U.S. exports to China could point to their own version of how best to secure a more democratic environment in China. They advised a soft-sell approach for change, one consisting of intensified pressures for gradual change in China exerted through a growing U.S. political and business engagement within that country. Advocates of this approach argued that harmonious diplomatic relations and increasing commercial relations over the long run would be the most effective means of bolstering the position of those elements of Chinese society that supported economic liberalization and democratic reforms. The spread of a market economy and expanded exposure to Western values, it was claimed, would prove to be a more effective facilitator of systemic political change in China than the isolation that would ensue from deteriorating bilateral diplomatic and economic relations.[9]

The international political perspective favored retention of MFN, good trade relations, and pursuit of bilateral cooperation in global affairs. Not only did China represent a potential superpower with one quarter of the world's population, but it was the wrong time for strained relations. The need for China's assistance in dealing with the delicate situation of North Korea's nuclear program coincided with President Clinton's need to make a decision on whether to link MFN to internal Chinese changes.

Throughout the MFN debate, the executive branch could not act without careful regard for congressional sentiment. Presidential discretion on the MFN issue was limited by existing as well as potential laws. For example, if either President Bush or President Clinton was committed to seeking a minimum of conditionality for MFN renewal, he had to weigh the possibility that Congress would again pass legislation mandating that MFN renewal should be made conditional on "significant" Chinese response. Such legislation was passed in 1992 in an effort by members of Congress to terminate what they deemed to be Bush's appeasement of China, a position that he viewed as a realistic calculation that the confrontational approach would backfire by alienating the Chinese leadership. The bill failed to become law only because Congress was unable to override Bush's veto.

In May 1994 President Clinton reversed the hard-line position on MFN renewal that he had assumed while running for office and extended MFN with only a few minor conditions. Although admitting that China had not achieved significant progress in reducing human rights abuses, he declared that the policy linking MFN and human rights had reached the end of its usefulness and it was time to take a new path toward achieving U.S. objectives. This decision reflected the simple reality that advocates of suspending MFN treatment in the absence of improved human rights conditions had been overwhelmingly eclipsed by advocates of commercial self-interests. The latter were effectively promoted by several forces. The first was the continued growth in the Chinese economy that created a fast-growing, increasingly lucrative export market for other countries. The specter of massive profits in turn inspired a vociferous and effective lobbying effort by the U.S. business community—an effort aided and abetted by Chinese officials' well-timed expressions of interest in placing huge purchase orders with such major U.S. corporations as AT&T and Boeing.[10]

In the end, the human rights advocates in Congress were caught in an untenable position between overwhelming support among constituents for delinking human rights from commercial relations and the realization that they could no longer rely on a presidential veto of a congressionally passed bill that would terminate MFN treatment and anger China. With much of the executive branch—mainly the Treasury and Commerce Departments—openly siding with the export community, President Clinton apparently decided that the risks of going against the clear majority on this issue were not worth the abstract benefits of demonstrating zero tolerance for internal Chinese humanitarian policies. Continuing news reports of widespread human rights abuses in China have sustained the controversy as to whether a hardline or soft-line MFN trade strategy best served the national interest.

Conclusion

U.S. foreign trade policy encompasses economics and political science. It has flexible boundaries and an expanding content. Trade policy is an economic process in the first instance. But its premium on judgment rather than scientific vigor, its propensity to help and hurt the fortunes of important sectors of the domestic populace, and the complex formula for the sharing of power by the executive and legislative branches mean that in the final analysis, U.S. trade policy is a political process. To a lesser extent, its formulation and conduct are influenced by a legislative process whose statutory output guides and constrains the executive branch's conduct of trade policy. However, trade laws are primarily a subordinate variable, one shaped by the synthesis of the two dominant variables: political and economic forces.

To understand the objectives, successes, inconsistencies, and imperfections of U.S. trade policy, one needs to understand and never lose sight of the economic, political, and legal factors involved. These include the economic logic for promoting and controlling imports and exports, the political realities affecting the decisionmaking process in what ostensibly is an economic realm, and the laws setting parameters for executive branch behavior in implementing U.S. trade policies. After outlining the history of these policies, we provide a detailed examination of economic, political, and statutory fundamentals. We conclude the book by integrating these three themes in search of comprehensive explanations—not a critique—of the major contemporary trade policy issues facing the United States.

For Further Reading

Baldwin, David A. *Economic Statecraft.* Princeton, N.J.: Princeton University Press, 1985.

Gilpin, Robert. *The Political Economy of International Relations.* Princeton, N.J.: Princeton University Press, 1987.

Lairson, Thomas D., and David Skidmore. *International Political Economy.* Fort Worth, Tex.: Harcourt Brace College Publishers, 1993.

Low, Patrick. *Trading Free—The GATT and U.S. Trade Policy.* New York: Twentieth Century Fund Press, 1993.

Spero, Joan Edelman. *The Politics of International Economic Relations,* 4th ed. New York: St. Martin's Press, 1990.

Walters, Robert S., ed. *Talking Trade—U.S. Policy in International Perspective.* Boulder, Colo: Westview Press, 1993.

Walters, Robert S., and David Blake. *The Politics of Global Economic Relations,* 4th ed. Englewood Cliffs, N.J.: Prentice-Hall, 1992.

Notes

1. In a more specific example of the winners and losers phenomenon, the creation of a free trade area with Mexico will help most U.S. makers of high-value-added industrial goods and some agricultural producers to increase shipments to that country while simultaneously hurting most U.S. labor-intensive, low-tech sectors and some agricultural sectors through the encouragement of increased imports from Mexico.

2. Stephen D. Krasner, "U.S. Commercial and Monetary Policy: Unravelling the Paradox of External Strength and Internal Weakness," *International Organization,* Autumn 1977, p. 645.

3. Another view, held by some economists, is that trade flows have a powerful influence on a country's long-term growth and development.

4. Some economists would argue that the expected dynamic benefits from trade liberalization may not be reaped equally by countries that would mainly import manufactured goods and export agricultural and primary products.

5. Some of the trade theories reviewed in Chapter 2 imply that even in the long term, some groups such as less skilled workers in the United States may suffer permanently lower real wages, other things being equal, as the result of a liberal import policy that increases imports of goods that account for employment of a large number of these workers. The result is a reduction in demand for their services. It is also possible that some unions lose leverage in demanding wage increases as the result of increased imports.

6. Keynesian macrotheory, however, implies that trade surpluses caused by increased exports can be good for employment in the short run, even though neoclassical microtheory disagrees.

7. Calculated from data in International Monetary Fund, *International Financial Statistics,* various issues. Trade as a percentage of GDP in member countries of the European Union is unusually high because of extensive intra-EU trade, which some economists no longer consider "foreign" transactions in the traditional sense.

8. For more detail on these events, see Stephen D. Cohen, *The Making of United States International Economic Policy,* 4th ed. (New York: Praeger, 1994), ch. 10.

9. There was a third, in-between option: to confine MFN renewal strictly to "acceptable" Chinese behavior on trade issues such as import barriers and thereby exclude U.S. political and social concerns from trade retaliation.

10. See, for example, "Backbone of the New China Lobby: U.S. Firms," *Washington Post,* June 14, 1993, p. A1; "China Steps Up Spending to Keep U.S. Trade Status," *New York Times,* May 7, 1993, p. A1; "Clinton's Renewal of Trade Status for China Followed Cabinet Debates, Congress's Sea Change," *Wall Street Journal,* May 31, 1994, p. A18; and "U.S. Firms, Anticipating Huge Market, Worry China May Lose Its MFN Status," *Wall Street Journal,* May 14, 1993, p. A8.

2 Historical Survey of U.S. Trade Relations

U.S. foreign trade policy has passed through a number of distinct periods. An appreciation of the causal factors responsible for the ebbs and flows of trade policy from the beginning of the republic into the 1990s is essential to gain a full understanding of where we are today and why. In briefly reviewing the history of U.S. trade policy, we analyze in this chapter both the fundamental changes and the persistent themes in economics, politics, and laws that have shaped the evolution of more than 200 years of U.S. trade policy.

A Conceptual Blueprint

In any democracy, trade policy over an extended period of time is the outcome of a series of intellectual debates and political struggles about the most desirable means to advance the long-term welfare of the country. The broad sweep of trade policy reflects changes in and a continually shifting balance of power among the four pillars that constitute this policy: domestic politics and domestic economics as well as international politics and international economics. The endless progression of shifting circumstances pertinent to each of these four factors as well as the ever-changing partnership in trade policymaking between the executive and legislative branches perpetually alter the cost-effectiveness calculation of the import or export policy status quo. Policymakers must reconcile political and economic priorities within a constantly changing trade policy equation. The substance of trade policy is therefore relatively fluid: The core question of how severe restrictions should be on imports and on exports at any given time is constantly being answered in different ways by different people and with different degrees of success. In some cases, lessons are learned only after major mistakes are committed. Experience has been an important teacher for U.S. government trade policymakers.

The broad concept that U.S. trade policy substance is the outgrowth of the need to reconcile competing ideas has been a constant. In a country like the United States—one that prides itself on pluralism and participatory government—it is not surprising that large numbers of senior economic and national security policy officials, elected politicians, candidates for public office, economists and political scientists, businesspersons, labor leaders, consumers, lawyers, and demagogues have collectively provided diverse input into the running debate as to how the government should regulate trade flows.

At the heart of the political economy of trade policy is the perennial rule of thumb that most trade decisions create winners and losers, both in the domestic body politic and in the economies of trading partners. When imports are allowed to enter freely, consumers and foreign producers benefit, but domestic producers of goods sensitive to import competition usually suffer. To protect their interests, import-impacted business executives and workers become a vociferous minority. They petition elected representatives for imposition of trade barriers that usually drive up domestic sales prices or reduce the availability of foreign-made goods or both. When domestic interests succeed in their efforts to get import barriers imposed, they are the winners and foreign producers and domestic consumers usually are losers.

As suggested in Chapter 6, success in convincing the U.S. government to impose import barriers (under conditions of fair foreign competition) is a function of the interplay among five major variables. The first is the number, economic size, and lobbying savvy of those special interest groups seeking restrictions on imports. The preponderant economic ideas and philosophy of key policymakers in the administration are the second variable, and these affect thinking about what makes immediate sense in terms of short-term import restrictions (as well as export restraints). Third are perceptions of intense congressional interest in a given import policy decision. The fourth variable is official perceptions of the severity of import competition. For countries other than the United States, an important financial variable in determining the utility of import restrictions is the strength of their balance of payments position and the availability of convertible foreign exchange necessary to pay for imports.

The final major variable is the intensity of internal and foreign countervailing political forces opposing restrictions on trade. Countervailing political forces to protectionist pleas in the United States did not have significant clout until the middle of the twentieth century, a tipoff to the tilt of U.S. import policy before that time. The first, more abstract countervailing force is the belief held by most modern-day trade policymakers that the competitive forces unleashed by the public's ability to choose freely between domestically and foreign-made goods are a social good that benefits the country as a whole. The second countervailing force consists of exporters—domestic producers with a vested interest in assuring minimal barriers on imports. Protectionism at home antagonizes foreign customers and can adversely affect other countries' ability to pay for imports (by denying them foreign exchange that would otherwise be earned from exporting to the protectionist country). Annoyance with protectionism has steadily increased among major exporters of manufactured goods in the large industrialized countries. The reason is that a growing percentage of these exporters are multinational companies desirous of maximum discretion to move goods and capital freely among their many subsidiaries in many countries as they see fit.

Historically, U.S. trade policy has been characterized by the consistent presence of controversy. The first phase of U.S. trade policy started with a relatively nonpartisan disagreement between free trade and protectionist ideologies about how best to promote domestic economic prosperity in a new country. The second phase emerged in the early 1800s in the form of a regional dispute between northerners and southerners. It in turn evolved into a new phase, lasting from the late 1880s until the 1920s, that was characterized by differences between Democrats and Republicans regarding the appropriate levels of tariffs (the former favored lower levels and the latter favored high tariffs). The common denominator of this period is that the debate was about domestic economics and politics exclusively. The issue was the overall structure of the U.S. economy and, more particularly, income distribution and the wisdom of taxing (via high tariffs) all Americans for the purpose of encouraging and protecting production in a limited number of import-sensitive sectors.

The modern era of U.S. trade policy was ushered in as the result of incredibly bad timing. The gradual (and unrecognized at the time) emergence of the United States after World War I as a major commercial and financial actor in the world economy collided violently with the decision in 1930 to adopt the most protectionist U.S. trade posture in history. An extremely harsh lesson was learned: Closing the now expansive, influential U.S. market to imports placed every country's economic growth at risk. This newly forged linkage between domestic and international economic prosperity caused a sea change in U.S. policy in 1934. But even then, all of the variables present in the contemporary U.S. trade policy equation were not yet in place. It was not until after World War II that the additional linkage between U.S. international commercial policy and an unprecedented confluence of U.S. international political and military objectives was recognized.

It is possible to argue (with only slight oversimplification) that in the 1990s, the U.S. policy debate has come full circle to entail an intellectual argument reminiscent of the 1790s: U.S. trade policy has become an ideological battleground between traditionalists, who still believe in minimum government interference in trade flows, and neointerventionists. The latter believe (not unlike Alexander Hamilton) in the need for government promotion of industry. They also accept the need to adopt new, more aggressive trade strategies in response to new global economic realities that have rendered obsolete most of the long-cherished assumptions of nineteenth-century free trade theory.

The First Stage of U.S. Trade Policy, 1789–1929

The transcendent features of the first stage of U.S. trade policy were the absence of presidential discretion in conducting trade policy, a gradual ratcheting upward of U.S. tariff rates, and an indifference to the operation of the global trading system.

The first substantive piece of legislation passed by the first Congress in 1789 was a tariff act. The bill's main purpose was to raise revenue—a critical need for a new country that had not yet implemented any generalized income or sales taxes and was forbidden by the Constitution to impose export duties. Although the notion of providing protection to the country's fledgling industrial base was not ignored in the bill, the fact that a low tariff rate of 5 percent was imposed meant that, by design, there was minimal discouragement of imports. Fiscal considerations remained a major, albeit declining, variable in the setting of U.S. tariff levels until the end of the nineteenth century. There was a simple reason for this connection: Until the twentieth century, tariff collections represented a high (at least 40 percent) proportion of total federal revenues.

Conspicuous by their absence for more than a century in the trade debate were two key factors: (1) concerns about key concepts of trade theory such as comparative advantage and (2) concerns about the impact of trade barriers on U.S. political and economic relations with other countries. This disengagement by the United States from concerns beyond the water's edge went largely unnoticed (until the 1920s) owing to the marginal external impact of a young country accounting for an inconsequential percentage of world trade.

An intellectual tug-of-war over trade policy between political heavyweights quickly erupted in the wake of the country's first tariff bill. In 1791, Alexander Hamilton, the first secretary of the treasury, produced his *Report on Manufactures* in response to the request that he study the efficacy of using protectionist measures to encourage the development of a domestic industrial base. The document strongly advised implementation of activist economic policies incorporating the use of high tariffs as well as federal "bounties" (i.e., subsidies). Hamilton, in the best tradition of mercantilism (see Chapter 3) believed that "Not only the wealth but the independence and security of a country appear to be materially connected with the prosperity of manufactures."[1] A thriving industrial base, he argued, also would have the advantage of increasing domestic demand for home-grown agricultural goods, thereby reducing the allegedly dangerously high degree of dependence by farmers on sales to foreign markets. His recommendations were rejected. The opposing views that carried the day were articulated by James Madison and Thomas Jefferson. They argued in economic terms that prohibitive tariffs would not be beneficial to the national interest. And they believed that politically, delegation of additional power to the central government for any reason—including guiding industrial development—should be kept to an absolute minimum.

Hamilton lost the battle but won the war. Over the span of the next 140 years, Congress by fits and starts increased the average level of tariffs. Although the periodic need for additional tax revenue was often a factor, the overwhelming determinant of the increasingly protectionist U.S. import policy was the responsiveness of lawmakers to industrialists' demands for protection against import competition.

The upward spiral of the average U.S. tariff rate during this period was directly related to the virtually nonexistent role of the executive branch in the formulation of U.S. import policy during the eighteenth century. The executive branch in trade matters was little more than a tax (tariff) collector. The concept of regular negotiations among governments aimed at reducing trade barriers was unknown. The president had absolutely no legal authority—and sought none—to reduce U.S. trade barriers on his own; all trade agreements signed with other governments had to be ratified by Congress. (A few relatively minor, limited-duration bilateral treaties providing for very limited tariff cuts were concluded in the late 1800s and early 1900s.) Trade policy continued to be defined by a profusion of tariff laws that raised and occasionally lowered the U.S. tariff schedule and thereby determined the openness of the U.S. market to foreign goods.

Conditions prevailing at the end of the War of 1812 led to the first of several legislated increases in the U.S. tariff schedule. The virtual absence of imports while the war was being fought had been a stimulant to the domestic manufacturing sector, most of which was located in the northern states. The subsequent resumption of imports of British-made goods and the burdensome debt load incurred by the U.S. government from waging the war led to imposition of a sharp rise in import duties in the Tariff Act of 1816. At this point, the tariff became part of a larger historical phenomenon: Rising tariffs became an irritant in the widening gulf between the North and South that culminated in the Civil War.

The failure of the 1816 Tariff Act to blunt the British export drive set the stage for passage in 1828 of the "Tariff of Abominations." This highly protectionist bill emerged as the result of a major political miscalculation. Opponents of increased protectionism quietly encouraged major tariff increases on every manufactured good they could think of, assuming that the bill would become so odious as to be rejected in the final vote. The strategy backfired in the face of the first major example of the inherent dangers of congressional logrolling in tariff legislation. A majority of members of Congress accepted tariff hikes on any number of goods (in some cases tariffs were equivalent to 100 percent of the value of the import) as a trade-off for enlisting support among colleagues for higher duties on commodities that they pushed on behalf of their own constituents. (The dark specter of this legislative version of "you scratch my back and I'll scratch yours" returned in 1930 to haunt U.S. trade policy in spades—see the next section.)

Although tariff levels were subsequently reduced by Congress in 1833, politicians from the South did not abandon their grievances concerning the intolerable costs of high tariffs imposed on them that were, for example, alienating foreign consumers of their tobacco and cotton. They had become reconciled to the notion that high tariffs could and would be imposed on them against their will. In the words of one historian, Southerners saw the tariff dispute as symbolic of the North's attacks on their economic and social systems.[2] Laws increasing tariff rates came pouring out of the Congress with great regularity beginning in 1861, when southern states began seceding from the Union, and continued to do so until well after the Civil War.

From the 1870s until well into the twentieth century, tariff levels were moved up or down in moderate degrees by a relatively rapid succession of new legislation. The direction of tariff modifications was determined mainly by which party controlled Congress. After the Civil War, the two major political parties "fell into an almost perfect equipoise. As Democratic and Republican leaders worked to slide the balance in their favor, they developed opposing stands on the issues, sometimes for no other reason than to create an appeal among the voters."[3] In general, the dichotomy between the Democrats' advocacy of lower tariffs and the Republicans' embrace of higher tariffs amounted to an intellectually barren period in U.S. trade policy. As one study concluded: "No conclusive evidence exists that either high or low tariff rates greatly affected economic conditions in that period. The whole controversy was frequently more an exercise in political, rhetorical and partisan faith than a well-considered, profound discussion of conflicting economic and trade strategies."[4]

It was not until after the conclusion of World War I that any great consequences flowed from the tendency of the United States to "internalize" import policy. The role of the U.S. economy in international trade relations heretofore had been sufficiently overshadowed by the larger European countries, mainly Great Britain, to enable the United States to go about the business of imposing tariffs with little regard to their external effects. Beginning in the mid-1800s, the country became, to use a basic term in political economy, a "free rider." It was content to enjoy the benefits of eased European trade barriers embodied by Great Britain's repeal in 1846 of its highly protectionist Corn Laws without reciprocating with its own liberalization.

Great Britain was then playing the classic hegemon role in the international economy. Its economic and international political strengths allowed it to set a more liberal trade tone to the global economic order as it more willingly accepted imports. Britain's decision at this time to chart a more open trade policy conforms perfectly to the model used in this book to explain the formulation of U.S. trade policy: a political and intellectual struggle among government policymakers to determine who will be winners and losers. Britain's trade policy was transformed in 1846 just as that of the United States would be exactly 100 years later. The political balance of power in Great Britain shifted from a land-owning aristocracy committed to smothering agricultural imports to industrialists who saw a connection among lower tariffs, expanding world markets, and the stimulation of their exports of manufactured goods.

The United States emerged in the post–World War I period as a bona fide industrial superpower, the world's number one exporter, and the world's most important import market for semifinished goods and raw materials.[5] The United States also became a major net supplier of capital to credit-hungry countries, moving in a relatively short span of time from international debtor to international creditor status. Unfortunately, the quick resumption after 1918 of an isolationist foreign policy assured that U.S. trade policy decisionmaking would remain mired within the gravitational pull of purely internal considerations—the priority that had prevailed for more than 100 years.

A disconnect resulted between the quick onset of U.S. international economic maturity and its continued international political immaturity: No longer would U.S. efforts to restrict imports have insignificant effects on global economic prosperity. The damage caused by the failure of the United States after World War I to provide a progressive voice in the international trade system was magnified by the economic inability of Great Britain to sustain its role of liberal trade–supporting hegemon.

The worldwide spread of the Great Depression appears to have been made more severe than it would otherwise have been because of the absence of an undisputed economic leader with a relatively open market. In the words of Charles Kindleberger, who popularized the thesis linking an open, liberal international economic order to the existence of an affluent hegemon: "When every country turned to protect its national private interests, the world public interest went down the drain, and with it the private interests of all."[6]

Going to Extremes:
Revolutionary Changes in the 1930s

U.S. trade policy was irrevocably changed by its spectacular roller-coaster ride during the first half of the 1930s. The shift started unsensationally enough with an effort to accommodate U.S. farmers' demands in the 1920s for higher agricultural prices. This effort effectively short-circuited what might have been a possible shift by the United States in the direction of a more open trade policy. The Underwood Tariff Act of 1913 had cut import duties (a move that was largely offset in terms of revenue by the statute's initiation of an income tax). President Woodrow Wilson's Fourteen Points program for the postwar world order had included a call for the early removal "of all economic barriers and the establishment of an equality of trade conditions among all nations consenting to the peace."[7] In the end, however, it was business as usual: Protectionism carried the day. Wilsonian foreign policy was rejected in the 1920 elections, a post–World War I economic boom fizzled, and the U.S. economy fell into recession.

The Fordney-McCumber Act of 1922 represented yet another embrace of the fallacious assumption that increased import duties could effectively address the farm community's distress over falling prices for agricultural goods, the main cause of which was excessive domestic production. The bill also doled out major tariff increases to industries, such as chemicals, that had flourished during World War I.

Although higher tariffs had consistently failed to turn around the fortunes of the U.S. agricultural sector, President Herbert Hoover early in 1929 yielded to intensifying political pressures and endorsed the idea of higher tariffs on agricultural goods as a means of boosting food prices. The utter lack of any compelling economic justification for providing this protection opened the door to a veritable army of lobbyists clamoring to get in on the act by urging higher tariffs on manufactured goods. Organized labor added its support. The result was the unleashing of an unprecedented exercise in logrolling: Votes in the House and Senate were freely exchanged to provide higher tariffs in response to nearly every constituent demand for relief from import competition. When the stock market crashed later in 1929 and economic conditions deteriorated within the United States, Republican leaders in Congress accelerated efforts to pass the new tariff act. They hoped the bill would switch demand to domestically produced goods. President Hoover urged restraint and was reportedly unhappy with the protectionist-laden bill that emerged. But he did sign it, dismissing bitter foreign complaints on the grounds that tariff legislation was strictly an internal matter.

The Smoot-Hawley Tariff Act of 1930 was a disaster of major proportions. The only silver lining was that the damage ultimately generated by the statute has literally scared policymakers around the world off of overt protectionism. To this day, it remains a textbook case of what *not* to do in trade policy. The average U.S. tariff duty was raised to 53 percent, an all-time high, and the number of dutiable items was increased sharply. The bill was viewed abroad as an unjust and unfriendly action by an economically strong creditor country and as a symbol of U.S. isolationism.[8]

The timing of the Smoot-Hawley legislation could not have been worse. As the depression spread from the United States, other countries wasted no time in retaliating in kind, with both higher tariffs and quotas. A tidal wave of fear and economic nationalism produced an unprecedented worldwide display of beggar-thy-neighbor policies in which all major trading countries were trying more or less simultaneously to dump their domestic economic problems on someone else. A proliferation of international financial controls and a series of competitive exchange rate devaluations further contributed to a gridlock of repressive international economic policies.

The ensuing global trade war produced all losers and no winners. As national economies spiraled downward, so too did the volume of international trade. Countries succeeded in reducing imports but at the cost of decimating their export sector, normally an economy's most productive and dynamic sector. Estimates peg the value of world trade in 1933 at just one-third of what it had been in 1929.[9] U.S. imports in 1932 had plunged by 70 percent from their 1929 level, but exports during this period also plummeted by about the same amount.[10] Although import-sensitive jobs were saved, relatively high-paying export jobs were lost.

The inevitable return to international economic sanity began with the traditionally low-tariff party, the Democrats, gaining control of the White House and Congress in 1932. The Democratic platform presented what was then a unique critique by politicians of higher tariffs: It vigorously condemned the Smoot-Hawley Act as detrimental to U.S. industry and agriculture by causing a loss of foreign markets as well as increases in domestic production costs. The platform went on to endorse reciprocal tariff-cutting agreements and other efforts to revive international commerce.

Initially, President Roosevelt was not personally committed to acting on this initiative. It was the unwavering zeal of Roosevelt's secretary of state, Cordell Hull, that was the catalyst for change. He deeply believed that an open trading system fostered a peaceful, cooperative, and stable international political order whereas a closed trading system produced international tensions and conflict. Having won President Roosevelt to the cause, Hull was entrusted with the task of gaining congressional approval for reciprocal trade agreements in which the United States would lower tariffs in return for comparable concessions by other countries.

Selling Congress on approving tariff cuts in 1934 amid massive unemployment at home would have been difficult to impossible without the astute, pragmatic marketing strategy adopted by the administration. Rather than asking for a sharp departure from the established trade policymaking process, Secretary Hull sought temporary negotiating authority in the form of an amendment to the Smoot-Hawley Act. Unilateral tariff cuts would not be part of the package. The export-enhancing—and by implication, job-creating—aspects of obtaining reductions in foreign tariffs were stressed. The need for the United States to make reciprocal concessions was downplayed. Even rarer were references to economic theory extolling the virtues of a country's being able to import goods more efficiently produced abroad. Furthermore, the administration accepted a congressional amendment to limit the tariff-cutting authority to three years, at which time the Congress would review the administration's performance before deciding whether to extend presidential tariff-cutting authority. In retrospect, many members of Congress were (and still are) happy to interpose the executive branch between themselves and special interest groups, letting the administration serve as the lightning rod for private sector petitions for import protection.

The Reciprocal Trade Agreements Act (RTAA) of 1934 is one of the pivotal turning points in international trading relations. For the first time, the executive branch was given authority to *enact* reductions of up to 50 percent in U.S. tariffs as long as other countries reciprocated in kind. (Previously, the executive branch could only make trade policy promises to other countries that were subject to formal approval by Congress.) Also for the first time in history, an ongoing series of bilateral negotiations commenced for the expressed purpose of reducing barriers to trade as a step toward expanding global production, employment, and efficiency.

Immediately after passage of the RTAA, U.S. trade negotiators got down to business with their foreign counterparts. By the early 1940s, bilateral trade agreements with some twenty-five countries, mainly in Europe and the Western Hemisphere, had been concluded. Because the most-favored-nation principle was included in the act, the tariff cuts implemented in each of these agreements were automatically extended by the United States on a nondiscriminatory basis to all other countries (which meant that the executive branch effectively was rewriting the U.S. tariff schedule). The average ad valorem tariff rate in the United States fell from over 50 percent in 1930 to about 37 percent in 1939.[11] Never before in world history had the direction of global trade relations moved so broadly and deeply toward reduced trade barriers.

Commercial trade relations were totally disrupted after the outbreak of World War II. However, the new postwar environment would expedite the relatively modest momentum toward liberalization generated in the 1930s. Throughout U.S. history, wars had been the major causes of shifts in trade policy. World War II was the last war to cause such a shift, but nothing before compared in magnitude to the revolutionary changes in U.S. international economic and political policies that it unleashed in the late 1940s.

The United States as Hegemon:
Internationalism Prevails in the 1950s and 1960s

The end of World War II found much of Europe and Asia in political disarray and economically devastated. The search for a lasting peace to prevent a third world war assumed even greater urgency following the advent of the cold war between the free world capitalist countries led by the United States and the totalitarian countries behind the Iron Curtain that were dominated by the Soviet Union. Economic growth in democratic countries became the transcendent international goal. To this end, U.S. international economic policy was commandeered as an instrument of foreign policy; administrations in the immediate postwar period were uninterested in attaching priority to enhancing domestic economic interests. The United States could literally afford to be commercially altruistic on a global basis. The unassailable strength of its economy in the initial postwar years made it immune to serious losses of jobs or domestic production from import competition.

By 1950, the application of U.S. international economic policy was clearly defined and sharply differentiated to serve two separate national security strategies. On the one hand, democratic countries in Western Europe and Japan received massive financial assistance (eventually to surpass $30 billion) from the United States to begin the rebuilding of their war-torn economies. Economic progress in those countries, in turn, would promote political stability and create a growing bulwark against the expansion of communism. The initial emphasis on aid was soon supplanted by efforts to maximize commercial relations with the objective of integrating the industrialized democracies into a thriving, harmonious, mutually rewarding, and nondiscriminatory international economic order. Later, the same strategy would be applied to friendly, less developed countries in Latin America and newly independent "emerging countries" in Asia and Africa.

At the other extreme, trade, capital, and advanced technology were denied to the hostile countries of the communist bloc in support of achieving larger national security goals. Export controls and the de facto excommunication of "expansionist" communist states from the international trading system by the United States and its allies became the economic dimension of containment. The minimization of East-West trade was viewed as being far more costly to the former than to the latter.

U.S. export policy in the immediate post–World War II period toward friendly countries was extraordinary in the degree to which it acquiesced to their discriminating against U.S. goods. U.S. long-term foreign policy goals generated an unprecedented state of international economic unselfishness that actively encouraged imports and ignored export expansion to an extent never seen before. The shortage of dollars in Western Europe and Japan sharply curtailed their ability to import, which in turn slowed their ability to rebuild the thriving, competitive industrial sectors sought by a paternalistic Uncle Sam. Furthermore, their ability to penetrate the U.S. market was minimal in light of the physical destruction suffered by factories in these countries during the war. In economic terms, the decision not to seek full reciprocity from trading partners in Western Europe and Japan was justified by the overwhelming U.S. economic dominance in the immediate postwar period. Some critics of contemporary trade policy contend that the U.S. government's approach toward export promotion has never progressed from the "Marshall Plan mentality" of the 1950s. In their view, the relatively low priority given by government officials to enhancing export performance is increasingly costly and out of sync with the decline in relative U.S. global competitiveness.

The executive branch's policy of assiduously encouraging imports and accepting the right of other countries to adopt quantitative and discriminatory import restrictions was vividly displayed during the 1947 negotiations to create the ill-fated International Trade Organization (ITO). State Department trade negotiators were rebuffed in their intensive effort to liberalize Great Britain's Imperial Preference system of tariff preferences extended to Commonwealth countries. But in the apparent belief that an unbalanced deal was preferable to no deal at all, the United States signed an agreement that, in the words of one critic, "cracked open only one market—its own." The State Department acknowledged that Washington gained concessions at Geneva with an estimated trade value of $1.19 billion but yielded concessions worth about $1.77 billion.[12]

The Senate and the U.S. business sector were deeply disenchanted by the numerous exemptions in the proposed ITO charter that would have permitted countries to impose quantitative and discriminatory (non-MFN) import barriers, mainly for balance of payments and economic development purposes. "There are more exceptions than rules in the ITO charter" was the gist of the criticism. As one scholar noted, U.S. trade seemed "to be the object of more restrictions and discrimination than ever before."[13] Shortly after the Congress failed to act in 1949 on the initial administration request for ratification of U.S. membership, the atmosphere on Capitol Hill toward the ITO deteriorated to the point that the Eisenhower administration decided it was pointless to resubmit the ITO charter to the next congressional session. With the ITO now effectively dead, the administration signed the General Agreement on Tariffs and Trade, which included most of the terms of the ITO, as an executive agreement. No formal multilateral organization existed to administer the rules of the trading system until the 1994 agreement to create the World Trade Organization (see Chapter 13).

The United States actively supported various efforts at regional economic cooperation among West European countries (initially, the European Payments Union, then the European Community, and since the early 1990s the European Union), despite the fact that they openly discriminated against exports of U.S. goods. Any effort to cement cooperation among West European countries was seen as a boon to the strength and solidarity of the Western alliance and therefore a relatively small price to pay for a few lost export opportunities. That European economic and political integration was viewed primarily in balance of power terms by the U.S. foreign policy establishment can be seen in the wording of President John F. Kennedy's speech of July 4, 1962: "We do not regard a strong and united Europe as a rival but a partner. . . . We will be prepared to discuss with a united Europe the ways and means of forming a concrete Atlantic partnership."[14]

Implicitly, a deal was struck. Western Europe accepted an international security and economic order that extended a nearly blank check to the United States to act unilaterally in the international arena however it saw fit to promote its self-interest—and without having to worry about the accumulating balance of payments deficits incurred, in part, from playing the expensive role of global superpower. The United States, in turn, condoned Europe's using the trade and monetary systems to promote its own regional economic prosperity, even if this resulted in the loss of some U.S. exports.[15]

U.S. trade policy toward Japan in the 1950s incorporated essentially the same strategy used toward Western Europe. Memoranda declassified in the early 1990s show that the National Security Council declared in 1952 and 1953 that the entry of Japanese goods should be "facilitated" because increasing access to the U.S. market was necessary to halt "economic deterioration and falling living standards" in Japan that "create fertile ground for communist subversion."[16] The Eisenhower administration accepted the need to negotiate trade agreements that were "favorable" to Japan and believed that "all problems of local industry pale into insignificance in relation to the world crisis." It therefore allegedly ignored the concept of reciprocity in its priority effort to resuscitate the Japanese economy by helping Japan to expand exports. One scholar has charged that the bilateral trade agreement signed with Japan in 1955 was an "egregious example of sacrificing domestic interests for foreign policy advantage." For national security reasons, it was "an unbalanced agreement" in which the Japanese "provided few major tariff concessions" while the United States "granted extensive tariff reductions covering almost all of Japan's major export items."[17]

The swan song for the State Department in its role as head of the U.S. trade negotiating team occurred in the Dillon Round of GATT trade negotiations that concluded in 1962. (The round was named for C. Douglas Dillon, then undersecretary of state and chief U.S. trade negotiator.) Eager to encourage the European economic integration process (this was the first multilateral trade negotiation in which the European Union, then known as the European Economic Community [EEC], negotiated as a single entity, supplanting national delegations from its member states) and seemingly oblivious of the need to protect domestic interests, the U.S. delegation again appeared to act on the notion that failure to achieve agreement was the worst possible scenario for trade negotiations. Rather than risk failure, the Kennedy administration agreed to several tariff concessions below the "peril point" levels recommended as the minimum necessary protection by the independent Tariff Commission (now known as the International Trade Commission). In addition, it made only a perfunctory effort to negotiate a partial liberalization in Europe's highly protectionist Common Agricultural Policy, which had only recently been implemented.

The failure of the Dillon Round to go beyond marginal tariff cuts sustained the administration's nightmare that the EEC's Common External Tariff would devastate U.S. exports in their most important foreign market and interfere with the Kennedy administration's grand design of a more integrated Atlantic Community. This situation led U.S. officials to propose a "wholly new approach" to trade negotiations that may have been an instinctive realization that the era of U.S. economic hegemony was coming to an end. A uniting Europe made the need for reduced trade barriers all the more important to U.S. exporters. Aided by the slogan "trade or fade," the Kennedy administration quickly convinced Congress to delegate to it the most extensive degree of tariff-cutting authority ever.

The Trade Expansion Act of 1962 authorized (on a reciprocal basis) across-the-board tariff cuts up to 50 percent with only a few exceptions. Duties of 5 percent or less could be eliminated entirely. In addition, authorization was extended to negotiate total tariff elimination on a reciprocal basis when the United States and the EEC accounted for at least 80 percent of world trade in a given product. (This provision was made largely irrelevant when Great Britain's membership application to the EEC was subsequently vetoed by the French.) Passage of the bill led to the initiation of the Kennedy Round of multilateral trade negotiations (named for President John F. Kennedy). The fact that the Trade Expansion Act provided tariff-cutting authority for only five years indirectly created a 1967 deadline for concluding the talks. At the last minute, the Europeans and the United States reached an agreement. This sealed the deal that produced history's largest single round of tariff cuts, about 35 percent on a worldwide basis. With average dutiable tariffs among the industrialized countries having been cut to less than 10 percent, nontariff barriers emerged as the dominant obstacle to trade in manufactured goods.

The Trade Expansion Act of 1962 contained two other significant innovations. The first was establishment of the adjustment assistance program that provides grants and loans to assist companies burdened by import competition to retool or diversify production and makes loans and grants directly to workers for retraining, relocation, or unemployment benefits. The adjustment assistance provision addressed a significant domestic political trend: emergence of the first serious doubts by U.S. labor unions about the virtues of a liberal trade policy for the United States. Organized labor was developing twinges of anxiety about the potential threat to jobs coming from the first stage of major inroads by foreign goods in the U.S. market. The adjustment assistance program joined the more import-restrictive escape clause provision (see Chapter 7) as a potential avenue of relief from fair foreign competition for U.S. companies and workers.

The second innovation contained in the 1962 act emanated from Congress's refusal to allow the State Department to remain the chief spokesman for the U.S. government in trade negotiations. The perception (if not the reality) existed that the increasingly sophisticated overseas competition facing the U.S. economy called for tougher negotiators, not the proverbial "striped pants cookie pushers" in the State Department beholden to cultivating the friendships of foreign governments. Congress demanded a more hard-nosed chief negotiator with a more balanced set of priorities, someone who would be willing to walk away from the negotiating table if unable to get a good overseas market access deal for U.S. producers. Accordingly, Congress created the post of Special Representative for Trade Negotiations in the Executive Office of the President, legislating that person's status as head of both U.S. trade negotiation delegations and interagency trade policy committees in the executive branch (see Chapter 5).

With the benefits of twenty-twenty hindsight, the conclusion of the Kennedy Round can be seen as representing the high-water mark through 1994 for liberal trade. By the end of the 1960s, momentous changes were surfacing in the international economy. Undisciplined macroeconomic policies were rapidly eroding relative U.S. economic strength, a trend that was hastened from another direction—the success of U.S. efforts to expedite the economic recoveries of Western Europe and Japan. The leadership provided by U.S. hegemony was in eclipse. The rising competitive threat from East Asia was beginning to be a source of alarm in Europe and the United States. The U.S. balance of payments deficits went from bad to worse. On the foreign policy front, the threat of Western Europe and Japan succumbing to the "red menace" had disappeared; so too had the national security justification for a soft-line U.S. acceptance of import barriers in these countries. The demise of the era of internationalism-driven U.S. trade policy was at hand.

The Agonizing Reappraisal of the 1970s

The end of the 1960s coincided with the beginning of the transition to entirely new phases of international economic relations and of U.S. trade policy. The size and strength of its economy, together with its military might, assured the United States of continued global economic leadership. But it was a challenge for everyone to adjust to U.S. leadership based on persuasion and compromise rather than hegemony. U.S. trade policy, meanwhile, was strongly influenced by a diminution of U.S. international competitiveness. The latter was induced by a relatively high rate of U.S. inflation and full return of Western Europe and Japan as major international competitors; achievement of this status was accelerated by their determination to keep their currencies' exchange rates undervalued against the dollar.

The impact of these trends was clearly visible in the gradual but steady decline in the U.S. trade surplus. This trend in turn generated growing doubts about the continued suitability of a liberal trade policy for the United States. Within months of the signing of the Kennedy Round tariff-cutting agreements, numerous quota bills were introduced on Capitol Hill in response to pleas from a number of manufacturing and primary product producers. Although nothing came of this 1968 offensive, the incoming Nixon administration's immediate initiation of efforts to limit imports of synthetic textile products (rayon, dacron, e.g.) was a metaphorical lighted match being tossed into a container of gasoline.

Frustrated with its inability to convince the Japanese to adopt "voluntary" export restraints on these newly popular textile products, the administration surprised everyone by eventually endorsing pending legislation that would have unilaterally invoked rigid textile quotas. The economic justification for such a harsh measure was dubious. Imports of synthetic fibers and apparel were indeed growing rapidly, but they still accounted for only a small fraction of total U.S. textile consumption because domestic production was also growing rapidly. Nevertheless, political factors won out. Congress revived the logrolling process of mutual back-scratching that had not played a significant role in trade legislation since the Smoot-Hawley tariff of 1930. The end result was arguably the most protectionist piece of trade legislation ever passed by the U.S. Congress. The Trade Act of 1970 included quotas on synthetic textiles, footwear, and a number of minor products. It also introduced a complicated trigger formula, which if met would have automatically extended escape clause relief to any and all petitioners demonstrating that they had been "substantially" injured by import competition. The bill passed both houses of Congress, but the congressional session ended before differences in the two bills passed could be reconciled by a conference committee; the likelihood of a presidential veto was never clear.

Dissatisfaction with the trade policy status quo was vividly displayed in the introduction of the radical Burke-Hartke bill in 1971. The bill was never acted on, but it was significant in that it symbolized the conversion of the politically powerful AFL-CIO (American Federation of Labor and Congress of Industrial Organizations) to a protectionist stance. The labor confederation at this time was suffering from a net loss of members, part of which was attributed to jobs lost to rising imports and increased overseas investments by U.S. corporations. The Burke-Hartke bill, largely written by the AFL-CIO, called for across-the-board import quotas and changes to U.S. international tax laws so sweeping that most foreign direct investment would have become immediately unprofitable for U.S. companies.

The probability that protectionist trade legislation would be enacted into law was reduced to nearly zero by a radical change in U.S. foreign economic policy orchestrated by President Richard Nixon. Beset on many fronts—frustrated with stagflation at home, jealous of growing prosperity and balance of payments surpluses in Western Europe and Japan, burdened by enormous defense expenditures to protect its allies, alarmed by currency crises involving enormous dollar sales in the foreign exchange market, and angered by continued gold losses in connection with the deteriorating U.S. balance of payments position—the Nixon administration became convinced that dramatic change was immediately needed. The twenty-five year tilt toward foreign priorities was judged to have become a prohibitively expensive liability that had to be shed.

The pendulum now swung dramatically back toward domestic needs. The international components of the New Economic Policy announced on August 15, 1971, to a stunned world centered on the imposition of a 10 percent surcharge on all import duties and the termination of the U.S. obligation to convert dollars held by foreign central banks into gold at a fixed price. The international financial markets suffered four months of chaos as massive sales of the dollar forced central banks one after another to suspend their obligation to keep exchange rates fixed. The Smithsonian Agreement of December 1971 permitted the return (at least temporarily) to fixed exchange rates after implementation of a multilateral exchange rate realignment of unprecedented proportions; the dollar was devalued and surplus countries revalued their exchange rates upward in an effort to restore U.S. trade competitiveness. The Nixon administration also demanded and received a commitment by the other industrial countries to initiate another round of multilateral trade negotiations. When it came to trade barriers, the United States considered itself more sinned against than a sinner. The U.S. government therefore believed it would be a major beneficiary of additional global trade liberalization efforts.

The advent of a new round of multilateral trade negotiations automatically produces the need for the executive branch to secure additional legislated authority to permit it to implement formally whatever trade liberalization concessions the administration had agreed upon in a multilateral trade agreement. The Trade Act of 1974 became another example of the post-1945 trend whereby major trade legislation replaced war as benchmarks for observing turning points in U.S. trade policy. Although more than twenty years have passed, many contemporary trade policy issues are rooted in the bill's innovative provisions. Broadly analyzed, its twin philosophies blazed the trail for what can be described as the occasionally contradictory two-track import policy pursued ever since by the United States: trade liberalization on a broad sector basis and import containment of selected, politically sensitive products. The Trade Act of 1974 contained yet another in a long-standing series of authorizations to the president to reduce tariffs. But in view of the success of past negotiations to reduce the vast majority of tariffs to the "nuisance" level, it was recognized from the start that the new round of trade talks would have to address nontariff barriers (NTBs) such as quotas, health and safety standards, and government procurement policies. Congress refused the administration's request for carte blanche authority (including the power to revise existing statutes) to reduce U.S. NTBs on a reciprocal basis. Instead, the fast-track system was born. Congress would show "good faith" by guaranteeing a floor vote on requested trade legislation changes within a minimum time period and without the option of any amendments (see Chapter 7).

On the protectionist side, the 1974 bill did not challenge the ideal of liberalized trade; it merely expanded the legal loopholes to the practice of liberal trade. The bill eased the qualifying language of the escape clause (a legislative provision providing temporary relief from fair foreign competition for companies able to demonstrate "injury" from rising imports) to make affirmative findings of injury or threat of injury much more likely. Congress tried to assure more leverage for domestic producers by voting itself the power to override any presidential decisions to ignore recommendations by the International Trade Commission under the escape clause for import relief. (The so-called legislative veto was subsequently declared unconstitutional by the Supreme Court.) In addition, the legislation introduced administrative reforms that favored U.S. plaintiffs in cases of unfair foreign trade petitions filed under the statutes on dumping (sales of imports at prices below their production costs or below their sales price in the exporting country's market) and countervailing duties (exporting companies receiving subsidies from foreign governments). The bill also provided conditional authority to the president to extend MFN treatment to countries not currently receiving it (the source of the complex situation with China discussed in Chapter 1).

The first of two important legacies of the Trade Act of 1974 was the successful conclusion of the Tokyo Round of multilateral trade negotiations. (In a shift symbolic of the decline of U.S. international economic hegemony, multilateral trade rounds are no longer being named after U.S. statesmen; instead, a round is named for the place where agreement has been reached to launch new negotiations.) In addition to reductions in industrial countries' tariffs to below an average level of 5 percent, participants took steps to curb NTBs. This consisted of agreement to abide by a series of "codes of conduct" regulating a number of internal government actions affecting trade flows (see Chapter 7). Another breakthrough was the initial effort in multilateral negotiations to deal specifically with the special trade problems of the less developed countries by authorizing the industrial countries to extend "differential and more favorable treatment" to them.

The second legacy of the 1974 act was the extension of more protection to U.S. interest groups seeking import relief, usually from the rapidly intensifying competition of Japan and the newly industrialized countries (NICS) of East Asia—Korea, Singapore, Taiwan, and Hong Kong. In what was essentially a compromise between the unilateral protectionism of the 1930s and the enthusiasm for trade liberalization of the 1960s, the United States and the EEC became the principal practitioners of what is commonly called "the new protectionism." The latter is epitomized by so-called orderly marketing agreements, also known as voluntary export restraints.

The agonizing reappraisal of U.S. trade policy introduced a search that continues to this day for an economic and political equilibrium between the extremes of pre-1934 protectionism and post-1945 internationalism. The initial surge in the 1970s toward legislated protectionism in the United States was rolled back by two developments: the sustained downward movement in the value of the dollar during the early 1970s and the willingness of the executive branch to impose ad hoc import restraints, on both a unilateral and a negotiated basis, on numerous products. Relative quiescence prevailed in U.S. trade policy at the beginning of the 1980s. But it would soon be shattered by an onslaught of unprecedented shifts in economic trends.

The 1980s and Early 1990s:
Is Free Trade Policy Obsolete?

U.S. trade policy was deeply affected by the revolutionary changes in domestic economic policy introduced in 1981 by the adoption of "Reaganomics." Sharp reductions in taxes and a rising budget deficit complemented by tight monetary policy produced an excess of national spending over production and an inadequate supply of saving, a situation that was offset by a soaring trade deficit and massive capital inflows, respectively. Despite the largest trade deficits ever recorded (peaking at $152 billion in 1987), the U.S. dollar continued to appreciate to levels that devastated the ability of many U.S. industrial and agricultural sectors to compete in the international marketplace. The Reagan administration obstinately preached the discipline of the free market.

In a stunning demonstration of the workings of the separation of powers in the U.S. government, Congress eventually forced the administration to alter its international economic policy by actively considering (but not passing) a progression of trade legislation with an increasingly anti-import bias.[18] The 1985 Plaza Agreement concluded by the major industrialized countries induced a significant drop in the dollar's overvalued exchange rate (thereby tending to make U.S. exports cost less in other currencies and to make foreign goods more expensive in dollar terms). Elsewhere, the administration formally added a major new theme to U.S. trade policy: reciprocity. The latter was originally popularized by Senator John Danforth (R., Mo.) in a bill that mandated the president seek comparable access to foreign markets as that provided to foreign goods by the United States.

Reciprocity, as interpreted by the Reagan administration, became the watchword of the larger, economically sound strategy of seeking to reduce the U.S. trade deficit by increasing exports rather than reducing imports. The propensity of the United States to turn the other cheek to foreign trade barriers, as it had done in the era of U.S. hegemony, was repudiated outright. The theme of a major trade policy pronouncement by President Reagan in September 1985 was the need for other countries to improve their allegedly inadequate commitment to a liberal trading order. He declared that he would "not stand by and watch U.S. businesses fail because of unfair trading practices abroad. I will not stand by and watch U.S. workers lose their jobs because other nations do not play by the rules."[19] Creation of government "strike forces" was announced to attack foreign barriers to U.S. exports and to secure the increasingly attractive symbolic lure of a "level playing field" in trade relations. These trade and monetary policy initiatives and the decline in the U.S. trade deficit mollified but did not satisfy the legislative branch.

Congress thereupon embarked on a three-year initiative to pass comprehensive trade legislation with or without executive branch cooperation. The end product was the Omnibus Trade and Competitiveness Act of 1988. This legal milestone in U.S. trade policy epitomized evolving U.S. trade philosophy as well as the tightening policymaking partnership between the executive branch and a more assertive Congress. The 1,000-page bill was devoid of unilateral restrictions on imports, a reflection of a remarkable consensus among politicians, economists, and the business community that protectionism was neither an appropriate nor efficient means to remedy U.S. trade problems. Instead, the omnibus trade bill was dominated by the usual delegation of authority to the president to reduce tariffs on a reciprocal basis in the impending round of multilateral trade negotiations and by proactive provisions. Most notable among the latter was the "Super 301" measure, an enhancement of the Section 301 provision dealing with overseas discrimination against U.S. exports (see Chapter 7), sounding the clarion call for a more aggressive policy of export expansion through more intensive official efforts to secure greater access to priority foreign markets for U.S. products.

The philosophy behind Super 301 and other activist provisions of the bill was an outgrowth of a prevailing belief on Capitol Hill that all presidents, past and present, lean too much in the direction of statesmanship. Many members of Congress believe that there is an ongoing presidential reluctance either to anger foreign friends or to be branded as a protectionist. This alleged tilt comes at the expense of domestic producers seeking relief from strong import competition and exporters burdened by foreign trade barriers. The trickiest part of drafting the 1988 trade bill dealt with finding statutory language that legislated the maximum degree of inflexible negotiating backbone for the president in pursuing overseas market-opening demands short of triggering a veto by overly restricting presidential discretion in administering trade policy.

The 1988 trade act also formalized the approach that the majority of U.S. foreign trade problems were transcending the tools of traditional trade policy and required more elaborate responses, such as better macroeconomic policy coordination among the Group of Seven industrialized countries (Canada, France, Germany, Great Britain, Italy, Japan, and the United States) and a system of exchange rates that accurately reflected relative national economic strengths. More important, the spreading fear that the United States was suffering a serious secular deterioration in its international competitiveness position, mainly at the hands of Japan, translated into numerous provisions going well beyond the boundaries of traditional trade bills and into programs (in effect, a limited industrial policy) designed to strengthen U.S. productivity, technology, and workers' skills. This new approach to trade strategy was well summarized by Laura D'Andrea Tyson just before she became chairperson of President Clinton's Council of Economic Advisers: "Even the most sensible and effective trade policies cannot compensate for domestic programs that remain impoverished both fiscally and intellectually."[20]

Whereas it spent the first twenty-five years after World War II unequivocally subordinating trade policy to geopolitical objectives, the United States since 1970 has consistently made exceptions to its traditional belief in liberal trade. Although most Americans strongly believe their country is still the world's single most important advocate of trade liberalization, many citizens of other countries would beg to differ. The first reason for the tarnished reputation of the United States as liberal trade champion has been its frequent willingness to restrict the further growth of selected imports when the market mechanism works to the disadvantage of domestic producers. This perceived tendency manifested itself in the 1970s and 1980s largely through demands that other countries "voluntarily" restrain their exports; in the 1990s the principal manifestation has been allegedly overly vigorous enforcement of the U.S. antidumping statute. The second factor debasing the U.S. image has been the repeatedly loud demands on major trading partners (most notably Japan and China in 1995) either to eliminate trade practices the United States finds odious or face retaliation. The previously discussed Super 301 statute epitomized foreign perceptions that some U.S. trade statutes have fueled an "aggressive unilateralism" in which the U.S. government, arrogantly and against GATT rules, establishes itself as trade policy judge, jury, and executioner.

More recently, an increasing number of influential U.S. voices have expressed concern that the intellectual core of free trade theory—the principle of comparative advantage—is no longer applicable. As explained in Chapter 3, these people believe in the radically new economics of high-technology industry, and they view the governmental-business cooperation model perfected by Japan to be capable of creating "induced competitive advantage," especially in knowledge-intensive industries. To the extent they are correct, even the most dynamic U.S. companies can falter in the face of new rules of international competitiveness.

The future of U.S. trade policy strategy will be defined by the outcome of an intellectual debate about new rules, new situations, and new tactics. The trade policy debate in the 1990s is *not* dominated by advocates of the extremes of a return to high trade barriers or an uncompromising internationalism that defined earlier, simpler times.

The Evolution of
U.S. Export Policy, 1949–1994

In terms of trade flows, exports literally move in the opposite direction of imports. Attitudes held by most people are equally opposite: Politicians and businesspeople revere exports for the jobs, profits, and foreign exchange earnings they generate, but, at best, they tolerate imports that compete with domestic production. Economists for more than 100 years have stressed the benefits accruing to a country by allowing a relatively free inflow of imports. Exports tend to be discussed by economic theorists only in the incidental context of being the means to pay for the most important element of trade: imports.

Although most other countries retain an "export or die" mentality, export policy in the United States remains more of an abstraction than hard reality. Commitment to boost exports receives relatively little sustained attention at the highest political levels. Export promotion strategy is normally subordinated to other concerns: import policy, national security, and domestic economic policy. This asymmetry is a function of four factors: the relatively low contribution of trade to U.S. GDP; the country's extraordinary lack of need to earn foreign exchange to pay for imports; the vast strategic interests of a global superpower that tend to overshadow commercial concerns; and the absence of domestic economic planning that precludes the need to expedite exports of industries targeted for international competitiveness. The volume of exports and their contribution to domestic economic activity are still largely ignored by the American public. Virtually no one realizes that the increase in U.S. exports from 1986 through 1990 generated almost 40 percent of the growth of U.S. GDP, and that in 1990 export growth accounted for more than 75 percent of GDP growth.[21] Most new jobs created in recent years in the U.S. manufacturing sector have been export-related.

An examination of the history of contemporary U.S. export policy is necessary at this point because the preceding sections of this chapter followed the common pattern of defining the evolution of U.S. trade relations in terms of import policy. This section provides this book with a distinctive element. Typically, one cannot find mention of export policy in the text or even in the index of international economics and trade books published in the United States.

The history of U.S. export policy since the end of World War II is characterized by inconsistencies and paradoxes, just as is import policy. Once again, there is evidence of the same trade policy philosophy: that for all countries the market mechanism should be maximized and government interference should be minimized. One administration after another has sought reductions in other governments' export enhancement programs (subsidies, highly concessional financing, foreign aid grants mixed in with official export loans, and so on) to get them lowered in magnitude and scope to U.S. levels, rather than to increase U.S. efforts to match the higher levels of such activities in other countries.

On the other hand, U.S. export policy, just like import policy, has repeatedly abandoned a hands-off strategy and become highly interventionist. The U.S. government has consistently discouraged and even prohibited exports to a degree unknown anywhere else. Its export policy relationship with the private sector frequently goes beyond uselessness into outright obstructionism. In a world in which export maximization is pursued with feverish activism everywhere else, the U.S. government's approach is—for better or worse—in a league of its own. This unusual pattern is partially the result of some U.S. policymakers remaining attuned to the Marshall Plan mentality of restoring *foreign* economic growth and political stability that dominated immediate post–World War II U.S. foreign policy.

To be sure, presidents since the 1960s have talked about the need for the U.S. government to assist in export promotion. But their actions usually have been inconsistent with their words. In some cases, new restraints were imposed faster than old ones were eliminated. (The major exceptions to official export lassitude have been the ongoing pressure on Japan for greater market access and the use since the mid-1980s of the Section 301 provision to reduce or eliminate foreign trade barriers on a product-specific basis.) A steady stream of criticism has suggested that most U.S. export promotion efforts are more a case of going through the motions than genuine reordering of policy priorities. One economist argued that export expansion packages have been announced with a regularity that "by itself suggests something less than total commitment by the government to these initiatives."[22] In the Jimmy Carter years, *Business Week* magazine claimed that "so feeble is Administration backing for the sales efforts of U.S. companies in global markets that many U.S. businessmen overseas are unaware that the U.S. even has an export policy."[23]

At a time when some high-tech goods for export can carry individual price tags in excess of $100 million, the availability of generous export financing terms—rather than price—can be the critical determinant of which company in which country gets the sale. Nevertheless, the U.S. government has subjected its Export-Import Bank and other export promotion programs to the same budgetary cutbacks accorded to all other agencies. In 1990, U.S. government outlays for all export promotion programs per $1,000 of exports were about one-third of those of the major European economies except for Germany.[24] But even this relatively low level of funding did not seem to be allocated on a coherent, reasoned basis. For political and historical reasons, the lion's share of export promotion outlays (about 75 percent of the dollar total) as of the early 1990s still went to agricultural commodities, not to advanced industrial goods. The former account for only 10 percent of total U.S. exports, and most of these concessional loans are made on behalf of large, competitive agribusinesses.[25] The General Accounting Office in 1992 decried the state of official export promotion efforts, claiming that "much more might be achieved with existing resources if they were allocated according to national priorities and were administered by a more rational agency structure. This is not now being achieved, with the export promotion effort spread amongst separate programs with separate budgets in separate agencies that are not integrated under any unifying strategy or rationale."[26]

The most dramatically negative and illiberal (i.e., interventionist) dimension of U.S. trade policy since 1949 has taken the form of a proliferation of export controls and sanctions. The latter have been imposed either for national security reasons or as retaliations designed to modify the behavior of other governments that has been deemed inconsistent with U.S. foreign policy objectives or ethical standards. The embrace of official export controls reflected the political defeat of the ideology of laissez-faire, first by the political ideology of fighting communism and later by the moral ideology of minimizing trade with governments that have "blood on their hands." "Since the end of the Second World War," concluded one scholar, "the United States has been the most prominent practitioner of peace-time restrictions upon trade and other economic transactions."[27]

Implementation of export controls following the onset of the cold war was a policy ultimately based on a straightforward and, to this day, noncontroversial premise: to deny or at least delay the ability of potential adversaries to obtain in the international marketplace both weapons and state-of-the-art dual-use commercial technologies, such as computers and machine tools, that readily could be adapted to enhance their military capabilities. U.S. cold war military strategy (successfully implemented, as it turned out) was based on the concept of the "force multiplier effect"—offsetting the Soviet bloc's numerical superiority in manpower and weapons with superior Western technology.

The major imponderable was and still is where to draw the line in using export controls to prolong and widen this technological superiority. In theory, exports of even the most innocuous civilian goods allow adversaries to divert resources away from production of these goods and into the military realm. The faction in the U.S. government that wanted to err on the side of caution and to inflict maximum economic injury on the Soviet bloc countries and China consistently dominated the policymaking process during the cold war era. Acting in its role of political and economic hegemon, the United States in the early 1950s was highly successful in convincing its relatively compliant West European and Asian allies to sign onto this rigid regime of economic denial through export control. Several factors contributed to Western unanimity on this subject lasting into the 1960s. During this time, other countries' fears of Soviet intentions were at their peak, the United States had undisputed leadership in most technologies, and it was easy to identify and isolate relatively limited numbers of sensitive dual-use technologies.

The Export Control Act of 1949 did more than provide the first legislative base for U.S. export controls in peacetime. It established the precedent for congressional allocation to the president of sweeping authority to restrict exports for the twin purposes of national security and foreign policy—power far in excess of any comparable presidential authority to restrict imports. From this legislative base, U.S. export policy evolved into strict adherence to utilizing economic sanctions in connection with protection of national security and promotion of foreign policy objectives. "Short supply" became the third legislated rationale for application of U.S. export controls with a view to preventing the aggravation of domestic shortages by limiting foreign sales.

After the 1960s, the U.S. export control effort was more pervasive and invasive than that of any other country. In the first place, the United States retained a far more extensive list of restricted goods and technologies (requiring the government's specific approval of export licenses) than the multilateral list maintained by CO-COM, the now defunct Coordinating Committee on Multilateral Export Controls. Second, the United States is unique in its extraterritorial application of export controls. U.S. law applies reexport provisions to U.S. corporate subsidiaries overseas and to independent foreign companies selling U.S.-made products, U.S.-made components incorporated into foreign-made goods, and even foreign products manufactured with U.S.-origin technology.[28] Many foreign companies have moved to "de-Americanize" their procurement practices in order to avoid the need to comply with what they regard as externally imposed, onerous restrictions. Finally, the U.S. export control system is widely perceived as being unduly nonresponsive to private sector interests because it is excessively complex (the Commerce Department's Export Administration Regulations fill 600 pages), overly secretive, slow-moving (eleven different federal agencies have some jurisdiction), and negative (in large part due to the Defense Department's extensive participation in the process).[29]

In a widely read analysis of the competitiveness and national security interrelationship, the authors of a National Academy of Sciences study in 1987 argued that U.S. export controls "encompass more products and technologies, are generally more restrictive, and entail more administrative delays and shipper uncertainties than those of the other major CoCom countries." Furthermore, several elements of U.S. controls were found to be weakening allied unity by "having an increasingly corrosive effect on relationships with many" friendly countries.[30] The costly domestic economic impact of U.S. export controls is suggested by the estimate that U.S. commercial exports valued at $21–$27 billion (and potentially as high as $40 billion) were going to be lost annually in the mid-1990s as the result of all identifiable U.S. government export controls and disincentives.[31]

By the late 1960s, the U.S. government's eager embrace of export controls was becoming progressively out of step. U.S. tactics increasingly deviated from the minimalist approach being adopted by all other major exporting countries, which imposed export controls only on the most sensitive dual-use items. As foreign companies began enjoying sales success in communist countries, U.S. industrial companies unleashed unstinting and loud complaints. They argued that severe U.S. export restraints were inflicting intolerably expensive inequities and competitive damage on them at the same time that U.S. export controls were becoming steadily less successful in denying the Soviet bloc access to advanced Western technology.

The executive branch, however, remained unwavering in equating the national interest with global political priorities, even as the export sector grew as a percentage of GDP.

Congress, as usual, felt the need to be responsive to intense pressure for trade policy changes being exerted by a wide segment of the private sector. There followed a long but only marginally successful legislative effort to force on the executive branch a more relaxed attitude on export controls, one that was more consistent with those of the other COCOM member countries.

The initial effort of Congress to reform export control policy was the Export Administration Act of 1969. Among other things, it directed the executive branch to limit the number of goods subject to export controls for national security reasons and declared that the foreign availability of a good should be an important criterion in determining export license approvals. The Export Administration Act of 1979 ordered the executive branch to take increased account of the foreign availability of any goods controlled for national security reasons and to first weigh a number of specific factors, dealing mainly with domestic costs and anticipated foreign impact, before imposing export controls for foreign policy purposes.

Despite additional efforts to ease the export control law in 1985 and 1988, Congress remained surprisingly unsuccessful in its efforts to legislate significant diminutions in the propensity of administrations to impose new export restraints and in the ability of the bureaucracy to arbitrarily deny export licenses for goods readily available from other countries. A primary reason for this was congressional unwillingness to deny the executive branch considerable leeway in export control policy in deference to the president's larger but ill-defined authority in foreign affairs. A second reason for the absence of significant change in the administration of export controls was that the executive branch won a battle of political will with the legislative branch. Successive administrations exerted a stronger, more focused commitment to achieving their preferred course of action; namely, they put the burden of proof on would-be U.S. exporters rather than on officials choosing to deny export licenses.[32] Furthermore, there were occasional White House end runs around the Export Administration Act to use the broader presidential trade restriction authority available under the International Emergency Economic Powers Act.

In point of fact, the imposition of export controls and sanctions did not abate. They proliferated. Throughout the 1970s and 1980s, an unrelated series of economic and political events triggered adoption of several important restrictive export actions having a major impact on U.S. external relations. Soybean exports were limited in 1973 because the Nixon administration erroneously perceived domestic shortages (thereby adding credence to foreign governments' defense of their protectionist agriculture policies on grounds of food security). President Carter angrily imposed controls on U.S. grain exports to the Soviet Union following the latter's invasion of Afghanistan at the end of 1979 (causing little deprivation but much redirected buying by the Soviets).

In perhaps the most futile of export sanction moves, President Reagan, frustrated with the lack of allied cooperation, in June 1982 imposed a second stage of trade sanctions to follow up those imposed on the Soviet Union during the previous December. In seeking to maximize the cutoff of U.S. goods and technology available for use in constructing the pipeline that would transport natural gas from Siberia to waiting customers in Western Europe, the new sanctions were applied on an extraterritorial basis. The governments of France, Germany, Great Britain, and Italy were furious with the additional application of restrictions to exports of energy-related goods and technology to the Soviet Union by overseas U.S. subsidiaries and by any foreign-owned company producing goods under licenses obtained from any company subject to U.S. jurisdiction. The additional U.S. dictum retroactively prohibiting exports of even those goods due to be shipped from factories in Western Europe to the Soviet Union under preexisting contracts was viewed as an unacceptable intrusion on European sovereignty. Threats of legal action by European governments against any locally incorporated companies complying with the new sanctions, combined with domestic opposition, forced President Reagan to rescind most of the pipeline-related controls a few months later.

Above and beyond export controls imposed for national security reasons against China and the Soviet Union and its "allies" in Eastern Europe, the United States imposed export sanctions on a number of other countries. In most of these cases, foreign policy reasons were the instigating force, and in several cases sanctions were imposed in association with United Nations resolutions. Countries targeted during the 1970s included South Africa, Cuba, Iran, North Korea, (North) Vietnam, Cambodia, Uganda, Ethiopia, Libya, Nicaragua, Chile, and Argentina.[33] During the 1980s and early 1990s, the trade sanctions list expanded (partly due to the addition of alleged support for terrorists as legal grounds for export controls) to include Iraq, Haiti, Serbia, Syria, and Panama. The first steps in a meaningful relaxation of the hard-line U.S. commitment to export controls did not begin to appear until the 1990s. Major changes in the international political landscape, primarily in the Soviet Union and South Africa, were the catalysts of this relaxation. The most tangible results were significant reductions in controls covering two key high-tech sectors: computers and telecommunications equipment.[34]

Conclusion

What is past is prologue. U.S. trade policy will always be evolving. The trade agenda will never be completed. New international commercial situations and the need for new responses are inevitable. Trade policy substance will remain in permanent transition because the relative importance of its four determinants cannot be held constant: the structure of the U.S. economy, the terrain of U.S. politics, the main goals of U.S. foreign policy, and the dynamics of the global economy. Formulas used to establish trade policy in one year are not necessarily appropriate for new contingencies and new variations of existing situations.

Surface changes notwithstanding, the core fundamentals will stay fixed. Much of U.S. trade policy will remain imperfect, impermanent, and inconsistent. It cannot be otherwise in view of the inherent imperfection of a democratic decisionmaking process forever struggling to establish an optimal hierarchy among legitimate yet conflicting economic and political, as well as domestic and external, priorities.

For Further Reading

Dobson, John M. *Two Centuries of Tariffs*. Washington, D.C.: U.S. International Trade Commission, 1976.

Hufbauer, Gary Clyde, Diane T. Berliner, and Kimberly Ann Elliott. *Trade Protection in the United States: 31 Case Studies*. Washington, D.C.: Institute for International Economics, 1986.

Hufbauer, Gary Clyde, Jeffrey J. Schott, and Kimberly Ann Elliott. *Economic Sanctions Reconsidered*. Washington, D.C.: Institute for International Economics, 1990.

Kelly, William B., Jr., ed. *Studies in United States Commercial Policy*. Chapel Hill: University of North Carolina Press, 1963.

Long, William J. *U.S. Export Control Policy: Executive Autonomy vs. Congressional Reform*. New York: Columbia University Press, 1989.

Mikesell, Raymond. *United States Economic Policy and International Relations*. New York: McGraw-Hill, 1952.

Schattschneider, E. E. *Politics, Pressures, and the Tariff*. New York: Prentice-Hall, 1935.

Taussig, Frank W. *The Tariff History of the United States*. 8th ed. New York: G. P. Putnam's Sons, 1931.

U.S. International Trade Commission. Annual reports on the *Operation of the Trade Agreements Program*.

Notes

1. Reproduced in *Powernomics: Economics and Strategy After the Cold War* (Washington, D.C.: Economic Strategy Institute, 1991), p. 135.

2. John M. Dobson, *Two Centuries of Tariffs* (Washington, D.C.: U.S. International Trade Commission, 1976), p. 51.

3. *Ibid.*, p. 56.

4. *Ibid.*, pp. 65–66.

5. Raymond F. Mikesell, *United States Economic Policy and International Relations* (New York: McGraw-Hill, 1952), p. 8.

6. Charles P. Kindleberger, *The World in Depression, 1929–1939* (Berkeley: University of California Press, 1973), p. 292.

7. Quoted in Dobson, *op. cit.*, p. 31.

8. Mikesell, *op. cit.*, p. 63.

9. Dobson, *op. cit.,* p. 74.

10. John Parke Young, *The International Economy* (New York: Ronald Press, 1963), p. 35.

11. Mikesell, *op. cit.,* p. 65.

12. Alfred E. Eckes, "Trading U.S. Interests," *Foreign Policy,* Fall 1992, p. 138.

13. Richard N. Gardner, *Sterling-Dollar Diplomacy* (New York: McGraw-Hill, 1969), p. 367.

14. Quoted in *European Community,* January 1970, p. 10.

15. Benjamin J. Cohen, "The Revolution in Atlantic Economic Relations: A Bargain Comes Unstuck," in Wolfram Hanrieder, ed., *The United States and Western Europe* (Cambridge, MA: Winthrop Publishers, 1974), p. 118.

16. Quoted in *The Washington Post,* July 18, 1993, p. H-1.

17. Eckes, *op. cit.,* pp. 139, 141.

18. For details of this process, see Stephen D. Cohen, *The Making of U.S. International Economic Policy,* 4th ed. (New York: Praeger, 1994).

19. Quoted in *Business America,* September 30, 1985, p. 3.

20. Laura D'Andrea Tyson, *Who's Bashing Whom? Trade Conflict in High-Technology Industries* (Washington, D.C.: Institute for International Economics, 1992), p. 2.

21. Data from General Accounting Office, *Export Promotion: A Comparison of Programs in Five Industrialized Nations,* June 1992, p. 10.

22. Penelope Hartland-Thunberg, "The Political and Strategic Importance of Exports," Center for Strategic and International Studies, 1979, p. 17.

23. "The New Export Policy Works Like the Old—Badly," *Business Week,* July 21, 1980, p. 88.

24. General Accounting Office, "Export Promotion, Governmentwide Strategy Needed for Federal Programs," congressional testimony of Allan I. Mendelowitz, March 15, 1993, p. 15.

25. General Accounting Office, "Export Promotion, U.S. Programs Lack Coherence," congressional testimony of Allan I. Mendelowitz, March 2, 1992, p. 2.

26. *Ibid.,* p. 3.

27. David Leyton-Brown, *The Utility of International Economic Sanctions* (New York: St. Martin's Press, 1987), p. 255.

28. Arvind Parkhe, "U.S. National Security Export Controls: Implications for Global Competitiveness of U.S. High-Tech Firms," *Strategic Management Journal,* January 1992, p. 54.

29. U.S. International Trade Commission, *Global Competitiveness of U.S. Advanced-Technology Industries: Computers,* December 1993, pp. 3–10.

30. National Academy of Sciences, *Executive Summary, Balancing the National Interest* (Washington, D.C.: National Academy Press, 1987), pp. 11, 16.

31. J. David Richardson, *Sizing Up U.S. Export Disincentives* (Washington, D.C.: Institute for International Economics, 1993), pp. 2–3.

32. For details on the history and analysis of executive–legislative branch relations in export control policy, see William J. Long, *U.S. Export Control Policy, Executive Autonomy vs. Congressional Reform* (New York: Columbia University Press, 1989).

33. Michael Mastanduno, "The United States Defiant: Export Controls in the Postwar Era," *Daedalus,* Fall 1991, p. 101.

34. As part of its new posture on export controls imposed for national security reasons, the United States participated in a 1991 COCOM exercise that dramatically relaxed controls on

shipments of dual-use technology by establishing a concise "core list" and sharply curtailed restrictions on shipments to Eastern Europe. President Clinton's September 1993 export initiative contained sixty-five measures designed to increase U.S. exports of goods and services from $628 billion in 1992 to $1 trillion by the end of the decade; as cited in "Remarks by the President in Export Commission Report Announcement," White House press release dated September 29, 1993, p. 2.

Part Two

Economics

3   Economic Theories of International Trade

As one prominent economist has written, the advocacy of free trade is "as close to a sacred tenet as any idea in economics."[1] In deference to most economists' strong views on this subject, political scientists, legal scholars, and editorial writers often take it on faith that free trade is the best policy for the nation and the world and view any departures from free trade as capitulations to interest group politics or nationalistic sentiments. Nevertheless, the economic theory of free trade is just that, a theory: a set of propositions derived from some underlying assumptions and principles. Rather than accept this theory on faith, it is important to understand its foundations—and its limitations.

To be sure, virtually all economic theories recognize that there are important gains countries obtain through their foreign trade. There is no support in economic theory for a policy of blanket protectionism of domestic industries or for walling a nation off entirely from foreign competition. But this does not necessarily imply that a pure laissez-faire attitude of governments toward their nations' trade relations is always and everywhere the best policy. There are valid economic arguments for an active government role in regulating or promoting particular types of economic activity among nations in specific ways under certain types of conditions. The case for *pure* free trade is full of qualifications and exceptions, and actual policy options are often less clear-cut than pure free trade versus protection anyway.

In this chapter we review the economic theories of international trade, emphasizing both their logical foundations and their practical limitations. This review takes a largely historical approach, beginning with the earliest theories and ending with the most recent. Throughout this chapter, attention will be focused on the assumptions of the theories and the conditions under which they apply. Without attempting to discuss the technicalities of these theories, we will still attempt to suggest some of their subtleties. The objective is to take trade theory out of the realm of religious faith and put it into the arena of intelligent, critical discourse where it belongs.

Mercantilism

The first systematic thinking on trade issues was that of the mercantilists. Mercantilist ideas were developed between the sixteenth and nineteenth centuries by a number of pamphleteers, philosophers, and government officials. The mercantilists were strong nationalists for whom the interests of the nation (and particularly of the monarchy) were primary. In general, the mercantilists advocated policies to maximize the wealth and power of the nation rather than the well-being of individual citizens.

In regard to trade, the mercantilists are most famous for arguing that a country had to have a positive *balance of trade* (a surplus of exports over imports) in order to increase its national wealth at the expense of other nations. The earliest mercantilists favored a trade surplus (positive balance of trade) because it would bring an inflow of gold and silver into the country, as foreigners would have to pay with precious metals in order to settle their accounts.

Later mercantilists were less interested in gold and silver inflows and more interested in encouraging domestic industry. In their view, a country with a trade surplus would have prosperous domestic industries providing employment for the laboring classes, and a deficit country would have depressed industries and high unemployment. These later mercantilists favored protectionism for domestic industries deemed vital for economic progress, to shield them from import competition and to help keep the balance of trade positive.

What united all the mercantilists was a belief that unregulated markets could not be trusted to maximize national advantages in trade, and therefore some kind of government guidance and control was necessary. Later economists criticized the mercantilists for assuming that trade was (in modern terminology) a *zero-sum game,* in which some countries (those with surpluses) could benefit only at the expense of others (those with deficits). Nevertheless, the conceptualization of the balance of trade was an important development in our understanding of international financial relations. It also foreshadowed the twentieth-century macroeconomic theory of John Maynard Keynes,[2] which holds that a high level of exports and a low propensity to import are helpful for stimulating aggregate demand and national income.

Classical Trade Theory and Comparative Advantage

Classical economic theories developed out of a critique of mercantilist ideas. Adam Smith devoted a large portion of his 1776 book, *The Wealth of Nations,* to an attack on what he called "the mercantile system" (from which the name *mercantilism* was later derived). Smith argued that the source of a nation's wealth lies in the productivity of its labor force, which was increased primarily by (1) the *division of labor* (specialization in different tasks) and (2) the *accumulation of capital* (investing in stocks of materials and equipment that could increase future production).

Smith was interested in promoting the welfare of individual consumers rather than the wealth and power of the national government. Government regulation was not, for the most part,[3] necessary, since the force of market competition could be relied upon to compel self-interested individuals to serve each other's needs through the social division of labor. For example, the butcher would supply the baker with meat and the baker would supply the butcher with bread, both acting out of self-interest. This same principle also applied to foreign trade: No government intervention was required to restrict or to promote it, since individuals in different countries would naturally specialize in those products that they could best produce and exchange them with each other, thus forming an international division of labor.

Smith argued that trying to maintain a positive balance of trade was foolish, since a nation could never grow rich by "beggaring" (impoverishing) its neighbors. As Smith put it, "if foreigners, either by prohibitions or high duties, are hindered from coming to sell, they cannot then always afford to come to buy."[4] Moreover, the protectionist policies advocated by the mercantilists would not lead to maximum production of national wealth. Any trade restrictions would force people to produce some goods domestically that could be obtained more cheaply abroad; the resources thus diverted could better be utilized producing other goods that the country could make more efficiently. Only if producers were left free to decide what goods to produce would the *invisible hand* of the market lead them to choose those products that they could produce with the lowest costs.[5]

Although Smith developed a powerful critique of mercantilist ideas, he did not really develop a convincing theory of international trade—an explanation of which countries export which goods and why. His notion that countries should specialize in those goods they can produce most cheaply has been referred to as the theory of *absolute advantage*. But this notion has an obvious flaw: How can a less developed nation, which cannot produce *any* goods more cheaply than it could import them, have anything to export? Thus, although Smith made a strong case against mercantilism and had some interesting ideas about the benefits of trade,[6] he did not satisfactorily explain how all countries can gain from trade.

Later classical economists developed a more general theory of trade than Adam Smith. The most important of these was David Ricardo, whose *Principles of Political Economy and Taxation* was first published in 1817. Ricardo is best known for the theory of *comparative advantage,* although this idea was also developed by others at the time. Ricardo formulated this theory in terms of comparative labor costs. Suppose that one country (say, Britain) can produce all goods more cheaply than another country (say, America), in the sense that in Britain it takes fewer hours of labor to produce each good. Nevertheless, Britain may be *relatively* more productive in some goods (e.g., cotton cloth), and *relatively* less productive in others (e.g., wheat). Then Britain has a comparative advantage only in cloth, and America has a comparative advantage in wheat (since it has a smaller absolute disadvantage in wheat).

BOX 3.1   An Example of Ricardian Comparative Advantage

A simple numerical example will help to illustrate Ricardo's theory of comparative advantage. In this theory, comparative advantage is based on labor costs, which are measured by the person-hours of labor required to produce each unit of output. The example assumes that there are two goods, wheat and cloth, and two countries (or regions), America and Britain, whose labor costs are as follows:

	Hours of Labor per Unit of Output	
Country	*Wheat (per bushel)*	*Cloth (per yard)*
America	8	9
Britain	4	3

These precise numbers are purely hypothetical, but in principle such labor costs could be calculated by measuring the total hours of production workers' labor in a factory or farm and dividing them by the number of goods produced. The amounts of labor time required in each country are determined mainly by its technology but could also be influenced by any natural resources or capital goods used in production that lessen the amount of labor needed to produce the final output.

Although Britain has lower costs in terms of labor hours for both goods, it has a relatively greater advantage in cloth and a relatively lesser advantage in wheat (British labor is three times as productive as American labor in cloth but only twice as productive in wheat). America, in turn, has a comparative advantage in wheat, since its labor is relatively more productive in that sector. American labor is one-half as productive compared with British labor in wheat, since it takes American workers twice as many hours to grow wheat (8 compared with 4). However, American labor is only one-third as productive as British labor in cloth, since it takes American workers three times as many hours for each yard produced (9 compared with 3).

Ricardo showed that if each country exports the good in which it has a comparative advantage, both countries will benefit from the trade even if one of the countries is absolutely more productive in both goods (see Box 3.1 for a detailed example).

The logic of comparative advantage is irrefutable, but some important caveats are in order. First, although both countries always gain from trade by specializing according to their respective comparative advantage, one country may get a relatively

BOX 3.1 (continued)

From this type of example, Ricardo concluded that a country does not have to have absolutely lower costs of producing a good in order to benefit from exporting it (and for the other country to benefit from importing it). Suppose, for example, that these countries can trade internationally at the ratio of one yard of cloth per bushel of wheat. America gains by exporting wheat and importing cloth since, in the absence of trade, domestic production possibilities dictate that Americans would get only 8/9 of a yard of cloth per bushel of wheat per yard of cloth in the absence of trade, and 3/4 is less than 1. In this way, both countries end up with more of both commodities to consume if they trade than if each country tried to produce both goods for itself.

To see the gains from trade from another perspective, consider an American worker who can spend her time producing either wheat or cloth. In 8 hours, the American can make 8/9 yard of cloth. But by devoting the 8 hours to wheat production, she can grow 1 bushel of wheat, which she can then trade for 1 yard of cloth (at the price of 1 yard for 1 bushel). Thus, the American can get more cloth by producing wheat and trading it for cloth than by making cloth at home. And the same logic applies to a British worker. If he works for 8 hours growing wheat, he will get 2 bushels. But if the British worker spends his time producing cloth, he can make $8/3 = 2\frac{2}{3}$ yards that he can then trade for $2\frac{2}{3}$ bushels of wheat at the price of 1 for 1.

---

greater *share* of the mutual gains if the *terms of trade*—the ratio in which the products exchange—turn in its favor.[7] This essentially means that one country gets a higher price for its export product and the other country has to pay more for its imports of that product, such as occurred when the Organization of Petroleum Exporting Countries (OPEC) raised the price of oil in the 1970s. In such situations, both importers and exporters of the product whose price increased still gain from the trade, but the exporters get a greater share of the gains and the importers get a smaller share.

Second, the theory of comparative advantage assumes that trade is balanced (i.e., exports equal imports in value) and that labor is fully employed, thus abstracting from two of the main concerns of the mercantilists. If trade is not balanced, some countries could be exporting goods in which they do not have a true comparative advantage (as, for example, in the case of a country with a trade surplus engendered by an undervalued currency, which makes its exports artificially cheap). If there is unemployment, then it is possible to increase the production of exports without producing less of import-competing goods, and increasing exports can raise employment just as the mercantilists claimed. Thus, the theory of comparative advantage has to assume that macroeconomic and monetary adjustment mechanisms succeed in keeping trade balanced and workers fully employed.

An even more fundamental qualification concerns whether the costs of production are fixed by unalterable conditions (e.g., some natural resource scarcity) in each country or could be changed by human effort. If, in our previous example, America could acquire improved technology and know-how from Britain (say, through the importation of textile machinery and the immigration of skilled textile workers), then perhaps America could become more efficient in cloth production. It is even possible that if the reduction in American labor cost in cloth production is large enough, America could achieve a comparative advantage in cloth.[8]

Thus, the policy recommendation that a country should always follow its *current* comparative advantage ignores the possibility that the country could improve its productivity in some import-competing sectors and thus transform its comparative advantage in the future. In order to achieve such potential improvement, however, temporary protection of the import-competing sector (cloth in America, in this example) or other government intervention (e.g., a subsidy) to promote its development might be necessary, if imports would otherwise wipe out the industry and prevent it from getting off the ground. This is the famous *infant industry* argument for protection, which can also be thought of as *dynamic comparative advantage* (developing the industries that will offer the greatest gains in the long run).[9]

Neoclassical Trade Theory

Early twentieth-century economists found Ricardo's explanation of comparative advantage based on comparisons of relative labor costs too simple. Led by Swedish economists Eli Heckscher and Bertil Ohlin, they developed a new theory to explain comparative advantage and thus to account for the fundamental question of why countries specialize in particular products for exports. This neoclassical theory of trade emphasizes the fact that goods are produced with inputs of various *factors of production* (such as capital, labor, and land) in different proportions, and that countries are differently "endowed" with supplies of these factors.[10] For example, in a comparison of clothing, wheat, and automobiles, one might say that clothing is labor-intensive, wheat is land-intensive, and automobiles are capital-intensive. Comparing three countries, say China, Canada, and Japan, we could say that China is labor-abundant, Canada is land-abundant, and Japan is capital-abundant.

Under certain conditions, these differences in factor supplies should determine the three countries' comparative advantages, and we should expect to find (as we actually do) the following pattern of trade: China would export clothing, Canada would export wheat, and Japan would export automobiles.[11] This proposition has become known as the *Heckscher-Ohlin theory* (H-O theory), or the *factor-proportions* theory of trade: A country will tend to export those goods that are produced with relatively large inputs of the country's relatively abundant factor of production.

At first glance this prediction seems sensible or even obvious and trivial, but in fact it is not as simple as it first appears. The H-O theory rests on a number of very strong theoretical assumptions, without which it is not even logically true. The theoretical assumptions required for H-O theory are quite technical, but many of them can be understood fairly easily. Some of the basic assumptions of comparative advantage theory in general are required for the H-O version as well as for the Ricardian model. For example, trade must be balanced and all resources (labor and other) must be fully employed.

More specifically, H-O theory also assumes that differences in *factor endowments* (relative factor supplies) are the *main* economic differences among nations—that is, that differences in other characteristics such as technological sophistication or consumers' preferences are not important.[12] Another key assumption is *constant returns to scale*. This means that there are no cost advantages (or disadvantages) from producing larger quantities of output in any given industry. However, economies of scale have become so important in today's world that they are the basis of new theories of international trade, which will be discussed further later in this chapter.

The Gains from Trade and the Costs of Protection

Traditional theories of comparative advantage (both Ricardian and Heckscher-Ohlin) imply that free trade is the most beneficial policy for a nation's consumers in the aggregate. That is, with free trade a nation's consumers usually have access to the most goods at the lowest prices, compared with any other trade regime (either partial protection or a completely closed market). Based on this logic, economists have argued that protectionist policies cause substantial losses to consumers. For example, one 1994 study estimated that tariffs (taxes on imports) and other trade restrictions in the United States cost U.S. consumers about $70 billion in 1990, or slightly more than 1 percent of the gross domestic product.[13]

There are, however, a number of important qualifications to such estimates. First, the consumer costs of protection are not the same as the net national costs, which are much lower. Consumers pay more for protected products, but producers in the protected industries get higher revenues, and the government receives tax revenues from the tariffs on imports. Thus, for example, in the previously cited estimate of $70 billion in consumer costs of protection, only about $11 billion represents a net loss in U.S. national income, after deducting the benefits accruing to domestic producers and the tariff revenue of the government. And $7 billion out of that $11 billion net loss is due to the windfall profits of foreign suppliers in industries that were protected by voluntary restraint agreements with the exporting nations (rather than by tariffs).[14] If tariffs had been used instead, the net national loss would have been only $4 billion. One could say that protectionism is, in effect, a gigantic transfer program that redistributes income from consumers to producers and governments.

There is another sense in which protection of import-competing industries is also costly. Aside from the losses to consumers, protection from imports in some industries can also hurt producers in other industries—including export industries. For example, if the United States protects the steel industry, and steel becomes more expensive, this raises costs for domestic manufacturers of automobiles, farm equipment, and other steel-using industries. Also, the fact that protectionism makes the imported goods more expensive in the domestic market gives producers incentives to produce more of those goods that are protected and (if labor and other resources are fully employed) therefore less of other products. However, this last effect may not be operative if there are unemployed resources that could be put to work in the import-competing industries.

There is no question that the main beneficiaries of free trade policies are consumers. But even then there are further qualifications. First, not all individuals share in the aggregate gains that a country's consumers as a group obtain from free trade. In the next section we discuss how the gains from trade are distributed and identify some of the chief winners and losers from trade liberalization. Second, there are cases in which free trade does not even maximize the aggregate consumer welfare of the nation. Some of these exceptional cases are discussed later in this chapter. And third, there are some potential benefits of protection that are not taken into account in the traditional analyses, such as the possibility that protecting the home market could allow domestic firms to improve their technology or reap greater economies of scale (as seems to have occurred in many Japanese industries in the 1950s and 1960s).

The Distribution of the
Gains and Losses from Trade

Even if free trade policies bring positive gains to a country's consumers in the aggregate, trade liberalization can also have profound effects on the distribution of income within a nation, and this can be a source of resistance to free trade policies by adversely affected groups. Trade redistributes income among different groups of people in the economy. Usually, these groups are distinguished by their factor ownership—that is, individuals are grouped according to whether they are owners of capital, labor, land, or other resources. Sometimes people are distinguished rather by whether they are producers or consumers of a particular product or by whether they are associated with export or import interests. In all of these cases, there are losers as well as winners from opening up to trade, and the losers generally stand to gain from protectionism. Thus, the fact that free trade usually brings aggregate gains to all consumers does not prevent some groups of consumers from being worse off with free trade.

The most famous theory of how trade affects income distribution is based on the logic of the Heckscher-Ohlin trade model. Recall that in the H-O theory, countries export the goods that are relatively intensive in their relatively abundant factors of production, and they import those goods that are relatively intensive in their relatively scarce factors of production. The reason for this is that the abundance of some factors of production makes them comparatively cheap (e.g., the low wages of labor in China), and therefore products made with relatively large amounts of these factors (e.g., labor-intensive clothing or toys) are cheaper and more competitive when produced with those cheaper inputs.

But as a country specializes in the goods that utilize an abundant factor, the demand for that factor rises and its *factor price* (wage rate for labor, profit rate for capital, or rental rate for land) rises. At the same time, as the country imports the goods that utilize a scarce factor more intensively, domestic production of those goods is reduced, demand for the scarce factor falls, and the price of the scarce factor decreases. As a result, the owners of the abundant factors gain and the owners of the scarce factors lose when a country adopts free trade; the reverse happens if a country abandons free trade and protects its import-competing sectors.

This result—that free trade hurts the scarce-factor owners and protectionism benefits them—is known as the *Stolper-Samuelson theorem* (named after economists Wolfgang Stolper and Paul Samuelson). According to this theorem, which is a part of the H-O model, the losses to the scarce-factor owners from free trade are absolute as well as relative—that is, the real income of the scarce-factor owners (as measured by how many goods they can afford to buy) is lower with free trade and higher with protectionism. This explains why owners of scarce factors of production (e.g., landowners in Japan or labor groups in the United States and Canada) are often in favor of protectionist policies. These distributional predictions of the H-O theory are summarized in Table 3.1.

It must be emphasized that in spite of the losses to the scarce-factor owners, free trade normally yields aggregate (net) gains to the country as a whole. For this to be true, it must be the case that the gains to the winners (abundant-factor owners) are greater than the losses to the losers (scarce-factor owners). This creates the possibility

TABLE 3.1 **Distributional Effects of Free Trade**

Theory (Perspective)	Winners	Losers
Heckscher-Ohlin theory (long-run)	Owners of abundant factors of production	Owners of scarce factors of production
Specific factors theory (short-run)	Owners of factors of production stuck in export sectors	Owners of factors of production stuck in import sectors
Partial-equilibrium model (specific industries)	Consumers of imported goods; producers of export products	Producers of import-competing products; consumers of exported goods

of *compensation:* The winners could pay off the losers, so that the latter would be no worse off with free trade, and still keep part of their gains. In this sense, free trade represents what economists call a potential *Pareto improvement,* after the early twentieth-century Italian sociologist Vilfredo Pareto. A Pareto improvement occurs when some people in a country are made better off while no one is made worse off. However, free trade is not likely to be an actual Pareto improvement; some people usually do lose from free trade in reality.

The reason for this disturbing conclusion is that there are severe practical difficulties in arranging compensation for those who would lose from free trade. First, in a free market system, there is no mechanism that compels the winners to compensate the losers. Ironically, some kind of government intervention would be required to make the winners pay compensation in order to prevent free trade (which is otherwise a free market policy) from harming some members of society. Second, some kinds of compensatory policies could lessen the *incentives* for producers to specialize and thus would reduce the gains from trade overall. For example, a tax on the profits of the export activity would be a disincentive to produce for export.

This raises a third problem with the compensation principle. Whether the losers from free trade deserve to be compensated at all is a value judgment that citizens and policymakers must make. If the losers are a wealthy class, such as a landed oligarchy, there is little moral justification for paying compensation. If the losers are members of a less affluent group, such as industrial workers or peasants, there may be a stronger moral case for paying compensation to them (although they may have less political strength to press their claims).

One fascinating implication of the H-O theory of trade is that under certain idealized conditions, perfectly free trade could completely equalize factor prices in all countries, even if the factors themselves are not mobile between nations (i.e., even if labor or capital cannot freely cross international borders). This is the *factor-price equalization theorem* developed by Paul Samuelson, which says that free trade in commodities alone could make workers, capital owners, and landlords receive the same real incomes for their land, capital, and labor in all nations. However, if any of the strong assumptions[15] of this theorem do not hold in practice, then trade will not produce a complete equalization of global income distribution. There is some evidence that trade does move the world in the direction of greater convergence in factor prices, but the world is still very far away from complete factor-price equalization, as evidenced especially by the persistent wide gaps in wages between rich and poor countries.

The H-O theory assumes that the factors of production are mobile between industries within a nation—that the same land, labor, and capital can be used with equal efficiency in all sectors of the economy, albeit in different proportions. For this reason, the distributional effects predicted by the H-O model pertain to *all* owners of a factor, *regardless* of the sector in which they are actually employed. For example, if U.S. labor would lose from free trade, this would include workers in export industries (e.g., farming or aerospace) as well as in import-competing industries (e.g., steel or apparel), because all the workers would be competing with each other for jobs and therefore (in a perfectly competitive labor market) would have to receive the same wage.

However, the H-O assumption that all factors of production are freely mobile between industries is not very realistic. There are many cases of factors that are adapted in some special way to a particular type of productive activity and that cannot be transferred to another line of activity (or would not be equally efficient if they were). For example, workers with industry-specific types of skills are not easily transferable to other industries. An autoworker cannot easily become a computer programmer, or a textile worker turn into an airplane mechanic—at least not without costly training (and some workers will find it hard to pick up new skills even with training). Similarly, most capital is invested in specific types of plant and equipment that cannot easily be converted from one use to another. A steel mill cannot be used to make textiles, nor can a tractor be used to make computers.

To the extent that productive factors are specific to particular industries, the conclusions of the H-O theory must be modified. Instead, the *specific factors theory* can be applied in these instances where factors are "stuck." This theory says that the owners of a factor that is *not* freely mobile across industries will gain or lose from trade according to whether the factor is used in an export sector or an import-competing sector, as shown in Table 3.1. Thus, for example, skilled technicians who make jet airplanes in the United States benefit from free trade policies because it exports airplanes, whereas less skilled (or differently skilled) workers who make furniture or sew clothing lose from free trade because the United States imports their products.

Finally, one can also analyze the distributional effects of trade policies in a framework of producer versus consumer interests. This analysis is based on a standard supply-and-demand approach, which economists call *partial equilibrium* (partial because it is applied to the market for only one good at a time).[16] According to this type of analysis (also shown in Table 3.1), the producers (workers and business firms) in any import-competing industry stand to gain from protectionism, which allows them to raise the price of their product and keep a larger share of the domestic market compared with free trade. Consumers of the same product stand to benefit from free trade, which allows them to buy the goods more cheaply. By the same logic, producers in export industries stand to gain from free trade (since they can get higher prices for their products if they export them), whereas consumers of exported goods stand to lose (since they will have to pay higher products for the goods).

In theory, the overall gains to the consumers generally exceed the losses to the producers from free trade in import-competing sectors, and likewise the gains to producers of exports exceed the losses to consumers of those products, so that there are positive net benefits of free trade to the whole country. But again, the politics of the situation need not support free trade policies. Usually, import-competing producers represent a concentrated set of interest groups, often located in a few regions of the country (such as the U.S. auto industry in states like Michigan), whose jobs and incomes are threatened by cheaper imported products. The consumers of imported goods, in contrast, are a widely diffused group of individuals for whom the extra costs of any particular protected product are neither apparent nor significant. Thus, import-competing producers are very likely to base their votes and political contributions on support for protectionist policies; consumers are more likely to base their political involvement on other issues that are more salient for them (including their economic interests as producers in whatever sector they work in).

The fact that many groups in society stand to lose from trade liberalization makes it hard to form a political coalition actively advocating free trade policies, even when the nation as a whole would stand to gain. One new and interesting exception to this generalization is in cases where the "consumers" are other industries that are able to organize effective political campaigns against protectionism in their supplier industries.

Exceptions to the Case for Free Trade

Although traditional trade theories generally imply that free trade is in the interest of all countries, even if it does not necessarily benefit all groups within a country, there are nonetheless some specific economic exceptions to the case for pure free trade even at the national level.

One important qualification to the theory of comparative advantage is the problem of *adjustment costs*. When we analyze the gains from trade in a comparative advantage model, we are essentially comparing an economy that has already fully adjusted to free trade with an economy that does not trade at all (or that has restricted trade).[17] This type of comparison does not take into account the social and economic costs of removing existing trade restrictions and making the transition to free trade. For example, after trade is liberalized in a country, some workers will lose their jobs at least temporarily and some capital equipment will have to be scrapped. The new jobs and industries that emerge may be located in different parts of the country, and this will require workers to move and governments to provide new social infrastructure (e.g., highways and schools) in the booming areas. Yet at the same time, tax revenues will be reduced, especially in the states and municipalities where factories are shut down and jobs are lost and that are likely to bear some of the greatest social costs (e.g., of increased welfare dependency and crime).

Adjustment costs are not a valid reason to maintain protected or inefficient industries in the long run, but they can be a justification for gradualism in trade liberalization. Adjustment costs can also be ameliorated through domestic social policies that help people through the hard times of the transition period. Programs such as labor retraining, job placement services, and even relocation assistance (for workers who need to move to areas with expanding employment) can help to offset adjustment costs and thus to make trade liberalization more politically palatable.

Even if we ignore adjustment costs, there are cases in which *market failures* cause free trade to be less than the optimal policy for a country even in the long run. Market failures are situations in which Adam Smith's invisible hand fails to operate properly, and the self-interested behavior of individuals does not lead to the greatest social good. There are many possible reasons for market failures, but one of the most important for trade policy involves *externalities.* Externalities are costs or benefits to some actors in the economy that are not accounted for by market prices. In cases where there are externalities of any kind, the free market will usually give the wrong "signals" to market participants about how much of the goods to produce, to consume, and to import or export. Whether governments should attempt to intervene in cases of externalities is a separate question, but in theory the right government policies (discussed subsequently) could improve on free market outcomes in these situations.

Externalities can be either negative or positive. For example, if a factory emits pollution that injures the health of people who live in the vicinity, but the factory owners do not pay for the costs imposed on the injured people and the people in turn do not receive any compensation for the health costs of the pollution, this is a case of a negative externality. Positive externalities are beneficial *spillovers* from one activity to another where the provider of the benefits does not receive compensation, and the beneficiary does not pay for the benefits obtained. An example might be the fact that knowledge generated in computer production can spill over into other lines of production, yet the benefits of the knowledge spillover may not be fully paid for by firms in other sectors that utilize that knowledge (and the computer firms that generate the knowledge are not paid for the benefits they create for others). Positive externalities are often asserted to be *dynamic,* which means they are realized only over a period of many years (e.g., the accumulation of know-how through experience with a production process). Such dynamic gains are often claimed for industries favored for infant industry protection in developing countries.[18]

In cases of goods that generate negative externalities, market participants will produce too much (because they are not forced to pay all the costs that their production creates). In cases of goods that generate positive externalities (including infant industries), the free market will induce too little output (because the market prices do not fully reward producers for the benefits they create).[19]

Although government policies have the potential to improve on the free market outcome in the presence of externalities, a *trade* policy (e.g., a tariff to discourage imports) is not the best way for the government to solve the problem. Rather, the best solution (which economists call a *first-best* policy) is a policy that directly attacks the *source* of the market failure. For example, a tax on the polluter's production or a subsidy to the computer firms generating positive externalities would be the best policies in the examples previously cited. These policies will affect trade but they are not trade policies per se; they are instead direct efforts to counteract the harmful externality or encourage the beneficial externality.

A trade policy is usually only a *second-best* policy in cases of externalities. If it is desired, for example, to encourage production of an import-competing product that generates a positive externality, then a tariff that protects the industry would be effective. It would not be as good as a subsidy to the producers, however, because the tariff imposes extra costs on consumers of the product (the tariff increases the price of the product, whereas the subsidy does not).[20]

The same type of logic that enables us to rank policy options in cases of market failures also allows us to rank policies in cases when there is a *noneconomic policy objective* (but no demonstrable market failure). Suppose, for example, that there is an overriding political pressure or national security need to maintain domestic production in a certain import-competing industry. If free trade is not an option politically, economic theory teaches that it is better to subsidize the producers directly rather than to use trade restrictions to keep out imports. The subsidy policy involves lower costs to society than trade protection (tariffs or quotas) would, since protectionism would make the goods more expensive for consumers and the subsidy does not. In this case, free trade would be the first-best policy, the subsidy is second-best, and the tariff would be third-best.

However, a subsidy is still a socially costly policy. Consumers must still pay for the subsidies through higher taxes, even though this costs them less than trade protection would. The subsidy also hurts exporters in other countries who have trouble competing with subsidized producers (thus the complaints of U.S. and other export-oriented farmers about the European farm subsidies). If free trade is to be achieved, it might be necessary to offer compensation or adjustment assistance as alternatives to continued subsidies.

In many of these cases the economic logic and the political-legal logic may collide. Even if economic theory suggests that a direct subsidy to producers is better than a trade policy (e.g., an import tariff or quota), it is often politically easier to adopt a trade remedy. For one thing, a subsidy costs the government money, whereas a tariff brings in tax revenue, which is important for any government trying to balance its budget. Politically, a tariff can be justified by blaming foreigners for a nation's problems; a subsidy requires admitting that the sources of the country's problems may be internal. Subsidization obviously violates free market ideology; trade protection can be supported by appeal to so-called fair trade principles. And both domestic laws and international agreements may prohibit subsidies in many instances (and can even invite foreign retaliation, such as through the imposition of countervailing duties, which are discussed in Chapter 7).

In all cases where some kind of government intervention (either a domestic industrial policy or a trade restriction) is theoretically superior to free trade, there are still important questions that must be asked about the political feasibility of appropriate and effective policy action. Most free traders today acknowledge the exceptional cases in which government intervention is theoretically desirable, but they claim that (1) the cases in which such policies would be appropriate are probably very rare in practice; (2) governments cannot be expected to have better information than private firms or individuals about what products should be promoted or discouraged; and (3) governments cannot be trusted to make policy decisions based on true economic rationality in cases of genuine market failures but will inevitably end up giving subsidies or protecting industries according to old-fashioned special interest politics.

Supporters of government intervention counter that (1) externalities and other market failures are actually fairly widespread, especially in high-technology industries; (2) governments can get the information they need if they make the effort (for example, through panels of experts) and can take a broader social perspective than any single firm or individual; and (3) it is worth the effort to design institutions that could make trade and industrial policy decisions rationally and that would be independent of special interest influence. Some advocates of *managed trade* argue that political involvement in trade relations is unavoidable, and therefore we should focus our attention on finding the best ways of intervening in trade when pure free trade is not a viable option.

Clearly, these questions of political economy are the cutting edge of current debates over the use of activist trade and industrial policies. Given the likely imperfections and failures of both markets and governments, the United States and other countries have to decide how much their governments should intervene in markets—including international markets. At least, economic theory suggests the need for careful cost-benefit analysis of any proposed interventionist policies.

Problems with Traditional Theories of Trade

Although the Ricardian and Heckscher-Ohlin (H-O) models of comparative advantage appear to offer powerful intellectual support for policies of free trade, their adequacy for explaining actual trade patterns in the contemporary world economy has increasingly been called into question. In the early 1950s, the invention of computers made it possible to conduct statistical tests of the validity of these theories. While the Ricardian theory seemed to give reasonably good predictions at the time (countries were exporting the goods in which they had relatively lower labor costs), the H-O theory did not fare as well.

As early as 1953, Wassily Leontief discovered that the United States did not export capital-intensive goods, as predicted by the H-O model, but actually exported more labor-intensive goods. This surprising result, which was dubbed the *Leontief paradox,* led many scholars to question the relevance of the traditional theoretical approaches to international trade. After dozens of studies of the United States and many other countries over more than four decades, more and more international economists have concluded that the H-O factor-proportions theory does not give generally reliable predictions of actual trade patterns.

In the years since the discovery of the Leontief paradox, other facts about global trade patterns have come to light that cast additional doubt on the general validity of all traditional models of comparative advantage, including Ricardian theory as well as the H-O model. Since these facts are inconsistent with the established theories, they may be labeled *anomalies* (although in another sense it is the economists' persistence in maintaining theories not supported by the facts that is perhaps more anomalous). At least six major anomalies have been discovered that have undermined faith in the traditional models of trade.[21]

The first anomaly was the rise of *intraindustry trade,* which means two-way trade between countries in very similar products. This generally consists of trade in manufactured goods between industrialized nations, often involving different styles, brands, or models of the same products (such as cosmetics, pharmaceuticals, and automobiles) or at least goods that are produced with very similar proportions of factor inputs (such as different types of electrical machinery or optical equipment). When countries simultaneously export and import such similar goods, this cannot be explained by comparative advantage theories, which imply that countries should be highly *specialized* in very *different* types of products—and in the case of H-O theory, that imports and exports should have very different production characteristics (factor proportions). Yet according to some estimates, as much as 60 percent of trade among the industrialized countries consists of intraindustry trade.[22]

A second problem for the traditional theories is the importance of *scale economies.* In many industries, it is cheaper to produce goods when there is a large volume of output. In many cases, this is because there is a large fixed cost (overhead) that has to be incurred regardless of how many units of output are produced, such as expenditures on research and development (R&D) or heavy machinery. As a result, the average fixed cost *per unit* falls as output increases. Some types of scale economies are *dynamic*—they accrue only over time. For example, in industries where there are important *learning effects* (figuring out better ways to do things by experience), costs fall as the cumulative amount of production (past and present) rises. Finally, some scale economies are *external* to individual firms—they obtain only at the local industry level. For example, the training of skilled computer technicians benefits all the firms in an area but not necessarily the firm that does the training because the workers can easily move from one firm to another.

In the presence of strong scale economies, the traditional logic of comparative advantage breaks down. This is because, fundamentally, a country can *acquire* a cost advantage in an activity that has scale economies simply by producing a lot of the product and thus reducing its average costs. As a result, the pattern of trade in industries that have scale economies cannot be predicted by reference to intrinsic country and industry characteristics, such as comparative labor costs or factor endowments. The actual pattern of trade is determined by historical accidents, such as which country started up an industry first.

Third, the Heckscher-Ohlin theory assumes that all countries have the same technological capabilities, but much research has shown that in fact this is not the case, and some countries typically have superior technologies in particular product lines or even in broad areas of manufacturing. This disparity immediately creates the possibility that many countries' exports of some products (especially manufactures) are determined by *absolute technological advantage* rather than by comparative cost advantage.

In some instances, acquired technological advantage can be viewed as a type of dynamic scale economy, in the sense that a country that specializes in a particular type of product becomes more proficient at producing it as producers discover new ways of reducing costs and improving quality. Some examples of this phenomenon would include the U.S. advantage in large jet aircraft, Germany's advantage in chemicals, and the fact that in the computer industry the United States has the lead in logic chips (microprocessors) and Japan has the lead in memory chips.

Fourth, traditional theories of international trade assume *perfectly competitive markets,* in the sense that there are large numbers of sellers of identical products, each of whom is too small to influence the market price. This may be a good characterization of many markets (e.g., textiles and agricultural commodities), but it is clearly not true in other cases where some form of *imperfect competition* prevails. For example, in sectors that are very costly for new firms to enter, markets are dominated by a relatively small number of large firms (such as Boeing, McDonnell Douglas, and the European Airbus consortium[23] in commercial jet aircraft production). These are called situations of *oligopoly,* in which firms have some power to set prices and to reap excess profits by charging prices in excess of average total costs. Another type of imperfect competition exists when there is *product differentiation* through brand-name identification or other ways of distinguishing different firms' products, a situation called *monopolistic competition*—monopolistic because there is only one producer of each brand or model, and competition because producers of different brands or models of the same type of product do have to compete with each other to some extent.

Fifth, whereas traditional trade theory assumes that business firms are nationally based, global trade today is largely dominated by *multinational corporations* (MNCs) with operations in two or more countries. For the United States, about 37 percent of merchandise exports and about 48 percent of merchandise imports are actually internal transactions or transfers within MNCs (counting both U.S. and foreign companies).[24] Hand in hand with the spread of MNCs has gone heightened capital mobility: the ability of firms to relocate their productive facilities to different parts of the world, depending on where it is convenient either for access to foreign markets or for sources of cheap inputs. Thus, to some extent, modern world trade is based on the strategic internal planning of MNCs rather than the arms-length transactions of the marketplace.

Sixth and finally, the apparent success of government *industrial policies* in enhancing export competitiveness in some countries, especially Japan and most of the East Asian NICs, has called into question the idea of trade following natural comparative advantage. In Japan, South Korea, Taiwan, and other aspiring developing nations of East Asia, governments have been involved with the private sector in a kind of partnership in which a variety of inducements and incentives are given to encourage particular lines of production, usually with an export orientation. Although it is controversial exactly how much these governments have aided their industries and how much the government assistance has accounted for their success (there are certainly cases of governments having made mistakes), it is increasingly recognized that many of their competitive successes were at least partly policy-induced. With the sole exception of Hong Kong, the East Asian examples make us realize that *export success* and *free markets* are not synonymous; many of the most successful exporters have used all kinds of government interventions to promote their exports while often simultaneously restricting imports.

New Trade Theories

In response to the unsatisfactory performance of the traditional trade theories (especially Heckscher-Ohlin) in explaining actual trade patterns, and in light of new trends in world trade and production not contemplated by traditional theories of comparative advantage, there has been a search for new theories of international trade. The development of the new theories began slowly in the 1960s and then took off in the late 1970s and 1980s when mainstream academic economists began to work out new models of trade based on new developments in economic theory (e.g., new models of oligopoly and monopolistic competition that could be applied to international trade). The new trade theories are exceedingly diverse and still evolving, which makes it difficult to generalize about them. What follows are brief summaries of some of the most important and influential theories that have emerged.

Monopolistic Competition and Scale Economies

This approach, pioneered by Paul Krugman and Kelvin Lancaster, focuses on the issue of trade in differentiated products (such as different brands of toothpaste). In this theory, it is usually assumed that each brand or type of good is made by a single firm in a particular country using a technology with scale economies (decreasing costs of production as output rises). Consumers are assumed to benefit from the availability of many different types of products; they have what might be called a "taste for variety."

The theory of trade with scale economies and differentiated products implies two types of gains from trade that are not found in traditional theories of comparative advantage: Consumers can get a greater variety of products from which to choose, and all workers can get higher real wages. The greater variety results simply from access to other countries' brands or types of goods. The higher real wages result from the fact that with scale economies, increasing output in order to serve world markets lowers the average cost of production, and as long as prices are reduced accordingly, workers can afford to buy more of the cheaper products.

This theory cannot predict the direction of trade. Since any country can become competitive in an industry or product line simply by producing enough of a good to drive costs down to a competitive level, which country will export which products is essentially arbitrary. Nevertheless, this theory does predict that there will be intraindustry trade because countries can exchange differentiated versions of similar products (e.g., different models of automobiles) with each other. And in this theory there is no group that loses from free trade as there usually is in traditional models (especially H-O); everyone can share in the benefits when costs are reduced by producing more goods for export (something that cannot happen in traditional theories that ignore scale economies).

However, one has to be careful because the monopolistic competition model (as developed by Krugman and others) makes just as many unrealistic assumptions as traditional trade models. For example, this model assumes *free entry*, which means that it is costless for new producers to enter industries in which there are any positive economic profits, and therefore economic profits are driven to zero. As a result, prices are always equal to average costs, and any cost reductions from producing for export are passed on to consumers. If there were barriers to entry, however, then existing firms would have some market power they could use to keep prices above average costs, and the benefits of trade liberalization to workers and consumers would be less certain.

Oligopolistic Rivalry and Strategic Trade Policy

Another type of model deals explicitly with the situation of trade with *oligopoly*, in which strong barriers to entry keep the number of firms in an industry small and those firms take each other's actions into account in forming their competitive strategies. Oligopolistic firms can reap excess profits by holding prices above costs of production. With oligopolistic rather than monopolistic competition, it becomes possible for government intervention to increase national income by allowing domestic firms to capture a greater share of the oligopolistic excess profits (often called *rents*) for the home country firm(s). This sort of intervention is called *strategic trade policy*, because the policy intervention allows the domestic firms to gain a better position in their strategic interplay with their foreign rivals. Strategic trade policy does not necessarily involve protectionism, but it may entail other forms of government intervention (such as subsidies) depending on circumstances.

Indeed, the precise type of government intervention required to give national firms a strategic advantage depends on the precise structure and behavior of the industry. In some cases, for example, it pays for the government to subsidize export production by the domestic firms; subsidization effectively lowers their costs and thus allows them to grab a larger share of the world market for themselves by underselling their rivals. If the extra profits thus obtained exceed the cost of the subsidy, then total national income is increased—at the expense of the foreign country, of course (although in this case global consumers benefit from more goods being available at lower prices).

Although the theory of strategic trade policy created great excitement when economists first developed it in the early 1980s, it is important to be very cautious in assessing the practical implications of this theory. For one thing, strategic trade policy only works at the expense of one's trading rivals, giving them incentives to retaliate (e.g., by subsidizing foreign companies, thus negating the home country's strategic advantage). Second, the conditions for strategic trade policy to work are very strict. If some of the assumptions of the theory, such as high entry barriers, do not hold in reality, then strategic trade policies will not achieve their objectives. Third, the government would need voluminous information in order to know which industries to select for strategic trade policies and exactly what policies to use to help those industries (e.g., what level of subsidy to pay and for how long).

The theory of strategic trade policy has nevertheless opened up new insights in the debate over managed trade and trade liberalization. Managed traders argue that if foreign countries (especially Japan) use strategic policy tools to advance their industrial interests, then the United States must respond in kind or else face losses of markets and income (corporate profits and high-paying jobs). Free marketeers respond that even if beneficial strategic trade policies are possible in theory, the U.S. government is unlikely to apply them successfully in practice.[25] If mistakes are made, whether out of ignorance or venality, the cost to the country could be very high. Managed traders in turn reply that the costs of doing nothing in response to foreign strategic interventions could also be very high, because in the presence of such interventions there can be no presumption that a free trade policy is in the national interest.

Free traders also argue that threats to retaliate against foreign trade practices could wreck the global trading system and produce a trade war and that the right response is to negotiate further trade liberalization, including international subsidies codes or antitrust agreements that could prevent governments from unduly aiding national firms. An intermediate position (between the managed traders and the pure free traders) is that although global trade liberalization should indeed be the ultimate goal, threats of U.S. strategic intervention or retaliation may be necessary to induce other countries to cooperate by giving up their own interventions.

In the end, a world with the potential use of strategic trade policies is a type of *prisoner's dilemma:* Each country can be better off if it intervenes and its rival does not, but then the rival will suffer, and if both intervene both could end up worse off; cooperation (in this case, international agreements to forswear strategic policies) is necessary to prevent anyone from being harmed.

Product Cycles and
Technological Gaps

One of the earliest alternative trade theories was the *product cycle model,* originally developed by Raymond Vernon in 1966. This model is based on the recognition that some manufactured products are new and innovative (e.g., supercomputers) and others are older and more standardized (e.g., steel). According to this theory, a few countries are the technological leaders that export the new and innovative products; other countries are followers that can export only mature or standardized products. Trade in new and innovative products is thus explained by absolute technological superiority, sometimes referred to as *technological gaps,* on the part of firms in the exporting nation.

The innovative leaders must have certain characteristics. For example, they must have high income levels so that their consumers can buy expensive new products. They must also have high wages (which induce a search for labor-saving devices), good communications between consumers and suppliers, and well-functioning capital markets to provide finance for innovations. Basically, these requirements restrict innovative leadership to a handful of countries, principally the United States and secondarily Germany and Japan. Those countries also receive special benefits from the effective monopoly that they have over the new products in the world market.

As products become older, their production becomes more routinized and mechanized, and cost factors become more important than proximity to the high-income market. Production initially shifts to other industrialized nations, such as Western Europe, Canada, or Australia, which are capable followers but not major leaders in innovation. The costs of production fall as there is greater use of labor-saving machinery and firms take advantage of scale economies. Eventually, the technology becomes completely standardized and production can be shifted to less developed countries where wages are lower and costs can be minimized. Foreign investment by multinational corporations may be a vehicle for transferring technology in standardized products to less developed countries.

Footloose Inputs and Absolute Labor Cost Advantages

Current trends suggest that the transfer of standardized manufacturing production to low-wage developing countries, originally described in Vernon's product cycle model, may be occurring at an accelerated pace. In today's world, both productive inputs (such as capital equipment) and technological knowledge are increasingly mobile. It is now possible to locate a factory in, say, China or Mexico, that uses completely up-to-date machinery and equipment and produces goods with world-class quality. Once the work forces are suitably trained, the labor in these transplanted factories can be just as productive or nearly as productive as in similar factories in the United States, Europe, or Japan. Yet the workers in the developing countries earn much lower wages and benefits. Mexican manufacturing workers, for example, received about $2 per hour in 1992, and Chinese workers made about $2 per day, compared with $15 per hour for U.S. manufacturing workers. As a result, in any production process where labor costs are very important, there is a clear incentive to move production to lower-wage sites when feasible. This may be done either through foreign direct investment or through sourcing from local suppliers in low-wage countries.

One should not exaggerate this point and claim that all or most manufacturing jobs are in danger of disappearing in the United States. There are many limits to the ability of corporations to relocate production to low-wage sites or even to source products from low-wage countries. In order to attract foreign investment, those countries must have reasonably stable governments, respect for property rights, and open capital markets. In order for local firms in those countries to satisfy foreign customers, they must uphold international quality standards. The low-wage countries also need adequate infrastructure, such as airports or seaports, roads or railroads, and communications facilities. Otherwise, transportation costs or lack of communication with suppliers could overwhelm any putative savings in labor costs.

These qualifications explain why some of the lowest-wage countries in the world, such as Bangladesh, Haiti, or much of sub-Saharan Africa, have not become major export platforms for labor-intensive manufactures. Also, the logic of low-wage competition applies only for labor-intensive goods or labor-intensive parts of the production process for which special skills and training are not important. In activities where either capital costs, raw materials costs, or *human capital* inputs (high skills and technical training) are more important than ordinary labor costs, it will not pay to move production to low-wage countries.

Nevertheless, there is some scope for low-wage competition to influence trade patterns, as the rapid growth of trade with countries like Mexico and China makes clear. By combining foreign capital and technology with domestic low-wage labor forces, these countries (and many others) can achieve *unit labor costs* (cost of labor per unit of output) far below U.S. (or European or Japanese) levels in certain types of activities, provided that they can guarantee adequate political and economic stability, transportation and communications facilities, and so on. Moreover, recent technological advances have made it possible to have globalized production, in which the production of a finished good can be broken down into many different parts and operations that can be done in different countries according to their unique advantages. Thus, labor-intensive operations (such as auto parts manufacture or television assembly) can be performed in low-wage countries, and other operations can be done elsewhere in the global factory system.

Traditional trade theory discounted this possibility by asserting that wage differences among countries always reflect differences in the productivity of labor, so that low-wage countries must also be low-productivity countries and therefore cannot gain overall competitive advantages by virtue of their low wages. There is much truth in this, even today. Even in new export powerhouses like China or Mexico, technology remains very backward in large areas of the domestic economy (especially agriculture, services, and handicraft manufactures), and the low wages do correspond to low *average* productivity.

What is new is the heightened mobility of capital and technology that makes it possible to create *export platforms* in which the productivity is far above the national average, yet the wages remain low because of low productivity in the rest of the domestic economy (and possibly repression of labor movements as well). Low wages alone are not a competitive threat, but low wages combined with high productivity in export activities can be.

In the long run, low-wage competition ceases to be a viable strategy for successful developing countries in which higher productivity becomes more diffused throughout the economy and wages eventually rise. Thus, in countries like South Korea and

Taiwan, wages have risen so much that these countries are no longer competitive in the simpler labor-intensive manufactures, which are now moving to lower-wage sites (such as China or Thailand). Following the earlier Japanese model, Korea and Taiwan are now moving into more advanced types of manufactures in which high quality and productivity make it possible to afford to pay higher wages. But with other poor countries still clamoring to get on the low-wage manufacturing bandwagon, this process will surely continue even after the present low-wage nations have advanced to higher levels.

Economic Integration and Trading Blocs

In practice, countries' trading policies are much more complex than a simple binary choice between free trade and protection. One of the most important complications in today's world is the potential for two or more countries to enter into trade agreements that give the signatories trading preferences in each other's markets while excluding other nations. Such exclusive agreements are called *preferential trade arrangements*. The European Union (EU) and the North American Free Trade Agreement (NAFTA) are examples of such preferential arrangements in contemporary trade.

In theory, there are four forms of economic integration, described here in ascending order of how deep the integration goes:

1. A *free trade area* is created when two or more countries abolish all (or most) trade restrictions among themselves without changing any of their own policies internally or externally. In particular, each country maintains its own structure of tariffs, quotas, and other protective devices against the rest of the world.
2. A *customs union* is a free trade area in which the member countries agree to establish common external policies (tariffs, quotas, and so on).
3. A *common market* is a customs union (and thus also a free trade area) in which factors of production such as labor and capital are allowed to move freely among the member countries, along with ordinary goods and services.
4. An *economic union* is a completely integrated market area in which there is a single set of "harmonized" domestic economic policies in all the member countries, along with all the other features of a common market.

Actual trading arrangements do not always fit any one model perfectly. For example, NAFTA appears to have merely created a free trade area among the United States, Canada, and Mexico. Indeed, NAFTA did not create a customs union; each of the three member countries retains its own trade barriers with nonmember countries. Yet NAFTA incorporates some features of a common market because it liberalizes restrictions on capital mobility (although not labor mobility) among the member states.

Economic theory offers several perspectives on the advantages and disadvantages of preferential trading arrangements. One simple benchmark is that joining a trading bloc (say, a free trade area, which is the simplest kind) is beneficial for a country if the gains from *trade creation* are greater than the losses from *trade diversion*.[26] The situation of Mexico in NAFTA can be used to give some (purely hypothetical) examples of these gains and losses.

Suppose, for example, that Mexican construction companies are now buying protected Mexican steel at $500 per ton, and under NAFTA they can buy imported U.S. steel at $450 per ton. This is pure trade creation, and it brings benefits to the Mexican economy (and Mexican consumers) in the form of cheaper steel (and cheaper products made with steel).

Now consider a Mexican manufacturing firm that is choosing between importing a Japanese machine that costs $1,000 and a Canadian machine that costs $1,100. If Mexico has a uniform tariff of 20 percent on imported machinery, the Mexican firm will buy the Japanese machine for $1,200 ($1,000 for the machine plus $200 for the tariff). If Mexico then joins NAFTA and the Canadian machine becomes exempt from the tariff, the Mexican firm will buy the Canadian machine for $1,100 since it has a zero tariff. In this example, the net gain or loss to Mexico is ambiguous. On the one hand, the Mexican firm pays $100 less for the Canadian machine than it paid for the Japanese machine with the tariff and as a result can afford to buy more machines; getting more machines at a lower price represents a gain from trade creation just as in the other example. On the other hand, in this case the Mexican government loses $200 in tariff revenue on each machine formerly imported from Japan; this is a loss due to trade diversion. Overall, whether Mexico benefits in this situation depends on whether the gains from the trade creation are larger or smaller than the losses from the trade diversion.[27]

Most studies have found that the diversionary effects of contemporary trade agreements are relatively small compared with the trade-creating effects. The issue of trade creation and diversion addresses only the static gains from forming a preferential trade arrangement, however. Countries forming free trade areas also hope to get dynamic gains as a result of scale economies, induced technological progress, and competitive pressures to improve quality. Scale economies may be especially important for smaller countries joining a preferential trading arrangement, such as Mexico in NAFTA or Belgium and the Netherlands in the EU. Producers in these countries can lower their costs by producing larger volumes for regional markets rather than just their own smaller national markets. Generally, the dynamic gains from scale economies and, more broadly, from rationalizing production in order to compete in a wider market area are thought to far exceed the static gains from trade creation (i.e., merely obtaining cheaper imports).

Conclusion

After more than two centuries, economists have developed an impressive body of theory of how international trade works, how nations gain from trade, and how the gains are distributed both among and within countries. Older theories emphasize the static gains from trade that occur when countries improve their efficiency by specializing according to their comparative advantages. Newer theories imply other types of gains, including the exploitation of scale economies and especially the dynamic gains that accrue from the development and diffusion of new technologies.

However, many of the theories also imply that political conflict over trade policy is inevitable, since the gains from trade are at best unevenly distributed, and in some cases particular groups or sectors stand to lose from trade liberalization. There are even cases in which government intervention is theoretically superior to free trade, such as the cases of externalities and strategic trade policies, although the ability of governments to properly identify such cases and to implement appropriate interventions remains in dispute.

The very diversity of trade theories, old and new, suggests that international trade is multifaceted, and no one theory can explain all of it. The Heckscher-Ohlin model gives important insights into trade in products whose production is tied to factor endowments, such as natural resource–based trade. For trade in manufactures, the models of product cycle and of technology gap emphasize that new products are exported by a small club of advanced nations whose firms have a virtual monopoly on technological leadership. The models of trade with scale economies and imperfect competition remind us that many competitive advantages in manufactures are essentially created advantages, deriving from some set of historical accidents and sometimes even from government policies. And when it comes to standardized manufactures, the Ricardian model comes back into its own: Nations tend to export those products for which they have relatively lower labor costs. Yet even here there is a new twist: Advantages in labor cost may be created through the acquisition of new technologies from abroad, a factor not considered by Ricardo.

The traditional models of comparative advantage emphasized how trade patterns were influenced by the internal characteristics of countries, which were taken as given in the analysis. The newer theories suggest the potentially more interesting question of how the external trade relations of nations affect the development of their industries and the structure of their economies. How does immersion in a global system of production and exchange affect a country's internal development and thus condition (or constrain) its future ability to gain from trade? This kind of question will probably be at the forefront of international economics as it enters its third century.

For Further Reading

Blecker, Robert A. ed. *U.S. Trade Policy and Global Growth: New Directions in the International Economy.* Armonk, N.Y.: M. E. Sharpe, Economic Policy Institute Series, 1995.

Collins, Susan M., ed. *Distributive Issues: A Constraint on Global Integration.* Washington, D.C.: Brookings Institution, 1995.

Dosi, Giovanni, Keith Pavitt, and Luc Soete. *The Economics of Technical Change and International Trade.* New York: New York University Press, 1990.

Krugman, Paul R., ed. *Strategic Trade Policy and the New International Economics.* Cambridge: MIT Press, 1986.

Lawrence, Robert Z., and Robert E. Litan. *Saving Free Trade: A Pragmatic Approach.* Washington, D.C.: Brookings Institution, 1986.

Lawrence, Robert Z., and Charles L. Schultze, eds. *An American Trade Strategy: Options for the 1990s.* Washington, D.C.: Brookings Institution, 1990.

Lindert, Peter H. *International Economics.* 9th ed. Homewood, Ill.: Irwin, 1991.

Porter, Michael E. *The Competitive Advantage of Nations.* New York: Free Press, 1990.

Tyson, Laura D'Andrea. *Who's Bashing Whom? Trade Conflict in High-Technology Industries.* Washington, D.C.: Institute for International Economics, 1992.

Notes

1. Paul R. Krugman, "Is Free Trade Passé?" *Journal of Economic Perspectives* 1, no. 2 (Fall 1987), p. 131.

2. See John Maynard Keynes, *The General Theory of Employment, Interest, and Money* (New York: Harcourt, Brace, 1936), especially ch. 23 ("Notes on Mercantilism, Etc.").

3. Although Smith is famous as an advocate of free market policies, he did recognize legitimate areas for government activity, including national defense, public education, and infrastructure construction (e.g., highways).

4. Adam Smith, *An Inquiry into the Nature and Causes of the Wealth of Nations,* ed. Edwin Cannan (London: Methuen, 1904; reprint ed. Chicago: University of Chicago Press, 1976), vol. 1, p. 486.

5. However, Smith recognized some exceptional cases in which interventionist trade policies could be justified. For example, he accepted the legitimacy of protecting domestic industries deemed necessary for national security reasons, as well as exempting exported goods from domestic excise taxes. Smith also advocated that trade liberalization should be slow and gradual in order to lessen the adjustment costs for those producers who would lose out to import competition.

6. Most significantly, Smith argued that by producing for a large global market, a country's producers could specialize more and thus increase the division of labor, which would make the nation's labor force more productive. This idea is the basis of some recent theories of trade that incorporate the principles of *economies of scale* (discussed later in the chapter).

7. In the example from Box 3.1, the international exchange ratio of 1 yard of cloth per bushel of wheat represents terms of trade of 1 to 1: It costs 1 yard of cloth to buy 1 bushel of wheat. If the price of wheat rises above 1 yard of cloth, then the terms of trade would be more favorable to the country that exports wheat (America) and less favorable to the country that imports wheat (Britain). Suppose, for example, that the terms of trade rise to 5 yards of cloth for every 4 bushels of wheat, or a ratio of 1.25 to 1. Both countries still gain from trade in this situation, but Britain gains *relatively less* while America gains *relatively more*.

8. In the example from Box 3.1, suppose America could lower its labor cost in cloth to 4 hours per yard. In this case, the comparative advantage in cloth would shift in favor of America, since its relative cost of producing cloth would fall from 9/8 to 4/8 = 1/2, which is lower than the British relative cost of cloth (3/4).

9. However, protectionism is not necessarily the best policy for helping an infant industry to develop. See the discussion of policies for *externalities* later in this chapter.

10. Most standard expositions of this theory use models of only two factors, such as capital and labor (or land and labor). But the theory was originally intended for application to multiple factors of production, and much new work has been devoted to models with more than two inputs.

11. These examples were chosen to be realistic and thus to portray the H-O theory in the best light. However, recent studies show that the H-O theory does not generally give accurate predictions of trade patterns, as discussed later in this chapter.

12. If this were not true, then trade patterns could violate the H-O prediction. For example, if Japan acquired a vastly superior technology in clothing production, so that clothing could be produced with very little labor, then Japan could potentially produce clothing more cheaply than China, which relies on its abundant labor and low wages to be competitive in clothing.

13. Gary Clyde Hufbauer and Kimberly Ann Elliott, *Measuring the Costs of Protection in the United States* (Washington, D.C.: Institute for International Economics, 1994).

14. In the case of a tariff, which is a tax on imports, the difference between the higher domestic price and the lower world price accrues to the government in the form of tax revenue. In the case of a voluntary export restraint, however, the foreign supplier gets to charge the higher price in the domestic market and thus pockets the difference between that price and the world market price in the form of excess profits (technically known as *quota rents*).

15. Some of the assumptions include identical technologies across countries, constant (nonincreasing) returns to scale, absence of transportation costs and other trade barriers, incomplete specialization, no factor-intensity reversals across countries, and perfectly competitive markets for goods and factors.

16. The crucial assumption of this model is increasing costs of producing greater quantities of a good, as reflected in an upward-sloping supply curve.

17. In economics jargon, the theory of comparative advantage employs the method of *comparative statics*, which consists of comparing two equilibrium states of the economy in which all parameters are held constant except one factor that is allowed to vary—in this case, the extent of trade barriers.

18. Note that the future benefits must not be capturable by the industry that generates them, or else (if capital markets are well functioning) the firms in those industries could get credit to finance their start-up operations, secured by the promise of future profits. Thus an argument for government assistance to an infant industry must allege either (1) that the benefits are external to the firms, so that they will not be captured in future profits; or (2) that there is a failure of capital markets to allocate credit efficiently (perhaps because such markets are themselves poorly developed).

19. The amounts traded will also be affected by externalities. For example, if a polluting factory is in an export sector, the country might actually be exporting too much of the product (thus creating too much pollution). Or, if an industry that generates a positive externality is in an export sector, then with free trade the country will be producing and exporting too little of the industry's product.

20. Similar principles apply in other cases of market failures. For example, if a country imports a product that is socially harmful (generates a negative externality) through its *consumption,* such as cigarettes, then the best policy is to tax consumption of the product rather than to restrict importation via a tariff. Or, if a country needs to develop a better-trained labor force in a certain industry, and private employers do not have sufficient incentives to provide enough training (perhaps because the workers could easily leave and take their skills to other firms), then the best policy is to subsidize training rather than to put a tariff on imports of the product (if it is imported) or to subsidize exports (if the good is exported).

21. However, three of these anomalies (imperfect competition, multinational enterprises, and industrial policies) were anticipated by theories of economic imperialism among dissident economists. For a good survey, see Anthony Brewer, *Marxist Theories of Imperialism* (London: Routledge, 1980).

22. This figure is cited in Peter H. Lindert, *International Economics,* 9th ed. (Homewood, Ill.: Irwin, 1991), p. 96, based on the study by O. Havrylyshyn and E. Civan, "Intra-Industry Trade and the Stage of Economic Development: A Regression Analysis of Industrialized and Developing Countries," in P.K.M. Tharakan, ed., *Intra-Industry Trade: Empirical and Methodological Aspects* (Amsterdam: North-Holland, 1983), pp. 111–140.

23. Airbus is a relatively new entrant, of course, having come on the scene since the late 1970s. But its entry was heavily subsidized by the European governments, which proves the point.

24. These figures include the intrafirm transactions of U.S. MNCs and their foreign affiliates plus U.S. affiliates of foreign MNCs and their parents or other affiliates abroad. The authors' calculations were based on data from the U.S. Department of Commerce, *Survey of Current Business,* July 1993, p. 45, and October 1993, pp. 54, 62.

25. See the earlier discussion of the political economy of government intervention in trade at the end of the section "Exceptions to the Case for Free Trade."

26. From a more mercantilist (or macroeconomic) perspective, however, trade diversion can actually be beneficial rather than costly to a nation joining a trading bloc. For example, giving a trading bloc partner incentives to buy more of a country's exports can help to improve that country's balance of trade. This can create jobs in an economy that does not have full employment to begin with.

27. Generally, the more elastic is the Mexican demand for machines (i.e., the more the quantity imported increases in response to the lower domestic price), the greater are the gains from trade creation. The larger is the cost differential between imports from member and nonmember countries, the greater is the potential for losses from trade diversion. With small initial protection, trade diversion is less of a problem.

4 Economic Determinants of a
Nation's Trade Performance

Publication of monthly and annual trade statistics attracts a great deal of attention. The size of a country's trade surplus or deficit is viewed by the public as a disproportionately important measure of the "success" or "failure" of trade performance. Most people view a trade surplus as an unequivocal good, and the bigger the better. In most countries, a trade deficit unleashes widespread distress that often leads to heated debate about the utility and "toughness" of existing trade policies. It is a gross oversimplification of sound economic theory to assume, as the majority does, that a trade surplus is necessarily rewarding for a country and a trade deficit is necessarily harmful. Most international economists would advise that less attention be paid to the arithmetic of trade performances and more emphasis be placed on the underlying causes of the overall trade balance as well as on product composition (i.e., what kinds of goods are being exported and imported).

This chapter has two objectives. First, on an implicit basis we seek to explain how and why the political significance of trade balance numbers greatly exceeds their economic importance. Our second purpose is explicit: to delineate the multitude of international and domestic economic factors that directly influence a country's trade performance. Collectively, these factors are sufficiently potent and numerous that they, not narrowly defined trade policy actions, are usually the critical determinant of the volume and value of a country's exports and imports. After examining the major domestic economic factors relevant to a country's trade performance, we then examine a series of external economic determinants.

The Significance of a Trade Balance

Trade balances share a basic characteristic of overall trade policy: Both are economic concepts containing sufficient complexity and ambiguity to convert them into political phenomena. Only an economist can be fully comfortable with the notion that rising imports and a merchandise trade deficit are not automatically damaging to a country's welfare. Economic theory specifically argues that major economic benefits can accrue to a deficit country, especially so to a less developed one seeking to eradicate mass poverty. Under most conditions, net benefits accrue to a country that is a net importer of real economic resources and that then finances this deficit through inflows of capital (not a real economic resource) in the form of foreign investments, loans to be repaid in the future, and grants. By way of example, Mexico was obliged to adopt growth-retarding austerity measures and run large trade surpluses during the 1980s because of the sudden drop in its ability to attract foreign bank loans and the need to repay the large amount of interest that had accrued on its old debt. When Mexican economic reforms began attracting a large net capital inflow in the early 1990s, the result was domestic economic stimulation and the ability to pay for a large trade deficit. It would have been as inappropriate to praise Mexico in the 1980s as a competitive nation (because of its trade surpluses) as it would be to express sympathy in the 1990s for its declining economic fortunes (because of its trade deficits).

The existence and extent of the benefits of sustaining a trade deficit can vary, with the product composition of imports being a major determinant. There is little net addition to a nation's long-term welfare if imports consist mainly of expensive luxury goods for the elites. On the other hand, imports dominated by capital goods can be a force in fostering infant industries and constructing a more dynamic export sector. In extreme cases, imports of food and medicine can literally sustain life.

The mammoth, uninterrupted U.S. trade deficits running from the mid-1980s through the mid-1990s are empirical facts. The precise severity of long-term economic problems associated with these record-shattering deficits, however, is open to conjecture. Even if one accepts the theoretical benefits of trade deficits just discussed, it does not necessarily follow that it is equitable and logical for one of the richest countries on earth to be a net taker of both real resources and capital from the rest of the world. However, as long as foreigners accept payment for their exports in dollars and as long as at least some of these foreigners retain dollar assets, the United States theoretically has no limits on the amounts or duration of its trade deficits.

Some societies seem to prefer to save rather than to increase their domestic consumption—in effect, they live below their means. It may therefore be assumed that some countries will be content to run perennial current account surpluses and remain net capital exporters; as such they will accumulate additional amounts of dollar-denominated assets (many of which will depreciate in foreign currency terms over time) in exchange for their real resources (exports). Surplus countries must take most of these dollar assets and invest them in or lend them to the United States. Trade surpluses can be attractive as a means of maximizing domestic employment, but many U.S. economists consider expansionary macroeconomic policies as the more efficient vehicle to achieve this goal.

The economic significance of the multilateral merchandise trade balance to the United States and other industrialized countries is further diluted by the increasing importance of international trade in *services*. Major examples of the latter include transactions in transportation, tourism, telecommunications and data transmission, insurance, banking services, and movie rentals. The balance in the trade of both goods and services, roughly equivalent to the current account, is a more representative arithmetic symbol of how well a country's business sector is doing in the world marketplace than just its net multilateral trade in merchandise. Economists are especially skeptical of negative assessments of a country's global economic position based only on a bilateral trade deficit, as best exemplified by the much publicized, long-running U.S. deficit with Japan.

Measuring international trade in goods *and* services seems especially appropriate for the United States in view of its relatively large and efficient services sector. Because of its traditional surplus in the services sector of the balance of payments, the overall U.S. current account deficit in recent years has been much smaller than the merchandise trade deficit. In 1992, for example, the U.S. international deficit on goods and private services (according to a newly adopted U.S. Commerce Department statistical measure of competitiveness) was $35.6 billion, less than one-half of the merchandise trade deficit of $84.5 billion (measured on the so-called f.a.s. [free alongside ship] basis—cost of goods as prepared for overseas shipment, excluding costs of shipping and insurance). A more detailed presentation of U.S. merchandise trade statistics can be found in the appendixes at the end of this book.

To many economists, the best definition of a country's competitiveness goes well beyond trade statistics. Competitiveness is deemed to be the ability of a country to produce goods and services that meet the test of the global market while its citizens simultaneously enjoy a standard of living that is both increasing and sustainable.

Domestic Economic Determinants of a Trade Balance

A nation's foreign trade position is in many ways the end product of developments originating within its domestic economy. There is an extremely close correlation between a successful set of domestic economic indicators—price stability, high rates of saving and investment, productivity increases, enlightened management, product innovation, and so on—relative to other countries and a strong, competitive foreign trade position in which exports exceed imports. Conversely, a country with a relatively weak set of domestic economic indicators usually suffers from global competitive weakness and a foreign trade deficit.

One very elementary short-term determinant of a country's trade balance is the domestic business cycle. During domestic economic booms, imports tend to rise in response to increases in aggregate demand, and export growth might soften as domestic producers rush to fill rising orders from domestic customers. Conversely, an economy in the depths of recession tends to import less, due to declining rates of domestic production and employment. If it has a sufficiently strong manufacturing base, a recession-plagued country may also experience an increase in exports as domestic producers intensify sales efforts in faster-growing foreign markets. Business cycle conditions within major trading partners, in turn, are important variables determining demand for a country's exports. It therefore was probably not coincidental that the temporary reduction in the U.S. trade deficit in 1991, caused by the relatively sudden onset of a combination of weak import demand and a strong spurt in exports, coincided exactly (when the necessary lag time is factored in) with the U.S. recession that began in 1990 and ended after the first quarter of the following year.

Differences in domestic growth rates among major economies are of special relevance to the United States in view of repeated statistical findings that the income elasticity of Americans' demand for imports is significantly higher than the income elasticity of foreign demand for U.S. exports.[1] These unequal *income elasticities* (defined as the percentage by which a country's demand for imports rises when national income rises by 1 percent) for U.S. imports and exports imply that, over time, if GDP growth rates for the United States are equal to or greater than those of its major trading partners, it will experience a widening trade deficit unless there is continuous depreciation of the dollar to temper import demand and reduce the overseas costs of exports.

When a national economy produces more than it spends on consumer and capital goods and on services, it will have a trade surplus in goods and services. Conversely, a national economy that spends more than it produces can accomplish this feat only through incurring a trade deficit (in goods and services). A simple national accounting identity, the saving-investment balance, summarizes this relationship: $X-M = S+(T-G)-I$. A country's current account, equal to exports (X) minus imports (M) of goods and services, will be equal to the pool of private saving (S) plus net government spending—taxes (T) minus government expenditures (G)—minus private investment (I).

Because of large federal budget deficits *and* languishing rates of saving since the early 1980s, this economic relationship has special relevance for contemporary U.S. foreign trade performance. Inadequate saving relative to these budget deficits and private investment caused the need for the United States to make up the shortfall by attracting capital inflows of more than $900 billion in capital on a net basis in the ten-year period beginning in 1984. A surplus on the capital account in a country's balance of payments always means a deficit on the current account. Table 4.1 demonstrates that although there is no 100 percent statistical match (because the current account balance cannot be measured precisely and because of minor differences in statistical measurements), the saving-investment difference is a good real-world indicator of the level and direction of the current account position. This shortfall of saving relative to investment partly explains the seeming paradox of a large, continuing U.S. trade deficit despite significant dollar depreciation. All of the appreciation recorded in the first half of the 1980s was reversed by the decline in the dollar's value between 1985 and 1992.

Despite this close relationship, the idea that the two deficits (budget and trade) are twins is at best oversimplified, at worst not necessarily accurate. In the first place, a budget deficit does not generate a trade deficit *if* domestic saving is sufficiently large to offset it, as was usually the case, for example, in West Germany. Second and

TABLE 4.1   U.S. Saving and Investment Disequilibrium, 1988–1994
(billions of dollars)

	Private Saving	Net Government Saving	Private Investment	Saving-Investment Imbalance	Current Account Imbalance
1988	802.3	− 98.3	793.6	− 89.6	− 128.2
1989	819.4	− 77.5	832.3	− 90.4	− 102.8
1990	854.1	− 136.1	808.9	− 90.9	− 91.7
1991	937.3	− 185.9	744.8	6.6	− 6.9[a]
1992	980.8	− 257.8	788.3	− 65.3	− 67.9
1993	1,002.5	− 215.0	882.0	− 94.5	− 103.9
1994	1,053.5	− 132.9	1,032.9	− 112.3	− 155.7

[a]Artificially improved by inclusion of U.S. government receipts of payments from allies in support of Operation Desert Storm.

Source: U.S. Commerce Department.

more significant, no causality is implied by a saving-investment imbalance; a country's international competitiveness can affect its levels of saving and investment. For example, it is possible that a country could experience an autonomous increase in its exports as a result of increased amounts of innovation, efficiency, foreign demand, and so on. A surge in exports (relative to imports) could induce higher levels of national saving, expanded tax revenues, and decreased government spending (e.g., lower unemployment benefits) by a sufficient magnitude to reduce or eliminate an existing current account deficit. Conversely, international competitive weaknesses can potentially depress domestic production by a sufficient magnitude to cause the budget deficit to rise and private saving to decline. A country must automatically import goods to meet the difference between production and spending only if it is already operating at full capacity. Third, a reduction in the federal budget deficit or an increase in the domestic saving rate or both would induce a reduction in the U.S. trade deficit but not necessarily by exactly the same order of magnitude. What is certain, however, is that as long as the U.S. internal saving-investment imbalance persists, the traditional trade policy tactics of import protectionism and export promotion will be inadequate by themselves to eliminate the U.S. current account deficit.

A major variable in the connection between domestic economic performance and the U.S. trade balance is the possibility that a substantial cause of the prolonged trade deficit is a secular decline in U.S. competitiveness. There are ample data to suggest that sectors of U.S. industry are having trouble competing in the international marketplace without being propped up by costly, undesirable trends like stagnant real wages for production workers and currency depreciation. A steady stream of negative assessments began with the conclusion in the 1985 report of the President's Commission on Industrial Competitiveness that America's "ability to compete in world markets is eroding" and that there is "compelling evidence of a relative decline in our competitive performance."[2] More recently, the first annual report of the semi-official Competitiveness Policy Council declared that U.S. competitiveness "is eroding slowly but steadily."[3] Robert Blecker, one of the coauthors of this book, has written that "declining competitiveness has contributed significantly to the persistently high trade deficits of the past decade" and that an improved industrial performance is a necessary ingredient of a high-income, high-growth correction of the trade deficit.[4] In another study arguing that there was more to the U.S. trade deficit than the saving-investment imbalance, the authors found that the basic economic adjustments facing the United States in the future are "linked to the microeconomic issues of competitiveness in particular products and the general performance of U.S. exports and import-competing industries."[5]

Explanations for the alleged erosion in U.S. industrial competitiveness begin with macroeconomic policy (excessive governmental absorption of the private saving pool, relatively high corporate borrowing costs because of high interest rates, and so on) and proceed to more specific trends, such as lagging productivity increases relative to other industrialized countries, inadequate U.S. outlays for corporate investment, and insufficient R&D expenditures in the nondefense manufacturing sector. More specifically, shortcomings in U.S. corporate performance and management strategies have been targeted as major causes of the competitiveness problem. Although many of the criticisms are narrowly focused on things such as the short-term time horizons of managers and on deficiencies in commercializing new technologies, a widespread damnation of the "attitudinal and organizational weaknesses that pervade America's production system" was contained in a respected report issued in 1989 by the MIT (Massachusetts Institute of Technology) Commission on Industrial Productivity. The multidisciplinary task force found weaknesses in the way Americans "cooperate, manage, and organize themselves, as well as the ways they use technology, learn a new job, and interact with government." The commission concluded that

> the setbacks many firms suffered are not merely random events or part of the normal process by which firms constantly come and go; they are symptoms of more systematic and pervasive ills. We believe the situation will not be remedied simply by trying harder to do the same things that have failed to work in the past. The international business environment has changed irrevocably, and the United States must adapt its practices to this new world.[6]

In a widely read book, Michael Porter of the Harvard Business School alluded to a comprehensive diminution of U.S. competitiveness over a wide range of industries: "U.S. industry, in too many fields, has fallen behind in the rate, character, and extent of improvement and innovation. . . . American industry is on the defensive, preoccupied with clinging to what it has instead of advancing."[7] That none of these negative trends is necessarily permanent was suggested in the competitive resurgence demonstrated by many U.S. high-tech companies in the 1993–1994 period.

Professor Porter's criticisms were contained in a larger study that sought to broaden the concept of competitiveness to include the roles of market structure, managerial strategy, and technological leadership. His thesis is that the degree of relative global competitiveness enjoyed by any given sector of a country's economy will be determined by the multiple interaction of four major factors in what he termed the "diamond" of competitive advantage: (1) factor conditions, (2) demand conditions, (3) related and supporting industries, and (4) firm strategy, structure, and rivalry. This view of factor conditions is different from the traditional Heckscher-Ohlin theory (see Chapter 3) because Porter emphasizes very specific factors such as workers with particular training and skills or appropriate types of equipment and infrastructure rather than broad factor inputs like labor and capital. In addition, he stresses that the most important inputs into production are created by real-world business conditions, not by unalterably endowed factors of production—an assertion that has implications for trade policy as well as for domestic industrial policy.

International Commercial Determinants

As explained in the previous chapter, comparative advantage in the manufacturing sector is determined by more than a country's relative endowment of the three traditional factors of production (land, labor, and capital). International competitiveness—and therefore the composition of a country's imports and exports—is also a function of new variables, as exemplified by technology, management savvy, product innovation, receipt by corporations of favorable government treatment, and efficiency of the transportation and telecommunications infrastructure. No one should be surprised at the large proportion of high-tech goods and agricultural commodities among U.S. exports or at the widespread presence of low-tech, non-state-of-the-art, labor-intensive goods among U.S. imports.

Market-restrictive trade measures are also important determinants of a nation's imports and exports. No sovereign country in the world adheres to a genuinely free trade policy in which private markets are left completely free to determine the volume and composition of trade flows into and out of the country. International trade "law" explicitly recognizes the right of a sovereign country to protect its producers from injury or threat of injury from either "fair" or "unfair" foreign competition (see Chapter 7). The United States, like all other countries, has erected an outer defense perimeter to discourage imports. One part of this barrier consists of tariffs, which are taxes on imports, imposed on thousands of different goods. Like those of all industrialized countries, U.S. tariffs are now relatively low, about 5 percent on average in 1993 and due to go even lower as the result of implementation of the Uruguay Round agreement. But as is true of all averages, this statistic hides a multitude of individual sins in the form of some very high rates. Tariffs in excess of 40 percent are imposed by the United States on imports of many textile and footwear items, for example.

Also like other industrialized countries, the United States in recent years has come to rely more on a broad array of *nontariff barriers* (NTBs). Like tariffs, these devices are imposed to restrict imports and thereby benefit local producers and workers. Prime examples of NTBs are the absolute quotas (and occasional tariff-rate quotas, through which higher tariffs are triggered after specified quantities of goods are imported each year) that the United States imposes on such goods as dairy products, wheat, animal feeds, sugar, cotton, peanuts, and watches. Other NTBs include unduly restrictive safety and health standards (such as the special set of technical specifications Japan imposed on imported skis because of its assertion that Japanese snow was different) and restrictive government procurement codes. Many less developed countries require importers to obtain licenses and post cash deposits with the government in advance of delivery as a way of allocating scarce foreign exchange.

The outer ring of defense from foreign competition is not always adequate to prevent politically powerful domestic producers from occasionally claiming injury and demanding protection. Consequently, all countries have a secondary defense perimeter for limiting imports (or increases in import flows). For some countries, this involves changing the rules in midstream and imposing new barriers (e.g., when the French insisted that all incoming Japanese videocassette recorders had to enter through one small, inland customs post). The United States is more likely to rely on an extensive array of existing import-limiting legislation.

Because of the frequent use of U.S. trade laws, some critics of U.S. trade policy have branded them as a subtle form of protectionism amounting to a de facto NTB. A number of foreign governments and companies have grown angry at what they feel has become the U.S. government's frequent and arbitrary imposition of antidumping duties on imports allegedly priced below what is considered fair market value. Foreign resentment on this issue was well summed up in the claim by Japan's semiofficial Industrial Structure Council that "U.S. law and practice ignores commercial reality when imposing anti-dumping duties."[8]

Furthermore, what are effectively the equivalent of import quotas exist in the form of negotiated "voluntary" export restraint agreements (also referred to as orderly marketing agreements) that establish quantitative ceilings of limited duration on foreigners' exports of specified goods to the United States. (See Box 4.1 for details about these agreements.) In most cases, the United States has utilized this policy option in lieu of unilaterally imposing import barriers under the escape clause. In what amounts to "negotiated protectionism," these agreements between exporting and importing countries have affected contemporary international trade in such products as automobiles, steel, machine tools, textiles and apparel, color televisions, and footwear.

U.S. trade policy also creates market distortions by placing restrictions and obstacles in the path of would-be U.S. exporters. The national security imperative and attempts to infuse U.S. morality into the international marketplace have led to an unprecedented network of official export restraints and disincentives that far exceed the relatively limited hindrances imposed by all other governments. Despite its deleteri-

BOX 4.1　The Political and Economic Allure
of Orderly Marketing Agreements

Voluntary export restraint agreements have existed for many decades, but their appearance in international trade relations has been commonplace only since the early 1970s. The prime reason for this change was the growing U.S. and European sensitivity to steadily rising imports from the suddenly highly competitive manufacturing sectors of Japan and the NICs of East Asia. Trade officials of importing countries find several characteristics of what are also known as orderly marketing agreements (OMAs) to be appealing. They allow the initiating country to temper the growth of specific imports without the stigma of adopting unilateral protectionist measures. In addition, when other countries respond to demands that they "voluntarily" restrain designated exports, the initiating country is absolved from the obligation contained in the General Agreement on Tariffs and Trade that newly imposed import barriers require the payment of compensation. The latter is provided in the form of requiring comparable reductions in import barriers on other products so that countries whose exports have been adversely affected by the new barriers can increase their shipments of different goods by a roughly equivalent amount.

Exporting countries usually prefer voluntary restraints to the unilateral imposition of import barriers by trading partners because they are thereby given some voice in determining numerical ceilings on allowable levels of exports. Additionally, most OMAs contain a formula for annual growth rates in the affected exports. In some cases, the affected industry in the exporting country can benefit by being able to charge higher prices than would have been possible in a free market situation. Restraining the quantity of shipments may enable exporters to raise their prices to more profitable "market clearing" levels at which restricted supply is in equilibrium with strong product demand by consumers in the importing country. When Japanese automobile makers restricted their exports to the United States in the early 1980s, continuing strong demand by U.S. consumers allowed these companies to fatten their profit margin significantly—collecting economic "rents," in the language of economists.

Finally, OMAs can be appealing to those who dislike trade restrictions because inherent in many of them are loopholes that are relatively easy to exploit, such as illegal transshipments from third countries not party to the agreement and production shifts to product variants not covered in the original agreement.

ous effect on U.S. business, the world's most extensive export licensing and control system arguably has been legislated and applied in pursuit of admirable goals. U.S. export controls have sought to promote national security and foreign policy objectives by withholding military hardware and advanced technology from unfriendly and aggressor governments; to limit the overseas proliferation of arms, nuclear materials, and hazardous substances; and to minimize inflation by limiting overseas shipments of goods in short supply domestically. Further U.S. export disincentives exist in the form of legislated imposition of rigid standards of conduct on U.S. businesses that no other country has seriously considered replicating. The major examples of this effort are the Foreign Corrupt Practices Act that flatly prohibits illicit payments to foreign officials in order to obtain business, vigorous antitrust laws, and antiboycott regulations on domestic businesses (see Chapter 7).

Even when unimpeded by their government, U.S. exporters are confronted by at least four important kinds of trade and economic obstacles that originate in other countries. The first is the thicket of foreign tariff and nontariff trade barriers that deters many tens of billions of dollars annually of potential U.S. exports. No precise estimates are possible, but the extent of these barriers is suggested by the length of the annual *Report on Foreign Trade Barriers* published by the U.S. Trade Representative's Office. The 1993 edition contains 270 pages of single-spaced text describing the barriers erected by more than forty countries and the European Union.

The second type of external barrier consists of illegal violations of U.S. companies' intellectual property rights—patents, copyrights, trademarks, and the like—by foreign companies that result in lost sales estimated by one U.S. government agency to exceed $40 billion annually.[9]

The third overseas obstacle to U.S. exports is the indirect barrier stemming from severe shortages of foreign exchange in most less developed countries (exclusive of Southeast Asia) and in the former Soviet Union that inflict limitations on imports through financial necessity rather than commercial malice. The most dramatic example of this syndrome was the events associated with the worst years of the debt crisis in Latin America, a major U.S. export market among developing countries. Unable to service escalating debt repayment obligations in the mid-1980s, one major South American country after another lost access to new commercial bank loans—their major means of attracting foreign capital. This diminished access to convertible foreign exchange to finance their current account deficits and an inability to quickly increase exports triggered an immediate and sharp decline in the ability of most South American countries to import. As seen from the other direction, U.S. exporters suffered a significant absolute drop in sales in one of their major export markets during most of the 1980s. Table 4.2 shows that U.S. exports to Latin America plunged so far in absolute terms during the mid-1980s that at the end of the decade, they still had not been restored to their 1980 levels. Conversely, dollar-hungry countries like Argentina, Brazil, and Mexico made incremental exports a sufficiently high priority as to cause U.S. imports from them to double over the course of the 1980s. Overall, U.S. imports from South America *increased* by 66 percent between 1980 and 1989.

TABLE 4.2   U.S. Merchandise Exports to South America in the 1980s and Early 1990s (millions of dollars)

1980	*1985*	*1990*	*1993*
17,130	10,780	15,067	23,422

Note: U.S. exports to Mexico, Central America, and the Caribbean countries are not included in the data cited.

Sources: United Nations Economic Commission for Latin America and the Caribbean, "Latin American and Caribbean Trade and Investment Relations with the United States in the 1980s," November 1991, p. 34. Data for the 1990s are from U.S. Department of Commerce, *U.S. Foreign Trade Highlights, 1993.* Data for all years are census-based numbers as collected by the U.S. Department of Commerce.

Table 4.2 also demonstrates the dramatic reverse of this process in the 1990s, when the abating of the debt crisis resuscitated U.S. exports to the region. As Latin American economic policy reforms created relatively quick turnarounds in domestic performances and enhanced international competitiveness, the ability of these countries to pay for imports from the United States also increased. (Although foreign exchange limitations continue to plague most of Africa and southern Asia, these countries have never been major markets for U.S. business. Consequently, the debt problem in the mid-1990s was no longer a serious drag on U.S. exports.)

A final category of obstacles to U.S. exports consists of measures originating within the borders of trading partners. De facto import barriers called "structural impediments" in countries such as Japan and Korea take a number of forms, including tightly knit corporate groups and discriminatory distribution systems. In former centrally planned economies, structural impediments include government-owned companies and primitive business law.

International Monetary Determinants: Exchange Rates

Events in the international monetary system in general and changes in the value of a country's currency relative to other currencies—its exchange rate—are also critical variables that influence a country's import and export flows. Exchange rates largely determine the local currency prices of imports, which begin as foreign goods denominated in foreign currency and are then quoted in a price denominated in local currency. They also determine the prices of a country's exports through conversion of the country's currency into the local currencies of overseas customers.

Changes in exchange rates, other things held constant, affect a nation's competitiveness. A depreciating currency normally causes imports to become more expensive—and therefore less attractive—and allows a country's exports to become more cheaply priced when expressed in the currencies of foreign customers. Conversely, an appreciating currency, other things being equal, allows imports to become more cheaply priced in terms of the stronger local currency while causing exports to become more expensive to foreign customers paying for these imports with their relatively weaker currencies. (Despite conventional mercantilist-tainted wisdom, economic common sense suggests that currency appreciation caused by rising national competitiveness is more attractive than depreciation in terms of aggregate national welfare. Other things being equal, moderate currency appreciation, by making imported goods and services cost less, enhances a country's real incomes and standards of living while reducing inflationary pressures.)

Figure 4.1 illustrates the close correlation between changes in the dollar's exchange rate over the 1975–1992 period and, with an appropriate lag time of two years, changes in the U.S. trade balance. The chart clearly demonstrates that dollar appreciation in the early 1980s led to a rapid increase in U.S. imports relative to exports. It also shows that the depreciation that began in 1985, with a two-year lag, is closely correlated with a reduction in the trade deficit as imports became more costly and U.S. goods became more price competitive in foreign markets. However, price changes in exports and imports were not sufficient to prevent the trade deficit in the early 1990s from remaining considerably worse than in the 1970s, prior to dollar appreciation.[10] The recessions in Germany and Japan, structural trade problems with the Japanese, continuing internal U.S. economic shortcomings, and the possibility of inadequate inflation-adjusted dollar depreciation were all contributing factors to the intractable and large U.S. merchandise trade deficit that continued into 1995.

Pre-1970s history provides a number of other case studies linking major shifts in U.S. trade performance with the dollar's exchange rate. Under the Bretton Woods fixed exchange rate system that prevailed from 1946 into early 1973, countries belonging to the International Monetary Fund were obliged to keep their exchange rates fixed (unchanged) relative to the U.S. dollar. This commitment would be unchanged unless and until countries encountered a "fundamental," or structural, balance of payments disequilibrium requiring a currency devaluation or revaluation as part of a mix of policy changes needed to correct it. As the other industrialized countries steadily recovered from World War II and thus steadily closed the competitiveness gap with the United States, their exchange rates should have, on average, appreciated against the dollar. Instead, the opposite happened. The real (inflation-adjusted) exchange rate of the dollar increased under the Bretton Woods system. This occurred because currency devaluations by other countries during the 1950s and 1960s were far more prevalent than upward revaluations, even among the other industrialized countries, whose balance of payments positions improved the fastest. Of the major balance of payments surplus countries during this period, only West Germany experienced significant currency appreciation.

The relatively subtle effects of this exchange rate phenomenon that prevailed in the early 1960s were overwhelmed by the severe and rapid damage inflicted on U.S. competitiveness in the latter years of that decade by the outbreak of relatively high

FIGURE 4.1   Impact of Exchange Rate Changes on the U.S. Merchandise Trade Balance (exchange rate lagged two years)

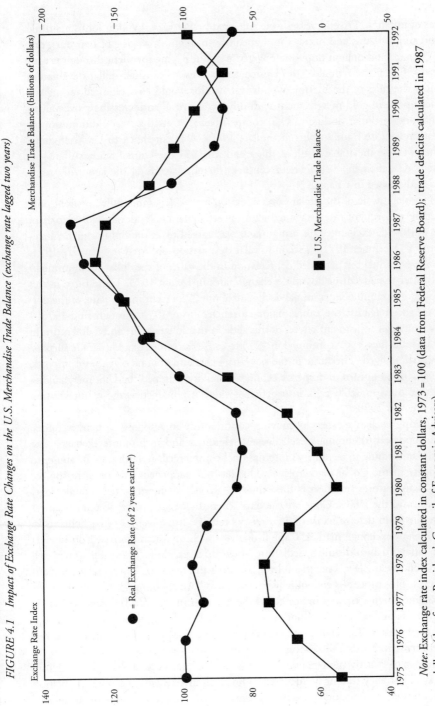

Note: Exchange rate index calculated in constant dollars, 1973 = 100 (data from Federal Reserve Board); trade deficits calculated in 1987 dollars (data from President's Council of Economic Advisers).

*For example, 1982 shows the 1982 trade balance and the 1980 exchange rate index.

rates of inflation. Price increases were triggered by President Lyndon Johnson's futile effort to have guns and butter simultaneously through his waging of two wars, one in Vietnam and one on domestic poverty, without paying for them through tax increases. Given the refusal of the United States even to consider dollar devaluation (under the rules of the Bretton Woods system, this would have required raising the official price of gold in agreement with other countries), an increasingly overvalued dollar and a secular decline in U.S. competitiveness caused a steady diminution of the merchandise trade surplus in the late 1960s. A major shock to U.S. self-confidence was the inevitable result of this trend: In 1971 the United States suffered its first trade deficit in the twentieth century (thereby launching the agonizing reappraisal discussed in Chapter 2).

The magnitude of the dollar's overvaluation by 1971 became fully apparent only after the subsequent three-stage reduction in its value. Dollar devaluation as part of the worldwide exchange rate realignment was agreed to in the Smithsonian Agreement of December 1971. A second dollar devaluation occurred in February 1973. Finally, a gradual but extended depreciation in the value of the dollar set in immediately after the advent of floating exchange rates in March 1973. These three moves resulted in a cumulative nominal decline of about 22 percent in the value of the dollar weighted against the other major currencies from 1971 through mid-1975.[11] The beneficial adjustment effects of this slide in the dollar's value and a downturn in the U.S. business cycle combined in 1975 to cause the return of a U.S. trade surplus. It was short-lived. The surge in the per barrel cost and volume of U.S. oil imports, along with an upturn in domestic economic activity, bumped the U.S. merchandise trade account in 1976 back into deficit—where it remained without interruption into the mid-1990s.

Floating exchange rates, by moving continuously in response to market forces, were supposed to eliminate exchange rate rigidities and to promote exchange rate levels conforming to a country's international commercial strength (i.e., its ability to compete in the global marketplace). This has not happened. The main reason for this disappointing situation is the explosive growth of international capital movements since the 1970s. Gone are the days when trade and current account balances were the main determinants of a currency's relative attractiveness to participants in the foreign exchange market. Capital flows—much of which are based on interest rate differentials and pure speculation—now drive exchange rates, sometimes well above and below levels suggested by a country's international commercial competitiveness. This process is colloquially referred to as "overshooting."

Recent rough estimates indicate that the turnover in the world's foreign exchange markets is approaching $1 trillion on a *daily* basis.[12] If this is taken as an accurate figure, the amount of foreign exchange market transactions necessitated by one year of world trade in goods and services equates to less than two weeks of total foreign exchange market activity. If poetic license is used, it can be said that the other fifty weeks of currency trading are devoted to financial investments and pure speculation about future exchange rate movements. This was the technical setting for the incredible dollar appreciation of the early 1980s.

Between mid-1980 and the end of February 1985, the dollar experienced what was by far the largest, most pervasive increase in value of any major currency in modern economic history. The genesis of this currency appreciation appears to have been the advent of Reaganomics, specifically the mix of expansionary fiscal policy (a large, growing budget deficit) and restrictive monetary policy (high interest rates) that dominated the U.S. economy in the early 1980s. The prevailing theory was that relative real interest rates in the United States needed to rise to whatever levels were necessary to attract the massive capital inflows from abroad to bridge the enormous gap ($100-plus billion annually) between U.S. saving (private and governmental) and investment. The combination of this interest rate differential, the relatively favorable business environment generated by the Reagan administration, and after 1984 pure speculation caused a major excess of dollar demand over supply. The dollar's exchange rate, or more simply its price, moved from an index number of 85 in mid-1980 to a peak of 165 at the end of February 1985—an astounding increase of 94 percent.[13]

Apparently irrelevant at this time in the minds of foreign investors anxious to acquire dollar-denominated assets was the damage imposed on U.S. exporters and import-competing companies by sustained dollar appreciation: Booming imports and stagnant exports caused the U.S. merchandise trade deficit to swell from $19.5 billion in 1980 to $118 billion in 1985. At least two major domestic causal factors were involved: the domestic saving-investment disequilibrium, which led to more spending than production, and pockets of secular decline in U.S. industrial competitiveness. However, most analysts agree that the infamous overvalued dollar was the leading cause of the unprecedented U.S. trade account deterioration in the 1980–1987 period. That dollar appreciation was not the exclusive cause is demonstrated by the fact that mammoth trade deficits persisted long after 1991, when the inflation-adjusted, multilateral trade–weighted value of the dollar fell below its preappreciation index of 1980.[14]

Patterns of Foreign Direct Investment

The direction and product composition of trade flows have become increasingly affected by the proliferation of global production facilities operated by multinational companies. The total world stock of *foreign direct investment* (FDI), defined as the acquisition of managerial control in a new or existing company by a corporation located in another country, is now in excess of $2 trillion. A conservative estimate of total merchandise produced and sold by the overseas subsidiaries of all companies of all countries would be about $5 trillion annually. During the 1980s, FDI increased at an annual average rate of 12.2 percent, more than twice the comparable rate of increase for world trade growth and more than four times greater than increases in world GDP.[15] FDI is part of the phenomenon of the end of national markets and the onset of market globalization that began in earnest in the 1960s. International manufacturing investment has become so pervasive that it can be said that large corporations now compete globally through location of production facilities as well as through exports.[16]

Belatedly, trade-related investment measures were added to the international trade negotiating agenda at the start of the Uruguay Round. Official investment policies that most directly alter trade flows are known collectively as *performance require-ments*—the most significant being host governments' requirements that a stipulated percentage of a foreign subsidiary's output be exported and that some minimum percentage of production utilize locally produced components. In some cases, foreign direct investments are established for the specific purpose of circumventing prohibitive import barriers.

Since the United States is the largest single source of inward and outward FDI, it stands to reason that its trade flows are significantly affected by intracorporate transactions (i.e., exports and imports negotiated between two branches of the same company in different countries). Using the broadest of several possible definitions, one can link an estimated $262 billion of U.S. exports in 1991, 62 percent of the total, with all transactions "associated with" U.S.-controlled nonbank MNCs. Exports by U.S. parent companies to their majority-owned foreign affiliates (a more accurate approximation of the direct linkage between trade and foreign investment) totaled $96 billion in 1991, almost one-fourth of total exports. Imports purchased by U.S.-based parent companies from their overseas subsidiaries in 1991 were valued at $78 billion, about 16 percent of total U.S. imports for that year. (Once again, a much larger figure of $216 billion, or 44 percent of total imports, materializes if the broader category of "trade associated with U.S. MNCs" is used.)[17]

U.S. trade flows are also materially affected by the upsurge of FDI that came into the United States during the 1980s. Although still a minuscule percentage of total corporate assets, foreign-controlled U.S. companies are relatively active in importing and exporting. U.S.-based affiliates of foreign MNCs exported an estimated $38 billion in 1990 to their parent companies (and an additional $53 billion to unrelated overseas companies). U.S. affiliates of foreign-controlled companies (many of which are wholesalers set up to do nothing other than import) in 1990 bought an estimated $137 billion from their parents and imported an additional $44 billion from unrelated companies. Japanese companies in the United States accounted for about one-half of all trade conducted by these foreign-controlled U.S.-based firms. Their total 1990 shipments from the United States (primarily by Japanese trading companies) of $39 billion accounted for 10 percent of total U.S. exports. However, their imports of $88 billion in the same year accounted for almost 20 percent of total U.S. imports.[18]

The propensity of large U.S. manufacturing companies to sell in foreign markets through overseas production has posed one of the longest-running conundrums in U.S. foreign trade policy debates: To what extent, if at all, does the half trillion dollars worth of U.S. FDI abroad displace U.S. exports? The lack of sufficient data to produce quantitative certainty has precluded scholars from making a conclusive, unanimous determination on whether FDI has caused a significant adverse (or favorable) impact on *net* exports.[19] Whereas some existing overseas export patterns are inevitably disrupted after a U.S. company opens an overseas subsidiary, new sales are just as inevitably generated as foreign subsidiaries buy components and product models from their U.S. parent that are not being assembled overseas. It probably is not a coincidence that U.S. exports remain strong in Western Europe, a major site of U.S. foreign direct investment, and are weak in Japan, where U.S. industrial FDI is relatively small. Whatever the exact answer, the growing effects of inward FDI on the merchandise trade balance has become an important new dimension of the already complicated effort to quantify the effect of MNCs on the overall U.S. trade picture.

A related, unresolved issue is whether a more accurate measure of U.S. international competitiveness would be produced if overseas sales of goods produced by foreign subsidiaries of U.S. manufacturing companies were combined with U.S. exports. The estimated figure in 1991 for total manufacturing sales by U.S. foreign subsidiaries was $760 billion,[20] a figure almost twice the value of total exports that year. If sales resulting from overseas production by U.S. MNCs were added to traditional exports, U.S. business firms would have a large "global sales" surplus even after necessary statistical adjustments were made (e.g., netting out estimated sales within the United States by local subsidiaries of foreign-owned companies). Although such an approach casts U.S. competitiveness in an improved light, it does not enhance domestic employment.

Conclusion

The economic importance of net trade balances is easy to exaggerate, even though exports and imports of goods and services have become important variables in national economic performance. Ironically, the importance of trade policy in determining a country's foreign trade performance—except in the short term—is also easy to exaggerate when other economic factors are considered. This chapter has sought to document the limitations of trade policy.

The relatively limited ability of narrowly defined trade policy to alter U.S. trade flows reinforces a larger thesis of this book: Foreign trade does not exist in a vacuum. Domestic economic factors and other international economic trends are more likely to exert the dominant influence on trade performance. This argument is supported by observing just how little impact the fundamental tools of trade policy—import restraints and export promotion—have had in the still fruitless quest, begun in the mid-1980s, to induce a return to equilibrium in the large U.S. trade deficit. Success or failure in official efforts to expand exports and constrain imports is increasingly being determined by the confluence of many forces outside the realm of trade policy as it is traditionally defined.

For Further Reading

Aliber, Robert Z. *The International Money Game.* 5th ed. New York: Basic Books, 1987.
Bergsten, C. Fred, Thomas Horst, and Theodore H. Moran. *American Multinationals and American Interests.* Washington, D.C.: Brookings Institution, 1978.

Blecker, Robert A. *Beyond the Twin Deficits: A Trade Strategy for the 1990s.* Armonk, N.Y.: M. E. Sharpe, Inc., 1992.

MIT Commission on Industrial Productivity. *Made in America: Regaining the Competitive Edge.* Cambridge: MIT Press, 1989.

U.S. Congress Office of Technology Assessment. *Making Things Better.* Washington, D.C.: Government Printing Office, 1990.

Notes

1. References to several studies of the relatively high U.S. income elasticity of demand for imports, including the pioneering work of Houthakker and Magee, can be found in Robert A. Blecker, *Beyond the Twin Deficits* (Armonk, N.Y.: M. E. Sharpe, Inc., 1992), pp. 62–64.

2. The President's Commission on Industrial Competitiveness, *Global Competition: The New Reality* (Washington, D.C.: Government Printing Office, 1985), pp. 1, 5.

3. Competitiveness Policy Council, "Rebuilding a Competitive America" (Washington, D.C.: Government Printing Office, 1992), p. 1.

4. Blecker, *op. cit.,* p. 1.

5. Rudiger Dornbusch, Paul Krugman, and Yung Chul Park, "Meeting World Challenges: U.S. Manufacturing in the 1990s" (Rochester, N.Y.: Eastman Kodak Company, 1989), p. 9.

6. MIT Commission on Industrial Productivity, *Made in America* (Cambridge: MIT Press, 1989), pp. 166, 42, and 8.

7. Michael Porter, *The Competitive Advantage of Nations* (New York: Free Press, 1990), p. 532.

8. "1993 Report on Unfair Trade Policies by Major Trading Partners: Trade Policies and GATT Obligations," Japanese Ministry of International Trade and Industry, May 1993, p. 14.

9. U.S. International Trade Commission, *Foreign Protection of Intellectual Property Rights and the Effect on U.S. Industry and Trade,* February 1988, p. H-3.

10. A complicating factor in recent years for the U.S. trade balance is that the real (inflation-adjusted) value of the dollar in terms of the currencies of the major U.S. trading partners has not shown much correlation to the purchasing power parity theory; the latter holds that exchange rates between two countries are not in equilibrium unless their domestic purchasing power for a range of goods (expressed in a common currency) is roughly equivalent.

11. Computed from unpublished Federal Reserve Board data for the weighted average value of the dollar, March 1973 = 100.

12. See references to various official surveys in *Financial Times,* April 1, 1993, p. 15; April 2, 1993, p. 15; and May 26, 1993, p. I.

13. Data from *Federal Reserve Bulletin,* various issues.

14. Data from *Economic Report of the President,* 1993, p. 470.

15. John Rutter, "Recent Trends in International Direct Investment," U.S. Commerce Department study, dated August 1992, p. 3.

16. Harry G. Broadman, "The Trade–Foreign Investment Linkage: Principles, Facts, and Policies," unpublished paper, dated Spring 1991, pp. 1–2.

17. Data from U.S. Department of Commerce, *Survey of Current Business,* July 1993, p. 45.

18. Data for all estimates of trade by U.S. affiliates of foreign companies from U.S. Department of Commerce, *Foreign Direct Investment in the United States: An Update,* June 1993, pp. 170–174.

19. See, for example, C. Fred Bergsten, Thomas Horst, and Theodore H. Moran, *American Multinationals and American Interests* (Washington, D.C.: Brookings Institution, 1978), p. 98; and the 1991 *Annual Report of the President's Council of Economic Advisers,* p. 259. For a different perspective finding that U.S. foreign direct investment overseas was damaging on balance to U.S. employment, see Norman J. Glickman and Douglas P. Woodward, *The New Competitors: How Foreign Investors Are Changing the U.S. Economy* (New York: Basic Books, 1989), pp. 317–324.

20. Data from U.S. Department of Commerce, *Survey of Current Business,* July 1993, p. 52.

Part Three

Politics and Administration

5 The Formulation and Administration of U.S. Trade Policy: Who Does What

Process affects substance. The organizational means by which a government makes trade policy often has an impact on the nature of that policy. Broad national values, in turn, affect the structure of the decisionmaking process. Policy decisions sometimes are bewildering unless one is familiar with the elaborate process used by senior policymakers to digest the relevant information, weigh the pros and cons of the various policy options available, react to strong pressures from concerned constituencies, and broker a final determination of how to proceed.

In this chapter we identify the relevant players in the government and the private sector, describe what they do, and explain how they go about doing it. Implicit throughout this discussion is the suggestion that different bureaucratic actors bring different priorities, institutional cultures, and constituencies to the policymaking process. In the next chapter we proceed to the second stage: a review of the various theories employed to explain why the policymaking process functions in the manner that it does.

The Basic Principles of U.S. Organizational Dynamics

At least five operational guidelines are essential for conceptualizing the complex, seemingly random process by which the U.S. government makes trade policy. The first guideline is recognition that there are several different kinds of decisions that vary in both nature and importance. Sometimes decisions involve abstract formulation of broad, long-term policy strategy (e.g., trade relations with Japan). More often, decisions involve narrow, specific administrative actions within existing programs that regulate import and export flows, such as how to respond to a petition seeking temporary relief from import competition.

The majority of trade policy decisions consist of relatively minor actions that either maintain the status quo or result in minor incrementalism (i.e., marginal modifications of existing policy). A typical policy action relates to a single country, a single product, or even a single company. Many of these issues in turn are handled at the office director or deputy assistant secretary level. At the other extreme are the relatively rare policy decisions that mark major turning points involving sweeping issues of dramatic importance such as passage of major new trade legislation, enunciation of U.S. negotiating objectives in multilateral trade negotiations, creation of a North American free trade area, or the imposition of an across-the-board tariff surcharge.

Some decisions involve ongoing trade relations and will have long-term effects (e.g., the semiconductor agreement with Japan). Others relate to one-time matters of limited duration (e.g., whether to support admission of China to the World Trade Organization). Some decisions involve proactive initiatives by the U.S. government, but it is more common to observe defensive reactions (e.g., retaliation against unfair foreign trade practices). Some decisions involve national security issues and entail negotiations with foreign governments (e.g., imposing trade sanctions in cooperation with other countries). Other decisions are mainly domestic in nature and involve U.S. government dealings with U.S. companies (e.g., proposed changes in trade legislation or the granting of export licenses).

The second guideline for conceptualizing the broad patterns of policymaking is realization that the extraordinary degree of decentralization in the U.S. government's trade policymaking apparatus has special implications for the nature of that policy. There is no one person or agency "in charge" of foreign trade policymaking. Uniquely with U.S. trade policymaking, there is not even a dominant *branch* of government. When it comes to trade policy, no other legislative body has as much influence and authority relative to the executive branch as does the U.S. Congress.

A basic, nearly universal characteristic of U.S. trade policymaking is the pursuit of compromise and accommodation on one or both of two levels—among the various executive branch departments and agencies having policy jurisdiction and between the administration and Congress. (The judicial branch makes very infrequent appearances when policies or administrative decisions are challenged in the courts.) An increasingly wide array of private sector interest groups constitutes an additional power center that is present at least in spirit, if not physically, when official policy deliberations are being conducted. The private sector actively exploits the U.S. government's belief that everyone affected by public policy has the right to be heard, especially in trade policy—which, after all, is administered mostly on behalf of the private sector.

Depending on the nature of the trade issue under consideration, any or all of these power centers may play a pivotal role. The resulting collectivity of control invariably affects at least the details of policy substance by instilling a premium on flexibility. The need to seek consensus within a decentralized policymaking process causes brilliant, optimal, make-everybody-happy trade policy decisions to be the exception rather than the rule. The nature of the decisionmaking process also causes policy inconsistencies in the trade field to be far more evident than an unswerving allegiance to a single guiding ideology.

The third operational guideline is an offshoot of the second: the need to appreciate fully the limits of presidential power in managing U.S. trade policy. An increasingly well-informed Congress is always a direct or indirect factor in every politically significant trade policy decision. No administration makes a major trade decision without keeping at least one eye on the legislative branch—the sole authority to pass trade legislation. On a day-to-day basis, every astute administration's approach to trade policy is tempered by the realization that if it acts too frequently in a manner contrary to prevailing congressional sentiment, it faces a clear and present possibility of being slapped with legislation that it did not ask for and does not support.

The fourth guideline is the unavoidable decentralization of trade policy authority within the executive branch. Given the fact that no single executive branch actor can monopolize any significant trade policy decision, coordination among many executive branch departments and agencies having jurisdiction in various foreign trade policy sectors is the inevitable organizational path to policy decisionmaking. Except for the rare instances of presidents interceding on their own to implement trade policy unilaterally, the watchword is interagency collaboration, or joint effort, in reaching policy decisions. The only question is how many different executive branch entities (the number can be as high as two dozen) have a compelling reason to participate in the inevitable interagency committees and working groups. Except for the infrequent instances when all agencies are in basic agreement, trade decisions are arrived at by a brokering process among competing coalitions of agencies sharing the same assessment of what actions will bring the most benefits to the most "deserving" constituencies.

A comparable situation exists in the legislative branch where the majority of all standing committees has jurisdiction over some facet of trade policy: import restraints, export restraints, export promotion, high-tech competitiveness, agriculture, foreign direct investment, and so on. Coordination in this case takes the form of joint hearings and two or more committees drafting different sections of the same statute. Another form of coordination between congressional committees is the conference committee, used to reconcile differences in bills passed by the Senate and House.

The final operational guideline is the propensity of the various bureaucratic actors to bring different perspectives and priorities to the interagency deliberative process. As explained more fully in the next chapter, the various executive departments and congressional committees have not been created to focus on the totality of U.S. interests and to represent everyone. Instead, they represent different constituencies or different sectors of the policy waterfront. Monolithic thinking in defining the national interest on trade policy issues is not a day-to-day characteristic of the governments of any large industrialized democracy. The notion that governments simply seek to advance their "national interest" is a gross generalization that is not a useful guide to explaining or predicting individual trade policy decisions. Reference to the national interest ignores the inherent difficulty of determining on a case-by-case basis which of several competing trade policy options would in fact most benefit the nation as a whole.

Inevitably, trade actions result in winners and losers—workers, companies, industries, foreign countries, and theories. The result is a high probability that at least two legitimate points of view about priorities will be advanced in connection with any significant decision on restricting imports, retaliating against trading partners, restricting exports, or subsidizing exports. Trade policy is ultimately a political process precisely because of the difficult task of choosing among conflicting but perfectly rational and legitimate viewpoints. The concept that trade policy spawns winners and losers begins with the pocketbook issue of whether jobs and production stay at home or go to foreigners in the form of imports or lost export opportunities.[1] Every sovereign government has exercised its right to interfere with free market forces. The pursuit of economic efficiency and the practice of free trade inevitably are tempered by concerns of social stability and equity, not to mention the assumption that popularly elected legislators are supposed to heed the desires expressed by their constituents.

Who dominates the making of U.S. trade policy? The answer is that relative clout varies over time, especially in the executive branch, depending on specific issues at hand, events (the advent of the cold war temporarily put the national security bureaucracy in the driver's seat), and the relative strengths of department heads. With regard to the latter, the key variables are the contrasting personalities, closeness to the president, understanding of how things work behind the scenes in Washington, and taste for bureaucratic intrigue among members of the cabinet.

On a different plane, the battle for domination in U.S. trade policy involves frequent clashes between foreign policy and domestic economic priorities. The result is passionate arguments between the national security bureaucracy and the economic bureaucracy over such issues as whether to impose export embargoes on "outlaw" countries (an especially difficult issue if "friendly" countries choose not to participate in economic sanctions), whether to renew China's MFN status, how far to go in protecting domestic "national security" industries from imports, or how aggressive to be in demanding greater market access in Japan.

The political process inherent in choosing among different values would be inescapable even if trade policy were made by a group of politically unaccountable economics professors. There may be general agreement on the broad virtues of free trade in the abstract. However, no academic unanimity exists on exactly which economic theories should prevail with regard to specific trade issues, to wit, the wisdom of unilaterally practicing free trade, how to determine proper candidates for infant industry protection, the existence of a significant U.S. competitiveness problem, and so on.

The Executive Branch

After passage in 1934 of the Reciprocal Trade Agreements Act, the executive branch assumed the lead in formulating and administering policy. However, executive branch authority here exists only to the extent permitted by congressionally passed legislation because the U.S. Constitution mandates that presidential authority in trade policy is derived from the Congress (see the next section). In effect, Congress has delegated the executive branch to handle the technical details of administering trade relations as well as to be the primary recipient of domestic political pressure from interest groups demanding import protection.

The executive branch's machinery to make trade policy exists on three different levels: the Executive Office of the President, the line departments and agencies, and interagency coordinating groups. The fact that the president is at the very top of the command structure does not necessarily mean he has been a major participant in trade decisions over time. Only on a few occasions have presidents taken time away from more pressing (and more appealing) matters of domestic politics and national security to take the initiative on a major trade matter. In most cases, presidential involvement in this area consists of approving a cabinet-level recommendation or arbitrating relatively rare cabinet-level stalemates.

Outside of the Oval Office, five White House groups are so heavily involved in trade policy formulation that they form a separate layer of bureaucracy paralleling the cabinet departments, an organizational idiosyncrasy found only in the United States. First and foremost is the *Office of the United States Trade Representative* (USTR)—the titular head of "overall" trade policy formulation, "chief" trade negotiator for the U.S. government, and designated "representative" of the United States in the major international trade organizations.[2] The USTR plays a major role in managing the interagency coordination process, and it has overall managerial responsibilities for the three-tiered network of private sector advisory committees on trade policy. The agency was described by an insider as seeing itself mainly as a policy broker and a problem solver.[3] The USTR is very much a creature of Congress, created because legislators in 1961 decided that the State Department needed to be replaced as the head of U.S. trade delegations by a more hard-nosed, domestically sensitive bureaucracy. Although USTR is intellectually aligned with the antiprotectionist articles of the GATT and is oriented toward negotiating agreements to reduce trade barriers, it is not a dogmatic free trade agency. It has remained mindful of its congressional heritage by its more than occasional willingness to recommend relief for import-impacted domestic industries. Congress elevated USTR to cabinet status in the Trade Act of 1974, but it is still so small (about 150 full-time staff) that it regularly utilizes the greater personnel resources of the cabinet departments.

USTR's role as primus inter pares among executive branch agencies charged with the development of U.S. trade policy has two important limitations. It has never been able to take the leadership role on all trade issues. The lines of command are sufficiently ambiguous and USTR's staff sufficiently limited that other agencies sometimes take the lead, either through a bureaucratic power grab or by mutual agreement. Second, as a presidential office, USTR by design has not been given authority to administer major programs affecting U.S. foreign trade relations (see the discussion of the Commerce and Agriculture Departments later in the chapter).

A second key White House player is generic: the *cabinet-level coordinating group for economic policy* favored by presidents since Richard Nixon. Created by executive order and having various names (Economic Policy Group, National Economic

Council, e.g.), this group represents the operational principle of cooperative policy-making at the highest political level. Usually, the president is formally the chairman, but in practice he is only an occasional attendee. Each of these groups has had roughly the same membership as well as the same indispensable responsibility: development of consensus among the ten or more members of the cabinet and senior presidential advisers having jurisdiction in economic policy formulation. For all but what are deemed the most crucial trade policy issues on which the president takes direct control, this is the final decisionmaking stop for foreign trade (and domestic economic) policy decisions.[4] Typically, a designated official of the senior coordinating council for economic affairs sends a memorandum to the president outlining its consensus recommendation, summarizing other policy options proposed, and asking for his formal approval.

The common denominator of the remaining three White House offices is that they are advisory bodies with a single constituent: the president of the United States. The *National Security Council* (NSC) is charged with coordinating international political and military policy (mainly between the State and Defense Departments) and providing independent foreign policy advice to the president. The person on the NSC's professional staff in charge of economic affairs has been an integral part of the interagency process deliberating any bilateral or multilateral trade issue affecting U.S. national security interests. It has been a commonplace occurrence over the years for the NSC and the senior economic policy group to engage in turf battles to determine which one would assume responsibility for managing the decisionmaking process for internationally sensitive trade policy issues.

The *Council of Economic Advisers* (CEA) has a broad mandate to provide the president with nonpolitical, technical advice on any economic issues affecting full employment and price stability. Since trade policy obviously impacts the domestic economy, the CEA member with international economic policy responsibilities or a senior staff member joins the interagency process when major trade issues are under deliberation.

The fifth and final White House entity with trade policy jurisdiction, the *Office of Management and Budget* (OMB), is not visible in trade policy on a day-to-day basis; most of its international activities are focused on defense and foreign aid policies. OMB's professional economists exercise clout in trade deliberations whenever budgetary expenditures or lost revenues are a consideration (e.g., officially subsidized export financing and reductions in tariff duties). It also can be influential in trade policy formulation by virtue of its responsibility for coordinating and clearing all executive branch agency responses to bills introduced into Congress and all testimony to congressional committees.

The line departments and agencies constitute the second layer of executive branch bureaucracy. By virtue of its responsibility to conduct U.S. foreign policy, the *State Department* provides the major assessment of the impact of trade policy options on U.S. relationships with other countries. Whereas the domestic agencies assess the impact on various sectors of the domestic economy, the function of the State Department is to worry about the responses to U.S. trade actions by its constituents (i.e., other countries, be they friendly or hostile). The validity of this external priority depends on how important one thinks a friendly, peaceful global environment is to assuring prosperity within the U.S. economy and on the extent to which one believes unfair foreign trade practices and foreign competition are a threat to U.S. national security. The State Department monitors trade policy both from its regional bureaus as well as from its Bureau of Economic and Business Affairs. A considerable amount of commercial negotiations and reporting is conducted by its economic officers stationed overseas in embassies and consulates. Although State long ago was stripped of its status as chief negotiator and coordinator of trade policy,[5] it still has the lead role in international aviation and maritime negotiations (major factors in international services trade) and is one of the three major actors in export control policy.

By virtue of its domination of domestic economic and balance of payments policies, the *Treasury Department* exerts a major voice in the formulation of trade policy. Its main function is to determine what trade actions would be best for its wide-ranging constituent—the overall domestic economy. The position of Under Secretary of Treasury for International Affairs has become very influential in all phases of U.S. international economic policy. Since import barriers tend to be inflationary, Treasury usually joins the other economics-oriented agencies like the CEA and OMB in preferring maximum competition from abroad. (Treasury was less charitable toward imports when the U.S. balance of payments deficits were soaring in the final years of fixed exchange rates; since 1973, the department has looked to floating exchange rates, not import barriers, to induce balance of payments equilibrium.) The department is especially influential in international agreements covering official export financing and in the interagency committee screening of new foreign direct investment in the United States for possible national security problems.

The *Commerce Department* lacks the broad policy clout of State and Treasury, but it plays an essential support role in trade policy by virtue of its administering a majority of the government's major trade programs and its speaking on behalf of the industrial sector in interagency groups. Whereas USTR has the lead role in macro trade policymaking, Commerce is influential in sectoral, or micro, policymaking and occasionally maneuvers its way into a leadership position on industry-specific trade issues such as steel and auto parts. On the import side, it administers the antidumping and countervailing duty laws. This responsibility involves investigating complaints filed by domestic producers to determine the existence of these two unfair foreign commercial practices: selling goods in the United States at less than fair value and governmental subsidies to exporting companies, respectively. Commerce officials will then calculate the amount of import duty needed to neutralize the unfair trade practice if one is found to exist—and if material injury to the domestic industry is proved (see Chapter 7). The department also monitors import control programs, be they unilateral quotas or voluntary export restraint agreements.

The Commerce Department also administers the two extremes of export programs. On the one hand, its U.S-based and overseas commercial attachés provide marketing data and advice to help U.S. businesses expand exports. On the other hand, Commerce has an active voice in setting U.S. export control policy, and it issues (or refuses to issue) export licenses in connection with contingencies authorized by the Export Administration Act (foreign policy or national security considerations and shortage situations). The department's influence is also felt through its administration of several newly instituted programs designed to enhance U.S. high-tech competitiveness (e.g., the Advanced Technology Program). Finally, Commerce provides the main body of executive branch expertise on the health of individual domestic manufacturing and service sectors and the impact of import competition on them.[6]

The *Agriculture Department* leads the field when the import or export of agricultural commodities is the subject at hand. Expertise and statutory authority to administer domestic farm programs assure this department the lead in agricultural trade decisionmaking and in setting the U.S. agricultural negotiating agenda in international trade talks. The Agriculture Department has a clearly defined constituency, but it has a problem in trying to please an agricultural community that is split between farmers who are import-sensitive (dairy, meat, sugar, peanuts) and those who are highly efficient, successful exporters oriented to free trade (soybeans, corn, wheat). Operationally, the department monitors import quotas, administers three separate subsidized export-financing programs for farm goods, and runs the Foreign Agricultural Service.[7]

The *Labor Department* monitors and is responsive to the interests, needs, and retraining of workers as they relate to international trade and foreign direct investment. The department's sole operational role in trade policy is administering benefits under the adjustment assistance program dispensed to qualifying workers whose jobs have been lost to imports.

A definitive list of all executive branch departments and agencies having a specialized jurisdiction in trade policy would be very long. To keep things manageable, what follows is a partial summary of those bureaucracies that occasionally can be a significant factor in trade policy formulation when certain narrowly defined issues are under consideration.

The *Energy Department* provides the primary source of expertise in dealing in general with international energy policy and in particular on issues related to the implications of U.S. need to rely on imports of petroleum, namely the global outlook for supply and prices. The *Defense Department* is concerned about any trade issue having immediate effects on military and national security matters; it is a key player in regulating exports of military-related goods. The *Interior Department* is concerned about U.S. import dependency with regard to minerals and metals. Negotiations involving international shipping and civil aviation issues would bring in the *Transportation Department.*

The growing nexus between trade policy and environmental concerns has expanded the responsibilities of the *Environmental Protection Agency* in U.S. trade delegations to multilateral trade talks. This linkage made it an influential actor in negotiating the free trade agreement with Mexico. The *Export-Import Bank* operates a multibillion-dollar program to provide subsidized financing and commercial loan guarantees to promote the export of U.S.-manufactured goods. As proof that virtually no agency is exempt from becoming an actor in the trade policymaking process, the *Federal Communications Commission* got involved when it determined which set of competing technical specifications would apply to high-definition television sets (HDTV) to be sold in the United States. The commission opted for a U.S.-developed technology; the result of the selection was to reduce the likelihood of imports of HDTV, a major technology of the future, from Japan, the acknowledged world leader in consumer electronics products.

The *International Trade Commission* (ITC) is statutorily independent of both the executive and legislative branches and has no formal policymaking role. It is a nonpartisan investigative body whose major responsibilities include determining whether petitioners for import relief under the escape clause, antidumping, and countervailing duty statutes are in fact being injured, as defined by these laws. To the extent that its commissioners do find injury or threat of injury, the imposition of new U.S. import barriers by the president may result. ITC decisions made in response to petitions for import relief can exert a major influence on U.S. trade relations. In a 1993 case involving upward of $4 billion in annual imports of flat-rolled carbon steel, trade relations with all major U.S. trading partners as well as the profitability of the domestic steel industry were significantly affected by the commission's final decision that came as a surprise to most observers. The ITC ruled that although some imports earlier determined by the Commerce Department to have been in violation of U.S. trade laws (because of either foreign subsidies or sales in the United States at less than fair value) were indeed inflicting material injury on domestic steel producers, most imports were not and therefore were not subject to import duties. The ITC also conducts investigations under what is termed the Section 337 provision to determine if imports are violating U.S. intellectual property rights.

The executive branch's third tier of decisionmaking consists of the interagency coordinating groups organized at the working level, in which all relevant bureaucratic actors have the opportunity to state their policy recommendations and to influence the search for consensus. Coordinating bodies start at the office level and extend up to the aforementioned cabinet-level committees. Virtually all trade-related decisions are made in one of them. On the import policy side, the most active are the Trade Policy Review Group (membership is at the undersecretary and assistant secretary levels) and the Trade Policy Staff Committee, which in early 1993 had created more than sixty separate working groups and task forces. Three different interagency groups deal with export control issues, and the Trade Promotion Coordinating

Committee attempts to bring cohesion to the government's decentralized export expansion programs scattered among eight different agencies.

The Legislative Branch

Article I of the U.S. Constitution empowers Congress "to regulate commerce with foreign nations" and to "lay and collect taxes, duties . . . and excises." For almost 150 years after the founding of the republic, Congress dominated trade policy through the passage of statutes producing progressively steeper tariffs. Shortly after succumbing to pressures for intensely protectionist trade legislation in 1930, Congress opted to earmark considerable trade policy authority to the executive branch. The assumption was that the latter was in a better position to balance pressure from domestic special interest groups for imposition of import barriers with advocacy of liberal trade policy from supporters who asserted that reduced barriers would provide the greatest good for the greatest number.[8] However, Congress has only "leased" authority to the executive branch to reduce import barriers and to impose export controls. Trade legislation grants circumscribed reciprocal trade liberalization authority on a limited-time basis (usually three to five years). Behavior of the executive branch has been affected by knowledge that it will periodically need to seek both renewal of existing authority and passage of new authority by Congress as future rounds of international trade negotiations expand efforts to reduce barriers.

To this day, Congress successfully cultivates the institutional image of an ardent protectionist while simultaneously granting a long succession of administration requests for new authority to reduce U.S. import barriers on a reciprocal basis. Congress, however, still remains a kind of court of last resort for domestic interest groups to argue that the executive branch is being too ideologically committed to free trade and is ignoring their plight. Congress is like a parent—under a watchful eye, it is indulgent of the desires of its offspring, but only up to a point. If the substance of U.S. trade policy is more pragmatic than consistent, part of the cause is the frequently shifting intellectual center of gravity in the management of U.S. import policy. The guidelines set out by Congress for the administration of trade policy are mostly unwritten, and frequently they have to be sensed by the political antennae of the White House.

On a formal basis, Congress influences trade policy by four means:

- passage of trade legislation (or refusal to pass legislation requested by the administration);
- approval of budgets and appropriations of funds;
- confirmation of senior policymakers;
- general review and evaluation (known formally as "oversight") of existing policies and programs.

U.S. trade officials now spend a considerable amount of time on Capitol Hill. Members of Congress for many years have argued long and hard that they are not content to be brought into the trade policy formulation exercise only at the very end of the process—that is, being asked to rubber stamp trade legislative proposals and trade agreement implementation authority drafted by the administration without consultation with key committees. It is now widely recognized that on trade issues Congress demands to be, in Washington jargon, "involved in the take-off as well as the landing." As part of its efforts to be better informed and to maximize dialogue, Congress has vastly increased the number of subcommittee oversight hearings on international commercial issues. These hearings provide a semiofficial forum to hear administration officials, business leaders, and academic experts defend or criticize current and proposed policies and programs, expound on international economic trends, and make proposals for adding new items to the trade policy agenda. Another manifestation of the new era in interbranch cooperation on trade policy was the literally hundreds of informal visits paid by administration officials to key congressional members for the purpose of providing private consultations while the Uruguay Round and NAFTA trade negotiations were still in progress.[9]

Congress has substantially increased its ability to collect international economic data independently and to propose trade legislation and second-guess policy proposals without reliance on executive branch resources. This endeavor reflects two basic factors: the overall congressional determination to constrain what in the 1970s was dubbed the imperial presidency, and the politicization of trade policy. The latter materialized as the encroachment of foreign competition and the decline in U.S. competitiveness made rising imports a pocketbook issue among an increasing number of voters. In addition to greatly enlarged professional staff capabilities on standing committees, members of Congress can draw on trade policy research and advice from hundreds of specialists working in four support agencies: the Congressional Budget Office, the Congressional Research Service, the General Accounting Office, and the Office of Technology Assessment.[10] When administration witnesses appear at oversight hearings, they expect and get pointed questioning on everything from basic philosophy through the more technical and intricate aspects of trade policy. This scrutiny in turn discourages perpetuation of policy by inertia and inattention.

Predicting the trade policy orientation and voting behavior of members of Congress is a tricky process requiring considerable information about what each individual member is hearing from constituents back home. Many years ago, trade ceased to be a partisan issue. Trade philosophy is predictable neither by a member's party affiliation nor by position along the political spectrum of liberal to conservative. (Political conservatives tend to favor liberal—that is, unobstructed—trade.) Members of Congress are influenced mostly by economic conditions in their respective districts.

As the saying goes, all politics is local, and members of Congress tend to correlate the national interest with trade policies that will benefit the people who elected them. Representatives with export-oriented multinational corporations and competitive high-tech companies in their constituencies will likely favor liberal trade policies. Members from textile districts would be more amenable to protectionist measures. Senators and representatives from states in the southwestern United States were favorably disposed to NAFTA because their geographical proximity to Mexico should accelerate exports from these states. Representatives from soybean-growing areas tend to be more liberal trade–oriented than those from dairy farm–intensive areas. However, the presence of large-scale foreign direct investments may reduce a member's protectionist ardor even if he or she represents an import-impacted constituency. Very few members can point to the complete absence among their constituencies of companies and workers opposed to protectionism; even fewer are themselves philosophically committed to protectionism. The bottom-line result is that congressional concerns about large U.S. trade deficits have focused on the same broad corrective strategy favored by the executive branch: increased domestic competitiveness and reduced foreign trade barriers so as to achieve greater reciprocity. Minimal support exists for turning to comprehensive import barriers.

If the focal point of trade policy decisionmaking in the executive branch is the interagency forum, the focal point in the legislative branch is the standing committee. Jurisdictional overlap occurs in both branches. Just as the majority of executive branch departments are involved at some point in making trade policy, a majority of congressional committees are involved at some point in drafting trade legislation. The major actors in import policy are the House Ways and Means and Senate Finance Committees. Jurisdiction over specialized import issues, export control policy, and export promotion programs is scattered among the agriculture, appropriations, banking, commerce, energy, and foreign relations committees in both houses. The exact allocation of committee authority reflects historical accident more than scientific formula. The Joint Economic Committee has no legislative duties but provides a unique forum for long-range examinations of trade issues as well as the links between trade and international financial and investment trends.

As trade legislation becomes more complex, the instances of overlapping committee jurisdiction increase. The epitome of this trend occurred when the conference committee was convened to finalize the text of the Omnibus Trade and Competitiveness Act of 1988. It consisted of 199 members representing 14 House and 9 Senate committees. Among efforts to expedite what can be a painfully slow legislative process are joint hearings occasionally held by two different committees.

The Private Sector: Special Interest Groups and Lobbying

What do owners of refrigerated warehouses, Florida alligator farmers, ladder builders, radio talk show hosts, operators of bed-and-breakfast inns, and lobbyists have in common? All of them have their own trade associations. These groups constitute some of the more than 7,000 trade and professional associations in the United States created to disseminate arguments promoting public opinion and public policies favorable to their interests.

When it comes to trade policy, the private sector is an informal partner in the policymaking process in all democratic countries. Special interests have organized themselves to be pivotal actors in the contest of ideas to determine what is and is not "good" trade policy. Since the practical business experience of the relatively small number of U.S. trade officials is very limited, and since trade policy is conducted more on behalf of the private sector than on behalf of national security considerations, no one asserts that the government should make trade policy in isolation. Presumably, there is consensus that trade policymakers should pay careful albeit detached attention to what spokespersons for hundreds of different special interests are recommending.

The private sector provides two invaluable sources of expertise in trade relations. The first is hands-on knowledge of current business conditions at the sectoral and individual corporation level. Aggregate trade statistics are too general to assure that trade actions do not have unintended consequences on a given industrial sector or company. The second source of expertise consists of former government officials who become Washington lobbyists and who often have detailed knowledge and institutional memory of programs and legislation exceeding that of incumbent officials.

On a day-to-day basis, lobbying consists mainly of two relatively innocuous endeavors. The first consists of simple public relations efforts designed to project a favorable public image for a given special interest group. The second is nothing more dramatic than trying to keep fully and immediately informed by carefully gathering information on what relevant institutions and people at home and abroad are saying and doing that might affect an interest group. When either a trade policy action or a vote on a trade statute is pending in Washington, one or more special interest groups will be directly affected. At this point, the intensity of activity escalates as part of a deliberate effort to influence government action. Interest groups, utilizing the right of free speech, present impassioned arguments, assemble data favorable to their argument, make allusions to their ability to deliver votes in the next election, and (also in conformity with law) make cash contributions to politicians' campaign war chests— all as part of the effort to assure that impending administrative and congressional actions are favorable to them.

The effort to influence trade policy in Washington, D.C., is crowded but still growing. It can be safely asserted that no conceivable interest group is without organized representation in some form. Every manufacturing sector, virtually every major corporation, the services sector, the farm bloc, unions, consumers, importers, exporters, and major foreign exporters to the United States have a permanent Washington presence. Efforts by special interest groups to convince policymakers and the public at large that their desires and needs are the most complementary with the broad definition of the national interest come from trade associations, political action committees, coalitions, alliances of coalitions, Washington representative offices, and embassies, as well as such "hired guns" as attorneys, public relations specialists, and assorted public policy consultants.

The extensive presence and output of lobbying by special interest groups on foreign trade issues can be observed empirically by reading congressional committee testimonies, special studies, articles on newspaper op-ed pages, speeches, news releases, reports on domestic lobbying released by the House and Senate (the total number of registered lobbyists in each house exceeds 6,000), and reports on lobbying on behalf of foreign interests released by the Justice Department (in its annual report on the Foreign Agents Registration Act). The extensive, high-powered pro and con lobbying campaigns undertaken in connection with the proposals to create NAFTA[11] and to extend MFN treatment to China on a conditional basis provide further proof of the inescapable—and appropriate—linkage between data provided by private advocacy and the government's trade policy decisionmaking process. U.S. trade officials publicly acknowledge their reliance on the private sector to inform them of individual overseas trade barriers that are deserving of official efforts to remove. The negotiating agenda with Japan has been largely written by U.S. corporate complaints about that country's trade practices.

The influence of the private sector as an informal power center in trade policy also can be observed in the operation of the permanent three-tiered network of private advisory committees statutorily created by Congress. The thirty-eight advisory committees and their more than 1,000 participants from all parts of the private sector (including environmental and consumer interest groups) are headed by the senior-level Advisory Committee for Trade Policy and Negotiations. The second level has grown to include seven policy advisory committees on agriculture, industry, investment, labor, services, defense, and intergovernmental relations (input from state and local governments). Thirty sectoral advisory committees dealing with industry, agriculture, and labor fill out the third tier of the groups.

The advisory committees are charged with counseling the administration's trade negotiator on the details of the private sector's attitudes on general trade policy and on specific negotiating objectives and also on bargaining positions in international trade negotiations. U.S. trade law formally stipulates that before the executive branch can submit trade legislation to Congress for approval under the fast-track process (see Chapter 7), the advisory committees must first produce written evaluations that assess whether the proposed agreement is in their judgment compatible with U.S. commercial interests. Since Congress is highly unlikely to enact legislation implementing a trade agreement that has been lambasted by a majority of the influential members of the private sector, members of the advisory committees collectively possess a de facto veto over key trade agreements (e.g., NAFTA and the Uruguay Round). No sensible administration would agree to a trade pact violently opposed by this legislatively created sample of informed private sector opinion: Congress would assuredly reject it.

Conclusion

A close reading of this chapter reveals a number of implicit suggestions that human beings, not organizations, make policy decisions. Knowledge of who does what in trade policy is not equivalent to understanding the reasoning behind decisionmaking actions, just as knowledge of the human skeleton and circulatory system is not equivalent to understanding human behavior. In the next chapter we examine "causality" by explicitly identifying the forces that tend to govern the behavior of government officials and that partially explain why the trade policymaking process functions as it does.

For Further Reading

Cohen, Stephen D. *The Making of United States International Economic Policy.* 4th ed. New York: Praeger, 1994.

Destler, I. M. *American Trade Politics.* 3d ed. Washington, D.C.: Institute for International Economics, 1995.

Lewis, Charles. *America's Frontline Trade Officials.* Washington, D.C.: Center for Public Integrity, 1990.

Pastor, Robert A. *Congress and the Politics of U.S. Foreign Economic Policy, 1929–1976.* Berkeley: University of California Press, 1980.

The United States Government Manual. Published annually by the U.S. Government Printing Office.

Notes

1. Politics is often defined as the determination of who gets what, when, and how. Trade policy fits this definition because a country's import and export actions affect which workers get and lose jobs and which companies prosper and which fail.

2. "Office of the U.S. Trade Representative," undated, photocopied paper prepared by USTR.

3. Not-for-attribution interview with USTR official, spring 1994.

4. On rare occasions, the cabinet-level coordinating group on policy is deadlocked and must turn to the president to approve one of the opposing policy options under consideration.

5. In passing the Trade Expansion Act of 1962, Congress insisted that the head of future U.S. delegations to trade negotiations no longer be the State Department. The latter was viewed by many on Capitol Hill as being too anxious to please foreign governments and not a sufficiently tough negotiator. Hence, Congress permanently created the USTR.

6. Details of the Commerce Department's ongoing activities can be found in annual reports that are publicly distributed.

7. The Agriculture Department also prepares and issues annual reports on its activities.

8. This theme is well developed in I. M. Destler, *American Trade Politics* (Washington, D.C.: Institute for International Economics, 1995), ch. 2.

9. Not-for-attribution interview with USTR official, fall 1993.

10. The General Accounting Office produced a steady stream of reports in the early 1990s on a number of trade issues, including NAFTA, the Uruguay Round, and export promotion programs. The Office of Technology Assessment produced several major studies of U.S. industrial competitiveness and of U.S. multinational corporations.

11. See, for example, the report issued in 1993 by the Center for Public Integrity (Washington, D.C.) entitled *The Trading Game: Inside Lobbying for the North American Free Trade Agreement.*

6 Decisionmaking Explained: The How and Why of Policymakers' Behavior

What makes the U.S. trade policymaking process tick? What explains the behavior of the U.S. government as it formulates and implements foreign trade policy? Why have the institutions described in the previous chapter acted as they have? All-inclusive or permanent answers to these questions are virtually nonexistent. There does not appear to be any single or permanent variable or official operating procedure that can be used to explain all of the major trade decisions made throughout U.S. history or even in the post–World War II era. In the words of a classic study of U.S. foreign trade politics, even "the theory of self-interest as a complete and all-embracing explanation of behavior breaks down when we realize that self-interest is itself a set of mental images and convictions."[1]

Substance and process are linked in the making of public policy. The purpose of this chapter is to verify the complementarity between these two aspects of U.S. trade policy. The nature of how trade policy is made—process—should be consistent with our central thesis about the substance of trade policy being the end product of a process of reconciling economic and political factors, domestic and foreign. The analysis that follows attempts to verify this consistency by reviewing the nature of trade decisionmaking, defined here as the process in which the government absorbs hard data and abstract perceptions and converts them into concrete policy actions (output). This process, in turn, can be described as consisting of two main components: the influences (inputs) on policymakers and the organizational mechanisms by which decisions are made.

The Inevitable Diversity of Trade Policymaking

The absences of fixed procedure and patterns of behavior are not surprising given the nature of U.S. trade policy. There is a constantly changing cast of policymakers who are coping with constantly changing circumstances and an ever-expanding agenda of substantive issues with varying degrees of importance. Balances of power among competing groups and ideas are also constantly shifting so that different constituencies have different degrees of power in Washington, D.C., at different times. The bottom line is that there is no single identifiable set of forces serving as the constant, underlying source of trade policymaking decisions. In other words, the decisionmaking process is too disparate to produce an iron-clad theory of cause and effect.

Whereas the surface content of international trade relations is economic in nature, there are several reasons for arguing that the processes of formulating and conducting trade policy are political in nature. Policymakers inevitably must select priorities from a number of logical, competing economic arguments. Given the absence thus far of economic absolutes and irrefutable econometric equations, trade policymaking is effectively an exercise in value judgments that will help some people and groups and hurt others. By influencing who gets production, jobs, and profits, trade policy meets the classic definition of politics. The importance, impact, and nature of trade policy actions are too diffuse to suggest that any one organizational configuration is appropriate to making decisions in all cases. To possess only a detailed understanding of the intricacies of international trade theory is to have only limited insight into understanding how legitimate, albeit conflicting, viewpoints and priorities must be reconciled.

Scholars using analytic techniques of political science have created a large body of international political economy literature in the effort to explain the force(s) that produces U.S. trade policy. The result is diversity, not a definitive explanation. Several theories focusing on quite different phenomena have been advanced.[2] In some cases, trade policymaking is conceptualized as a specialized form of foreign policymaking; in some cases, it is viewed as a specialized form of domestic economic policymaking. Some models view government structures as the controlling, or independent, variable determining policy output. Others look to the policy environment, both domestic and foreign. Still other models attempt to synthesize these two approaches. There is no intent here to praise the relevance of some models and dismiss others. Nor is the intent here to express concern that the existence of what are often largely incompatible theories dangerously diminishes our ability to comprehend the act of trade policymaking.

Rather, the intent here is to argue that all of the explanatory models cited subsequently in this chapter have *some* relevance in explaining a complicated phenomenon with many variations. The central thesis of the analysis that follows is that no one concept can explain the totality of the complex and fluid process of trade policymaking. No single model developed thus far can do more than explain some import policies and perhaps some export policies as well. No single model identifies a constant cause-effect relationship, individually or collectively, among the vast array of past import and export policy actions. Nor has any single model demonstrated possession of infallibility in predicting future trade policy. The use of selective case studies to demonstrate the applicability of any given model is not inconsistent with the thesis that trade decisionmaking cannot be anything other than a diverse, multidimensional policy process. It continues to defy a single explanatory formula, as one study of U.S. import policymaking concluded:

The models focusing exclusively on short-run, direct self-interest are insufficient for explaining the wide range of behavior patterns observable in the trade policy area. Models that include behavior based either on long-run self-interest or concern for the welfare of other groups and the state are also necessary to account for the actions of voters and public officials.[3]

Admittedly, a finite number of variables are inherent in trade policy decisions. There are a number of basic guidelines and, to use a phrase of Max Weber's, "general laws and events" that can be used to identify recurring patterns of U.S. trade policymaking behavior. Policymakers must be responsive to, among other things, the economic ideology and political needs of the president and his senior advisers, the foreign policy objectives of a global superpower, public opinion, and the forcefully articulated demands of interest groups. The dominant economic ideology of U.S. foreign trade policy since the late 1930s is easy to identify: It has been liberal trade—the pursuit of reduced barriers to the flow of international commerce. However, a single decisionmaking model placing primary emphasis on this belief system is not plausible in view of the number of exceptions to a market-oriented trade policy that consistently appear in the decisionmaking process.

Thus there are critical questions: Why have these deviations to the guiding philosophy been made? Equally fundamental, which domestic and international economic or political consideration will dominate in a particular policymaking situation? What is on the minds of policymakers that causes the interests of one constituency to triumph over others? The answer to each question is imprecise: It depends on the combination of personalities and the circumstances at hand. With so many of these combinations possible in a decisionmaking exercise, the relative importance of any given variable is in a constant state of flux. So too is the U.S. government's trade policymaking apparatus, which is somewhere between haphazard and ultraflexible in nature. The key to understanding the functioning of the trade policymaking system is to recognize that varying circumstances associated with any given decision dictate that different actors will be in charge, different behavioral patterns will dominate, and different constituencies and perceptions will be given priority treatment. The process that has evolved to reconcile the conflicting interests associated with trade decisions lacks—appropriately—the precision, single-mindedness, and conformity to repeatedly use identical criteria and a fixed set of procedures to calculate which needs and objectives get priority attention.

Theories of trade decisionmaking do not even agree on a basic frame of reference. At the risk of a modest amount of oversimplification, the analysis that follows divides the main explanatory theories into two categories. The first consists of those that emphasize political and economic pressures on policymakers. These theories focus on preexisting forces that allegedly heavily influence the course of governmental deliberations to resolve a specific trade issue. The second category (examined separately) encompasses theories that emphasize the discretionary role of the state and focus on organizational mechanisms within the government.

The Government as Reactive Decisionmaker

By law, government officials are in charge of creating and conducting trade policy. However, this does not automatically mean that they possess sufficient freedom of action to be an autonomous, independent, and activist force in trade policymaking. One theoretical approach to trade policy decisionmaking is to identify the most important force shaping the actions of trade officials. This approach has resulted in construction of several models pinpointing different dominant factors that, in fact, have at various times been instrumental in shaping consensus among policymakers. Three of the major identifiable influences on policymakers are discussed here: domestic political forces (interest group politics), global political and economic structures (international regime constraints), and the state of the economy (market conditions).

Interest Group Politics

Private sector activism is brought to bear to some degree on virtually every U.S. trade policy decision. The occasions when the U.S. government imposes trade barriers on a major imported product are dramatic and attract a relatively large amount of publicity. All things considered, a somewhat exaggerated, oversimplified viewpoint emerges that portrays U.S. trade policymaking as being ultimately controlled by organized domestic political forces demanding and receiving protection from import competition. U.S. trade policy is viewed by this theory as being less shaped by resolute, activist politicians than by a Darwinian struggle among special interest groups. The sources of policy are the outcomes of the raw exercises of political power by these groups and the success of their intellectual efforts to convince legislative and executive branch officials that their interests are synonymous with the national interest. Carried to its logical conclusion, this model portrays the U.S. government as a "disinterested referee," providing but not controlling a venue for interest group lobbying. In the end, governmental agencies are seen to be acting as conduits between private sector trade demands and foreign governments.

Some scholars assert that "money talks" and that "policy outcomes on any particular issue are a function of the varying ability of groups to organize and give their interests prominence in the policy process."[4] Examples of this extreme interpretation occasionally materialize but on such a limited basis that this theory is open to the criticism that it can be nothing better than a partial explanation. Overall, the direct impact of special interest groups on U.S. trade policy in the 1990s is laced with nuance. Extensive empirical evidence of a widespread, lobbying-induced protectionist bias in contemporary U.S. trade policy is not currently available.

In a very few instances, representatives of the private sector have been allowed to write technical portions of pending statutes.[5] U.S. government demands for specific market-opening measures by Japan almost always originate from specific private sector complaints.

Examples of long-term domination of the import policymaking process by the same interest groups are becoming increasingly rare. It does happen that less competitive industries can convert political clout into trade barriers that benefit the few and penalize the many, but in recent years this has not been a commonly recurring event. It is no longer commonplace for the absence of an effective countervailing political force on behalf of liberal trade to render the U.S. government powerless to resist the import protection demands of such industrial behemoths as the apparel, steel, and automobile sectors.

In some cases, lobbyists in the United States have earned their fees by performing a genuine service to society as a whole, most notably by educating unaware policymakers about unfair and restrictive foreign trade practices. In two important cases, interest group agitation inspired the incorporation into the U.S. trade policy agenda of two new objectives for which there was no significant domestic opposition or criticism. Protection of intellectual property rights emerged as a concern of the U.S. government only after a sustained educational process. Initiated by two coalitions of companies adversely affected, lobbying efforts demonstrated how U.S. industry was annually losing tens of billions of dollars in sales to foreign violators of U.S. copyrights, patents, trademarks, industrial designs, and so on—in most cases to illegal, "back alley" foreign producers. Earlier, efforts by lobbyists from companies in the services sector had educated key U.S. trade officials about the reality and heavy cost of foreign barriers against their exports, something not previously recognized in Washington. The result was that U.S. trade policy priorities expanded to include the economically sound goal of broadening the definition of multilateral trade liberalization to include services as well as merchandise goods.

Further clouding any simple model of protectionist policies derived from interest group politics is the recent wave of private sector activism opposing protectionist trade policies.[6] The emergence of an energetic, politically significant lobbying effort on behalf of a more liberal world trading order, mainly by large U.S. MNCs, is an important explanation for the relatively limited U.S. recourse to protectionism from the 1980s through the mid-1990s despite a string of gargantuan trade deficits. These companies were galvanized into active lobbying in the early 1970s as U.S. infatuation with protectionism began to blossom. MNCs seek profit maximization unbothered by national borders and thus disdain restrictive national measures. Another reason that restrictions imposed by the U.S. government on international trade and investment flows are anathema to these MNCs is their fear that these measures will trigger retaliation by foreign governments against their exports and their foreign subsidiaries. More recently, the liberal trade lobby in Washington has grown from the wholesale entrance of foreign corporations, especially Japanese, that spend freely to hire talented local lobbyists to point out the costliness of depriving U.S. consumers and companies of maximum product choice in the marketplace.

The potential ability of a liberal trade lobby to dilute the impact of the traditional protectionist emphasis of special interest groups was recognized as early as 1963: "The stereotype notion of omnipotent pressure groups becomes completely untenable once there are groups aligned on both sides. The result of opposing equipotent forces is stalemate."[7] To the extent that both sides of a trade issue are pressed by high-powered interest groups, diametrically different positions will be supported by politically powerful interest groups having conflicting economic interests. The proliferation of trade policy lobbying activities in Washington has become so extensive that "lobby gridlock" periodically materializes. When conflicting lobbying efforts effectively neutralize each other on a specific issue, the administration and Congress are free to concentrate on their own value systems to define optimal trade policy.

A relatively new source of industry-versus-industry conflict arises in cases when "downstream" users of intermediate products and components oppose protectionist measures that would increase their production costs. Fearful of their own import competition, end users of steel, such as makers of construction equipment, have been vociferous critics of export restraint agreements by other countries that would limit steel shipments to the United States. (To the extent that domestic steel users do not have the same access to cheap foreign steel as do their foreign competitors, they lose price competitiveness.) The 1,200-member Coalition of American Businesses for Stable Steel Supplies provided argumentation in early 1993 against even the imposition of dumping duties to penalize what a government investigation found to be steel imports being sold at less than fair value.

Another example of the end-user phenomenon was the public cleavage in the U.S. electronics industry twice displayed in the intense struggles by domestic assemblers of personal computers to reverse dumping duties imposed on two price-sensitive components—memory chips and flat panel display screens. Rather than risk losing market share in a fiercely price-competitive product, several U.S. personal computer companies warned of the need to move their production offshore. If they did so, they could buy low-priced Japanese components abroad and avoid U.S. dumping duties; although imports of an individual component might be subject to U.S. antidumping duties, such goods are exempt when imported as parts of an assembled final product. The dynamics of interest group confrontation also were exhibited when the U.S. retail industry campaigned on several occasions against barriers on imported apparel. Barriers against foreign-made apparel reduce retailers' ability to provide customers with relatively low-priced (despite some high price markups) and therefore better-selling clothing.

The limits of interest group politics are further demonstrated by the fact that in some cases, corporate lobbying has been an utter failure. Some of the largest, most influential U.S. corporations have since the 1970s unsuccessfully tried to coax officials to relax U.S. export controls to the lower levels prevailing in Western Europe and Japan. Even in the post–cold war atmosphere of 1993, corporate megapower AT&T was denied an export license for sales to China of state-of-the-art high-speed telephone transmission switches (presumably because intelligence agencies would have encountered more difficulty eavesdropping).[8] In late summer 1993, Iran Air was reported to have placed a $1 billion order for jumbo jet commercial aircraft with Airbus Industrie because the Clinton administration refused to approve export licenses for the U.S. aircraft originally eyed by the Iranians.[9] This rejection brushed aside considerations that Boeing is the number one U.S. exporter, that the General Electric Corporation that would have supplied engines for the 737 aircraft is one of the country's largest companies and third-largest exporter, and that the Clinton administration had publicly recognized aerospace as a vital domestic industry. Power lobbying could not dislodge the government's priority of retaining economic sanctions imposed on Iran in retaliation for its alleged support of international terrorism.

Assessments of the impact of special interest group lobbying are further clouded by the inherent difficulties of quantifying effective rates of protection. It is not as easy as it appears to noneconomists to declare certain interest groups as victors in their efforts to significantly squelch import competition. Although outsiders complain of the ability of the textile and steel industries to garner considerable import protection, most representatives of those industries lament publicly that they have been the recipients of loophole-ridden import restraint programs that are too little and too late. In point of fact, many of the voluntary export restraint agreements that have largely displaced implementation of unilateral U.S. import restrictions have been relatively easy for foreign companies to circumvent, by using illegal transshipments or partially assembled goods, for example. The introduction of new commercial products not covered by bilateral restraint agreements negotiated under the Multifiber Arrangement has been a major reason that despite alleged protectionism, imports have maintained a slow but steady increase in their share of the U.S. textiles and apparel market.[10]

Finally, the ability of private sector lobbying to affect the substance of U.S. trade policy often has nothing to do with the popular notion that companies possessing large economic size and political clout are rewarded with import barriers. The power of a small but determined and well-organized group to buck the larger public interest is vividly displayed in the case of long-standing U.S. import quotas on sugar. They are imposed at great cost to domestic consumers—an estimated $1.4 billion annually in higher prices according to one study[11]—and to U.S. foreign policy. A number of friendly, relatively poor countries, mainly in the Caribbean, have seen a sharp curtailment of their potential sugar exports to the United States. The winners in this case are a small number—about 15,000—of U.S. sugarcane and sugarbeet growers concentrated in just four states.

A final case study suggests that the political clout to influence U.S. trade policy can be wielded by a cleverly orchestrated, well-financed alliance of domestic importers and a large foreign company. After a massive lobbying effort in 1987 and 1988, Congress backed down from its stated intention to punish the Toshiba Corporation for what was perceived to be a serious national security transgression. (A Toshiba subsidiary company had violated Japanese export control laws and sold sophisticated machine tools to the Soviet Union that were used to make quieter submarines.) The proposed five-year comprehensive import ban on Toshiba products wilted in the face of a well-orchestrated uproar by U.S. companies concerned about the dislocations they would incur if unable to continue importing electronic components from that company. Members of Congress also heard repeatedly from angry constituents employed at Toshiba subsidiaries in the United States that the proposed ban would cause most of them to be laid off.

An objective, scholarly assessment of the impact of interest groups on U.S. trade leads to another set of imprecise conclusions. Interest group politics, like all other models of trade policymaking, is not ubiquitous in the policymaking process. A continuously changing mix of variables seems to determine on a case-by-case basis exactly what will be official responsiveness to the input of interest group lobbying.[12] Sometimes the U.S. trade policymaking process is very responsive to such pressure, sometimes the opposite phenomenon occurs, and sometimes there is a halfway response. No known model can accurately predict which of these responses will occur. Powerful private sector pressure groups seeking either erection of import barriers or relaxations of export controls are regularly rejected by policymakers because of economic ideology or national security reasons. Even in decisions where the interest group politics model dominates, no reliable prediction of the outcome of policy substance is possible.

International Regime Constraints

Another model of trade policymaking argues that trade policy decisions are ultimately grounded in interrelationships and interactions among sovereign states, all of which are using international economic relations to maximize their wealth and influence. Larger states will also be looking to use trade relations to increase their power on global issues. A major variant of this approach is the notion that the discipline of international regimes encourages countries to cooperate and constrain aggressive behavior. U.S. trade officials, like their foreign counterparts, regularly subordinate domestic considerations to international standards of trade behavior, most of which are codified in the General Agreement on Tariffs and Trade (see Chapter 8). Perhaps the principal reason that countries generally conform to GATT's antiprotectionist provisions, which are less than absolutely binding, is to discourage other countries from imposing their own trade barriers. Some argue that international regimes make cooperation rational in what is essentially a confrontational world. Since trade is a continuous process and not a one-shot event to be won, long-term efforts to cooperate within the framework of liberal trade–oriented rules can ensure the maximization of wealth for everyone. This consideration is likely to be at the back of the minds of U.S. trade officials when they point to GATT-imposed obligations as justification for not responding to domestic pressures for implementation of protectionist measures.

On other occasions, U.S. trade rules have been modified to meet international norms. The U.S. government responded in 1979 to intense foreign pressure and added an injury test to its 1897 countervailing duty statute designed to protect domestic interests from imports receiving foreign government subsidies (see Chapter 7). The imposition of countervailing duties solely on the basis of detecting an illegal subsidy was deemed inconsistent with the international standard: Both injury *and* existence of an unfair trade practice must be demonstrated prior to imposition of retaliation by the importing country.

Another argument associated with the global structures model is the theory that a country's position in the global economic order decisively shapes its international commercial policy. Most notable and demonstrable are the two instances of international political and economic hegemons, Great Britain in the nineteenth century and the United States in the twentieth. At the height of their global power, both countries identified their interests with creating and supporting liberal (nonrestrictive) trade regimes.

Market Conditions

Yet another approach to explaining policy substance is to emphasize market conditions. One version of this theory argues that changing international market conditions can make it "economically irrational for a government to continue prevailing policy."[13] This approach would explain the need for radical changes in U.S. trade policy in 1971 and 1985 when exchange rate distortions caused a deterioration both in the level of U.S. industrial competitiveness and in the trade balance. The market conditions model is appropriate to explain the tendency for governments to be relatively resistant to protectionist pressures during periods of high domestic economic growth and low unemployment. It also explains their tendency to be predisposed to imposing protectionist measures during periods of slow or negative growth, a propensity best illustrated by the beggar-thy-neighbor policies employed during the depression years of the 1930s. Yet another example of the utility of this model is that it apparently explains why the U.S. government did not react harshly to Japan's failure in fall 1994 to agree to relax internal market regulations impairing the ability of U.S. automobile companies to export to Japan. The U.S. automobile industry at the time was producing at full capacity in an effort to meet unexpectedly strong domestic demand. A simple check of market conditions would have suggested that there were relatively few U.S.-made cars available in the short to medium term for incremental exports, no matter what the Japanese government did.

The Government as Active Decisionmaker

When U.S. governmental entities convene to formulate general policy or to make a specific decision, they cannot escape being influenced by a varying mix of external stimuli: the previously described constraints as well as perceived opportunities. Decisionmakers cannot and do not act in a value-free vacuum. Nevertheless, it is not a given that these stimuli are the independent variable in determining policy substance. A second, broad school of thought just as legitimately argues that the controlling variable is the manner in which government entities organize themselves to sort out the various constraints, opportunities, conflicts, trade-offs, and perceptions that are inherent in the trade policy decisionmaking process.

The substance of trade policy is often a direct by-product of what a number of officials collectively determine is best for the country, favored constituencies, the global economy, and their personal situations—not necessarily in that order. Few persons aspire to the senior levels of U.S. trade policymaking for the money. Their usual motivation is self-confidence in having intellectual and problem-solving abilities that are well above average. They also tend to possess a conscious or subconscious enjoyment of the exercise of power. For these reasons, U.S. trade officials view themselves as capable of making reasoned and calculated choices, not as being prisoners of externally imposed constraints.

There is no standard operating procedure by which the U.S. government formulates and implements trade policy. The choice of exactly which of several possible organizational procedures is utilized can have implications for policy substance. The delicate balance among the four components of trade policy—domestic and international economics plus domestic and international politics—can be tilted in one direction or the other depending on which government entities are involved and which have leadership roles.

The purpose of this section is to introduce the three most widely used government organization–oriented models of trade policy decisionmaking. The determination of which one of these models is used depends on yet another set of variables associated with the issue to be decided. The variables include the issue's political and economic importance and notoriety (at home and abroad), complexity, legal implications if any, and whether it creates new policy or is merely refinement of an existing one.

The Presidential Fiat Model

The simplest, most dramatic model of U.S. trade policymaking consists of the relatively rare phenomenon of the president taking an early and dominant role. Presidents are usually too preoccupied with national security and domestic social and economic issues to get deeply involved in the arcane minutiae common to most trade dilemmas. When they do get involved, presidents usually come in at the very end of the process to approve a recommendation from their cabinet or, less frequently, to mediate an irreconcilable dispute. Only on rare occasions, typically in response to dramatic unfolding events, have presidents intervened at the onset of an international trade issue by making a forceful declaration of policy intent that immediately and unequivocally dictated the nature of subsequent U.S. actions. Staff work and interagency consultations are minimal to nonexistent prior to a presidential fiat. In this case, the president speaks first, and then the bureaucracy is ordered into action to provide the support necessary to implement the president's publicly stated position. Criticism may be directed toward the substance of the policy produced by this model but not its lack of clarity and quickness. In studies of national security policy decisionmaking, clear-cut control of the policymaking process by the head of government is known as the unitary, or rational actor, model.[14]

Examples of the presidential fiat model in the international trade realm include President Nixon's ordering his senior economic aides to join him at Camp David on an August weekend in 1971 where he guided and approved dramatic overnight decisions that reversed several major domestic and international economic policies. The so-called New Economic Policy, among other things, immediately invoked a 10 percent surcharge on all import duties and suspension of convertibility of dollars held by foreign central banks into gold—after only a cursory calculation of the likely international impact and repercussions of these measures. A second example is the personal anger and shock at the Soviet invasion of Afghanistan that led Jimmy Carter immediately to order an economic retaliation by banning the export of 17 million metric tons of wheat previously ordered by the Soviet government—a move that financially hurt U.S. farmers as well as Soviet consumers.

A few weeks after the 1993 inauguration, the Clinton administration issued a detailed blueprint for enhanced government support for and involvement in the effort to strengthen the U.S. high-technology sector, an endeavor aimed in large measure at increasing U.S. international competitiveness. This technology initiative originated in the White House because it was a direct outgrowth of Clinton's and Vice President Al Gore's personal economic philosophy that was graphically spelled out in their campaign promises to alter economic policies.

Presidents are far more likely—except in the weeks immediately prior to a close race for reelection—to respond to deeply held, preexisting values, ideologies, and concerns for the country's broader, longer-term interests than they are to crass political manipulations. Since each Oval Office incumbent possesses a different mix of personal beliefs and experiences, there is no predictable, preordained tilt in trade policy substance when the presidential fiat model is utilized. President Bush took the lead in articulating his administration's position on China's MFN status. His unwavering opposition to imposing conditions on the extension of MFN tariff treatment appeared to be based on deeply held personal convictions directly related to his earlier experience as ambassador to China.

The Bureaucratic Politics Model

The presence of top-down leadership in the form of active presidential involvement in U.S. trade policy decisionmaking has been and still is the exception rather than the rule. Since presidential time and energies normally are concentrated in other policy sectors, most trade policy decisions are made at or below the cabinet level by an interagency group, sometimes numbering in excess of twenty. Participating agencies in interagency trade policy deliberations have steadily grown in number as the impact of the growing trade sector has impinged on more policy jurisdictions.

Interagency trade committees and working groups in the U.S. government operate mainly as meetings of institutionalized interests possessing different perspectives.

They seldom have the benefit of an unambiguous, self-evident strategy to guide selection of optimal policy decisions that everyone deems to maximize the national interest, the definition of which may also escape agreement. Decisionmakers are usually confronted with the need to reconcile conflicting policy proposals that normally emerge in the absence of a specific directive from the president. Repeatedly, a bargaining process involving compromises and trade-offs among different strategies becomes central to the interagency trade policymaking process.

When the absence of quick consensus leads to interagency brokering of decisions, decisive strategy and brilliantly conceived tactics tend to be the exception in trade policy, not the rule. The dynamics of bureaucratic politics explain why most interagency decisions ultimately produce trade policy that more closely resembles a "line of least resistance" approach—accepting something all participants can live with—rather than inspired brilliance.

But why, exactly, is the interagency coordinating process usually afflicted with disagreement rather than blessed by an easy consensus? No executive branch trade policy official, except the president and vice president, represents the country as a whole and has responsibility for the entire policy spectrum. All trade officials work for bureaucratic entities that have been established for and work on behalf of specifically defined institutional constituencies, not the country as a whole. In the trade area, these focal points include domestic economic price stability, the industrial sector, the environment, foreign policy, agriculture, jobs and wages, and human rights. An important part of job performance evaluation for employees of line departments and agencies is how well individuals represent their chosen constituency in interagency meetings.

An analogous form of bureaucratic politics is practiced in Congress. Quite literally, constituents influence members' votes. The economic interests of the district or state that voted members into office, not political ideology or party, is usually the determining factor as to their outlook on trade issues.

The core principle of the bureaucratic politics model of decisionmaking is that the government seldom engages in monolithic thinking.[15] Rather, in a field with few absolute guidelines, different ministries and agencies with divergent missions, agendas, and priorities all bring distinctive mind-sets about the meaning of "good policy" to the interagency policy coordinating process. From ministers down to the junior staff level, members of ministries and agencies in all countries tend to perceive a linkage—self-serving but usually genuinely believed—between defense of their seemingly very important constituency's needs and desires and the enhancement of the overall national interest. Nominees for cabinet posts deemed to be unsympathetic or antagonistic to the constituency that they would represent seldom pass the Senate confirmation process (which explains why Wall Street bankers do not become secretary of agriculture and Kansas farmers do not become secretary of the treasury).

The bureaucratic politics model does not necessarily depict venal or inappropriate behavior. There has never been and probably never will be unanimity as to whether there is a fixed ranking of U.S. trade policy objectives and, if so, what the order of priorities is. What is the relative importance of economic efficiency versus social equity? How important are increases in domestic prosperity relative to achievement of a prosperous, stable global economic environment? Is clear and present threat of U.S. retaliation a cost-effective method of forcing other countries to buy more U.S. products? Can protectionist moves be beneficial in the long term by allowing an import-impacted industry to restructure itself into a world-class competitor? Is it appropriate for the United States to express its dislike for the policies of the Iranian government by denying Boeing export licenses to that country for potentially hundreds of millions of dollars of commercial aircraft shipments—aircraft the European makers of Airbus can and will happily sell to Iran? These are rhetorical questions. There are very few simple, clear-cut answers to the major issues of trade policy.

The bureaucratic politics model predicts a consistent general pattern of organizational behavior, but its appearance in a given decisionmaking exercise does not preordain any specific policy substance. There is no way of knowing beforehand whether a single viewpoint will dominate and, if so, which one. The intraexecutive branch balance of power ebbs and flows as in all political arenas. The appearance of inconsistency in U.S. trade policy is partially attributable to the fact that no department or coalition of departments has sufficient power, resources, or wisdom to claim permanent authority to establish U.S. trade priorities and determine winners and losers in the private sector at home and abroad.

In most cases, institutional attitudes toward trade issues are consistent and predictable. Certain agencies invariably view trade policy as a tool of foreign relations efforts to influence the attitudes and actions of other countries, friendly and unfriendly. The foreign affairs bureaucracies, namely the State Department and the National Security Council, typically support liberal import policies because an open trading system would best promote a stable system and harmonious relations among like-minded countries. Conversely in the export sector, these two agencies plus the Defense Department typically support illiberal export controls as a means of exacting a price overseas for what is deemed undesirable or dangerous foreign behavior. Officials in the foreign affairs bureaucracies are not totally insensitive to the well-being of domestic workers and companies. However, they know that they are not paid to worry primarily about this constituency and that no one else in the trade bureaucracy can be expected to speak out on behalf of the global political environment— one of several perfectly legitimate concerns in making "good" trade policy.

It is necessary to examine the institutional "essence" of the coordinator of U.S. trade policy, the office of the U.S. Trade Representative, to understand its sometimes paradoxical behavior. Its primary mission is to successfully negotiate reciprocal trade liberalization agreements with other countries. Engaging in trade acts that would anger other governments is hardly conducive to encouraging such agreements. Nevertheless, the USTR takes a hard line on demanding reductions in overseas barriers to U.S. goods, and on occasion it sides with the protectionist faction in import policy debates. USTR's bureaucratic behavior is rooted in the mutually accepted concept that it was born of congressional initiative and that it could be terminated by

Congress if it loses touch with domestic constituencies. Translation: It must occasionally recognize the need to limit the injury inflicted on U.S. producers by severe import competition—to provide a safety net for the adverse effects of reduced U.S. import barriers. Furthermore, most USTR officials feel that they alone have the primary role of creating executive branch consensus on policy and not the task of imposing a particular point of view.[16]

The growing linkage between domestic economic performance and the foreign trade sector means that in terms of sheer numbers, the contemporary U.S. trade policymaking process is dominated by so-called domestic agencies with specific, sometimes competing, jurisdictions. The macroeconomic agencies—the Treasury Department, the Council of Economic Advisers, and the Office of Management and Budget—generally advocate liberal trade positions but for reasons that differ from those of the foreign policy bureaucracies. The economic policy agencies are dominated by professionally trained, free market–oriented economists. They tend to equate their mission to enhance the overall U.S. economy with a relatively unrestrained flow of imports, a trend that maximizes competition and price stability within the domestic economy.

The perception of its having an institutional predisposition to tolerating increased imports was the reason the Treasury Department was stripped of its authority over investigating allegations of dumping and foreign governmental subsidies. The Commerce Department, viewed as being institutionally more sympathetic to the domestic industries that are affected by these unfair foreign practices, was given this responsibility in the 1980 reorganization of the U.S. trade policymaking apparatus.

The bureaucratic perspectives of Commerce and Agriculture are simple: Both departments advocate policies that will strengthen and benefit what are arguably vital sectors of the economy. For the Commerce Department, this means industry and services; for the other department, this means the agricultural community. When they confront individual trade decisions, however, their mission is complicated by the dichotomy in both of their constituencies: Some subsectors are internationally competitive and export-oriented, and some are relatively inefficient and import-sensitive. The result is that these departments sometimes vigorously support liberal trade policy options, but selectively recommend exceptions in the form of limited import restraints on specific goods. There is much less ambiguity on the export side: Both Commerce and Agriculture are wholeheartedly supportive of export expansion. They dislike domestically imposed controls and take an activist stand against trade barriers maintained by U.S. trading partners.

When participating in trade policy deliberations, officials of the Environmental Protection Agency are sensitized to the physical and legal need to temper economic considerations whenever necessary to assure conformity with domestic environmental protection laws. For them, the U.S. national interest is not measured primarily in terms of financial considerations and conformity with international trade agreements to avoid imposition of new trade barriers.

Clear-cut examples of bureaucratic politics abound in the record of U.S. trade policy. The trifurcated approach long taken by the executive branch toward trade relations with Japan is symptomatic of the "internal harmony" that exists among an institutional mind-set, a constituency's interest, and perception of what course of action would most likely serve the national interest. The macroeconomic agencies, for the most part, believe that retaliatory import barriers would, on a net basis, hurt the U.S. economy and are a far less desirable means of reducing the bilateral deficit than free market forces. The national security agencies soft-pedal economic priorities because their primary goal here is to prevent commercial squabbles from damaging political relations with a key ally. Last, the "trade warriors" of the USTR and the Commerce Department retain their long-held advocacy of a hard-line trade policy to belatedly force Japan's (allegedly) unfair import and export practices into conformity with U.S. norms for proper trade behavior.

A schism between those bureaucracies inclined to favor liberal trade and those leaning toward protectionism is virtually inevitable when the executive branch—regardless of who is president—is deciding on whether to restrict imports under an escape clause proceeding (presidential discretion is allowed because no unfair trade practices are involved) or whether to renew a voluntary export restraint agreement. During a 1976 deliberation on possible imposition of barriers on footwear imports, the usual pattern of dissension was joined by an unusually animated Defense Department, not an agency that normally gets excited about commercial trade policy. Its conclusion that the free trade approach would serve the national interest was based on a classic example of bureaucratic politics. Spain and Italy, two major shoe exporters, were sites of important military bases (furthermore, the Communist Party in Italy, a NATO ally, was making significant advances at this time). Constituency needs dictated that Defense be more concerned about the health of the Italian and Spanish economies than with the problems of the U.S. footwear industry.

Contradictory facts hampered the decision as to whether to extend for another five-year period the voluntary export restraint agreements, negotiated in the mid-1980s on behalf of the U.S. steel industry and due to expire in fall 1989. Parts of the bureaucracy felt that the steel industry had received too much protection for too long. The opposing faction urged continued import restraints on the grounds that many foreign steel producers had not abandoned unfair trade practices (dumping and governmental subsidies) and that the domestic industry had taken great strides in nearly completing efforts to become more productive and internationally competitive. So ambivalent was the situation that President Bush was called upon to break the resulting cabinet deadlock. His decision to prolong the restraints for two and one-half years makes sense only in arithmetic terms: It was the midway point between the two major policy recommendations—no extension of the restraints and a full five-year extension.

A major example of Congress acting on its perception of the bureaucratic bias occurred in 1962. A provision in a new trade law it enacted divested the State

Department of authority to lead U.S. trade delegations because Congress perceived it as being too soft on foreign interests at a time when U.S. international competitiveness was on the wane. Legislation passed in that year transferred this leadership role to the newly created USTR.

Bureaucratic wrangling over trade policy priorities and definitions of the national interest is not ubiquitous in interagency decisionmaking exercises. Occasionally, there is easy consensus. This was the case when the decision was made to retaliate against Japan when it was seen to be violating conditions agreed upon in the 1986 semiconductor agreement.[17] On other occasions, a single agency or a single policymaker so dominates an issue that others quietly back off. Letting Treasury Secretary John Connally take the lead in setting international economic policy strategy in the wake of the New Economic Policy pronouncement exemplifies this situation.

Congress and the Interbranch Politics Model

The relatively large percentage of U.S. trade policy that consists of the executive branch dutifully carrying out the spirit and letter of laws written by the legislative branch is one of the unique aspects of the U.S. political system. Unlike in a parliamentary form of government, the president as head of the executive branch has little legal scope to act on his own in conducting trade policy. He depends on Congress for legal authority to commit the United States to most trade agreements. If the president flagrantly disregards strong congressional trade sentiments, he risks a reprimand in the form of passage of statutory language that he opposes.

Any effort to model trade decisionmaking strictly within the executive branch (or the private sector) would ignore important realities. The cumulative effect of numerous statutory provisions devised by Congress is that an administration has limited discretion to act as it sees fit in the realm of foreign trade. The modern-day partnership between Congress and the administration and the fusion of their distinctive institutional perspectives embody a uniquely complex, multifaceted trade policymaking process. Presidents administer trade policy and tend to embrace a liberal trade policy that complements the role of world statesman. Members of Congress write trade laws and tilt toward giving thorough hearing to the demands of voters back home. Each remains uneasy about and at times distrustful of the perceived bias in the other's trade policy inclinations.

The Omnibus Trade and Competitiveness Act of 1988 contains numerous provisions designed by Congress to modify the executive branch's trade policy behavior. Key provisions seek to increase the likelihood of presidential retaliation against discriminatory foreign trade practices and to enhance U.S. industrial competitiveness. Passage of these initiatives reflected a uniquely congressional sentiment that certain trade policy changes—mainly in the form of greater presidential resolve to attack foreign trade barriers—had become necessary. These initiatives in turn were part of the larger trend of congressional efforts dating back to the 1930s to fine-tune the substance of contemporary U.S. trade policy.

Fearful of repeating its excessive acceptance in 1930 of interest group demands for protectionism, Congress since 1934 has used a network of statutory provisions to establish what it considers to be an economically progressive, politically responsive system of import policymaking. Congress has seen fit to relinquish some of its constitutional power to the executive branch and to the independent International Trade Commission. By design, Congress has seen to it that the executive branch takes most of the heat in carrying out the delicate task of determining how to respond to the unending procession of private sector demands for trade actions that favor their interests. As I. M. Destler has observed: "The system allowed members so inclined to advocate, even threaten, trade restrictions, while nicely relieving them of the need to deliver on their threats. Indeed, its main result was not protection for industry but protection for Congress—insulation of its members from trade pressures."[18]

To this day, Congress pursues its trial-and-error effort to codify into U.S. trade laws just the right tension between broad pursuit of trade liberalization and the conditional availability in appropriate situations of protectionist measures and retaliatory sanctions. Congress is an unabashed advocate of "fair" trade, a pleasant-sounding concept lacking both opponents and precise meaning. The trade legislation it has passed since 1934 is characterized by an intricate set of counterweights and shock absorbers. Congress has long encouraged the executive branch to pursue a basically liberal trade policymaking posture. But at the same time that trade barriers are being reduced, a "fair" hearing about eligibility for legislated relief mechanisms is guaranteed to those domestic sectors that are losers from the inflow of imports. Furthermore, U.S. exporters are made happy by congressional efforts to force the administration to be more aggressive than it might otherwise be in threatening grave consequences for trading partners that discriminate against U.S. commerce. In effect, the post-1934 trade policy system has utilized an intricate system of congressionally designed political pulleys and levers to sustain a precarious balance of power unofficially and informally designed to block the reemergence of the once-dominant protectionist coalition.

A system of counterweights also has been inserted in export policy. On the one hand, the executive branch has been delegated authority to impose U.S. export controls and sanctions on unfriendly countries. Simultaneously, however, Congress has pushed offsetting relief in the form of efforts to increase the access of U.S. goods to friendly foreign markets. An examination of the evolution of U.S. export legislation demonstrates patterns similar to those that characterize import legislation: modest interbranch differences in trade philosophy and congressional efforts to restrict the executive branch's freedom of maneuver in a manner consistent with Congress's perception of the national interest. Not wishing to usurp the administration's power to decide when to impose export controls for national security and foreign policy purposes, Congress has progressively put the burden of proof on those executive branch officials advocating export restrictions. Over the years, the Export Administration

Act (previously named the Export Control Act) repeatedly has been amended in response to complaints by major exporting companies that they have lost billions of dollars of overseas sales to foreign competitors operating under much more relaxed export control systems. As part of a philosophical effort to dictate the right range of executive branch behavior, recent versions of export control legislation have ordered progressive reductions in the list of controlled items and have required that the overseas availability of an item be taken into account when an export license is being reviewed.

The interbranch politics model of trade policymaking is visible in three different permutations. The first is the harmonious variant in which the two branches bargain cooperatively with one another. No bill submitted under the so-called fast-track authority has yet been defeated. Since this procedure calls for an all-or-nothing, yea-or-nay, no-amendments vote on legislation to ratify proposed trade liberalization agreements, informal interbranch negotiations have always been conducted prior to the administration's submission of such legislation. Administrations have made the concessions and adjustments necessary to assure congressional passage *before* formally submitting such legislation. A second example of harmonious interbranch relations is the tactic frequently used by the U.S. government since the 1970s to goad Japan into responding to trade concession demands. In its role as "bad cop," a seemingly furious Congress threatens to run wild and pass highly protectionist, anti-Japanese trade legislation. This prospect encourages the Japanese to cut a preemptive deal with the more reasonable, less protectionist "good cop" as played by the administration.

Interbranch politics on other occasions become adversarial in nature. Occasionally, Congress passes trade legislation actively opposed by the administration. President Carter's imposition in 1980 of import duties on petroleum was thrown out by legislation banning it. The restrictive provisions in the 1974 trade bill governing extension of MFN status to countries not yet receiving it were deemed excessive by the Ford administration and almost resulted in a presidential veto of this major piece of otherwise acceptable legislation. At other times, Congress has delayed or refused to pass trade legislation submitted by the administration.

A detailed examination of U.S. trade policymaking reveals a third variant of the interbranch model: executive branch positions and attitudes being modified in *anticipation* of congressional action that would go against administration desires. The Reagan and Bush administrations secured a tightening in voluntary export restraints under the Multifiber Arrangement by pointing to the need to sustain presidential vetoes of several textile quota bills. The latter seem to have been passed mainly to induce such an administrative tightening of imports, not with the expectation of being enacted into law. The Reagan administration chose the protectionist option of imposing higher tariffs in an escape clause decision involving shakes and shingles from Canada. Because this action was taken in the midst of free trade agreement negotiations between the two countries, it appeared on the surface to be a case of bad timing. This decision makes sense, however, when one learns that it came, not coincidentally, on the very day that the House was voting on protectionist amendments very much opposed by the administration.[19]

Conclusion

The convergence of economics, politics, and laws that defines the substance of U.S. trade policy is also at the core of its formulation. Through the use of conceptual models and case studies, we have sought to demonstrate in this chapter the inherent diversity and inconsistency that characterize the policymaking actions of the executive and legislative branches as they go about the daunting task of seeking to maximize economic logic within the constraints of political reality. Process affects substance—especially in a policy sector that perpetually must reconcile domestic and external economic and political priorities. This rule of thumb explains why the organizational dynamics outlined in this chapter previously appeared, either subtly or clearly, in the historical sweep of U.S. trade policy presented in Chapter 2. It also explains why the footprints of these same dynamics will reappear in later chapters in the analyses of major contemporary issues in U.S. trade policy. These same dynamics will almost certainly appear in the future when the U.S. government grapples with the emerging issues discussed in the last two chapters.

The lack of precision by which trade policy decisions are arrived at is not a weakness that can be overcome by better organizational arrangements or by new scholarly models. Diversity and inconsistency are inherent in any U.S. policy that is short on absolute or permanent truths. Given U.S. political and economic ideologies, there may well be merit in having a trade policymaking system so flexible and diverse that it discourages the potentially destabilizing prospects of fixed ideas, unassailable power centers, and permanent winners and losers.

For Further Reading

Baldwin, Robert E. *The Political Economy of U.S. Import Policy.* Cambridge: MIT Press, 1985.

Bauer, Raymond A., Ithiel de Sola Pool, and Lewis A. Dexter. *American Business and Public Policy.* Chicago: Aldine-Atherton, 1972.

Destler, I. M., and John S. Odell. *Anti-Protection: Changing Forces in United States Trade Politics.* Washington, D.C.: Institute for International Economics, 1987.

Ikenberry, G. John, David A. Lake, and Michael Mastanduno, eds. "The State and American Foreign Economic Policy." *International Organization,* 42 (Winter 1988), special issue.

Odell, John S. "Understanding International Trade Policies: An Emerging Synthesis." *World Politics* 43 (October 1990), pp. 139–167.

Notes

1. Raymond A. Bauer, Ithiel de Sola Pool, and Lewis A. Dexter, *American Business and Public Policy* (Chicago: Aldine-Atherton, 1972), p. 226.

2. Two excellent syntheses of this literature can be found in G. John Ikenberry, David A. Lake, and Michael Mastanduno, eds., "The State and American Foreign Economic Policy," *International Organization,* 42 (Winter 1988); and John S. Odell, "Understanding International Trade Policies: An Emerging Synthesis, *World Politics* 43 (October 1990), pp. 139–167.

3. Robert E. Baldwin, *The Political Economy of U.S. Import Policy* (Cambridge: MIT Press, 1985), p. 174.

4. Ikenberrry, Lake, and Mastanduno, *op. cit.,* p. 7. Also see Mancur Olson, *The Rise and Decline of Nations* (New Haven: Yale University Press, 1982).

5. See, for example, Stephen D. Cohen, *The Making of United States International Economic Policy: Principles, Problems, and Proposals for Reform* (New York: Praeger, 1994), p. 131.

6. See, for example, I. M. Destler and John S. Odell, *Anti-Protection: Changing Forces in United States Trade Politics* (Washington, D.C.: Institute for International Economics, 1987); and Helen Milner, *Resisting Protectionism: Global Industries and the Politics of International Trade* (Princeton: Princeton University Press, 1988).

7. Bauer, de Sola Pool, and Dexter, *op. cit.,* p. 398.

8. "AT&T Falls Victim to Cold War Trade Limits," *Washington Post,* August 6, 1993, p. G3.

9. "Iran Seeking Jets from Airbus Industrie," *Washington Post,* August 8, 1990, p. D9.

10. Data from U.S. International Trade Commission, *U.S. Imports of Textiles and Apparel Under the Multifiber Arrangement: Annual Report for 1991,* September 1992.

11. U.S. General Accounting Office, "Sugar Program—Changing Domestic and International Conditions Require Program Changes," April 1993, p. 3.

12. Interest groups today are most likely to "capture" the bureaucracy with a protectionist request if the cost of such an action is so scattered over a wide enough group that no one is seriously and noticeably impacted; hence, no major oppositional lobbying effort is likely to be instigated. I thank my colleague, Renee Marlin-Bennett, for this observation.

13. John S. Odell, *U.S. International Monetary Policy: Markets, Power, and Ideas as Sources of Change* (Princeton: Princeton University Press, 1982).

14. See, for example, Graham T. Allison, *Essence of Decision: Explaining the Cuban Missile Crisis* (Boston: Little, Brown, 1971).

15. See, for example, Morton H. Halperin, *Bureaucratic Politics and Foreign Policy* (Washington, D.C.: Brookings Institution, 1974); and Stephen D. Krasner, "Are Bureaucracies Important? (Or Allison in Wonderland)," *Foreign Policy* 7 (Summer 1972), pp. 159–179.

16. Not-for-attribution interview with USTR official, summer 1994.

17. Stephen D. Cohen, *Cowboys and Samurai: Why the United States Is Losing the Battle with the Japanese, and Why It Matters* (New York: HarperBusiness, 1991), p. 62.

18. I. M. Destler, "Protecting Congress or Protecting Trade?" *Foreign Policy,* Spring 1986, p. 98.

19. Not-for-attribution interview with U.S. trade official, spring 1987.

7 Legislation Regulating Imports and Exports

Countries regulate the import and export of goods and services through tariffs and various forms of nontariff barriers (NTBs). The U.S. Constitution grants solely to Congress the explicit power "to regulate commerce with foreign nations." For various reasons, as noted in the previous chapter, Congress has delegated by statute some of its authority over trade to the executive branch or to independent agencies.

This chapter provides a description of statutes affecting the regulation of imports and exports. The first section deals with statutory language enacted to give the president authority to reduce import barriers. These laws are the vehicles for achieving progressive reductions in global barriers to trade flows. The second and third sections explain statutes bestowing authority on the president to restrict or inhibit imports; these laws are the vehicles for achieving the basic political necessity of providing limits to the degree of domestic damage inflicted by a liberal trade policy. Two sections are necessary in order to correspond to the internationally accepted distinction between providing protection to domestic producers and workers from injury induced by "fair" foreign competition as opposed to injury induced by "unfair" forms of foreign competition. The laws guiding presidential policy responses on matters of import relief are significantly different according to whether the foreign trade competition being reviewed is classified as fair or unfair. The remainder of this chapter is a summary of the relevant statutes and regulations concerning export promotion, market-opening measures, and export restrictions.

Trade Liberalization Measures

Since the adoption of the onerous Smoot-Hawley Tariff Act of 1930, the U.S. Congress has repeatedly approved statutes authorizing the president to negotiate bilateral and multilateral trade agreements reducing barriers to trade on a reciprocal basis (see Chapter 2). Beginning with the 1934 Reciprocal Trade Agreements Act, Congress has delegated to the president specific authority to negotiate reductions in existing tariffs. Although the Constitution gives Congress the exclusive power to impose import and export duties, Congress may delegate this power to the president if it prescribes when and how he may raise or lower tariffs. Congress could not, for example, unconditionally give the president all of its power to impose import duties without instruction as to the purposes of the delegation (what some courts refer to as an "intelligible principle" to guide the president) and without limitation.[1] Although the president has inherent authority to talk to foreign governments about any issue, including international trade, the president may not implement such agreements in domestic law without the explicit authorization of Congress either before or after such negotiations occur.

Examples of legislation designed to expand trade include the 1962 Trade Expansion Act, the 1974 Trade Act, and the 1979 Trade Act. The Trade Expansion Act of 1962 authorized the president for five years to negotiate reciprocal reductions in most ad valorem tariffs up to 50 percent and specified that some tariffs could be eliminated entirely. The Trade Act of 1974 gave the president five years to negotiate reciprocal reductions on some tariffs to zero and other tariffs by 60 percent. The 1979 Trade Act implemented the NTB reductions negotiated by the Tokyo Round of the GATT.

Since 1974, Congress has repeatedly authorized the president to negotiate reciprocal reductions in tariffs and NTBs subject to "fast-track authority."[2] Fast-track authority allowed the president to introduce legislation modifying existing tariffs and NTBs for approval by Congress, which agreed not to introduce any amendments to the legislation and to vote on it within a limited period of time. Members of Congress cannot use parliamentary maneuvers to delay the legislation from reaching a floor vote under the fast-track procedure. It is a self-imposed limit on the rules by which each house of Congress operates. Either house of Congress could terminate the fast-track rule by a simple majority vote restoring the usual rules of procedure. All of the legislation implementing the Caribbean Basin Initiative (CBI), the U.S.-Canada Free Trade Agreement, the North American Free Trade Agreement (NAFTA), and the Final Act of the Uruguay Round of the GATT was submitted to Congress under the fast-track procedure.

Relief from Fairly Priced Imports

Imports may be subject to tariffs for the purposes of protecting domestic employment, raising revenue, or adjusting import prices that are otherwise deemed "unfair" to domestic competitors. Additionally, restrictions may be imposed for political purposes to pressure exporting countries to change their policies or form of government or to protect domestic national security by fostering self-sufficiency. Import tariffs are usually imposed as a percentage of the value of the import, in which case they are called "ad valorem" tariffs. Alternatively, import tariffs may be imposed on the quantity of imports, in which case they are called "specific" tariffs, or tariffs may combine an ad valorem rate and a specific duty, in which case they are called "compound" tariffs.

Governments increasingly rely on NTBs to discourage imports. NTBs may operate by means of a quota or a voluntary restraint agreement negotiated with the exporters or the exporting countries either to restrict the quantity of an imported product or to prohibit an import altogether. Such restrictions may be intended to protect domestic producers or workers; to deter infringement of domestic trademarks, patents, or copyrights; or to protect the public from fraudulent, deceptive, or injurious products. Even though the GATT prohibits quotas, except in certain circumstances, quotas continue to exist. For example, the United States restricts the quantity of imported sugar by statute and has negotiated voluntary limits on imports from other countries of steel, automobiles, and textiles.

When importers of a particular good increase their share of the domestic market—despite the existence of tariffs or NTBs—domestic producers of that good may be forced to cut back production or to lower the price of their goods in order to remain competitive. In either event, domestic producers may experience reduced profits and may be forced to lay off workers. Domestic producers may need to redesign their own products or marketing strategy or to improve productivity in order to recapture their domestic market share. Or the domestic producer may decide to shift into an entirely new line of products rather than face foreign competition. These adjustments may take months or even years to complete. Meanwhile, the loss of profits and jobs may weaken domestic producers to the extent that they can no longer afford the necessary adjustments, and the domestic industry may fail.

Of course, this kind of competitive pressure is generally regarded as healthy in a market economy so long as prices are determined by genuine market forces rather than by manipulation. Nevertheless, a threatened domestic industry may pressure the government for protection against import-induced injury.

Consistent with the GATT's escape clause,[3] which permits countries to respond to the needs of domestic industry for temporary adjustment to foreign competition, Section 201 of the Trade Act of 1974 as amended[4] provides relief for a domestic industry hurt by imports. According to Section 201, if the U.S. International Trade Commission (ITC) determines that an increase in imports is a "substantial cause of serious injury or threat" to a domestic producer of a like or directly competitive product, then the president can take any appropriate action to assist the domestic producer to adjust to the foreign competition. Section 201 provides an escape valve from rising protectionist pressure, but a domestic producer faces a heavy burden to convince the ITC that it deserves help.

First, a domestic producer has to show that its product is "like or directly competitive" with the imported product. Two products may perform somewhat the same function and compete for customers—such as a passenger car and a motorcycle—but they are not necessarily alike or directly competitive. Is an imported passenger car like a domestically built small truck? Is an imported small car like a domestically produced large car?[5] These are the kinds of questions the ITC must tackle at the outset of a Section 201 action.

Second, a domestic producer has to prove that imports have increased either in the sense that the absolute number of imports has increased or if the number of imports has remained steady or even declined, imports have increased relative to domestic consumption. The significance of the latter definition of increased imports is that if imports are taking a larger share of the domestic market, they may be hurting domestic producers.

Third, a domestic producer must show that it has suffered a "serious injury or threat thereof," meaning that the producer must point to evidence of significant unemployment, idle factories, an inability to earn reasonable profits, increased inventories, and similar economic indicators. There is no simple definition of what is sufficiently "serious" to warrant action by the ITC, but the members of the ITC historically have expected a high threshold of injury or threat before recommending action to the president.

Finally, a domestic producer must show that the increase in imports is a "substantial cause" of the injury. In determining causation, the ITC will weigh all of the contributing causes of unemployment or low profitability in an industry. The domestic producer must prove that imports are at least as important a cause of injury as any other contributing cause of injury. If, for example, increased imports account for 40 percent of injury, a shift in consumer preference accounts for another 40 percent of injury, and decreased consumer demand accounts for 20 percent of injury, then increased imports are no less important than any other cause, and this element of the claim is satisfied.[6] Since 1980 (when the ITC in a controversial decision refused import relief from Japanese and German passenger car imports for the domestic automobile industry), there have been very few 201 petitions brought to the ITC, and only a handful have resulted in an affirmative determination from the ITC.[7]

The process for obtaining a 201 remedy is provided in the statute. Basically, any trade association, firm, union, or other entity representing a U.S. industry may file a petition with the ITC, an agency independent of both the legislative and executive branches, requesting relief.[8] Alternatively, the commission can act at the request of the president, the USTR, and certain congressional committees or on its own initiative. The commission has 120 days after the filing of a petition to determine if positive adjustment relief should be granted. There are six commissioners, three each from the two major parties, appointed by the president with the consent of Congress to nine-year terms. The ITC is supported by a large staff of professional economists and lawyers. The ITC is not bound by its own precedents, so commissioners can use contradictory principles to decide similar cases. The ITC's decisions are reviewable by the New York–based Court of International Trade, whose decisions can be appealed to the Federal Circuit Court of Appeals, which sits in Washington, D.C., and from there to the U.S. Supreme Court.

If the ITC determines that an increase in imports is a substantial cause of serious injury or threat of serious injury to a U.S. producer of a like or directly competitive product, the commission will recommend to the president import relief, which may consist of tariffs or tariff increases, quotas, or voluntary export restraint agreements.

The president is free to undertake any combination of these relief actions or none at all if he believes it is not in the national economic interest.

Even though Section 201 relief requires domestic producers to meet a heavy burden of proof, the law in its present form represents a substantial liberalization compared to the pre-1974 version. In 1974 as part of an overall revision of the trade laws and an extension of the president's authority to negotiate the Tokyo Round of the GATT, Congress rewrote Section 201 to make it more readily available to U.S. industries hurt by imports. For example, the prior law required U.S. producers to show that imports were the major cause of injury (i.e., more than 50 percent responsible for it). The 1974 revisions require the U.S. producer to show only that imports are no less important a cause of injury than any other cause (even if imports, for example, are deemed to be only 20 percent of the cause of injury, assuming no other factor is greater than 20 percent of the cause).

The escape clause is often defended as a means of buying time for domestic industry to adjust to changes in the international market. Yet there is serious doubt that Section 201 in fact facilitates adjustment. In order to obtain import relief, producers are required to prove causation and injury. They may show that over time they can restructure the industry to regain competitiveness, but they are not required to do so. If the president determines that an industry cannot adjust to become competitive internationally, the president may deny the industry relief.

Aside from the escape clause, other import relief measures available to U.S. industries include "adjustment assistance" (financial compensation to workers and industries displaced by imports), relief from imports that threaten national security, and relief from market disruption. Adjustment assistance programs for industry are administered by the Departments of Labor and Commerce. By statute, if the secretaries of these departments determine that increased imports are an important cause of declining sales or production in an industry and of job losses for a significant number of workers in that industry, the federal government will provide limited temporary financial support for workers, firms, and communities and for retraining and job placement.[9] Additional funds have been made available for workers whose jobs are lost as a direct result of the increased trade from NAFTA. Of course, in many cases it may be difficult to determine the actual cause of job losses, and it is hard to defend special privileges for workers whose unemployment results from foreign competition when many workers are idled by domestic competition. Adjustment assistance is sometimes criticized as "too little, too late" or as government assistance to pay for an industry's "funeral expenses," but most economists prefer adjustment assistance to import restraints as a form of import relief.

Agricultural producers may benefit from specialized adjustment assistance programs.[10] Under the Agricultural Assistance Act, if the secretary of agriculture determines that agricultural imports harm any domestic program to benefit farmers, the secretary will recommend to the president an investigation by the ITC. The ITC can recommend appropriate relief to the president. It is far easier for agricultural producers to obtain relief than it is for most manufacturers under Section 201, although both statutes provide comparable forms of relief for injured producers.

Producers of goods related to national security have special import relief available to protect them from foreign competition under Section 232 of the Trade Expansion Act of 1962. Under Section 232 an interested party representing a domestic industry or a head of any agency or department can request the secretary of commerce to conduct an investigation to determine whether imports of any good threaten the national security. The secretary has 270 days to make a recommendation to the president to restrict imports, and if the president concurs, the president can take any appropriate action to restrict imports. For example, in 1959 President Eisenhower invoked Section 232 to impose import quotas on oil out of concern that the country's increased dependence on foreign oil was threatening the domestic oil industry and thus U.S. security in the event of a disruption in foreign oil supplies. The quota remained in effect through 1973, although President Nixon substantially liberalized the import restrictions in the early 1970s.

Special import relief is available to domestic industries affected by imports from nonmarket economies that cause "market disruption."[11] Market disruption occurs when imports from a nonmarket economy are increasing rapidly, either in absolute numbers or relative to domestic production, so as to be a significant cause of material injury or threat of material injury to a domestic producer of like or directly competitive goods. The purpose of this rarely used provision is to respond quickly to situations in which command economies overproduce certain goods and then are forced to dump them at very low prices on the world market. Ordinarily, such situations might be handled through the antidumping laws, but the difficulties of determining production costs when using the antidumping laws against nonmarket economies led to the need for a more expedient remedy for U.S. industry. With the end of communist rule in the Soviet Union and Eastern Europe and the transition to a market economy in other countries like China, the market disruption remedy is unlikely to be frequently invoked in the future.

Unfairly Priced Imports: The Problem of Dumping

When imports are sold either at a price less than the same goods are normally sold for in their home market or at a price below production costs, it is called "dumping," and the importing country can impose duties to raise the price of the import to a "fair price." Sellers may dump goods in order to eliminate a temporary surplus—especially if the goods are perishable or are obsolete because a newer model of the same product becomes available. Temporary discounts are unlikely to hurt domestic competitors. A more serious problem occurs if the seller is engaging in long-term "price discrimination." To understand the problem of dumping it is useful to think about price discrimination. Sellers engage in price discrimination because they know that some people are willing and able to pay more for the same product or good if it is offered to them in a different location or at a different time.

Although price discrimination is a familiar feature of a market economy, it may distort competition if a seller is able to use a high-priced market to subsidize sales in another market. In that situation the risk is that a seller may use "predatory" dumping to sell goods at a price below the market price in order to drive competitors out of business. In the short term, consumers might benefit from lower prices, but if competitors go out of business, the remaining seller may be able to set a monopoly price. In the domestic market, unfair competition is prohibited by state and federal law.

In international trade, such competition is difficult to monitor and prohibit because of the difficulty of obtaining information about prices and gaining jurisdiction over foreign parties. Even though the law prohibits certain anticompetitive acts, such legal cases are difficult to prove, expensive to litigate, and time-consuming. By the time a domestic producer is able to prove that a foreign party has engaged in anticompetitive pricing, the domestic producer may be out of business. Moreover, the risk of dumping is greater where there may be barriers to reexporting. For example, if a European widget manufacturer sells widgets in the European Union (EU) for $5.00 and in the United States for only $1.00, an enterprising person might think to buy up the cheap imported widgets and reexport them to the EU, selling them there for something less than the price charged by the original manufacturer, say $4.50, and still making a healthy profit. On the other hand, if the EU has a high tariff against imported widgets or has trademark laws that prevent anyone other than the original manufacturer from selling that manufacturer's trademarked goods, then the lower-priced imported widget may be kept out of the European market; in this case, price discrimination is maintained between the two markets.

For these reasons, the trade laws provide a special remedy for dumping. In the United States, any U.S. producer or association representing a group of workers or industry may initiate an investigation to determine if an import is being sold in the United States at less than its "fair value" and causing or threatening material injury to or materially retarding the establishment of a U.S. industry.[12] If the regulatory authorities determine dumping and material injury exist, they will impose a dumping duty on imports equal to the difference between the "fair value" and the price at which the good is sold for export to the United States (U.S. purchase price). This price differential is called the "margin of dumping."

Determining the dumping margin involves a complex series of calculations performed by the Department of Commerce International Trade Administration (ITA). The procedure for obtaining a dumping duty begins with the simultaneous filings of petitions with the ITA and the ITC. The ITA sends out a lengthy questionnaire to all interested parties to collect information concerning the price and volume of each sale of the particular import both in the foreign and the U.S. markets over a period of at least six months.

First, the ITA must determine the "fair value" of the import. Fair value is usually defined as the wholesale price paid in the ordinary course of trade for consumption in the foreign market, otherwise referred to as the "home market price." If the imported product is not sold in the home market, then the ITA may calculate the fair value by determining the price that the good is sold for when exported to another large industrialized export market similar to the U.S. market.[13] Alternatively, the ITA may construct a fair value by determining the cost of production and adding in a fair profit margin. ITA must use a constructed value if it determines that the home market price is less than the actual cost of production or if not enough information is available to determine the home market price.[14] Once a fair value is determined, the U.S. purchase price is usually calculated from the purchase price paid by the U.S. importer to the foreign producer for export to the United States.[15] Next, the ITA must make certain adjustments to ensure that in comparing the fair value and the U.S. purchase price, the goods are sold in the same circumstances, in the same condition, on the same terms, and subject to the same expenses for packing and transportation.[16]

Within 160 days of the filing of the petition, the ITA must make a preliminary determination as to whether it is likely that imports are being sold at less than fair value.[17] Whether the preliminary determination is affirmative or negative, the ITA then has another 75 days to make a final determination as to whether dumping exists.

Concurrently with the ITA's determination of dumping, the ITC must determine whether a U.S. industry has been injured.[18] There is little science in the methods used by the ITC to determine if a U.S. industry is materially injured or threatened with material injury. The law defines "material injury" as "not immaterial," which means that a relatively low degree of injury might satisfy the standard depending on the discretion of the commissioners. In making this determination, the ITC is not bound by its own precedents.

One issue that has divided the ITC in recent years is the requirement that material injury results "*by reason of*" imports. The traditional analysis used by the ITC, referred to as the "bifurcated" analysis, asked first whether injury had occurred and second, whether it was caused by imports. Applying the traditional analysis, the commissioners would focus on whether there was sufficient evidence the industry had suffered material injury. Some commissioners in the 1980s began to reinterpret the statute to stress the causation requirement. The new "unitary" analysis asks the single question "*but for* the presence of imports in the market, would the U.S. industry be in better condition?" The unitary analysis *presumes* injury exists. Unlike the traditional bifurcated analysis, it focuses on the relationship, if any, between the condition of the U.S. industry and the presence of imports. To illustrate, if imports are sold at 30 percent less than fair value, the unitary analysis would ask what would happen to the U.S. industry if the price of imports were 30 percent higher. Of course, if the imported goods were identical to the U.S. products, a 30 percent increase in the price of imports would help the U.S. industry. But if consumers prefer the imports for reasons other than price—such as styling, quality, or brand names—then consumers may be willing to pay more for the imports and the U.S. industry would not necessarily be helped by an increase in the price of imports. Thus, the outcome of the unitary analysis depends upon the "elasticity" of consumer demand for imports. ITC commissioners have used both the traditional bifurcated analysis and the new unitary analysis in determining material injury, and consequently the methodology for determining injury has been inconsistent.

If the ITC and ITA both reach affirmative determinations of injury and dumping, respectively, then the Customs Service will impose a dumping duty in the amount determined by the ITA to be the margin of dumping. The dumping duty is expressed as a percentage of the value of the import and varies for each foreign producer. If the ITA determines that certain producers do not engage in dumping, those producers' imports will be exempt from the dumping duty.

Calculating a dumping margin is highly complex and involves many judgment calls. Reasonable persons will not agree on what prices to include in the weighted average, what constitutes differences in the circumstances of sale, when sales in the home market may be below the cost of production, what prices are reasonable in constructing a fair value, how to identify a surrogate country, or what adjustments may be appropriate. Small differences of opinion may result in substantial differences in the final dumping margin. The unpredictability of the dumping laws makes it difficult for a foreign producer to know how to price exports to the U.S. market. If the producer sets the price too high, it will not be able to compete in the U.S. market, but if the price is too low, the producer may be subject to a costly dumping proceeding that could end in a dumping margin. A U.S. industry may intimidate an importer into raising prices merely by the threat of filing an antidumping action. Even a minor producer in a small developing country may be subject to a dumping margin because a U.S. industry can ask the ITC to "cumulate" the adverse effects of competition from many different small producers in many countries for purposes of determining material injury. The problem for foreign companies is the uncertainty in setting a price that is both competitive and "fair" because the determination of a fair price is so complex and discretionary. Thus, the U.S. antidumping laws are frequently criticized by foreign governments as arbitrary, capricious, and protectionist.

The antidumping law was intended to prohibit certain unfair pricing that might have the effect of driving U.S. producers out of business. However, the calculation of the dumping margin is not based on what economists call a "predatory price"—one intended to hurt competitors. The dumping law at best ensures only that foreign producers charge the same price everywhere, regardless of competitive forces.

Another form of unfair import pricing may result when foreign producers receive subsidies from their governments. Subsidies may enable importers to sell in the United States at prices below those that market forces would have dictated. The result is that U.S. consumers may benefit from the exporter's subsidy, but U.S. workers and producers may be injured by unfair prices. To offset the effect of the subsidy, the U.S. countervailing duty laws provide for the imposition of an additional duty equal to the net amount of the subsidy. In effect, the countervailing duty is designed to raise the import price to the estimated price it would have been without a subsidy.

The countervailing duty neutralizes the effect of the foreign subsidy on the import's price. At the same time, the countervailing duty adds to the receipts of the U.S. Treasury Department roughly the same amount as the estimated cost of the subsidy for each export to the exporter's treasury.

U.S. producers or an association representing U.S. workers or a U.S. industry can petition the ITA or the ITC for a countervailing duty.[19] The ITA must determine the net amount of a subsidy, and the ITC must decide if a U.S. industry has suffered a material injury or the threat of it.[20] Prior to 1979 a countervailing duty could be imposed without a finding of material injury or threat of material injury. After the adoption of a GATT code on subsidies (described in the next chapter), the United States in 1979 amended the countervailing duty law to require a finding of material injury or threat of material injury as to imports from countries that became members of the code. Imports from nonmember countries may still be subject to a countervailing duty without the additional requirement of proving material injury or threat.[21] The procedural time frame for preliminary and final determinations of a subsidy is similar to the procedure previously described for determining a dumping margin.

The law distinguishes between export subsidies and domestic subsidies.[22] *Export* subsidies are defined by reference to the illustrative list of export subsidies attached to the GATT code on subsidies. These include direct payments to producers contingent upon export, currency regulations that benefit exporters, the provision of products or services on preferential terms for use in producing exports, the exemption or remission of direct (income) taxes in connection with exports, the remission of indirect (excise) taxes in excess of the amount actually paid on their production, and export credits at below-market rates.[23] In each of these instances the payment of a subsidy or the provision of a good or service is contingent upon the export of a good.

The law defines *domestic* subsidies as a government grant or bounty to a specific enterprise, industry, or group of enterprises, such as loans or investments on terms more favorable than the market rates, preferential rates on goods or services, the payment of funds or forgiveness of debt, or the assumption of any expenses of the producer. It is unclear whether exemptions from government regulations, such as environmental restrictions or labor laws, may constitute a subsidy even though there is no budgetary outlay of government funds. For purposes of U.S. law, domestic and export subsidies are treated the same. As described in the next chapter, the GATT treats domestic and export subsidies differently.

Export subsidies are usually easier to identify than domestic subsidies. A domestic subsidy must benefit a specific firm or industry in order to be considered an unfair trade practice. A government program that benefits all industries, such as one for public education, roads, or police protection, is not a countervailable subsidy. The key test is whether the subsidy is generally available. Several reasons are advanced for why generally available subsidies are not countervailable. One argument is that if a subsidy is generally available, it is too difficult to calculate the net amount of the subsidy per import. Another argument is that if governments imposed countervailing duties on all or most imports from a particular country, it could trigger a trade war.[24]

Section 337 of the Tariff Act of 1930 prohibits unfair methods of import competition that threaten or substantially injure U.S. industry and the import of goods that infringe on U.S. patents, copyrights, or trademarks.[25] Section 337 principally provides owners of intellectual property rights a quick remedy against infringing imports. Section 337 also provides a remedy against unfair competition by importers. For example, it has been used to prevent predatory (unfair) pricing by importers.[26] In addition, Section 337 offers a remedy against other conduct outlawed by the U.S. antitrust laws, including price fixing, restraints on trade, and attempts to monopolize, and may be used to prevent fraudulent practices that may confuse consumers, such as deceptive labeling or pricing or misrepresenting the origins of a good.

The popularity of Section 337 is due both to its versatility and to the expedient process for obtaining relief. A successful 337 action can result in an order totally excluding an import from the United States or in an order to cease and desist any unfair trade practice. A U.S. industry can file a Section 337 complaint with the ITC. Within twenty days the ITC must decide whether to refer the matter to an administrative law judge employed by the commission for investigation or to dismiss the complaint. If the matter is sent to an administrative law judge, the judge has nine months to reach a decision. The hearing before the administrative law judge is less formal than a proceeding in a trial court. The evidentiary rules allow more evidence than would be admitted in most U.S. courts. If the administrative law judge finds that unfair methods of competition have injured the complainant or that the complainant's intellectual property rights have been violated, then the judge will recommend action to the ITC. The latter then has twelve months either to issue an order excluding the import or to issue a cease and desist order. If the ITC decides to exclude the import while the investigation is still pending, it may allow the importer to bring in imports upon posting a bond until the investigation is completed. If the ITC issues a cease and desist order, then the importer may be subject to fines in excess of $100,000 per day. If the importer violates the cease and desist order, then the president has sixty days to disapprove the ITC's order before it will take effect.

Although Section 337 is a relatively quick and inexpensive way to prevent infringement, legal experts do not generally regard it as an ideal way to litigate complex antitrust suits because of the lack of time for discovery of new evidence. From a policy perspective, Section 337 is interesting because it can be used by the ITC both to encourage competition by prohibiting unfair business practices and to restrict competition by protecting patents, trademarks, and copyrights. Moreover, unlike other trade statutes that are principally intended to protect jobs in the United States, Section 337 protects investors' expectations that their intellectual property rights will be respected. By protecting a trademark for a particular product, a manufacturer may be saving the jobs of workers employed abroad. Section 337 is unique to the United States, and in 1988 a GATT expert panel found that Section 337 violated GATT national treatment rules by treating imports that violated intellectual property rights differently from domestic products that violated the same intellectual property rights. Section 337 was amended by the Uruguay Round Agreements Act of 1994 to conform to the GATT panel report. The amendments allow foreign defendants accused of import practices in violation of Section 337 greater procedural rights before the ITC.

Export Promotion Laws

The impact of export policy is no less important than the impact of import policy on domestic employment. Yet laws governing exports are sometimes overlooked in discussions of trade policy. Perhaps one explanation is that unlike import policy, export policy tends to be formulated on a case-by-case basis depending on political relations and national security considerations as well as economic interests. Whereas the antidumping and countervailing duty provisions, for example, are fairly technical and provide relatively objective criteria for determining when to impose tariffs, the statutes governing exports afford the executive branch broad discretion to decide how to regulate exports in a given situation. There are three broad categories of government programs to examine: export promotion laws, market-opening laws, and export restrictions.

The U.S. government has a variety of programs for promoting U.S. exports. The most important of these is the Export-Import Bank, which provides financing to foreign purchasers of U.S. exports. The Export-Import Bank was originally created by executive order in 1934 but was later chartered by Congress as a U.S. government corporation under the Export-Import Bank Act of 1945.[27] The Treasury Department financed the bank with lending in excess of $1 billion on which the bank pays interest. The Export-Import Bank lends to foreign purchasers on easier terms than might be available from a commercial bank. Export credits are a form of export subsidy, but all major industrial countries maintain export credit programs. From its creation through the early 1990s, the Export-Import Bank has provided about $200 billion in financing for U.S. exports.

There are a variety of other programs operated by the government to assist small- and medium-sized businesses that seek to enter foreign markets. Among these programs are the Department of Commerce's programs for providing information and counseling to exporters. Programs administered by the Department of Agriculture to promote the export of U.S. farm products include Public Law 480,[28] which provides food assistance to poor countries on concessional terms; the Food Security Act of 1985, which promotes agricultural exports generally; and the Commodity Credit Corporation, which provides guarantees to U.S. banks against defaults on loans for agricultural exports. The Internal Revenue Code also encourages exports through special provisions affording favorable tax treatment for export sales by U.S.-controlled companies deemed to be either foreign sales corporations or domestic international sales corporations.[29]

The Export Trading Company Act of 1982[30] authorizes the formation of export trading companies between banks and commercial companies to provide export services to U.S. producers. The act lifts certain restrictions that would otherwise prevent banks from participating in a commercial business and possible antitrust restrictions on companies that provide export services. The purpose is to make export services more widely available to small- and medium-sized companies. The actual number and significance of export trading companies that have been formed as a result of the act have been modest.

Market-Opening Laws

Section 301 of the Trade Act of 1974[31] is a powerful tool for opening foreign export markets to U.S. producers. Under Section 301 the U.S. Trade Representative (USTR) is authorized to retaliate against foreign trade policies that hurt U.S. exports. Section 301 may be invoked in two forms. First, if the USTR determines that any policy or action of a foreign country is inconsistent with any international agreement granting the U.S. trade concessions or is "unjustifiable" and restricts U.S. trade, the USTR is required to take action to enforce U.S. trade rights. A policy or action is "unjustifiable" under the act if it violates either an international trade agreement, such as GATT, by denying the United States some legal right (such as most-favored-nation treatment) or if it violates U.S. intellectual property rights. The USTR is not required to retaliate if there is a GATT panel determination that no rights under GATT have been violated, if the foreign country is taking some remedial steps or providing compensation to the United States, or if retaliation would have an adverse effect on the U.S. economy or national security.

Second, if the USTR determines that any internal or external policy or action of a foreign country is "unreasonable" or discriminatory and restricts U.S. trade, then the USTR may retaliate. A foreign country's policy or action is deemed "unreasonable" if it denies fair opportunities for competing or establishing a business in a foreign market, fails to provide adequate protection for intellectual property rights, allows domestic firms to engage in anticompetitive behavior, subsidizes exports, or constitutes a practice of denying labor rights that are internationally recognized. (The U.S. semiconductor industry considered filing a 301 petition in the mid-1980s against Japan on the basis that Japanese semiconductor companies were colluding to keep U.S. semiconductors out of the Japanese market.) If a foreign country subjects imports to different regulations than apply to domestic products in violation of the national treatment principle, such practices may be deemed "discriminatory." Unlike the mandatory action discussed previously, in these circumstances the USTR is free to exercise discretion in deciding whether to retaliate.

Whether retaliation is mandatory or discretionary, action can include suspending or withdrawing from any trade agreement, imposing tariffs or quotas on foreign imports, or negotiating a new agreement to eliminate the offending policy. Petitions to the USTR for redress or retaliation may be filed by any interested party, including any representative of an industry or group of workers. The USTR can also initiate an investigation on its own without a petition. Section 301 can be used against a wide range of foreign trade practices, including practices that restrict the export of services as well as goods and that restrict foreign investment. For example, if a foreign government discriminates against U.S. construction companies in accepting bids for a major public works project, the USTR could retaliate by restricting the imports of an unrelated product from that country. In principle, the value of the imports affected should approximate the value of U.S. exports affected, but the USTR has broad discretion to decide on the appropriate target goods and form of retaliation.

In 1988, Congress, concerned by the persistent U.S. trade deficit and frustrated by a sense that the president was not aggressive enough in opposing foreign trade barriers, transferred authority to retaliate from the president to the USTR and strengthened Section 301 by adding two provisions known as "Super 301" and "Special 301." Super 301[32] required the USTR to initiate Section 301 investigations against major foreign barriers to U.S. exports. If an agreement with the foreign government either to eliminate these practices within three years or to provide compensation to the United States could not be obtained, the USTR was required to retaliate. Super 301 led to the Structural Impediments Initiative (SII) with Japan and other market-opening negotiations with foreign trade partners. The SII was successful in persuading Japan to initiate certain changes in its system of domestic distribution and to increase enforcement of competition law. The authority established under Super 301 to retaliate lapsed in 1990, but several members of Congress have called for renewing this provision in some form to ensure that the executive branch has maximum leverage to attack foreign barriers to U.S. exports. In 1994 President Clinton renewed Super 301 by executive order in response to the persistent trade deficit with Japan and the collapse of the negotiations with Japan to remove barriers to the Japanese market. When Japan refused U.S. demands to import a minimum of U.S. automobiles and automotive parts, President Clinton announced in May 1995 that the United States would impose 100 percent tariffs on imports of certain Japanese cars and car parts under Super 301.

Under Special 301,[33] the USTR is required to maintain a priority list of countries that fail to enforce U.S. intellectual property rights. A Special 301 investigation may be initiated against any country on the priority list unless the USTR determines that such an investigation would be harmful to U.S. economic interests. If the foreign country does not take steps to protect U.S. intellectual property rights, the USTR may be required to retaliate. Special 301 led to a range of agreements with developing countries, such as Thailand, to bolster enforcement of intellectual property rights. These agreements are especially important to the U.S. film and sound record-ing industries in preventing piracy of their products.

Export Restrictions

The basic framework for restricting most commercial exports and technical informa-tion is the Export Administration Act of 1979 (EAA),[34] which was renewed in 1985 and 1993 and may be amended in 1995. The EAA designates certain authority to the executive branch to control exports for reasons of (1) preventing foreign adver-saries from obtaining sensitive technology or information that could undermine na-tional security, (2) promoting foreign policy objectives, and (3) preserving com-modities that are in short supply (see Chapter 2).

Under the EAA, exporters of goods and technical information are required to ob-tain licenses from the Office of Export Administration of the Department of Commerce. The export of most commercial goods is permitted by a general license, except for goods destined for certain countries subject to almost total embargoes (which in 1995 included Cuba, Libya, Iran, Iraq, North Korea, and Serbia). Some sensitive goods and technical data require special licenses to export. These goods are identified on a commodity control list maintained by the Commerce Department. The Commerce Department will issue licenses for listed goods and information only if it is satisfied that the items will not be diverted for military uses by a foreign adver-sary. U.S. participation in the Coordinating Committee on Multilateral Export Controls (COCOM) is authorized under the EAA. For more than four decades, CO-COM coordinated export controls among the North Atlantic Treaty Organization (NATO) countries and Japan aimed at preventing the communist countries from ob-taining sensitive technology. COCOM was dissolved in 1994 following the end of the cold war. In 1995 the industrialized countries, including Russia and those in central Europe, continued a series of negotiations to reconstitute a multilateral orga-nization to coordinate and control the export of both conventional weapons and other technologies and products that may be useful in creating weapons of mass de-struction.

The EAA has also provided authorization for export controls connected to specific foreign policy objectives. For example, President Carter prohibited grain exports to punish the Soviet Union for its invasion of Afghanistan in 1979, and other export restrictions have been imposed on Iran, Libya, South Yemen, and Syria for support-ing international terrorism. Export controls on commodities in short supply have been invoked only rarely in response to specific shortages. Exports of Alaskan crude oil and certain timber cut from federal lands are restricted under this provision, for example.

In response to the Arab boycott of Israel and efforts by Arab governments to pun-ish foreign companies that do business with Israel, the Congress amended the EAA in 1977 to prohibit any U.S. firm or individual from participating in any boycott organized by a foreign government against a friendly country.[35] The antiboycott provisions would, for example, prohibit U.S. companies either from refusing to do business with any Israeli, U.S., or other firm or individual in compliance with the Arab boycott or from providing information requested by Arab governments to assist the boycott. Some U.S. companies have been subject to severe penalties for violating the antiboycott provisions. These provisions, like those in the Foreign Corrupt Practices Act (discussed subsequently), are regarded by some members of the business community as an unwarranted intervention in the policies of foreign governments that places U.S. firms at a commercial disadvantage in exporting to these countries. Any U.S. person or firm that knowingly or willfully violates any provision of the EAA may be subject to substantial criminal fines or imprisonment up to ten years. The Commerce Department may also impose civil penalties up to $10,000 per violation.

Exporters whose economic interests have been adversely affected by the imposition of export controls and some members of Congress have been critical of the broad operational authority granted to the president under the EAA. In both the 1985 and 1988 revisions of the EAA, Congress has tried to reduce the overall regulatory burden to exporters, to streamline licensing requirements, and to restrain the president from imposing foreign policy controls in the future. Two important amendments in the 1988 act allowed the export of low-technology items previously included on the commodity control list and of technology that is otherwise available from foreign producers. Despite these efforts at restricting the president's discretion to control exports, the executive branch has been able to continue implementing export controls with relative autonomy.

In 1994 the Clinton administration introduced a revised EAA intended to refashion the legislation in light of changes since the end of the cold war. In particular, the administration sought changes to strengthen existing multilateral export control regimes and the government's authority to prevent the spread of unconventional weapons, reform and streamline the licensing system, and tighten penalties on individuals who violate export controls. These revisions were opposed by some of the business community as overly restrictive. Congress continued to debate revisions to the EAA in 1995.

The president has special authority delegated from Congress to respond to imminent threats to the national or economic security of the United States under the International Emergency Economic Powers Act of 1977 (IEEPA).[36] The IEEPA was intended to apply in times of war and other national emergencies and to limit the much broader discretion that had been granted by the Trading with the Enemy Act of 1917[37] (discussed later in this section). IEEPA provides that if the president declares that a national emergency exists involving an unusual and extraordinary foreign threat to the U.S. national security, foreign policy, or economy, he is authorized to investigate, regulate, or prohibit any transaction subject to U.S. jurisdiction involving any foreign property. The IEEPA has been invoked in response to a wide variety of foreign policy crises: The president froze assets belonging to the government of Iran following the seizure of U.S. hostages in 1979; prohibited most trade with Nicaragua because of the policies of the Sandinista government; and imposed a range of economic sanctions against South Africa, Libya, and Panama. Despite its intentions to limit presidential authority, the IEEPA has been used broadly to authorize restrictions in situations that are less than imminent national emergencies.

Another statute regulating exports indirectly is the Foreign Corrupt Practices Act of 1977 (FCPA),[38] as amended by the Omnibus Trade and Competitiveness Act of 1988. The FCPA resulted from a congressional investigation into the payment of bribes by U.S. companies to foreign governments and agents in order to obtain sales contracts. The statute prohibits any U.S. firm or its employees, agents, officers, or directors from corruptly giving anything of value directly or indirectly to a foreign official, foreign political party, or foreign party official or candidate in order to gain business. The act does not apply to "grease payments" intended to obtain a routine government service from a clerical employee, such as a customs official. It also requires U.S. firms to disclose any such payments in accordance with the Securities Exchange Act of 1934.[39] Violations of the FCPA may result in substantial civil or criminal fines against both the individuals and firms involved and imprisonment up to five years. Many U.S. exporters have criticized the FCPA, claiming that it uniquely disadvantages U.S. exports while foreign companies continue to engage in bribery of foreign officials.

In addition to these provisions is a range of other measures that may be invoked to regulate exports. The Trading with the Enemy Act of 1917 (TWEA) prohibits trade with any enemy during wartime. Prior to the enactment of the IEEPA, the TWEA was amended to permit presidential control of both domestic and foreign transactions in emergencies even during peacetime. Thus, the TWEA was repeatedly invoked in circumstances that seemed far removed from its original purposes. For example, presidents have declared national emergencies under the TWEA to issue emergency banking regulations in 1933 (which remained in effect as late as 1977) and to deal with a balance of payments problem in 1971. Under the TWEA, the Treasury Department has issued Foreign Asset Control Regulations that are still effective against Cuba, Vietnam, and North Korea.

The Atomic Energy Act[40] authorizes the Atomic Energy Commission to license the export of nuclear materials and technology, and the Arms Export Control Act of 1976[41] authorizes the State Department to license certain defense-related exports. The Narcotics Control Trade Act of 1986[42] gave the president authority to impose certain trade restrictions against countries that refuse to cooperate with U.S. efforts to control illegal narcotics trade.

Finally, in addition to the unilateral export controls authorized by statute, the president has authority under the U.N. Participation Act of 1945[43] to impose economic sanctions whenever the United States is called upon by the Security Council to apply sanctions under the U.N. charter. Under this authority the president has imposed economic sanctions against Rhodesia, Iraq, and Serbia in compliance with appropriate Security Council resolutions.

Conclusion

U.S. laws regulating imports have been shaped by two fundamental and occasionally contradictory impulses. On the one hand, the economist's faith in the benefits of free trade has led to laws liberalizing the flow of imports to the United States. On the other hand, the political need to respond to domestic producers and workers injured by imports has led to laws restricting the flow of imports. Restrictions on fairly priced imports are intended to allow U.S. industries time to adjust to changes in the international marketplace so as to regain competitiveness. In practice, these laws provide relief to uncompetitive industries as a way of buying off their opposition to free trade policies generally. The philosophy underlying this approach is that a little protection is better than a lot of protection.

Export policy can be expected to play an important role in overall U.S. trade policy even as the United States dismantles the export regulations of the cold war era. Export laws have both promoted exports and restricted certain exports to some countries on grounds of national security, foreign policy, and scarcity. In general, export policy has been characterized by repeated efforts by Congress on behalf of constituents to limit the president's discretion to restrict exports. Nevertheless, the president has retained broad authority to restrict exports on a variety of noneconomic grounds and under circumstances that fall far short of real national emergencies—another reminder of the heavy political component of U.S. trade policy.

For Further Reading

Carter, Barry. *International Economic Sanctions: Improving the Haphazard U.S. Regime.* New York: Cambridge University Press, 1988.

Hufbauer, Gary C., and Jeffrey J. Schott. *Economic Sanctions in Support of Foreign Policy Goals.* Washington, D.C.: Institute for International Economics, 1983.

————. *Economic Sanctions Reconsidered: History and Current Policy.* Washington, D.C.: Institute for International Economics, 1985.

Jackson, John H., William J. Davey, and Alan O. Sykes, Jr. *Legal Problems of International Economic Relations.* 3d ed. St. Paul: West, 1994.

Long, William J. *U.S. Export Control Policy: Executive Autonomy vs. Congressional Reform.* New York: Columbia University Press, 1989.

Lowenfeld, Andrew. *International Economic Law: Trade Controls for Political Ends.* 2d ed. New York: Matthew Bender, 1983.

Stephan, Paul B., III, Don Wallace, Jr., and Julie A. Roin. *International Business and Economics: Law and Policy.* Charlottesville, Va.: Mitchie, 1993.

Swan, Alan C., and John F. Murphy. *Cases and Materials on the Regulation of International Business and Economic Relations.* New York: Matthew Bender, 1991.

U.S. Department of Commerce Bureau of Export Administration, Office of Technology and Policy Analysis. *Annual Foreign Policy Report to the Congress,* published annually.

U.S. House of Representatives Committee on Ways and Means. *Overview and Compilation of U.S. Trade Statutes,* published annually.

U.S. International Trade Commission. *Summary of Statutory Provisions Related to Import Relief.* USITC publication, published annually.

Notes

1. See, for example, *Star-kist Foods, Inc.* v. *United States,* 275 F.2d 472 (Court of Customs and Patents Appeal 1959).

2. Trade Act of 1974, 19 U.S.C. 2191–2193. For a good discussion of the fast-track authority, see Harold Hongju Koh, "The Fast Track and United States Trade Policy," *Brooklyn Journal of International Law* 18 (1992), pp. 143–189.

3. GATT Article 19, discussed in Chapter 8.

4. 19 U.S.C. 2251.

5. The ITC found that small and large cars were "directly competitive" but were distinct from small trucks. *Report to the President on Certain Motor Vehicles and Certain Chassis and Bodies Therefor,* U.S. ITC investigation No. TA-201-44 (December 3, 1980).

6. When U.S. car manufacturers brought a 201 action against Japanese and German imports in 1980, the ITC determined that the recession of the late 1970s was a more significant factor in explaining the domestic industry's problems. The difficulty with the commission's decision in that case is that the recession itself was aggravated by the high unemployment in the U.S. car industry, and the recession also made less expensive, more fuel-efficient cars more attractive to the U.S. consumer. The recession was both cause and effect of the increase in imports that hurt the U.S. automotive industry. By treating all of the economic indicia associated with a recession as a single cause, the ITC established a principle that would make it difficult for producers in any industry during a recession to prove that imports are a more important cause of injury than the recession itself. The ITC's decision not to recommend a 201 remedy for the U.S. automobile industry greatly angered members of Congress, and Congress amended 201 in 1988 to prohibit the ITC from aggregating the causes of declining demand associated with a recession. See Section 202(c)(2)(A) of the 1988 Trade Act. President Reagan responded to the demands of the automobile industry for adjustment relief by negotiating a voluntary export restraint agreement with Japanese and European car manufacturers under which they agreed not to export more than a set number of cars to the United States annually.

7. These included relief from imports of motorcycles, shingles, and stainless steel.

8. In addition to determining 201 petitions, the ITC determines when unfairly priced goods cause material injury to U.S. industry, investigates allegations of unfair methods of competition (as described in the next chapter), and studies and makes recommendations to the president and Congress on trade policy.

9. Section 221 et seq. of the Trade Act of 1974, 19 U.S.C. 2271.

10. Section 22 of the Agricultural Assistance Act.

11. Section 406 of the Trade Act of 1974, 19 U.S.C. 2436, as amended.

12. Section 731 of the Tariff Act of 1930, as amended, 19 U.S.C. 1673.

13. The law assumes that a foreign producer that is not producing for its home market could not be dumping in more than one large export market at a time.

14. The calculation of a fair value is especially complicated in nonmarket economies because all prices are artificially set by the central planners. A constructed value based on the cost of labor or materials in a nonmarket economy may also be artificial because these costs are also

determined by the central planners. Instead, the ITA will construct a value based on the cost of labor and materials in a surrogate market economy at the same level of development as the nonmarket economy. For example, in constructing a value for glassware manufactured in China, the ITA might look at the cost of labor and materials in another large developing South Asian economy like India, assuming India's glassware industry employed comparable technology. Alternatively, the ITA could construct a price based on the surrogate country's export price to other market economies, including the United States.

15. In fact, there may be many different prices paid by different importers for different volumes of the import. For example, many producers offer high-volume discounts, or producers may offer seasonal discounts. The ITA will calculate a weighted average price from many individual transactions over the six months prior to filing the petition. The U.S. purchase price may not reflect a real arms-length transaction price when the foreign producer sells to a related U.S. company. For example, if Toyota of Japan sells cars to Toyota of the United States, the price is not necessarily the same as would be negotiated between two unrelated parties in an ordinary market transaction. Therefore, when goods are imported to the United States by a related party, the ITA will calculate the U.S. purchase price based on the price paid by the first unrelated party to the importer. This price is called the "exporter's sales price," and it must be adjusted in order to determine what price an unrelated party would have paid to the foreign producer on export to the United States. Any value added by the importer once the good enters the United States and the cost of any sales commissions or promotional costs for selling the good in the United States must be deducted from the exporter's sales price.

16. If the U.S. purchase price includes the cost of shipment, insurance, or U.S. tariffs, these costs will be deducted in order to ensure that in comparing the U.S. purchase price and the fair value, the ITA is comparing the goods under the same circumstances of sale. If the foreign producer extends interest-free credit for buyers in the domestic market, then the added cost to the goods sold in the home market must be deducted from the home market price unless the same credit terms are available for U.S. buyers.

17. If the preliminary determination is affirmative, then importers may be required to post a bond in the amount of the estimated dumping duties. By posting a bond, the importer gives the government security that the amount of estimated dumping duties will be paid if a final dumping determination is affirmative.

18. Initially, the ITC has 45 days to make a preliminary determination as to whether the U.S. industry has suffered or is threatened by a material injury or may be materially retarded by reason of imports. If the ITC decides that no injury or threat occurred, the whole proceeding, both at the ITA and at the ITC, stops (as a practical matter, the ITC almost always makes a preliminary determination of injury). Then the ITC has another 45 to 75 days to make its final determination.

19. Section 731 of the Tariff Act of 1930, as amended, 19 U.S.C. 1673.

20. Once the ITA determines that a subsidy exists, valuing the net amount of the subsidy is more complicated than merely dividing the nominal amount of a grant by the number of imports. For example, if a producer receives $1 million from the government for new equipment, what is the life of the subsidy? Generally, the ITA assumes that the subsidy continues to benefit the producer for the life of the equipment but not necessarily in the same amount each year. Arguably, the amount of the subsidy may diminish over time as the equipment ages and depreciates, or it may increase as the producer has additional cost savings to reinvest each year. Another consideration is the time value of money. If a producer receives $1 million annually for ten years, it is not the same as receiving $10 million in the first year, because the producer

would prefer to have the money sooner to invest. Therefore, it may be necessary to calculate the present discounted value of the stream of future payments, and this approach requires the ITA to make assumptions about future interest rates.

21. Section 303 of the Tariff Act of 1930, as amended, 19 U.S.C. 1303.

22. Section 771(5) of the Tariff Act of 1930, as amended, 19 U.S.C. 1677.

23. GATT Subsidies Code, Annex Illustrative List of Export Subsidies, reprinted in 18 I.L.M. 579 (1979).

24. For some time it was uncertain whether a nonmarket economy's imports could be subject to a countervailing duty. After much controversy, the U.S. courts held that imports from a nonmarket economy were not countervailable because the idea of a subsidy was meaningless in a nonmarket economy in which prices are artificially set by central planners (*Georgetown Steel* v. *U.S.,* 801 F.2d 1308 [Fed. Cir. 1986]). It remains unclear, however, how this decision will apply in practice to those economies in transition to a market, such as China. One possibility is treating each industry differently depending on whether it constitutes a "market bubble" in an otherwise controlled environment.

25. Section 337 of the Tariff Act of 1930, as amended, 19 U.S.C. 1337.

26. USITC, *In the Matter of Certain Welded Stainless Steel Pipe and Tube,* Inv. No. 337-TA-29 (1978).

27. 12 U.S.C. 635.

28. Title I of the Agricultural Trade Development and Assistance Act of 1954, 7 U.S.C. 1701–1736d.

29. Internal Revenue Code Sections 921-7, 991-7.

30. 15 U.S.C. 4001–4003, 12 U.S.C. 1841–1843.

31. 19 U.S.C. 2411.

32. Section 301 of the Trade Act of 1974 as amended by the Omnibus Trade and Competitiveness Act of 1988, 19 U.S.C. 2411 et seq.

33. Section 182 of the Trade Act of 1974 as added by the Omnibus Trade and Competitiveness Act of 1988, 19 U.S.C. 2242.

34. 50 U.S.C. 2401.

35. Section 8 of the Export Administration Act of 1979, 50 U.S.C. 2401 et seq.

36. 50 U.S.C. 1701–1706.

37. 50 U.S.C. App. 5(b).

38. 15 U.S.C. 78a–78ff.

39. 15 U.S.C. 77b–78hh.

40. 42 U.S.C. 2011–2296.

41. 22 U.S.C. 2751–2796.

42. 19 U.S.C. 2491.

43. 22 U.S.C. 287c.

8 The International Legal Framework: The General Agreement on Tariffs and Trade

Among the fundamental international norms that govern world trade is the General Agreement on Tariffs and Trade (GATT), the basic framework for international trade in goods.[1] Originally, GATT was a part of the charter of the International Trade Organization (ITO). While the ITO was still being negotiated, the United States proposed that the parties agree to an interim protocol that would give effect to the GATT rules within the charter. The Protocol of Provisional Application was signed by 22 governments in 1947, and 106 governments had signed as of 1993. Although the protocol was never submitted to the U.S. Senate or to any other national legislature for adoption as a treaty, it was the legal foundation that bound the parties to the GATT rules prior to 1995. In 1995 the Uruguay Round agreement replaced the protocol as the basic GATT framework and created the World Trade Organization (WTO). These developments are discussed in Chapter 13. This chapter will focus on the basic GATT framework, which has existed since 1947 and remains in effect under the new WTO.

The GATT in Domestic U.S. Law

One of the perplexing issues raised by GATT is its legal status. Clearly, for purposes of international law, the GATT is a treaty binding the United States and all the contracting parties to its provisions. The status of GATT under domestic or national law is less clear. In the United States and most other countries, the GATT has no direct effect on the rights or obligations of individuals before national courts. In other words, an individual cannot assert a right to import or export under the GATT. A related but more complex question is whether a federal or state law in conflict with the GATT takes precedence over the GATT in a U.S. court. The Senate never adopted GATT as a treaty. Congress has adopted legislation for the purposes of implementing U.S. obligations under GATT; for example, Congress has authorized lowering U.S. tariffs. Moreover, Congress reiterated in every trade bill prior to 1988 that nothing Congress did to implement GATT should be read as approving it. To the extent a federal statute that predates the GATT is inconsistent with the GATT, it nonetheless remains good law enforceable in a U.S. court.[2] If Congress were to adopt a statute inconsistent with the GATT, even though the United States may be in violation of its international obligations, a U.S. court must apply the federal law. One example of how U.S. federal law preempts the operation of the GATT involved the U.S. Marine Mammal Protection Act.[3] Under that act the United States banned the import of yellowfin tuna from Mexico, Venezuela, and Vanuatu because these countries commonly used nets that trapped and killed dolphins. Mexico complained to the GATT that the United States had imposed an import barrier in violation of the GATT, and a GATT panel agreed. Yet even though the United States law clearly violated the GATT, the United States continued to enforce it domestically pursuant to the statute.

There is some uncertainty as to whether and how the GATT may affect state laws that are contrary to it. Under the U.S. Constitution, a treaty approved by the Senate supersedes inconsistent state law, but GATT is not a treaty approved by the Senate. A few state courts[4] and some commentators in the United States assert that under the U.S. Constitution, obligations undertaken by the president under GATT are like treaty obligations and may supersede contrary state law.[5] Even if GATT is not quite the same as a treaty approved by the Senate, the powers to regulate foreign commerce and to conduct foreign relations lie exclusively with the federal government. A state law that interferes with foreign commerce or embarrasses the president in the conduct of foreign relations may be preempted. For example, if California passes a law restricting the sale of imported electronic equipment in violation of the GATT, it could complicate U.S. foreign economic relations. A U.S. court would be likely to strike down such a law because the Constitution gives the power to regulate foreign commerce exclusively to the Congress and prevents states from imposing trade restrictions on their own.

The Substance of the GATT's Rules

The GATT's language is especially vague, obtuse, and technical. Its thirty-eight articles and multiple annexes and codes are considered almost unreadable, but the most fundamental obligations of GATT are clear. First, Article 2 of the GATT requires that once a contracting party has agreed to make a tariff concession, it cannot unilaterally raise the tariff at a later time. For example, if the United States agrees to reduce the tariff on foreign footwear, that tariff concession is fixed, or "bound," at the lowered rate. The GATT has sponsored a series of eight multilateral negotiations referred to as "rounds." These sessions have achieved significant reductions in tariff rates that are now bound.

Article 1, the so-called most-favored-nation provision, requires that any advantage given to any product of any contracting party shall be granted to like products of all contracting parties. In essence, contracting parties agree not to discriminate among the imports of any contracting parties. If the United States permits imports of shoes from another contracting party like the EU tariff-free, then it cannot impose a tariff on shoes from Brazil because Brazil is entitled to be treated as favorably as any other contracting party to the GATT.

Article 3 requires that contracting parties must afford the products of any other contracting party the same treatment as national products with regard to all national laws, regulations, and taxes. The basic requirement of national treatment is different from the MFN clause in two respects: First, national treatment applies to imports even after they have entered the territory of a contracting party, whereas the MFN clause applies only at the point at which goods enter the territory. Second, national treatment compares how imported goods are treated relative to national goods, whereas the MFN clause compares the treatment of imports from different contracting parties.

These three obligations—to maintain negotiated tariff rates, to extend the same tariffs to all contracting parties, and not to discriminate against imports relative to domestic goods in national regulations and taxes—form the core of the GATT. They work together to ensure that tariff and nontariff barriers to trade are minimized so that market forces will determine the pattern of trade. The GATT is based on the liberal market assumption that discriminating among foreign producers would distort the market price of goods and the pattern of trade in a way that would reduce the world's welfare.

Consider one example of how that might work. Assume that during a given GATT round the United States maintains a 10 percent tariff on imported pasta products, and the EU maintains a 6 percent tariff rate on imported leather shoes. Perhaps the EU is prepared to lower its tariff on U.S. shoes to 2 percent if the United States will eliminate its tariff on pasta. If the United States cuts its pasta tariff to zero, U.S. shoe exporters will be able to sell more in the EU. But other shoe producers in Argentina, for instance, will also benefit because the EU is required to extend MFN treatment to Argentina. Similarly, other foreign pasta producers in Chile will benefit from being able to export to the U.S. tariff-free. Thus, the effect of the GATT is to generalize the tariff concessions. Argentina and Chile have received something for nothing out of the negotiations, but the assumption is that no country loses in a world of lower tariff barriers.

Two other important GATT obligations facilitate the nondiscrimination principle of the GATT. Article 5 guarantees that contracting parties will grant free transit through their territory for the products of any other contracting party. If a U.S. company wants to export widgets through Mexico to Costa Rica, Mexico cannot impose a tariff or nontariff barrier to the export of the goods through its territory. Article 11 of GATT prohibits all quantitative restrictions on exports and imports with certain exceptions. Quantitative restrictions or quotas are a particularly pernicious nontariff barrier to trade because no matter how hard the exporter tries to compete by lowering price, it cannot get around a numerical quota. The GATT recognizes that quantitative restrictions may be used in some limited circumstances to prevent exports of essential goods in short supply or to protect agricultural prices. Despite Article 11, the United States has long maintained quantitative restrictions on certain imports such as automobiles and steel products. It has not technically violated Article 11, however, since the quotas are "voluntarily" imposed by the foreign exporters to limit their sales in the U.S. market. It may seem odd that foreign companies would agree to limit their exports to the United States, but the U.S. executive has implicitly threatened to take protectionist action against imports if the quotas are not agreed to and enforced. Similar quotas have been in effect in the EU to limit the sale of Japanese cars.

The GATT obligations summarized here are qualified by numerous exceptions, which have the effect of making the GATT more ambiguous than it may at first appear. Although a detailed listing of all the qualifications written into the GATT would require a more extensive treatment, a brief summary of some of the most important exceptions to the GATT's obligations gives an idea of what those qualifications involve.

First, as a concession to the former colonial powers, the GATT allows "historical preferences" between former colonies and their former rulers to continue. This exception was especially important for the United Kingdom, which extends preferential tariff treatment to other countries in the British Commonwealth, and for France, which maintains special economic relationships with its former colonies in Africa.[6]

Second, the GATT allows countries to impose "antidumping" or "countervailing" duties on imports that are "unfairly priced." These terms are explained later in the discussion of the GATT codes.

Third, the GATT allows countries with fixed exchange rates to take actions to limit imports if required to prevent an imminent loss of foreign reserves.[7]

Fourth, the GATT allows developing countries to use subsidies, tariffs, and quotas when necessary to improve development.[8]

Fifth, the GATT "escape clause" allows countries to use tariffs and quotas to protect domestic industries that suffer or are threatened by serious injury as a result of an unexpected increase in imports.[9]

Sixth, the GATT exempts measures necessary to protect public morals; human, animal, and plant life or health; intellectual property rights; and national artistic or historic objects. Also exempted are measures to prohibit fraud or to safeguard goods that are in short supply.[10]

Seventh, the GATT allows certain measures for national security in order to prevent the export of secret information, nuclear materials, and armaments and to enforce restrictions in time of war or mandated by economic sanctions imposed by the United Nations.[11]

Eighth, the GATT allows countries to grant preferential treatment to the goods of other countries within a customs union or free trade area.[12] For example, the EU is a customs union in which all of the member states maintain one uniform tariff on imports from non-EU countries. Within the EU, there are no tariffs on goods originating from another member state. The United Kingdom may impose a 5 percent tariff on a widget that originates from the United States but no tariff on a widget from France. That contradicts the principle of MFN treatment, but it is an important GATT exception that has allowed the EU to become a powerful trading bloc. Similarly, the United States and Canada share a free trade area; thus there are no tariffs on goods originating in either country. A free trade area differs slightly from a customs union in that the United States and Canada do not impose a common external tariff. Like the EU example, the U.S.-Canada free trade area is a permissible exception to the principle of MFN treatment.

Ninth, in exceptional cases, the GATT establishes a mechanism for opting out of any GATT obligation if two-thirds of the contracting parties agree to waive the obligation as it applies to a particular party.[13]

In sum, prior to the creation of the WTO in 1995, the GATT was more of a framework of rules for negotiating and conducting trade than it was an organization. The GATT did not have any enforcement arm as such. Instead, the GATT relied on the good faith of the contracting parties to carry out their obligations or face the risk of reciprocal sanctions imposed by other trading partners. If one contracting party undertook a measure that another contracting party objected to on the basis of the GATT, the offending party was required to consult with the complaining party.[14] If the parties failed to resolve their differences, a party claiming that its rights under the GATT were "nullified or impaired" could refer the matter to the GATT secretariat for an investigation and report to the other GATT parties.

Under the original GATT, the investigations were undertaken by panels of experts appointed by the GATT Council. Typically, these panels took years to complete their reports, which were carefully worded to avoid any diplomatic embarrassment. Usually, the reports concluded with some recommendations to the parties to resolve their dispute. The reports were unpublished and did not become official until the GATT Council accepted the recommendations contained in them. In effect, a panel report was nonbinding, since any party to the dispute could block adoption of the report by the Council. As a practical matter, diplomatic pressure usually compelled parties to accept the report.

After the report was accepted and published under the 1947 GATT, parties sometimes failed to conform their behavior to the recommendations of the panel. For example, in the U.S.-Mexican tuna dispute previously described, a GATT panel determined that the U.S. ban on tuna violated the GATT, but the U.S. government continued to enforce the ban. Mexico and the United States were then engaged in sensitive negotiations leading to the North American Free Trade Agreement. Rather than risk those negotiations by confronting the United States or asking for compensation from GATT, Mexico agreed to settle its claim and change its fishing practices. In another case, two GATT panels determined that EU subsidies for oilseed production nullified and impaired benefits negotiated for by the United States and recommended that the EU terminate such subsidies. Yet the EU continued to subsidize oilseed production until the United States threatened to take unilateral trade action against the EU that might have wrecked the Uruguay Round of the GATT. These examples show that often the 1947 GATT relied on unilateral action or threats of unilateral action to compel parties to resolve GATT complaints.

In an extraordinary case under the original GATT, the participating countries could "compensate" the complaining party by authorizing the complaining party to suspend its obligations to the offending party.[15] This procedure, known as "nullification or impairment" proceedings, was used frequently and primarily by industrial countries against other industrial countries. The United States was often a complainant or a respondent. Approximately half of all disputes were settled before a report was actually issued. Although parties refused to comply in a few cases, only once did the GATT actually authorize compensation for a complaining party by allowing that party to suspend its obligations to another party.[16]

It should be noted that a party claiming nullification and impairment was not expected to allege that an actual violation of a GATT rule had occurred. It was sufficient to claim that a benefit bargained for had been denied, even if the offending party had not breached its GATT obligations. Consider this hypothetical: Japan agreed to eliminate all tariffs on foreign automotive parts and then provided a domestic subsidy for Japanese automotive manufacturers that allowed those manufacturers to significantly undercut the price of imported parts. In effect, Japan would deny the United States and the EU the benefits they bargained for in eliminating the tariff, because U.S. and EU exporters would still be unable to increase their market share in Japan. Note that in this hypothetical, Japan did not violate any GATT rule by providing the domestic subsidy. Nevertheless, the United States or the EU could claim that a benefit anticipated under the GATT had been nullified or impaired, and accordingly, it could seek permission from the GATT to suspend some other obligation owed to Japan.

The dispute settlement mechanism was significantly strengthened by the Uruguay Round agreement. Panels will be appointed by a dispute settlement body consisting of all WTO member states. A panel will be composed of three independent experts. The panel has six months to issue a report, which may be reviewed by an appellate body. Once the appellate body adopts a report, it is automatically effective without requiring a vote of the WTO membership. If a party fails to conform to a panel report, the opposing party can request the dispute settlement body to authorize compensation or suspension of trade concessions.

The GATT has served as an important forum for negotiating reductions in tariff and nontariff barriers to trade. The first six rounds of the GATT led to significant cuts in tariffs, and the seventh, the Tokyo Round, concluded in 1979 with a series of codes to reduce and eliminate nontariff barriers. These codes are referred to as the "multilateral trade negotiations" (MTN) codes, and prior to the WTO in 1995, GATT parties could choose to sign on to any of these codes. (After 1995 all GATT parties were required to participate in all of these codes.) The most important of these are the codes on subsidies, antidumping, standards, procurement, and customs valuation. All the codes were revised by the Uruguay Round agreement in 1995. An exhaustive description of each of these codes is beyond the scope of this chapter, but following is a brief summary of their function.

The codes on subsidies and antidumping were intended to elaborate on Articles 6 and 16 of the GATT. These provisions of the GATT allowed states to levy tariffs on imports that are "unfairly priced." There are two situations in which imports may be unfairly priced. The first case is when an exporting country pays a subsidy to a manufacturer, producer, or exporter so that a good can be exported at a lower price. In this event the GATT allowed an importing state to levy a "countervailing duty" in an amount equal to the net subsidy per import. The code on subsidies included rules defining subsidies and specifying how countervailing duties should be determined. Most important, the subsidies code required that before a government imposed a countervailing duty, it must have determined that the unfairly priced import caused or threatened material injury to a domestic industry in the importing country. Finally, the code provided for consultation and dispute settlement. The material injury requirement was an important limitation on the levying of countervailing duties. Prior to the WTO, exporting countries that were not parties to the subsidies code could have their exports subject to countervailing duties in the United States even though there was no evidence of material injury. Thus, there was an advantage to participating in the code for countries that exported to other code members.

The subsidies code referred to three kinds of subsidies: export subsidies on primary products, export subsidies on nonprimary products, and domestic subsidies. The code allowed countries to grant export subsidies on nonprinting on certain primary products including agriculture, fish, and forestry products so long as subsidies did not result in any country gaining "more than an equitable share of world export trade" in that product. As a practical matter, this limitation on primary product export subsidies was meaningless. Domestic subsidies were also permitted so long as they did not result in "serious prejudice" to another country's interests or "nullify or impair" the benefits of GATT for another country. Only subsidies on the export of manufactured or secondary products were prohibited. Although the code did not authorize countervailing duties on domestic subsidies or export subsidies on primary products, U.S. law did not distinguish between domestic and export subsidies or between primary and secondary products.

The Uruguay Round revised the subsidies code to provide a new dispute settlement procedure and further clarify what subsidies are prohibited or subject to countervailing duties. Agricultural subsidies are now covered by a new agreement on agriculture that requires countries to reduce substantially export subsidies on farm products over a six-year period.

The second case of an unfairly priced import concerns dumping, which occurs when an exporter exports a good at a price that is less than the fair value of that good. In this case the importing country is allowed to impose an antidumping duty, if the dumping causes or threatens material injury to a domestic industry in the importing country. The concept of "fair value" or "normal value" is complicated, but in general, the fair value or normal value is the price of a good sold in the ordinary course of wholesale business in the home market of the exporter. In essence, the antidumping duty is used by the importing country to raise the price to the same level as that of the exporter's home market.

It may seem strange that an importing country would want to raise the price of imports and thereby reduce the welfare of its own consumers. However, the danger is that dumping may put domestic competitors out of business and allow the foreign exporter to occupy a dominant position in the importing country's market. If that happens, the exporter may be able to set a much higher noncompetitive price. Thus, even though the dumping law appears to raise prices, it does so in the interests of maintaining more competitive prices in the long term.

The antidumping code set out how to determine the difference between the fair price and the export price, which represents the margin of dumping, and the degree of injury or threat thereof. The code also created a procedure for consultation and dispute settlement, which was revised by the Uruguay Round.

The code on standards, also known as the code on technical barriers to trade, ensured that imports were guaranteed national treatment in relation to all technical regulations and that such regulations were not intended to create barriers to trade and did not otherwise have the effect of creating an unnecessary barrier to trade. For example, in 1985 the European Union (EU) restricted the sale of meat containing certain hormone additives. This restriction prevented many cattle ranchers in the United States from selling in the EU. The United States challenged the EU restrictions based in part on the code on standards, and the EU defended the restriction based on grounds of protecting human health from possible carcinogens. The code provided a framework for challenging and defending the restriction. The United States did not seek a GATT panel but instead unilaterally imposed tariffs on agricultural imports from the EU.

In addition to the substantive provisions, the standards code set out procedures for the adoption of standards by national governments and for "transparency," a term that means standards must be clear and accessible to importers. The Uruguay Round updated the code and encouraged parties to adopt uniform international standards whenever possible.

The government procurement code was intended to open up the procurement practices of governments to allow imports to compete on a more equal footing with domestic products. Government expenditures represent roughly one-fourth of the world's gross national product, and thus the importance of this market for exporters should not be overlooked. Most governments tend to discriminate in favor of domestic products in their procurement. For example, in the United States there are both federal laws that prevent the government from buying certain kinds of goods, such as sensitive technology, from foreign sources and state "Buy America" statutes that give preferences to domestic products over imports.

The government procurement code prohibited discrimination against imports, required consistent and transparent procedures for government procurement, and provided for consultation and dispute resolution. The code applied to the purchase of goods costing more than about $200,000 but only to purchases by national governments; it did not apply to purchases by the military or national security agencies. In the U.S.-EU negotiations, the Europeans argued that since some of their governments provided functions that were not provided by the U.S. government, those agencies should not be covered. For example, telecommunications services, utilities, and railroads are typically government-owned in the EU. The United States insisted that if these agencies could be excluded by the Europeans, analogous functions of the U.S. government should be excluded. As a result, the United States excluded purchases by the Departments of Transportation and Energy and by the Tennessee Valley Authority, COMSAT, and Amtrak.

The Uruguay Round agreement on government procurement expanded the coverage of the code to include government procurement of services as well as goods in excess of approximately $175,000. In addition, it extended coverage to procurement by state and local governments and state-owned public utilities. In effect, the new provisions opened up the market for government procurement by tenfold.

The code on customs valuation was intended to standardize the methodology for determining the value of imports for purposes of levying tariffs. Obviously, differences in the ways that governments value imports can significantly affect the amount of tariff paid. For example, if an import is subject to a 10 percent tariff, the difference between valuing the import at $100 and $125 is equivalent to raising the tariff from 10 percent to 12.5 percent.

In addition the provisions previously discussed, the Uruguay Round added a number of agreements. Among the most significant Uruguay Round achievements were new agreements on sanitary and phytosanitary(SPS) measures, trade-related investment measures, trade-related intellectual propety rights, and trade in services. The SPS agreement is designed to harmonize national health regulations protecting humans, animals, and plants and to establish international standards. The agreement on trade-related investment measures (TRIMS) requires national treatment for foreign investors and prohibits all national laws that prevent foreign investors from importing goods. For example, it prohibits laws that require foreign investors to use materials that meet certain local content requirements. The agreement on trade-related intellectual property rights (TRIPs) recognizes the growing importance of patents, trademarks, and copyrights in international trade. The TRIPs provisions establish basic principles for the uniform enforcement of intellectual property rights to deter trade in counterfeit goods. For example, member states are required to provide adequate protection for exporters of sound recording or computer software against unauthorized use of their copyrights.

Finally, the general agreement on trade in services (GATS) expands the GATT from a framework of regulations for the import and export of goods to reach barriers to trade in services as well. GATS contains a general framework of principles for eliminating barriers to trade in services. First, it applies national treatment to services like banking, insurance, transportation, communication, tourism, education, and consulting. Second, it provides detailed national schedules of commitments to liberalize specific service industries within certain time periods. Third, it incorporates several annexes concerned with reducing barriers to specific service industries, such as financial services.

Conclusion

The GATT provides the framework for conducting trading relations among signatory countries. The GATT prohibits contracting parties from engaging in discrimination against imports and ensures that contracting parties are able to enjoy the benefits they bargain for through the GATT. The GATT codes have helped to reduce nontariff barriers to trade. By facilitating the free movement of goods on a nondiscriminatory basis and by lowering tariffs, the GATT has expanded the range of market forces and allowed more countries to benefit from the gains from trade. The Uruguay Round of the GATT is intended to contribute further to the growth of world trade, particularly through the establishment of the WTO.

For Further Reading

Barton, John, and Bart Fisher. *International Trade and Investment: Regulating International Business.* Boston: Little, Brown, 1986.

Curzon, Gerald. *Multilateral Commercial Diplomacy: The General Agreement on Tariffs and Trade and Its Impact on National Commercial Policies and Techniques.* London: Michael Joseph, 1965.

Dam, Kenneth. *The GATT: Law and International Economic Organization.* Chicago: University of Chicago Press, 1970.

Dillon, Thomas J., Jr. "The World Trade Organization: A New Legal Order for World Trade?" *Michigan Journal of International Law* 16 (1995), pp. 349–392.

GATT Secretariat, Final Act Embodying the Results of the Uruguay Round of Multilateral Trade Negotiations, December 15, 1993.

Hudec, Robert. *The GATT Legal System and World Trade Diplomacy.* New York: Praeger, 1975.

Jackson, John H. "The General Agreement on Tariffs and Trade in United States Domestic Law." *Michigan Law Review* 66 (1967), p. 249.

———. *The World Trading System: Law and Policy of International Economic Relations.* Cambridge: MIT Press, 1989.

McGovern, Edmund. *International Trade Regulation: GATT, the United States, and the European Communities.* 2d ed. Exeter: Globefield Press, 1986.

Notes

1. The term "goods" refers to tangible merchandise, which is sometimes called "visible trade." Goods must be distinguished from the category of internationally traded services ("invisibles"), which include professional services (such as legal counseling or financial services), transportation, interest payments, renting and licensing property rights (such as the copyright to a musical work or a trademark like "McDonald's"), foreign tourism, and education for foreign students. Originally, the GATT was exclusively concerned with trade in goods. During the Uruguay Round the GATT contracting parties agreed to principles governing international trade in services and intellectual property rights as well.

2. The Protocol of Provisional Application says that the contracting parties must apply GATT Articles 3 through 23 "to the fullest extent not inconsistent with existing legislation." Thus, even by it own terms, the GATT does not preempt federal trade statutes existing prior to 1947. The MTN codes adopted in 1979 did not grandfather existing legislation, so this required Congress to pass implementing legislation to modify then-existing law. It should be pointed out that if the Congress had not passed implementing legislation, United States courts would have had to enforce the existing law, even though that law was inconsistent with the 1979 codes.

3. 16 U.S.C. 1371–1377.

4. See, for example, *Bethlehem Steel Corp.* v. *Board of Commissioners,* 276 Cal. App. 2d 221, 80 Cal. Rptr. 800 (1969); *Baldwin-Lima-Hamilton Corp.* v. *Superior Court,* 208 Cal. App. 2d 803, 25 Cal. Rptr. 798 (1962); *Hawaii* v. *Ho,* 41 Hawaii 565 (1957).

5. Rest. 3rd, Restatement of the Foreign Relations Law of the United States, Part VIII, Chapter One, Introductory Note; John H. Jackson, "The General Agreement on Tariffs and Trade in United States Domestic Law," *Michigan Law Review* 66 (1967), pp. 249, 259–260.

6. Article 1(2).

7. Article 12.

8. Article 18.

9. Article 19.

10. Article 20.

11. Article 21.

12. Article 24.

13. Article 25(b).

14. Article 22.

15. Article 23.

16. John H. Jackson, "GATT Machinery and the Tokyo Round Agreement," in William Cline, ed., *Trade Policy in the 1980s,* (Washington, D.C.: Institute for International Economics, 1983).

Part Four

Major
Contemporary
Issues

---

9 Japan: America's Strongest Economic Competitor

The notion that the single most important bilateral relationship in the world today is the one between Japan and the United States continues to gain wide acceptance among foreign affairs specialists. For the first time in history, economic forces, not military or political factors, define what is arguably the international system's most important bilateral relationship. The end of the cold war has brought into focus the critical importance of the economic and technological competition between the world's two largest, most dynamic economies. Though peaceful, this competition entails enormous stakes involving future trends in domestic standards of living and in international influence.

Unfortunately, the escalating importance of national economic strength and the mutual complaints about the fairness and intentions of the other side have introduced an uninterrupted series of frictions into the relationship between the two economic superpowers. To the dismay of defenders of Japan, there is a growing acceptance among U.S. politicians, businesspeople, and trade policymakers of the need to adopt a hard-line trade policy toward Japan, even if it risks straining political relations with the most important ally the United States has in the western Pacific. To the dismay of critics of Japan, U.S. pressures on Japan to alter its economic practices are still not strong enough.

In the meantime, two of the most important, most vexing U.S. trade policy questions remain unanswered. First, why has the strongest, most successful foreign competitor of the United States been able to surpass it in one industrial sector after another? The two most likely explanations are either unfair Japanese trading practices or an inadequate U.S. industrial performance. Second, what should be the primary response of the United States to its structural and very large trade deficits with Japan? The main alternatives are either efforts to make domestic companies more competitive or unambiguous threats to retaliate if specific demands for internal Japanese economic reforms and market-opening measures are not met.

A major reason for the lack of precision in evaluating the true nature of U.S.-Japanese trade relations is the failure to untangle two separate, albeit related, problems: (1) a widespread inability of many U.S. manufacturers to compete head-to-head with their Japanese counterparts, and (2) the singular difficulty of exporting even the most efficiently produced manufactured goods to Japan caused by indirect, informal trade barriers. A more economically balanced and politically harmonious

U.S. trade relationship with Japan presupposes domestic and trade policy initiatives that separately address both of these problems.

Unique Aspects of U.S.-Japanese Trade Relations

Japan's role in U.S. trade policy is extraordinary because Japan's role in the global trading order is extraordinary. When calculations are made regarding national economic accomplishments and the relative importance of other countries to U.S. trade relations, Japan invariably comes in at the top of the list. It was the first non-Western society to become an international economic superpower. No other country since the mid-1970s has challenged U.S. industrial leadership more than has Japan, and no other exporter of manufactured goods has competed as successfully in the U.S. market.

Neither is there any other country that poses as big a challenge to U.S. preeminence as an economic and technological superpower. For no other country can it be said that "most studies by U.S. experts share the conclusion that Japan's high technology capabilities are now on par with or ahead of the United States in many fields."[1] The prospect of Japan's domination of the high-technology sector has been the single greatest reason for arguing that the definition of U.S. national security must be broadened to include industrial, financial, and technological strength.

No other country has generated as much anger and frustration among its trading partners for allegedly not opening its markets to the extent that other countries' markets are open to Japanese goods. Japan holds the number one global position for success in exporting an increasingly sophisticated array of manufactured goods. But it also holds the top position in any list of "underachievers" when it comes to importing manufactured goods, as measured as a percentage of either total imports or total domestic manufacturing. Only in Japan does a leading national political figure argue that it should become a "normal" country.[2]

Because perceptions regarding Japan's role in the global trading system dominate irrefutable realities, that country can be placed at the top of two seemingly mutually exclusive categories:

- international trade aggressor, a country hell-bent for international commercial conquest and domination, possessing an uncompromising double standard regarding market access for foreign-made manufactured goods;
- victim of foreign jealousy and misunderstanding, a country unjustly chastised for being a paragon of economic excellence, unappreciated for its ability to provide capital to a capital-starved world by virtue of its being the only major country saving more than it is spending.

Japan would far and away be at the top of any list of foreign countries directly contributing to the development of new themes in U.S. trade policy since the mid-

1970s: orderly marketing agreements, reciprocity of market access, enhanced government technology policy, managed trade, results-oriented trade, strategic trade theory, voluntary import expansion efforts, and so on. Furthermore, Japan has had a virtual monopoly in inspiring improved production processes among U.S. manufacturing companies over the same period: quality control; just-in-time delivery from a few carefully chosen, highly trusted suppliers; development of new products through joint efforts among R&D technicians, product designers, parts suppliers, and production line workers; reduced middle management; increased authority for production line workers, and so on.

Japan comes in first in any list of countries posing obstacles to the design of an optimal set of U.S. trade policies. In short, it is extraordinarily difficult knowing just what solutions are most appropriate for solving "the Japan problem."

Japan in the early 1990s was perennially number one among all countries in terms of the size of its multilateral (i.e., worldwide) trade surpluses and in accounting for the largest U.S. bilateral trade deficits. The serious systemic imbalance experienced by the United States with Japan is manifested on the surface by the large, long-running U.S. trade deficits with that country. Despite the empirical size of Japan's trade surpluses (see Table 9.1), there is intense controversy as to their significance and costs to the United States and to the true source of the large disequilibrium constantly plaguing the world's most important bilateral trade relationship.

Lost in the ensuing exchanges of charge and countercharge is the fact that the U.S. trade deficit with Japan is not a cause of problems but rather an effect. Despite

TABLE 9.1   Bilateral U.S.-Japanese Trade Balances (billions of dollars)

	U.S. Bilateral Deficit	U.S. Imports from Japan	U.S. Exports to Japan	U.S. Exports to Japan as a percentage of U.S. Imports from Japan
1970	1.2	5.9	4.7	80
1980	9.9	30.7	20.8	68
1986	55.0	81.9	26.9	33
1987	56.3	84.6	28.3	33
1988	51.8	89.5	37.7	42
1989	49.0	93.6	44.6	48
1990	41.1	89.7	48.6	54
1991	43.4	91.6	48.2	53
1992	49.4	97.2	47.8	49
1993	59.3	107.3	47.9	45
1994	65.6	118.8	53.3	45

Source: U.S. Department of Commerce trade statistics from various publications.

having taken on a life of its own, the bilateral deficit is merely a surface manifestation, first of contrasting domestic economic performances, second of market access problems in Japan, and third of aggressive Japanese exporting. Japan remains content with a large, seemingly nonstop bilateral surplus, but U.S. public opinion views the deficit as an intolerable burden generated by Japan's commercial perfidy. Most Americans would declare a victory and turn their attention elsewhere—if only these deficits were to disappear.

Five points are necessary to make important qualifications to the raw trade numbers presented in Table 9.1. First, the U.S. bilateral deficit has been unusually impervious to repeated efforts aimed at its elimination. It has persevered unabated for a quarter of a century despite the application of all known balance of payments adjustment measures—exchange rate changes, efforts to stimulate imports through increased Japanese aggregate demand and GDP growth, countless reductions of Japan's import barriers, Japanese voluntary export restraints (in effect, negotiated export quotas), relaxations of Japanese business regulations, and so on. Second, this bilateral deficit has been disproportionately large from the late 1980s through the early 1990s. In most of these years, Japan has accounted for more than one-half of the entire U.S. multilateral trade deficit; in 1992 the figure was almost 60 percent of the total. Third, the value of U.S. imports from Japan (expressed in nominal terms) exaggerates the effects of the rising dollar prices of Japanese exports caused when the yen appreciates. In other words, the volume of Japanese exports in recent years has grown more slowly than their dollar-denominated costs. Fourth, in the late 1980s the growth rate of U.S. exports to Japan exceeded that of U.S. imports from that country. However, this moderately faster rate of export growth was not sufficient to generate a sustained reduction in the net deficit because it could not overcome the arithmetically distorting effect of U.S. imports from Japan in the mid-1980s being *triple* the value of U.S. exports to that country. A fifth factor is the macroeconomic reality that Japan spends less than it produces and the United States spends more than it produces. In other words, Japan's rate of saving is much higher than that of the United States. Because Japan's aggregate saving exceeds its aggregate investment and the United States as a nation invests more than it saves, the former is assured of a *multilateral* trade surplus in goods and services and the United States is assured of a *multilateral* trade deficit.

The exact significance of the bilateral trade deficit numbers is open to conjecture. From a political point of view, they are dynamite, a negative trend arousing emotional fervor in many Americans. From an economic theory point of view, the numerical size of the U.S. trade deficit with Japan is overshadowed in importance by its product composition. Whereas more than one-third of U.S. exports to Japan are raw materials and foodstuffs, the vast majority of U.S. imports from Japan are relatively sophisticated manufactured goods. The national wealth and living standards of the United States would not be maximized in the long run to the extent that it imports sophisticated, high-value-added, expensive industrial goods made by highly skilled, highly paid foreign workers, and then pays for these imports by exporting an equivalent dollar amount but a greater volume of relatively cheap, low-tech goods (scrap metal, scrap paper, logs, cotton, used clothing, tobacco) produced by relatively low-paid, low-productivity workers. In economic terms, the United States would be experiencing unfavorable *terms of trade* under such circumstances. In any event, it is important to note that most economists dismiss bilateral trade balances as being relatively unimportant. Since trade deficits with some countries will be offset by surpluses with others, only multilateral balances are seen as being economically significant.

Wisely or unwisely, the overriding priority of U.S. trade policy vis-à-vis Japan since the early 1970s has been clear and unswerving: to reduce or eliminate the bilateral deficit. This has proved to be a deceptively difficult, elusive goal—for equally difficult and elusive reasons.

Is Japan the Innocent Victim of Overly Aggressive U.S. Trade Policies?

U.S. trade policy cannot rest on the flat assertion that Japan is the overwhelming cause of the bilateral trade disequilibrium and resulting frictions. Even if it is assumed that unusually large bilateral U.S. trade deficits in fact represent a serious economic problem, it cannot be taken as a given that they are due to unfair Japanese trade practices. A noted economist, Jagdish Bhagwati, has argued that the "better-crafted" econometric studies "certainly do not support the thesis that Japan imports too little, nor do they indicate a special and extraordinary effect of informal trade barriers that make Japan a fit case for unusual treatment in the world trading system."[3] The Japanese are quick to point to the U.S. domestic disequilibrium, the saving-investment imbalance discussed in Chapter 4, that suggests a large U.S. trade deficit is inevitable unless the federal budget deficit is sharply reduced or the rate of private saving is sharply increased.

One school of thought exempts Japan from criticism regarding the trade disequilibrium on the grounds that this imbalance should be viewed as reflecting several factors for which the Japanese need offer no apologies. Japan's bilateral surpluses with the United States, to some extent, reflect an intense outpouring of hard work by the industrial sector and clever governmental policies that make the Japanese economy relatively strong and competitive, the free-will preference of U.S. consumers and companies for Japanese goods, and the failure of many U.S. companies to endure the long, expensive, and demanding process required to successfully crack the difficult Japanese market—one that is not welcoming of any newcomers, be they Japanese or foreigners.

The Japanese point out that on a per capita basis, they buy more U.S. goods than Americans buy Japanese goods, and that no other country has come close to matching Japan's efforts since the late 1960s to unilaterally reduce its trade barriers. Defenders of Japan are literally correct when they assert that its levels of *formal* import barriers compare favorably with those of other industrialized countries. Most Japanese are very critical of U.S. industry, citing factors ranging from its inadequate levels of increases in investment and productivity to its lack of concern with the manufacturing process. Akio Morita, the founder of Sony, once wrote that "America no longer makes things, it only takes pleasure in making profits from moving money around."[4]

Another key argument against retribution in the form of hard-line U.S. trade policies is the assertion that Americans tend to use Japan as a scapegoat because it is easier to criticize Japan's alleged misdeeds. The alternative is the painful admission of U.S. economic shortcomings and adoption of the difficult measures necessary for reversing the allegedly largely self-inflicted decline in U.S. industrial competitiveness.

Is the United States the Unwitting Victim of Overly Aggressive Japanese Trade Policies?

At the other end of the spectrum from the "apologists" is a critical school of thought collectively dubbed the "Japan bashers." (Both labels are oversimplifications and reflect the emotional nature of bilateral frictions.) Critics contend that a serious problem exists due to the combination of unfair Japanese trade practices and a radically different form of market mechanism operating within Japan. A 1989 report of the president's Advisory Committee for Trade Policy and Negotiations concluded that in "response to the question, 'Is there anything different about Japan's pattern of trade, especially manufactures trade?' . . . studies suggest the answer is an unqualified yes."[5]

The more severe critics accuse the Japanese of being "adversarial" traders, an outgrowth of their mind-set that elevates trade relations from mere commercial considerations to life-and-death matters of utmost concern for national power and self-esteem. The result is seen to be a fanatical drive to maximize exports and an aversion to any imports that would interfere with industrial targeting and traditional ways of doing business. In other words, mercantilism has become a priority goal of state policy. Well-informed adherents of this approach note that all of Japan's trading partners (except for oil exporters) have the same problems with and make the same criticisms of Japan's export success and its relative paucity of manufactured imports. The global nature of discontent with Japanese trade practices undermines the Japanese dismissal of bilateral problems with the assertion that the problem is one of insufficient U.S. efforts and skills in exporting.

The already long and still-growing list of accounts detailing the extraordinary difficulties of exporting manufactured goods to the Japanese market is given credence by Japan's trade statistics. By any measure, import patterns for manufactured goods deviate from the international norm. Japan's relative industrial strength and relatively high dependency on imports of raw materials can explain some but not all of this discrepancy. In 1990, the market share of Japan's imports of manufactured goods, which accounted for 5.9 percent of its total consumption of manufactures, paled in comparison to the shares for the United States (15.3 percent) and Germany (15.4 percent excluding intra–European Union trade,[6] about 37 percent including intra-EU trade). Furthermore, Japan is unique in being the only major industrialized country where this import penetration figure is not increasing; among major industrial countries, Japan's industrial sector is the only one not becoming increasingly intertwined with the international economy. Japan is the only major country (at least through the end of the 1980s) whose ratio of total imports to GDP has declined.[7]

Economists have paid increasing attention to Japan's presence at or near the bottom of international measures of *intraindustry trade* (whereby a country imports and exports similar products, e.g. chemicals and automobiles). Uniquely, Japan imports very little of the goods it exports, and these levels have been stagnant.[8] Finally, Japan is probably the only industrialized country that consistently has run large trade surpluses in manufactured goods with all of the newly industrialized countries of East Asia whose export prowess has led them to be dubbed "export platforms."

Curiously, the best single statistic demonstrating why Japan's trading partners are furious with its trade practices is seldom mentioned: Japan's multilateral surplus in manufactured goods. In 1994 it reached a record-shattering $237 billion,[9] surpassing previous records, also held by Japan. The more frequently cited overall surplus is always smaller than Japan's balance on manufactured goods because of the country's enormous imports of raw materials and agricultural goods. Japan's contention that it must be a major exporter of manufactured goods to offset its dearth of natural resources is valid to a point but does not explain why Japan needs to export manufactured goods worth about *twice* as much in dollar terms as its imports of primary products.

The Japanese market is not "closed" to imports. But critics assert that the indirect barriers faced by all countries in exporting manufactured goods to Japan remain so serious and deep-rooted that the Japanese economy effectively constitutes a unique form of capitalism. This "revisionist" perspective is hotly contested on the ground that any market economy is subject to certain basic disciplines, and by inference, cultural factors cannot dominate the underlying forces of the market mechanism. Those who wish to demonstrate genuine, serious problems of market access in Japan point to overt trade barriers, such as the total ban on rice imports that was modestly eased in 1994, and questionable product standards, such as the ruling that skis exported to Japan needed to meet special performance standards on the grounds that Japanese snow was different. Far more important are numerous indirect barriers that are fully consistent with a country that seems driven to minimize its dependence on imports of advanced technology. Obstacles to exporting manufactured goods to Japan include the existence of an industrial policy that fosters targeted industries through financial support and import discouragement; the widespread existence of cartels that apportion market share; the propensity of member companies of the large industrial groups (*keiretsu*)[10] to buy from one another; the importance of pre-serving long-term business relations; a restrictive distribution system in which Japanese companies apply severe pressure on retailers to sell only their goods; restrictive Japanese government procurement practices; the belief that most Japanese products are more reliable than foreign goods; the relative dearth of foreign direct investment (foreign-controlled companies) in Japan; and so on.

The Domestic Foundations of Japan's Export Success

The bilateral trade problem is rooted in domestic economics. Japan and the United States share the same general economic ideology, but there are important differences in their application of it. Throughout the post–World War II period, Japan has subordinated everything to the unanimous national consensus that its war-ravaged economy had to be rebuilt, enlarged, modernized, and strengthened. Much of U.S. industry was content to rest on its laurels after World War II, confident that its global dominance would last indefinitely. Because short-term sacrifice had to be made for long-term gain, Japan's entire economic system was tilted in favor of producers and away from consumers. The speed and degree of its incredibly successful effort to achieve industrial strength surprised and impressed everyone, but in the process, the Japanese economy came to be viewed abroad as "a sort of perpetual-motion machine that generates trade surpluses, cranking out a surfeit of exports . . . while drawing in a relative paucity of imports."[11]

The international priority for Japan was to maximize its relative industrial strength and win commercial wars; for the United States, it was to maximize its military strength and win the cold war. The fact that both countries successfully achieved their priority international goal is crucial to understanding why the two have been amenable to spending twenty-five years unsuccessfully pursuing what was in fact the secondary objective of more balanced bilateral trade.

Nothing has illuminated U.S. nondefense industrial shortcomings more than the sight of Japanese industrial sectors one after another surpassing their U.S. counterparts on the way to becoming world-class competitors. Although most Americans focused on dirty tricks as the secret of Japan's spiraling exports, the main impetus came from favorable developments within the Japanese economy.[12]

Japan's contemporary economic success does not so much reflect accident or conspiracy as it does a mix of cultural values, management strategies, production know-how, and official policies that mutually reinforced one another in a uniquely favorable environment for industrial growth and strength. An unrivaled positive synergy developed with the Japanese doing a lot of things right and making relatively few mistakes in rebuilding their shattered economy. There is no single secret to their success. The whole is larger than the sum of its parts. Japan had to draw on a number of strengths in order to overcome a number of serious obstacles to achieving economic strength—a dearth of raw materials, labor immobility and a rigid seniority system, corporate collusion in lieu of unrestrained competition, and so on.

Culture and history are the first important source of Japan's economic success. Relevant Japanese cultural values can be discerned on three different levels:

- Strong belief in hard work, frugality, honesty, and education.
- Group loyalty and collective goals (in lieu of self-aggrandizement), mutual trust and obligations, simultaneous competition and cooperation, social harmony, and respect for hierarchy.
- Ambiguous attitudes toward non-Japanese that hinder foreign penetration of the inner sanctum of what is viewed as Japan's unusually distinctive social order. There appears to be a strong, deeply rooted belief throughout Japan's history in the need to preserve the essence of "Japanese-ness" by minimizing dependence on the outside world. When viewed closely, the Japanese seem intent on controlling, to the maximum extent possible, the terms upon which foreign ideas, goods, business practices, or technology penetrate their society.

The second factor in Japan's economic success, and possibly the most important, has been the accomplishments of its manufacturing sector, particularly in learning how to make goods better and cheaper. Management has been brilliant in adopting a long-term orientation stressing growth and market share rather than immediate profits. This strategy has been facilitated by the fact that Japanese corporations in the post–World War II era generated most of their capital needs from bank borrowing. Because they did not need to sell much common stock to the public, these corporations did not have to be as responsive to shareholders clamoring for short-term profits and higher dividends as did most of their U.S. counterparts. Another singular trait of Japanese companies is never, never being content with any given level of manufacturing productivity. Management's stress on engineering and detail eventually allowed Japanese companies to become world leaders in what is called *process technology*, the totality of the manufacturing process that begins with new product development and ends with its final assembly on a production line. Whereas Japan intensively studied U.S. economic methods in the early post–World War II era, by the 1980s the student-teacher roles in the manufacturing sector had been reversed. There is also a dark side of Japan's corporate pursuit of competitiveness: consistently holding workers' wage increases below their productivity increases (in order to minimize unit labor costs) and consistently making harsh price and delivery demands on vulnerable, dependent, and intensely loyal subcontractors.

Economic policies are the third component of Japan's economic success. Since the end of the U.S. occupation, the Japanese have been singularly focused on maximizing economic growth and the competitiveness of the industrial sector. Whereas the role of the government has waned in the years since Japan's emergence in the early 1980s as an international economic superpower, it is no oversimplification to say that government policy priorities remain focused on encouraging and supporting big business. Unlike most government planners in the world, Japan's bureaucrats usually seek consensus with senior industrialists, listening as well as advising, about future economic means and ends. In so doing, they have been unsurpassed in providing the private sector with (infinitely) more positive support than negative interference. Disdainful of the notion that the market mechanism works best when left alone, the Japanese government has been instrumental in successfully nudging the invisible hand of the marketplace toward the development of state-of-the-art, high-growth industries. The approach has included such measures as R&D subsidies, monetary policies that emphasize low interest rates to corporate borrowers and encourage bank lending to favored industries, tax incentives, encouragement of market allocation schemes to maximize corporate specialization, buy-Japanese government procurement practices, and various forms of administrative guidance.

Additional internal factors of consequence still contributing to Japanese economic strength include an unusually high rate of saving that tends to constrain the costs of borrowed capital to corporations, a methodical searching for and licensing of newly developed foreign technology, and a relatively low rate of national expenditures for military purposes. Important external factors start with the successful U.S. efforts to cultivate a liberalized international trading system after World War II; not even the strongest company can expand exports in the face of rigid quotas imposed by other countries. Depending on the United States for its defense allowed Japan to keep military spending low and to channel resources into the more productive commercial sector.

The Goals and Strategy of U.S. Trade Policy Toward Japan

Bilateral trade relations had an inauspicious beginning. The first, partial opening of the Japanese market was made possible only after a determined show of military force in 1853 by Admiral Perry and his well-armed "black ships." Except in the years immediately following World War II, when the United States was dedicated to aiding Japanese economic recovery, bilateral trade relations have never been marked by great cordiality. The contemporary era of U.S.-Japanese trade began in the late 1960s when declining relative competitiveness forced the U.S. government into repeated demands for voluntary export restraints to slow rapid rises in Japanese shipments. First came the demand for restraints on steel products, and soon thereafter came three years of contentious negotiations on restraining exports to the United States of synthetic textile products.[13]

The late 1960s marked the beginning of a transition period. One Japanese industrial sector after another began to expand its share of the U.S. market. The two countries began a gradual reversal of roles as dominant industrial competitor in the international marketplace, a switch quantitatively visible in the form of the fade-out of U.S. trade surpluses and the onset of progressively larger Japanese multilateral and bilateral surpluses. There ensued a quarter of a century of nonstop bilateral negotiations in which the United States initiated demands and Japan responded. The Japanese would have preferred to be left alone and to change little. However, as the second-place finisher in head-to-head trade competition, the United States embarked on a noisy but idealistic crusade to create "a level playing field" by converting what was perceived as an unrepentant trade sinner into a paragon of Western-defined economic virtue. Optimists can point to upward of forty agreements by Japan either to reduce trade barriers or to restrain its export machine—nearly all of which came only after the U.S. application of what the Japanese call *gaiatsu,* foreign pressure. In effect, U.S. trade negotiators became the equivalent of the only effective opposition party in Japan, dragging reluctant Japanese politicians and bureaucrats kicking and screaming into altering what had been a winning formula: an import-discouraging, export-maximizing trade regime that directly contributed to Japan's economic success. The statistics show that in many cases, Japanese import liberalization measures led to increases in U.S. exports of goods that had been previously afforded a high degree of protection.[14] The result was creation of tens of thousands of U.S. jobs and tens of millions of dollars of corporate profits. On the other hand, cynics can point out that in other cases, import liberalization measures were deliberately undermined by the quiet imposition of new kinds of barriers.

Pessimists look at twenty-five years of deal making and see scant progress. U.S. trade policy toward Japan is still based on frustrations about limited market access and fears of excessive Japanese exports from overly aggressive, highly competitive corporations. Clyde Prestowitz, a noted "basher," has analyzed the situation this way:

> Nothing in U.S. law or tradition . . . anticipated the possibility of trade and industry being organized as part of an effort to achieve specific national goals. . . . The United States understood military competition . . . but not national industrial competition. The result was a series of negotiations that never focused on the main issues and that dealt with symptoms instead of causes.[15]

One variant of the critical school of thought derides U.S. negotiators for being repeatedly outfoxed by Japanese negotiators possessed of a greater sense of institutional memory and a rigid determination to minimize foreign presence among favored industries in Japan. Despite the size and importance of the Japanese market, many U.S. firms are considering focusing their export efforts elsewhere (see Box 9.1). Other critics lament that U.S. policy has been marginalized because the U.S. government has emphasized narrowly defined trade measures painstakingly negotiated on a product-by-product basis (following complaints from domestic producers) rather than securing broad structural changes in Japanese economic ideology, business practices, and economic policies. A related criticism holds that U.S. negotiating efforts are continually undermined by a well-financed, seemingly pervasive Japanese lobbying presence in the United States, as well as by a U.S. bureaucracy split three

**BOX 9.1   If the Japanese Market Is So Tough
to Penetrate, Why Bother?**

The consensus that the Japanese market is notoriously difficult for foreign companies to flourish in leads to the logical question of whether U.S. businesses would not be well advised to concentrate scarce personnel and capital resources on penetrating booming markets elsewhere in Asia. There are a number of reasons for asserting that the answer is no—the Japanese market is too important to be given lip service or ignored outright. It is easy to overlook the fact that in many sectors, U.S.-made goods can compete effectively in the Japanese market in terms of price, quality, and technological sophistication. At least four reasons can be cited to justify constant, uncompromising efforts by both the U.S. private sector and government to maximize the exports of competitive U.S. companies, especially manufacturers of high-value-added goods, to Japan:

1. It is the world's second largest market for most manufactured goods and the largest for some products, notably semiconductors. As such, successful exporting to Japan is an important means to the critically important end of sales maximization. The latter is essential to achieving the economies of scale necessary to minimize production costs and maximize price competitiveness. Maximizing sales volume also generates the profits that encourage expenditures for research and development and for outlays on new plant and capital equipment, both of which are essential business strategies in retaining global competitiveness in high-tech goods.
2. If a company can succeed in the most customer-demanding (and arguably most byzantine) market in the world today, it can succeed anywhere. In short, Japan is an ideal testing ground for mastering all aspects of the marketing process.
3. Experience suggests that it is unhealthy and in some cases even fatal for foreign manufacturers to allow their Japanese competitors to operate in a protected home sanctuary. The absence of foreign competition has seemed to support the recurring pattern of high prices within the Japanese market being used to offset rock-bottom prices of exported goods.
4. A full-scale business presence in Japan is essential to achieve quick, full knowledge and understanding of the increasing numbers of technological and scientific innovations occurring in Japan, a country that has clearly transcended its old reputation of being an unoriginal copycat.

ways among those who view preserving good political relations with Japan as the un-equivocal top policy priority, those who are ardent free traders, and a minority of trade hard-liners.

The U.S. government's negotiating tactics have been criticized from the opposite direction—for allegedly demonstrating gross hypocrisy by readily imposing import barriers when political pressures are intense. Charges of hypocrisy are also leveled against the United States for its propensity to lecture Japan out of one side of its mouth about the glories of liberal trade while simultaneously demanding out of the other side that Japan "voluntarily" restrain exports because U.S. producers cannot compete. The need to form cartels to allocate export shares among Japanese compa-nies under an orderly marketing agreement (OMA) contributes to the "Japan Incorporated" syndrome that is so repugnant to market-oriented Americans. Similarly, some critics view the United States as an incessant whiner that prefers bul-lying a stoical Japan rather than enduring the painful process of accepting the conse-quences of America's allegedly fading international economic power and deteriorat-ing social fabric.

Still another strain of criticism is directed at both countries. One variant decries their excessive embrace of bilateralism (Japan's trade liberalization has been all but totally directed at goods of interest to the United States) that denigrates the spirit of multilateral, nondiscriminatory trade negotiations. Another variant scoffs at both sides' willingness to continually deal with surface issues and symptoms while disre-garding the need to correct the causes of a deeply rooted systemic problem.

Evaluations of results differ, but there is no denying that the chronology of bilat-eral trade relations since the late 1960s consists of nonstop tensions ameliorated from time to time by a negotiating process built around U.S. demands and Japanese responses—symbolic and real. The best means of making sense of the dozens of ma-jor events transpiring over two and one-half decades of frenetic activity, as partially summarized here,[16] is to appreciate the consistency of two transcendent themes run-ning in tandem: repetition and agenda expansion. The first theme is visible in the sheer volume of two generic trade actions repeatedly adopted by the Japanese to avoid retaliation by the United States: (1) market-opening measures designed to pro-vide various degrees of greater market access for U.S.-made goods and (2) voluntary export restraints that have given the Japanese a political voice in implementing the economic equivalent of U.S. import quotas. The second theme is a constant expan-sion of the negotiating agenda as the United States tries one new gambit after an-other, partly out of cunning and partly out of desperation. The common denomina-tor of both themes is the cumulative failure to accomplish their objective of restoring U.S. competitiveness and trade balance parity on a sustained basis with Japan.

The first phase of Japan's import liberalization began in the late 1960s. The initial targets were the country's most conspicuous, most expendable trade distortions. Most of Japan's numerous import quotas, a throwback to its postwar protectionist posture, were illegal under GATT rules and were phased out. Also disposed of was its extensive array of increasingly superfluous export incentives. Unilateral tariff cuts and reductions in barriers to inward foreign direct investment soon followed. During the mid-1970s, bilateral tensions temporarily abated. The U.S. government was (temporarily) content with the initiation of Japanese liberalization efforts. Yen appreciation against the dollar led to (temporary) reductions in the bilateral trade deficit. Last but far from least, universal economic strains associated with OPEC's sudden, massive increase in petroleum prices took center stage on the international economic agenda.

But then Japan's admirable trait of responding to economic crises (it must import virtually all of its oil) with harder and smarter work habits—as opposed to the ineffectual initial responses of the United States to the domestic impact of the two oil shocks—kicked in. The rise of Japan's relative industrial competitiveness soon resumed. At the same time, the Trade Act of 1974 (see Chapters 2 and 7) made it easier for Americans to gain relief from import-induced injury. The first tangible result of these events was an OMA signed in 1976 that imposed quantitative limits for three years on Japanese exports of specialty steel products. One year later, an OMA was signed that imposed a temporary ceiling on Japanese exports of color televisions to the U.S. market. It was later revealed that one reason for the upsurge in imports of Japanese televisions was a systematic effort among Japanese producers to engage in market rigging and dumping.[17]

Negotiations held during 1977 and 1978 produced the first modest efforts to utilize macroeconomic policy to stimulate Japanese imports by means of enlarging the country's aggregate domestic demand. The dubious logic of setting specific quantitative GNP growth targets for a free market economy not surprisingly meant that the Japanese failed to fulfill their commitments. Nevertheless, the need for Japan to adopt expansionary macroeconomic policy has remained a recurring theme in debates about U.S. bilateral trade strategy.

The 1980s began with two exercises in smoke-and-mirrors tactics by Japan as it appeared to reduce barriers on imports of U.S. cigarettes and telecommunications equipment. Failure to see any hints of increased market access for these products necessitated several more years of unstinting U.S. government follow-up efforts to remove discrimination against imports. A third key event of the early 1980s was Japan's bowing to U.S. pressure to brake its growing U.S. market share in automobiles and agreeing to voluntarily restrain its exports. The Reagan administration could not legally demand an automobile OMA because the International Trade Commission had rejected the escape clause petition alleging that increased imports amounted to a "substantial" cause of injury to the domestic automobile industry.

Japan's automobile export quota began in 1981 as a fixed-duration arrangement of three years. Demonstrating Japanese acceptance of the adage that discretion is the better part of valor, it lasted until 1994, by which time it had evolved into a genuinely voluntary, unilateral export ceiling that was too high for most Japanese automobile companies to meet. The arrangement limiting Japanese automobile exports was among the costliest import-restrictive programs ever pursued by the United States. The politically induced shortage of Japanese cars quickly gave a green light to producers in both countries to accelerate price increases in the U.S. market. The billions of dollars of cumulative price increases that resulted, combined with the relatively few American jobs saved, suggested that it would have been far more efficient simply to provide massive subsidies to displaced automobile workers.[18] Furthermore, the surging profits enjoyed by Japanese automobile companies helped to finance their development of better production techniques and larger, more upscale cars, previously the domain of U.S. producers. Other events in bilateral relations during the early 1980s displayed traces of black humor. U.S. pride in baseball as the national pastime induced a long emotional conflict over alleged Japanese barriers to imports of U.S.-made aluminum baseball bats. In June 1982 an FBI sting operation led to the arrest (and conviction) of Japanese businessmen for buying stolen IBM business secrets.

What followed during the mid-1980s might be loosely described as a frenzied but inconclusive trans-Pacific game of policy tennis. On one side, the Japanese government feverishly served up one market-opening package after another. They had little impact in reducing the bilateral U.S. trade deficit. In response, an increasingly impatient Congress feverishly served up but never enacted a number of restrictive bills aimed squarely at Japan. They included demands for reciprocity, local content rules, and retaliation against countries running large, persistent bilateral surpluses with the United States; also incorporated was a sense-of-the-Congress resolution that Japan was an unfair trader. This process eventually led to the enactment of the Omnibus Trade and Competitiveness Act of 1988 containing provisions on market-opening measures and enhancing U.S. competitiveness that were inspired mainly by perceived problems with Japan.

During the second Reagan administration (1985–1989), additional Japanese voluntary export restraints were implemented on steel and machine tools. Reagan's second term also produced several important innovations to go along with the old standbys, Japanese import-opening and export-restricting measures. The market-oriented sector-selective (MOSS) negotiations begun in 1985 were the first formal acknowledgment that random, case-by-case efforts to secure lower Japanese trade barriers on individual products had been excessively time-consuming and not cost-effective. The MOSS talks were designed to address all identifiable trade barriers in several industries in which the United States was internationally competitive but relatively unsuccessful in exporting to Japan: electronics and computers, telecommunications equipment, medical equipment and pharmaceuticals, and forest products. Automobile parts were added later.

A second innovation was the successful effort beginning with the Plaza Agreement by the Group of Seven industrial countries in early fall 1985 to coax the foreign exchange markets into causing significant yen appreciation relative to the dollar. Another new element on the agenda consisted of the three unique aspects of the pathbreaking semiconductor agreement signed in 1986: a comprehensive series of minimum prices imposed on U.S. imports of Japanese semiconductors, agreement by Japanese producers not to dump in third-country markets, and a loosely defined 20 percent market share goal in Japan for foreign semiconductor producers—the first official foray into managed trade. A fourth new wrinkle came shortly after when the United States for the first time in the post–World War II period hit Japan with unilateral sanctions—as retaliation for alleged violations of the agreement.

The Bush administration actively pursued the market access issue, inducing the Japanese to agree to more than a dozen new import liberalization actions covering computers, supercomputers, government procurement procedures, automobiles and automobile parts, glass, legal services, cellular telephones, paper, and other goods. A separate avenue of pressure exerted on the Japanese to open their markets was a direct outgrowth of a new statute. The Bush administration had little choice but to focus a bright spotlight on Japan's restrictive trade practices in the wake of Congress's initiative in writing the Super 301 provision into the 1988 trade bill.[19] Japan had been the primary inspiration for the legislative branch's handing the executive branch an additional lever for overseas market-opening efforts, and U.S. trade negotiators successfully pressed for Japanese import liberalization measures in three priority sectors—supercomputers, communications satellites, and forest products.

As part of the effort to limit the number of Japanese economic practices challenged under the high-profile, high-tension Super 301 process, the Bush administration initiated a relatively low-profile effort to address the underlying domestic causes of the bilateral competitiveness and trade disequilibria. The Structural Impediments Initiative was established in 1989 and immediately broke new ground in terms of one sovereign country scrutinizing the internal affairs of another—a reflection of just how far economic interdependence between the two countries had progressed. The Japanese discussed the possible need for changes in their business structure, goods-pricing mechanism, working hours, land use policy, and distribution system. The U.S. side, among other things, discussed how to increase U.S. rates of saving and investment, reduce the federal budget deficit, lengthen the time horizons of business executives, and improve the educational system. At best, marginal reforms were initiated in response to the suggestions of the other country.

The Clinton administration tried to initiate change in the means of achieving the permanent ends of contemporary U.S. trade policy toward Japan. The administration came into office knee-deep in bilateral agreements put into place by its predecessors, but it rejected this policy legacy by adopting a much more aggressive, results-oriented trade strategy toward Japan. A major new set of demands was pressed that centered on establishing specific numerical targets for a reduction in Japan's current account surplus and for increased levels of imported manufactured goods. The rationale for the latter demand was the cumulative cynicism among trade negotiators that past Japanese liberalization measures had had relatively little trade impact and that specific measures of change were necessary to assure Japanese credibility. Japan, however, adamantly refused to commit itself to any more quantitative trade targets on the grounds that they constituted managed trade.

The two countries' differences were briefly reconciled in a deliberately ambiguously worded agreement, concluded during the July 1993 Group of Seven economic summit meeting, that introduced yet another new dimension to the bilateral negotiating process. As part of a multifaceted "framework" process (dealing with such issues as Japanese compliance with past bilateral agreements, Japanese government procurement, and foreign direct investment), Japan agreed to work toward a "highly significant" decrease in its trade surplus. The agreement also stipulated that there would be an emphasis on "objective criteria, either qualitative or quantitative or both," to measure future Japanese progress in opening its markets. Diplomatic translation: Tangible increases in U.S. exports would be a more important means of evaluating the outcomes of future negotiations than the degree to which Japan lowered import barriers. Prophetic words about this "understanding" were written by *New York Times* reporter James Sterngold: "President Clinton described it as a new start, full of new ideas; knowing Japanese bureaucrats said it was merely a continuation of the old, incremental negotiating process. Both sides conceded that, as a mere framework for future bargaining, it may take years to produce results."[20]

Ironically, it did produce results but in a wholly negative and unexpected way. A meeting between Prime Minister Morihiro Hosokawa and President Clinton in early 1994 ended in abject failure when the Japanese categorically rejected U.S. demands for accepting the quantitative indicators formula to determine market-opening measures in four priority sectors: insurance, automobiles and automobile parts, telecommunications equipment and services, and hospital equipment. Japan's refusal was based on its assertion that compliance with the Clinton administration's demands would be tantamount to engaging in managed trade—a policy it adamantly opposed. The United States was unwilling to accept abstract promises from Japan about market liberalization, and Japan was unwilling to begin accepting the minimum market share formula applied to semiconductors on a potentially open-ended basis. In a break with precedent, the two heads of government agreed that no agreement would be better than an unsatisfactory agreement, and the bilateral economic summit ended in failure.

Lengthy negotiations on these issues continued at the ministerial level. They achieved a qualified success in easing import entry in four sectors (Japanese government purchases of telecommunications equipment and medical equipment; insurance; and flat glass) thanks mainly to the arrival of the September 30, 1994, deadline for retaliation by the United States under its trade laws. Both sides immediately had different interpretations regarding the language in the procurement agreements describing plans to engage in an "annual evaluation of progress in the value and share" of Japanese imports; the objective was to determine if, over the medium term, there had been "a significant increase in access and sales." The U.S. side expressed satisfaction that a general system of performance indicators was in place; the Japanese side emphasized that it could not be held accountable for any specific measure of import increases. In a fitting metaphor for this and many other Japanese-U.S. understandings, several Japanese newspapers likened it to a *tama-mushi-iro*, a Japanese insect whose color changes depending on the angle from which it is being viewed.[21]

The determination of the Clinton administration in mid-1995 to impose retaliatory trade sanctions if the Japanese did not further open their market for U.S.-made automobiles and auto parts led the two countries to the brink of what arguably was the most widely discussed and most widely feared *near*-trade war in history. The

Clinton administration issued an ultimatum after a protracted period of unsuccessful efforts to achieve its goals of relatively limited regulatory changes in Japan's distribution system for new automobiles and a renewal by Japanese auto makers of their pledge to buy a minimum amount of U.S.-made auto parts. Having completed an investigation of relevant Japanese trade barriers under the Section 301 provision of the 1974 Trade Act, the administration announced that in the absence of an agreement by June 28 it would impose unilateral retaliation in the form of prohibitive 100 percent tariffs on imports of Japanese luxury cars—valued at nearly $6 billion annually.[22] The Japanese promptly announced that they would file a grievance against the United States in the World Trade Organization, given that they rejected the accuracy of the U.S. complaint and the legality of unilateral U.S. retaliation.

The ensuing bilateral negotiations, held under a bright spotlight of international media attention, achieved a successful, albeit very ambiguous, last-minute resolution. Both sides declared victory by virtue of a significantly dissimilar interpretation as to what actions had been agreed to, what criteria existed to determine Japanese compliance, and how the pact would be enforced. Any doubts that only the most tenuous of truces in bilateral trade frictions had been consummated were dispelled when the Clinton administration within a few days announced initiation of another Section 301 negotiation to determine whether collusion in the Japanese distribution system systematically discriminated against exports of U.S.-made film.

An irony of the high-stakes automobile dispute was the tendency for larger conceptual issues to be overshadowed by media attention on the relatively narrow issue of the potential for U.S. automobile makers to sell more new cars in Japan. Of enormous importance to the world trading system were many unanswered questions. For instance, was the United States truly putting at risk the recently established World Trade Organization (see Chapter 13) by threatening to bypass the latter's dispute settlement mechanism in favor of unilateral trade sanctions? The ill-defined settlement of the auto issue failed to achieve a conclusion on whether the U.S. recourse to "aggressive unilateralism" in the face of lingering and unique market access problems in Japan is justified and productive. Also left unresolved was the question of whether existing multilateral trade rules can be applied to a country's internal competition policy, in this case the alleged distortions in Japan's business structure favoring domestic suppliers of automobile parts. Nor was there any answer to the question as to why the tremendous appreciation of the yen relative to the dollar was not sufficient to cause Japanese automobile companies to eagerly and voluntarily increase purchases of relatively low-cost U.S.-made auto parts without prodding.

Conclusions and Outlook

Deep-rooted differences and problems have frustrated more than twenty-five years of efforts to minimize bilateral economic frictions. U.S. policy toward Japan cannot escape two long-term dilemmas that will survive anything less than a permanent rupture in bilateral trade relations. The first is how best to reduce U.S. competitive shortcomings relative to Japan. This, however, is mainly an internal U.S. objective that must be achieved through an improved domestic economic performance. The second is how far and how hard to press in making additional, legitimate market-opening demands on the Japanese without risking major damage to the U.S. economy and major harm to an old political alliance. The latter is in increased danger of erosion because of the swift reduction in the two countries' common fear of the Soviet Union's successor states. Further complications emerged in 1993 when Japan's changing political landscape produced an untried, loosely knit ruling coalition to replace the known commodity of the once invulnerable, long-ruling Liberal Democratic Party.

U.S. trade strategy vis-à-vis Japan presumably will avoid the two extreme options, neither of which has a major domestic constituency. One is imposition of widespread unilateral import barriers in the effort to punish restrictive Japanese import practices and to prevent further dislocations and unemployment in the U.S. economy. Although attractive to a few hard-liners, overt protectionism not only would contradict U.S. efforts to push for a more liberalized trading system but also would hurt the U.S. economy. U.S. companies would have reduced access to critically needed, cheap Japanese components; U.S. producers would be encouraged to raise prices and delay product innovation; and Japan could retaliate against many U.S. exports by buying comparable goods from third countries.

The other extreme option is to revert to a soft-line stance by summarily abandoning the long-running U.S. demands for changes in Japanese policies. Although this strategy is not very popular in Washington, some persons advocate it because they believe that the Japanese already have been sufficiently accommodating in opening their economy—to the point that the United States must now get its economic house in order.

After more than a quarter century of long, hard and at best marginally successful efforts, Japan stubbornly remains the most difficult market for foreign manufacturers to crack. The United States has consumed vast amounts of political capital in its incessant, less than successful, and perhaps misguided efforts to change Japanese economic policies and trade practices as a means of correcting the structural bilateral trade disequilibrium. "Success" is still not in sight. It is as unlikely that Japanese economic behavior can be converted to the U.S. style as it is that U.S. economic behavior can be converted to the Japanese style. The two countries still do not share a common definition of basic economic concepts like competition, openness, and regulation. Barring an unexpectedly strong and permanent resurgence in U.S. industrial strength, future administrations are likely to be faced with the same problems and frustrations with Japan as their predecessors.

For Further Reading

Bergsten, C. Fred, and Marcus Noland. *Reconcilable Differences? United States–Japan Economic Conflict.* Washington, D.C.: Institute for International Economics, 1993.

Cohen, Stephen D. *Cowboys and Samurai: Why the United States Is Losing the Battle with the Japanese, and Why It Matters.* New York: HarperBusiness, 1991.

Gibney, Frank, *Miracle by Design: The Real Reasons Behind Japan's Economic Success.* New York: Times Books, 1982.

Holstein, William J. *The Japanese Power Game.* New York: Plume Books, 1991.

Johnson, Chalmers. *Japan: Who Governs? The Rise of the Developmental State.* New York: W. W. Norton, 1995.

Lincoln, Edward J. *Japan's Unequal Trade.* Washington, D.C.: Brookings Institution, 1990.

Okimoto, Daniel. *Between MITI and the Market.* Stanford: Stanford University Press, 1989.

Prestowitz, Clyde, Jr. *Trading Places: How We Allowed Japan to Take the Lead.* New York: Basic Books, 1988.

Notes

1. National Research Council, "Science, Technology, and the Future of the U.S.-Japan Relationship," 1990, p. 7.

2. The source of this quotation is Ichiro Ozawa, a prominent member of one of Japan's new reform parties; see, for example, Richard P. Cronin, "Japan's Ongoing Political Instability: Implications for U.S. Interests," Congressional Research Service report, dated July 8, 1994, p. 2.

3. Jagdish Bhagwati, "Samurais No More," *Foreign Policy,* May-June 1994, p. 11.

4. As quoted in *Fortune,* September 25, 1989, p. 52.

5. "Analysis of the U.S.-Japan Trade Problem," report of the Advisory Committee for Trade Policy and Negotiations, February 1989, p. 77.

6. "Major Findings and Policy Recommendations on U.S.-Japan Trade Policy," report of the Advisory Committee for Trade Policy and Negotiations, January 1993, p. ii.

7. International Monetary Fund, *International Financial Statistics Supplement on Trade Statistics,* 1988.

8. See Edward J. Lincoln, *Japan's Unequal Trade* (Washington, D.C.: Brookings Institution, 1990), pp. 39–47.

9. Official Japanese trade statistics collated by the Japan Economic Institute, 1995.

10. The major *keiretsu,* such as Mitsui and Mitsubishi, are descendants of the giant conglomerates broken up after World War II by U.S. occupation forces. The various companies composing the modern Japanese business group are still closely bonded to one another on the basis of extensive holdings of each other's stock (i.e., partial ownership), interlocking directorates, regular meetings among senior company officers, tradition, and so on.

11. "Reform May Reshape Japan's Edge in Trade," *Washington Post,* June 27, 1993, p. H1.

12. For greater details on the multiple sources of strength in the Japanese economy, see Stephen D. Cohen, *Cowboys and Samurai: Why the United States Is Losing the Battle with the Japanese, and Why It Matters* (New York: HarperBusiness, 1991), chap. 4.

13. U.S. demands for voluntary export restraints by Japan date back to the 1950s, when restraint agreements were negotiated on cotton textiles and several minor items, such as bicycles and baseball gloves.

14. See, for example, "Analysis of the U.S.-Japan Trade Problem," report of the Advisory Committee for Trade Policy and Negotiations, February 1989, pp. 92–98.

15. Clyde Prestowitz, *Trading Places* (New York: Basic Books, 1988), p. 47.

16. For a more detailed chronology of events, see Cohen, *op. cit.*, chaps. 2 and 3.

17. Prestowitz, *op. cit.*, pp. 202–205.

18. See, for example, U.S. International Trade Commission, "A Review of Recent Developments in the U.S. Automobile Industry Including an Assessment of the Japanese Voluntary Restraint Agreements," February 1985; and Robert W. Crandall, "Import Quotas and the Automobile Industry: The Costs of Protection," *Brookings Review*, Summer 1984, pp. 8–16.

19. The Super 301 provision of the 1988 Trade Act ordered the executive branch to identify "priority foreign countries" on the basis of major trade acts and practices that discriminated against U.S. exports. Upon being placed on this very public target list, these countries would be on notice to commence negotiations to reduce or remove these barriers or face U.S. retaliation (see Chapter 7).

20. "Clinton Discovers That Even Japan Can Go for a Populist," *New York Times*, July 11, 1993, p. IV–1.

21. *New York Times*, October 3, 1994, p. D1.

22. The choice of expensive luxury cars as targets of retaliatory tariffs was probably made with the idea—correct as was later proved by opinion polls—that this move would minimize a backlash by middle-income American consumers opposed to any and all price increases in popular, widely used goods.

10 European Union–United States Trade Relations

In 1945, the economies of continental Europe again lay in ruin, ravaged by the unprecedented devastation of World War II. War-weary Europeans began casting a jaundiced eye toward a once-hallowed institution, the nation-state, deeming it guilty of directly aiding and abetting the unrestrained growth of nationalism—the primary cause of three major wars among western European countries since 1870. The concept of seeking European economic union and political confederation was an idea whose time had arrived. European "visionaries" found an increasingly receptive audience. "The intensification of efforts toward European unification after the Second World War sprang from the realization that there was no other sure way to put an end to Europe's sorry history of conflict, bloodshed, suffering and destruction."[1]

Beginning with the Roman Empire, dictators attempted to unify Europe forcefully by military conquest. Whereas all of these efforts failed, there is every indication that the positive-sum game of voluntary economic integration may be the first formula to successfully bring about European unification. The imperative of regional economic cooperation has created a totally unprecedented, still-evolving supranational institution whose final power, configuration, mandate, impact, and membership are impossible to predict. In the meantime, what is now called the European Union (EU) already has become the world's largest trading bloc (as measured by total trade flows),[2] a development that has created problems and opportunities alike for the international trading system. As the largest trading partner of the United States, the EU has posed an extraordinary predicament for U.S. policymakers. On the one hand, U.S. national security objectives have been advanced by the steadily rising affluence and political harmony among its major European allies that have been the principal rewards of the pursuit of economic integration. On the other hand, U.S. economic interests have paid a price in the form of commercial discrimination by an increasingly large and powerful customs union (a free trade area with common institutions).

Knowing exactly what to call the collective institutions of the European integration process has become difficult. *European Union* is slowly becoming the term of choice, but it is not yet the official or the universally used collective designation for the European economic institutions. The older term of *European Community* is still widely used, technically correct in referring to European trade policymaking, and applicable to events of the 1970s and 1980s. For the sake of consistency and to bypass this "identity crisis," the newer term *European Union* is used both in this chapter and throughout the book. [*Authors' note*]

Unique Aspects of
U.S.–European Union Trade Relations

The United States and Western Europe created and for many years dominated the post–World War II international economic order. Linked by similar cultural, political, and economic traditions as well as mutual fear of Soviet expansionism, the countries making up the so-called Atlantic Community developed a tightly interdependent economic relationship along with a tightly knit military alliance. It was no exaggeration (at the time) when Robert D. Hormats, then a senior U.S. State Department official, declared in 1981 that the U.S.–West European relationship "remains at the heart of our foreign policy and our international economic policy."[3]

The EU is a large, affluent market that assures it a high-priority role in U.S. trade policy. With a population of about 370 million people, the fifteen member countries of the EU as of the beginning of 1995 were collectively one-third more populous than the United States and about three times more populous than Japan with its 124 million people. The EU's gross domestic product in 1993 ($6.2 billion measured in nominal terms at then current exchange rates) was approximately the same as the total output of the United States and almost 50 percent larger than Japan's GDP ($4.2 billion).[4] By the early years of the next century, the EU's membership—theoretically open to any democratic country in Europe—could easily be well above twenty. As of early 1995, several countries (e.g., Cyprus and Malta) were in various stages of negotiating membership. Turkey long ago requested membership, but Greece's opposition has blocked active consideration. Norway and Iceland remain prospective members. On the horizon, the stronger central European economies Hungary, Poland, and the Czech and Slovak republics—and the three Baltic republics can be expected to seek membership. Well into the next century, the former Soviet republics in Eastern Europe and the weaker central European states will all be potential members.

The current EU represents a gigantic presence in world trade. It collectively accounts for nearly 40 percent of total world trade when intra-EU trade is included in this statistic; combined EU–European Free Trade Association (EFTA) trade accounts for almost one-half of total world trade. (EFTA is an industrial free trade area comprising West European countries unwilling to be part of the EU's pursuit of full economic and political union.) The United States accounts for slightly more than 10 percent, so it and Western Europe together account for about 60 percent of total world trade.

Collectively, the EU's fifteen member states are the largest trading partner of the United States. The United States is the EU's second largest trading partner, behind the combined countries of EFTA. In 1992 the United States accounted for 17 percent of total EU exports and 18 percent of EU imports.[5] U.S. exports of $103 billion to the EU in 1992 were the equivalent of 23 percent of its total exports; imports from the EU of $94 billion were the equivalent of 18 percent of all U.S. imports.

To obtain a complete accounting of bilateral U.S.-EU economic relations, it is also necessary to examine bilateral trade in services and foreign direct investment, both of which are of unusually large magnitude. Recorded exports of services by U.S. companies to the EU in 1993 were $55 billion, almost one-third of total services exports; U.S. imports of $48.5 billion from EU countries represented almost 40 percent of global U.S. services imports in the same year.[6] Extensive overseas production is the other major aspect of U.S.-EU commercial relations. U.S. foreign direct investment in EU countries, valued at $201 billion at year-end 1992, accounts for slightly more than 40 percent of all U.S. direct investment on a worldwide basis. These U.S.-controlled overseas companies at year-end 1991 had assets of about $840 billion and sold goods and services in and outside of the EU estimated at more than $750 billion annually.[7] The $219 billion value (on a historical-cost basis) of EU countries' foreign direct investment in the United States represented 53 percent of total inward foreign direct investment at year-end 1992.

The classic question involving U.S. exports in the critically important EU market is whether their impressive growth (U.S. exports more than doubled in value between 1985 and 1992) have been *because* of the creation of the European customs union or *despite* it. On the one hand, as the world's preeminent trading bloc, the EU is the greatest living proof of the economic theory describing the dynamic, or follow-on, benefits of trade liberalization. When trade barriers are removed among countries, efficient companies tend to thrive in their expanded sales market, and inefficient companies either adjust, specialize, or go bankrupt. Furthermore, a "virtuous" cycle can be unleashed for years as increases in both trade and competition tend to spur real economic growth by way of increased real incomes, which in turn encourage more trade, then further income increases, and so on. Hence, the well above average growth rates in imports, exports, and domestic growth exhibited by EU countries after internal tariff barriers were removed were not a coincidence.

On the other hand, a customs union is inherently discriminatory against goods produced in nonmember countries—except in the limited cases when absolutely no tariff or nontariff barriers are imposed on imports. The absence of internal trade barriers gives a competitive boost to the goods of other member countries, as does imposition of a common external tariff and common nontariff barriers. Furthermore, the subsidies given to some EU domestic production and to agricultural exports also affect world trade flows.

While happily observing the international economic and political benefits of an increasingly prosperous, cohesive, and self-confident Western Europe, U.S. trade policymakers have placed strong emphasis on achieving maximum market access for its goods to EU member countries. This has been done through efforts to minimize the trade-diversion effects that inevitably accompany the removal of internal trade barriers following creation of a regional free trade bloc. Market access initiatives have been pursued in both multilateral trade negotiations seeking trade liberalization and in bilateral demands that the EU comply with its obligations under GATT to compensate for any higher levels of trade barriers imposed on U.S.-made goods when new countries join the EU.

Since the inception in 1958 of what is now called the European Union, U.S. trade policy has experienced a mixed record of successes and failures in efforts to maximize the benefits and minimize the commercial costs of the building of an integrated European market. The latter's contribution to greater European prosperity has advanced U.S. foreign policy objectives while simultaneously increasing certain categories of U.S. exports. At the same time, however, the unavoidable downside of the EU is that it has closed off or threatened to close off the lucrative European market to other categories of U.S. goods, especially agricultural exports. The result has been a steady state of acrimony and threats of retaliation and counterretaliation. In short, U.S. trade policy has never encountered anything like the EU's unique institutions and programs that were created explicitly to implement an unprecedented effort in collective sovereignty and regional economic integration.

The EU's Institutional Framework: Evolution and Operation

The member countries of the EU are exceptions to the rule that sovereign nations conduct their own external trade policies. As a supranational institution the overriding purpose of which is to provide the framework for an economically integrated Europe, the EU was empowered by the Treaty of Rome, which created the Common Market in 1958 to conduct external trade relations on behalf of its member countries and to harmonize economic policies. Optimists see the European Union as a work still in progress. They assume that the body of community law will continue expanding and that EU law's expanding control over member countries' economic policies will continue proliferating until the process causes a spillover into the political realm. The result would be the emergence of a federally administered "United States of Europe."

It is, however, still much too early to predict the ultimate breadth and depth of Europe's regional unification. No one knows the timetable, nature, and extent of unification or the ultimate number of member countries. Failure to evolve beyond a discriminatory trade bloc is theoretically possible, as indeed is dismemberment. However, the EU already benefits from its status as the world's best symbol of "nonnationalism": individual nation-states recognizing that they can achieve far greater economic reward for their citizens in a collective effort than by individual action.

Encouraged by their success in creating the European Coal and Steel Community (ECSC) in 1951, Belgium, France, the Federal Republic of Germany, Italy, Luxembourg, and the Netherlands signed the Treaty of Rome six years later that subsequently created what was originally called the European Economic Community (EEC). Through common institutions and a harmonization of national economic policies, the EEC was designed to move to an "ever closer union" in Europe via pursuit of four economic freedoms: the free movement of goods, services, capital, and workers. Implicit in the aspiration to forge regional economic integration was the desire to submerge historically costly European nationalism into positive mutual co-operation. More specifically, regionalism was viewed as essential to (1) channeling German energies away from nationalism and in a positive direction and (2) to avoid the disastrous mistakes made after World War I to isolate and punish the defeated Germans. In July 1967 the EEC, the ECSC, and a third institution, the European Atomic Energy Community (Euratom), were merged to create what was known for the next twenty-five years as the European Community (and subsequently labeled the European Union).

The overall goal of converting individual European economies into an integrated common market has been pursued by the promulgation of new EU law through numerous regulations and directives, changes in national laws of member states, and treaties amending the Treaty of Rome. The most important of these amendments were the Single European Act of 1986 and the 1992 Treaty on European Union, popularly known as the Maastricht Treaty. The latter formally placed Western Europe on a path to political union and to economic and monetary union. The clearly defined effort to go beyond economic integration and seek common European foreign and defense policies was the genesis of the loftier term *European Union* for use as the umbrella designation for all pillars of the European unification movement.

The European Union has grown physically as well as administratively and legislatively. Neighboring countries took notice of the early successes of the EEC. The original six members accelerated their initial schedule for phasing out internal tariffs eighteen months ahead of schedule in mid-1968; intra-EU trade increased 168 percent between 1958 and 1964 while total world trade grew by only 58 percent.[8] Because they literally could not afford to be left behind, the United Kingdom, Denmark, and Ireland successfully negotiated full EU membership at the start of 1973. Membership later expanded to twelve with the accessions of Greece (in 1981) and Spain and Portugal (in 1986). Austria, Finland, and Sweden officially became EU members at the start of 1995. Additional territorial expansion occurred in 1990 when the five *Laender* (states) of the former East Germany were absorbed after German unification.

International trade flows and U.S. exports have been further altered by the EU's long-standing geopolitical strategy of offering favorable market access to the goods of a number of countries physically near or having historical ties to the bloc's member countries. The EU's "extended family" is now nothing less than global in nature. The gradual process of achieving industrial free trade with the EFTA countries, culminating in the EU-EFTA free trade agreement previously mentioned, began in 1973. The EU's Mediterranean policy consists of cooperation and association agreements providing nonreciprocal duty-free market access for manufactured exports, agricultural concessions, and financial assistance to Turkey, Malta, Cyprus, Algeria, Morocco, Tunisia, Israel, Egypt, Jordan, Lebanon, Syria, and the former republics of Yugoslavia. (External pressure, mainly from the United States, forced the EU to request the withdrawal of concessional import treatment extended to exports of its goods by the less developed Mediterranean countries that had secured preferential market access treaties; the United States argued that trade discrimination benefiting relatively wealthy EU countries was totally unjustified.) A much more limited degree of preferential market access is provided by the "Europe Agreements" signed in 1991 with Hungary, Poland, and what was then Czechoslovakia. Through the Lomé Convention, the EU extends financial aid and one-way elimination of customs duties on a large number of goods to sixty-nine less developed African, Caribbean, and Pacific countries that were once colonies of European countries.

Like all nonmember governments, the United States deals not with individual European governments but with a supranational institution, the EU Commission. The latter is the EU's version of an executive branch, modified to meet the extraordinary requirements of the evolving transfer of national economic sovereignty to regional control. The commission is currently headed by twenty commissioners, one of whom is appointed as the president. Although each member country selects a predetermined number of commissioners (two by France, Germany, Italy, Spain, and the U.K. and one each by the other ten members), once in office they are charged with acting on behalf of the EU's needs and goals, independent of instructions from national governments. The nineteen commissioners working under the president each have assigned portfolios, not unlike those of traditional cabinet ministers. The commissioners are supported by some 13,000 "Eurocrats," a large transnational civil service based mostly in Brussels (hence the use of *Brussels* as a shorthand reference for the EU).

The commission has the sole right to *propose* new actions and programs to advance the development of EU objectives and policies. It is solely responsible for implementing and administering those initiatives (after they are approved by the European Council). As part of its overall responsibility to ensure that the principles of the EU treaties and laws are respected and properly implemented, the commission possesses investigative powers, controls EU spending, and represents the EU countries in international trade negotiations.

Approval, the critical gap between proposing and implementing policy, is the power held by the EU's Council of Ministers. It is composed of cabinet ministers who represent their home countries. The council's ministerial composition varies according to the issues (e.g., trade, environment, finance) under discussion at each meeting. Discussions on matters of major importance (e.g., acceptance of new members and amendments to the major treaties) require unanimous approval to pass. In most cases, a qualified majority, defined as at least sixty-two votes (out of a total of eighty-seven allocated on a weighted basis to EU members) cast by at least ten member countries, is sufficient for approval. The council represents the residual link between national sovereignty and communitywide action. As such, it is the key decisionmaking institution in approving (but not conducting) the EU's negotiating position in trade relations with the United States in both multilateral and bilateral forums.

The other major EU institutions, the European Parliament, the European Council (twice yearly meetings by the member countries' heads of government), and the

Court of Justice, are predominantly internal in nature, exerting no day-to-day direct impact on U.S. trade interests.

The "living" institutions of the EU are its common policies that serve as the paths to the end of a single European market. Common policies are necessary to harmonize economic practices among member states in such a way as to make national borders in Europe as irrelevant to the planning and conduct of business on the Continent as state borders are to economic transactions within the United States.

The most important of these common policies for the EU is the virtually completed trade policy involving internal free trade and erection of common import barriers and export incentives. The common commercial policy is supplemented by a number of internal common policies in various stages of finalization. For example, to promote a common business environment among member countries, the EU has pursued harmonization of fiscal policy by aligning national rules on indirect taxes such as value-added sales taxes and excise taxes.

Achievement of a genuine single market in Western Europe is inconsistent with constant fluctuations among the exchange rates of the EU member countries, just as the United States could not function as a single economic entity if each state had its own exchange rate. Hence efforts are being made to create a common monetary policy, the first step of which takes the form of efforts to keep the values of EU member countries' exchange rates fixed against one another. This effort has collided violently with the technical problems inherent in keeping exchange rates fixed between countries whose domestic economic trends are moving in opposite directions. Massive exchange rate speculation in 1992 and 1993 caused the de facto suspension of the fixed exchange rate rules of the European Monetary System (an interim step to monetary union). However, the long-term prognosis is good for eventual attainment of monetary union. Achievement of the so-called Stage III sometime early in the next century would bring about monetary union through the creation of a single European central bank that would manage a single European currency, the Ecu, the projected replacement for the national currencies of all EU countries.

The imperative of economic policy harmonization has also inspired efforts in pursuit of

- a common transport policy dealing with trucking, railway, aviation, and inland waterways regulation;
- a common competition policy to prevent corporations from forming cartels or gaining abusive dominant market position as well as to prevent member governments from bestowing special treatment on favored businesses;
- a common research and technology development policy through which financial and scientific resources are pooled in joint efforts to achieve technological advances in high-tech industries;
- a common environmental policy to maximize consistency in national laws limiting pollution, regulating the disposal of hazardous wastes, protecting natural resources, and so on;

- a common energy policy built upon the absence of internal barriers and efforts to seek security of supply.

Common regional and social policies are also in force with the objective of reducing income disparities between the various regions of the EU. In order to promote equity and to minimize internal economic distortions, the European Social Fund and the European Regional Development Fund are used as vehicles to channel regional development loans to and sponsor labor enhancement programs in the EU's poorer regions.

As part of the larger framework of the European Union, an effort is under way to define and implement a Common Foreign and Security Policy. The objective is to foster common policies and joint actions in the international political sector—up to and including a common defense policy.

The last but far from least significant common economic policy is the Common Agricultural Policy (CAP). Often called the "political glue" holding the EU together, the CAP has been the single biggest irritant in U.S.-EU trade relations since the 1970s. It began as a political and economic bargain between France and Germany. French farmers received a Continental market for their produce as well as subsidies that were paid for largely by West Germany's contribution to the EU budget. As stated in Articles 39 and 40 of the Treaty of Rome, the major objectives of the CAP are ensuring adequate incomes for farmers, raising agricultural productivity, stabilizing agricultural markets and providing for food security, and providing reasonable prices for consumers. On a more practical level, EU farmers have long possessed political clout disproportionately greater than their numbers. European governments have perceived great political benefits from meeting the economic demands of this vociferous swing vote demanding higher prices for farm goods, and urban consumers have never mobilized to force reforms in the relatively high costs of the CAP.

The mechanics of the CAP, first implemented in 1962, are built on the notion of uniform prices throughout the EU for all major crops produced in member countries. To oversimplify slightly, a target price is established for each product that, until the reforms of 1992, triggered official market intervention to provide a guaranteed minimum price—at levels sufficiently high to please European farmers—for an unlimited amount of production of any commodity covered under the CAP. This commitment had the domestic effect of dramatically increasing EU agricultural production, turning the region from a net importer of most commodities in the 1960s to a self-sufficient or surplus producer of many commodities in the 1980s.

The internal market distortions unleashed by the CAP have had two important implications for international agricultural trade in general and U.S. trade flows in particular. First, given the fact that politically selected EU target prices normally are well above world prices for agricultural goods, a "variable levy" is employed to impose whatever level of tariff protection is necessary to discourage the entry of competitive imports by raising their prices above target prices (again, this is a slight oversimplification of the process). To the extent that lower-priced imports are allowed into any region or country guaranteeing farm prices higher than world prices, unrestrained import inflows would cause massive hemorrhages from the local treasury. The latter would be forced to finance official purchases of vast unsold amounts of domestic production. Even with the protectionist effects of the variable levy, the EU commits more than $25 billion annually, about 60 percent of its total budget, to agricultural support programs.

The second international implication of the CAP is its use of export subsidies to reduce the growing stockpiles of surplus agricultural production, colorfully referred to in such terms as "butter mountains" and "wine lakes." Since the CAP for many years set minimum prices for most crops without effectively limiting production, overproduction became a constant problem, one that was at least partially relieved by exporting at "discount" prices (i.e., dumping). The EU's export subsidy pays farmers the difference between their (relatively high) support prices and world prices, thereby making commercial price competitiveness irrelevant.

The Tokyo Round of GATT trade negotiations in the 1970s permitted agricultural export subsidies so long as they were not used by countries to earn a more than "equitable" share of world markets. Throughout the 1980s, the United States objected strenuously to EU export subsidies, arguing that they constituted an unfair trade practice and reduced U.S. world market share beyond a reasonable amount. After failing to persuade the EU to restrain its agricultural export subsidies, the U.S. government countered by introducing its own export subsidy program in 1985 in an effort to respond in kind. Limitations on agricultural export subsidies were later agreed to in the Uruguay Round (see Chapter 13).

The EU has strongly defended the CAP, something it believes to be a cornerstone of postwar West European cooperation. Spokespersons point out that even with the variable levy, the EU has remained a large and growing overall market for U.S. agricultural exports, mainly for commodities not covered by the CAP. Between 1960 and 1980, the U.S. agricultural surplus with the nine countries that were EU members after 1973 rose from $1.4 billion to $7 billion.[9] Although it moved from being a net importer to a net exporter of some agricultural goods, the EU contends that this occurred in part because of CAP financing for rationalization and increased productivity among its farmers. The EU also argues that U.S. farmers receive extensive subsidies, and that their troubles during the 1980s should not be blamed on the EU but rather on high U.S. interest rates, the strong dollar, and increasing competition for export markets from some developing countries.

Family Feuds

Beneath the complexity and volume of the occasionally strained U.S.-EU trade relationship is the larger reality of a strong bond of friendship. Based on shared economic, political, and social values as well as a stoical tolerance of the other side's occasionally shrill rhetoric, this bond has withstood a long series of highly publicized trade disputes. Almost all of these problems have been satisfactorily resolved by an effective, if sometimes slow to materialize, system of conflict resolution that has minimized interruptions of trade flows. In most cases, amid the sound and fury of trans-Atlantic accusations and recriminations, amicable settlements eventually are reached to dramatically pull the two sides back from the early stages of yet another trade war.

Although the often colorful U.S.-EU fights grab the headlines, the real tenor of economic relations was captured in an official EU publication: "The bulk of . . . economic activity between our two, essentially open, economies proceeds in a smooth and trouble-free manner."[10] Similarly, a U.S. government statement made one year later in 1993 noted that "while the United States is often openly critical of a number of EC trade practices . . . the EC does have a largely open trading regime."[11] It is for these reasons that the European Union and the United States have been able to join forces to guarantee the successes of a long line of GATT-sponsored multilateral trade negotiations to reduce and eliminate governmental trade barriers.

The ugly side of bilateral relations is illustrated by occasional disdain for *specific* economic policies pursued by the other side. Frustration has produced such hyperbole as a U.S. undersecretary of state in 1986 publicly asserting that the Common Market was "probably the most disruptive factor in the world trading system."[12] Former West German Chancellor Helmut Schmidt, angry at U.S. monetary and fiscal policies in 1984, claimed that "the economic mess today is a greater danger . . . to the coherence and political stability of the alliance than the Soviet threat."[13]

From the beginning, the United States provided enthusiastic, unqualified support to efforts to create European economic unification. Regional cooperation was viewed as a means of promoting peace in Western Europe and of assuring the economic strength and political stability needed to counter the military threat from the east. During the ten years following the creation of the EU in 1958, the benefits from attaining U.S. geopolitical objectives heavily outweighed the moderate commercial costs of trade discrimination against U.S. goods. The upsurge in European economic growth created a visible triumph over the dismal economic conditions in communist-controlled Eastern Europe at the same time that it stimulated U.S. exports to the EU. The prospect of selling to a single European market attracted waves of profitable U.S. foreign direct investment (the value of such investment in EU countries jumped from $6 billion in 1960 to $201 billion in 1992).[14] Furthermore, the successful conclusions of the U.S.-inspired Dillon and Kennedy rounds of multilateral tariff reduction negotiations in the 1960s suggested that (except in agriculture) the EU was more outward- than inward-looking.

The end of the U.S.-EU honeymoon coincided with the fading of the so-called golden age of international economic prosperity and the decline of U.S. trade fortunes, both of which materialized in the late 1960s. The 1970s brought a global upsurge in inflation, international monetary instability, two energy crises, and an embrace by both Western Europe and the United States of more protectionist attitudes. Most West European countries witnessed declines in both their economic growth rates and their optimism about the future. Changing priorities in U.S. international economic policy caused a fundamental shift in the U.S. government's calculation of its national interests vis-à-vis Western Europe. It was time for the United States to emphasize the enhancement of domestic economic interests.

The thrust of U.S. trade policy toward the EU in the 1970s therefore shifted from unequivocal advocacy to suspicion, occasional hostility, and a legalistic determination to have the customs union conform fully with its obligations under the GATT, such as paying compensation whenever "bound" tariffs (duties previously reduced as the result of official agreements in GATT trade negotiations) are raised. Despite its emphasis on nondiscriminatory, most-favored-nation treatment, the GATT sanctions the creation of customs unions (as well as free trade areas) with the stipulations that "substantially all" internal trade be liberalized and that the level of trade barriers mutually imposed on nonmembers will "not on the whole be higher or more restrictive" than the level of barriers prevailing among the member countries prior to creation of the customs union. In addition, the United States, believing itself to be the leading practitioner of liberal trade policies, embarked on a crusade to have the EU behave in a similar manner so as to prevent creation of the dreaded "Fortress Europe."

The resulting tensions and Europe's profound disagreement with the U.S. reading of the situation generated a surface mood of animosity and recurring conflict. A basic quantitative measure of this atmosphere is the frequency with which the EU and the United States have utilized the GATT dispute settlement process in an attempt to resolve bilateral disagreements. The two sides squared off as the "defendants" and "plaintiffs" in almost one-third (twenty-six of eighty) of what were in effect international lawsuits heard by GATT tribunals between 1960 and 1985. The two trade powers filed more complaints against each other in these tribunals than were filed by any third party.[15]

The series of trade frictions that have dominated bilateral U.S.-EU trade relations since the early 1970s have a few similarities with U.S.-Japanese trade relations (e.g., vociferous U.S. concerns about market access) but for the most part have been different. In the first place, U.S. trade policy initiatives and complaints toward the EU have been more heterogeneous in that they frequently deal with issues outside the range of traditional protectionism. Transatlantic trade relations have lacked the relatively neat, continuous symmetry of U.S. demands for an end to closed Japanese markets and demands that the Japanese adopt voluntary export restraints.

A second distinction is the overwhelming preponderance of disputes involving sectors other than newly developed, advanced technologies. Unlike in the Japanese-U.S. relationship, EU-U.S. trade frictions have mostly involved agriculture and mature industries like steel; the dispute over Airbus (discussed later) is the main exception. A third basic difference from the Japanese problem is the relative absence of disputes involving U.S. perceptions of excessive export zeal and unacceptably large bilateral trade balance disequilibria. Finally, neither the United States nor the EU has accused the other of practicing a distinctive brand of capitalism or behaving like an "adversarial trader."

A classic example of the sui generis, dispute-escalation-followed-by-settlement nature of post-1960s U.S.-European trade relations involved the high-level 1981–1983 disagreement over appropriate economic strategy toward the Soviet Union. Specifically, the Reagan administration opposed the assistance given by several West European countries to the Soviet effort to build a natural gas pipeline from Siberia to feed into the West European gas network. EU countries strongly opposed President Reagan's year-end 1981 extension of existing U.S. export controls toward the Soviet Union to include energy-related equipment and technology.

West Europeans were livid when the administration shortly after the June 1982 Versailles summit meeting dramatically expanded the U.S. export ban on oil and gas equipment to include sales to the Soviets by overseas subsidiaries of U.S. companies and by foreign firms producing such equipment under U.S. licenses. This decision not only involved the issue of extraterritoriality, but it also was invoked retroactively to goods already under contract, thereby precipitating "an almost unprecedented clash of legal, economic, and political interests across the Atlantic."[16] U.S. companies operating in Europe were placed in a classic "damned if they do, damned if they don't" situation. They were threatened with legal sanctions both by the U.S. government if they defied U.S. export controls and by European governments if they reneged on preexisting sales contracts to export energy equipment to the Soviets.

The Reagan administration eventually backed down in the face of united European opposition that threatened to cause a major schism in the Atlantic alliance. However, the EU and the United States never did resolve their sharp differences of opinion on four major points of political economy: whether economic cooperation or isolation was the best means of modifying undesirable Soviet behavior; whether the Europeans were setting themselves up for a dangerous degree of vulnerability to a Soviet cutoff of natural gas supplies; whether Soviet export sales of gas would significantly strengthen the Soviet economy by increasing the USSR's ability to pay for imports of Western technology; and whether the United States was being hypocritical by continuing to sell agricultural goods to the USSR.

Steel is the longest-running bilateral bone of contention in the manufactured goods sector. It is an unusually clear example of how the policies of both parties to a trade dispute can look bad. On the one hand, the United States engaged in long-running demands on its trading partners to limit steel exports to the U.S. market. On the other hand, the EU began in the 1970s to create its own version of market distortions by extended interventionist programs to cope with domestic excess capacity and declining competitiveness in steel. Consider this partial chronology of steel-related frictions:

- Stung by the first significant inroads of foreign competition, the U.S. steel industry in 1968 convinces the government to negotiate voluntary export restraints by West European and Japanese producers that lasted through 1974.
- Faced with impending imposition of severe U.S. penalty duties on imports of European steel found to be selling below fair value and benefiting from govern-

mental subsidies, the EU agrees in 1982 to limit steel shipments to an average of 5.44 percent of total U.S. consumption of specified steel products through the end of 1985.

- Unable to convince the EU countries to voluntarily restrict exports of specialty steel products not included in the 1982 agreement, the United States unilaterally imposes higher tariffs and quotas on European specialty steel as part of its efforts to reduce injury to the domestic industry. The EU retaliates by imposing import barriers on a comparable amount of U.S. manufactured goods.

- In September 1984 President Reagan announces that he will reject import relief recommended under the escape clause statute but states that the prevalence of unfair trade practices by foreign steel companies must be addressed through voluntary export restraints by all countries that are major steel exporters to the United States. A new bilateral steel pact broadens product coverage of the 1982 agreement and sets new limits for the market share of EU member countries in the United States; it is extended for two and a half years beyond its fall 1989 termination date.

- An early 1986 agreement ends a unilateral U.S. quota imposed on imports of semifinished steel from the EU as well as the latter's retaliatory barriers imposed on several U.S. goods.

The major exception to the rule that U.S.-EU trade frictions do not involve the key high-tech industries of the future is the dispute arising from U.S. assertions that the Airbus Industrie consortium became a successful competitor in the lucrative but expensive-to-enter commercial aircraft market only by exploiting substantial official subsidies provided by its four government owners (France, Germany, the U.K., and Spain). The Europeans downplay the impact (and amount) of the subsidies and assert that Boeing and McDonnell Douglas have benefited greatly from indirect U.S. government subsidies associated with U.S. defense and space programs.

Two events caused an escalation of U.S. demands for European subsidy restraints. Worldwide, new orders for commercial aircraft sharply declined in the late 1980s as airline profits went into a nosedive. In addition, U.S. patience with subsidies evaporated in the face of the German government's 1988 agreement to prevent foreign exchange losses being incurred by the new private German participant in the Airbus consortium.[17] A GATT panel found this arrangement to be in violation of the GATT subsidies code, but U.S. negotiating leverage was still limited by the difficulty of direct retaliation in a situation where the vast number of Airbus exports went to third-country markets. The Airbus issue was largely resolved by a 1992 U.S.-EU agreement. Among other things, it limits direct European governmental support to 33 percent of total aircraft development costs, eliminates production subsidies, limits indirect subsidies to commercial U.S. aircraft producers from the Department of Defense and NASA, and increases financial reporting of governmental involvement in aircraft development programs.[18]

To examine the most enduring and acrimonious West European–U.S. trade dispute, one involving traditional questions of import barriers, it is necessary to look beyond the industrial sector.

Food Fights

The United States has never brought a formal GATT challenge about the legality of the EU's Common Agricultural Policy despite two major grievances: The CAP has caused a multibillion-dollar loss of U.S. farm goods exports to Western Europe, and it has spurred the rapid ascent of the EU as a major agricultural competitor in world markets. The U.S. government has never publicly released any official estimates of lost agricultural exports to Europe on a cumulative basis. The cumulative cost of the CAP to U.S. farmers is impossible to precisely quantify because it neither closed the European market to all U.S. agricultural products, nor was its restrictive impact on affected commodities uniform or immediate.

The U.S. government's disdain for the external effects of the CAP is clearly demonstrated in the 1986 congressional testimony of Thomas Kay, at the time administrator of the Foreign Agricultural Service. He said that after generating large agricultural surpluses in a period of sagging world demand, the European Union (which he referred to as the European Community) "has then used export subsidies to dump its surpluses, causing serious damage to U.S. export earnings in third country markets. ... EC export subsidies have significantly depressed world grain prices."[19] As noted previously, the U.S.-EU disagreement is not over the existence of agricultural subsidies because by international agreement they are legitimate as long as they do not lead to an "inequitable" world market share. The disagreement has literally centered around the possibility that EU subsidies had gone too far in expanding agricultural exports.

The long, mostly unsuccessful U.S. efforts to chip away at the CAP's trade-distorting effects have fallen into three separate categories. One consisted of many years of futile demands for reduced EU agricultural export subsidies.

The second set of initiatives entailed repeated demands, backed by threats and occasional acts of retaliation, that the EU provide either reductions in import barriers or adequate compensation (reduced trade barriers in other goods) for U.S. exports lost because of inflexible agricultural import barriers. The first major skirmish in the U.S.-EU agricultural trade conflict, the aptly named "Chicken War," served notice that future disagreements could easily escalate beyond words into action. In 1962 the initiation of the CAP's variable levy raised a bound tariff on frozen poultry, thereby causing U.S. exports to fall as fast as they had earlier increased. When the EU refused to meet U.S. demands for compensation owed under GATT rules, the United States in 1963 retaliated by raising tariffs (on an MFN basis as required by GATT) on a number of goods of export interest to EU countries. These higher duties were still in effect as of 1995. One of them, on light trucks, was hurting Japanese companies by the 1980s more than the Europeans.

The frequency and relatively similar patterns of subsequent U.S. trade offensives against lost agricultural export potential in EU countries are suggested through the use, once again, of a partial chronology:

- A citrus-pasta dispute begins in the 1970s when the U.S. government cites EU tariff preferences extended to citrus fruits imported from some "associated" Mediterranean countries as discriminatory against U.S. citrus exports. When the EU blocks adoption of a GATT dispute settlement report supporting the U.S. complaint and recommending that the United States receive compensation, the U.S. government retaliates in 1985 by increasing tariffs on imports of EU pasta. (Pasta was targeted because at the time it was the subject of a separate dispute; U.S. trade officials had claimed that EU exports of pasta, a nonprimary product, were being aided by illegal subsidies.) After a failed cooling-off period and EU counterretaliation against U.S. lemons and walnuts, a comprehensive resolution is reached in August 1986.

- When Spain and Portugal enter the EU on January 1, 1986, a protracted fight and a near trade war erupt over the amount of compensation due the United States for lost agricultural exports, mainly corn and sorghum, resulting from those countries imposing the more protectionist CAP variable levy in lieu of their national tariffs. In an effort to break yet another impasse, the U.S. government announces a timetable for imposing 200 percent tariffs on an assortment of processed foods carefully selected to assure an adverse impact on the exports of all EU members. Undaunted as usual, the EU responds by threatening to counterretaliate with increased duties on U.S. corn gluten feed and rice. Once again, the mutual desire to deescalate trade tensions prevails. An interim agreement on a formula for compensation by the EU is initialed on January 30, 1987, just hours before U.S. sanctions are scheduled to be imposed.

- In early 1988, disagreement over market access in the EU for oilseeds puts the United States and the Europeans on the path to a trade war that could have spilled over and had disastrous consequences for the Uruguay Round of multilateral trade negotiations. U.S. trade officials demand an end to CAP subsidization of oilseeds on the grounds that the subsidies are discriminatory and result in excess European production that in turn impairs the trade benefits due U.S. soybean producers from the EU's 1961 agreement to reduce to zero its duties on imports of soybeans and soybean meal. In their efforts to reverse the steady drop in the U.S. share of the EU oilseeds market, U.S. trade officials twice receive favorable rulings on their grievance against the Europeans from GATT dispute settlement panels but cannot secure a satisfactory response from the EU. The United States loses patience and announces a firm deadline of December 5, 1992, for the first installment of prohibitive tariffs (200 percent) on EU countries' agricultural goods that eventually would affect U.S. imports valued at $1 billion annually, an amount equal to the alleged damage to U.S. soybean exports by the EU's domestic subsidies.[20] Two weeks before the U.S. retaliation deadline, the two sides reach a settlement, the main thrust of which cuts back European production of oilseeds by a sufficient amount to assure that an increase in imports (presumably from the United States) would be necessary to maintain existing consumption levels.

- In the wake of the implementation of its Third Country Meat Directive in the late 1980s, the EU begins steadily to reduce the number of U.S. meat processing plants certified as meeting its new sanitary and hygiene standards. By the end of 1990, the EU effectively bans imports of U.S. beef and pork by removing all U.S. meat plants from its export-eligible list. U.S. meat producers attack the effective loss of a $100 million annual export market by alleging that the European inspection requirements are discriminatory trade barriers having no scientific justification and exceeding standards applied by the EU on domestic meat plants. Several months of meetings produce an agreement in November 1992 resolving differences on technical standards and procedures, thereby reopening the door to U.S. meat exports.

The third category of the long U.S. campaign to limit CAP-inflicted damage on U.S. agricultural exports consisted of efforts to negotiate a liberalization of barriers to agricultural trade in multilateral negotiations. This tactic was a failure for the better part of thirty years. In the Dillon Round of MTNs (1960–1961), the United States was unsuccessful in securing agreement for guaranteed access to the EU market for U.S. agricultural goods at then-existing U.S. export levels. The most significant EU agricultural concession achieved in these talks by the United States was securing duty-free exports of soybeans and corn gluten feed.[21] (This trade concession led to the 1990s conflict previously mentioned.)

In the Kennedy Round of multilateral trade negotiations (1963–1967), the United States failed in its efforts to bring domestic agricultural policies under the purview of the GATT and to liberalize the EU's agricultural trade policy. At U.S. insistence, a separate negotiating committee was created in the Tokyo Round (1973–1979) to deal exclusively with agricultural trade barriers. However, the EU's continued resistance to any substantial progress in this sector limited its agricultural concessions to little more than reduced tariffs on tobacco, beef, and poultry.[22] The long-frustrated U.S. goals of reducing CAP import barriers and export subsidies finally met with success in the Uruguay Round agreement in 1993.

Completing the Common Market:
The Europe 1992 Exercise

The euphoria surrounding the early economic success of the EU gradually gave way to a spreading malaise in the early 1980s. A growing number of West Europeans were dissatisfied with their countries' domestic economic performance and became concerned about their flagging high-technology competitiveness relative to the

United States and Japan. Skepticism about the future was conveyed through colorful new terms like *Europessimism* and *Eurosclerosis*. As seen by the business community and government officials alike, the most effective means of preventing Europe from becoming an "industrial museum" was to exploit what is perhaps the European Union's greatest advantage—market size—by removing the final layer of intra-EU trade restraints: nontariff barriers. But the move toward economic integration had stalled. As the EU commission reported in 1981, "The substance of what has been achieved is . . . being jeopardized and undermined by the fact that old barriers have survived for too long and new barriers have been created."[23] Thus was born the "European Community 1992" exercise to "complete the internal market."

Myriad nontariff barriers and other obstacles to the uninterrupted flow of commerce were delaying the creation of a genuinely integrated market in which manufacturers could design and sell identical goods anywhere in Europe with little regard to national borders. Instead of being able to adopt pan-European marketing plans, EU and non-EU firms alike faced higher costs associated with producing for twelve national markets, each with distinct testing and certification requirements, import licensing procedures, product safety standards, and so on. Germany's rigid specifications on the ingredients of beer that could be sold in that country and the mountain of paperwork required by truck drivers to haul freight from one end of the EU to the other became symbols of residual trade barriers.

The genesis of the 1992 plan for a final phase of internal trade liberalization was the EU Commission's white paper entitled "Completing the Internal Market." Issued in June 1985, the report put the economic cost of the inefficiencies associated with an unfinished common market at the equivalent of about $250 billion and laid out a comprehensive strategy for achieving full economic integration. The paper contained 280-plus legislative proposals (dubbed "directives") for approval first by the Council of Ministers and then by each member state in the form of new national laws. In this way they would be guaranteeing the "four freedoms": free movement of goods, services, capital, and people throughout the EU. The directives sought to dismantle barriers in three broad categories: (1) physical barriers, such as customs inspections and diverse immigration laws; (2) fiscal barriers, such as disparate rates of direct and indirect taxation; and (3) technical barriers, such as national differences in product standards, limitations on international capital movements, regulation of the services sector, and controls on corporate behavior (e.g., antitrust law). The Single European Act, which took effect on July 1, 1987, established both a blueprint and timetable (the end of 1992) for completion of the single market exercise. To this end, it amended the Treaty of Rome, most importantly by replacing unanimity with qualified majority voting in most areas related to the completion of the internal market.

Once fully operational and in their final form, the specific economic reforms that composed "EC 1992" are expected to create increased production efficiencies, more vigorous competition, and enhanced diffusion of technology throughout the region. In *The European Challenge, 1992: The Benefits of a Single Market,* a widely read 1988 semiofficial report, Paolo Cecchini estimated the prospective gains from the single market program to be a one-time increase in EU gross domestic product of 4.3 percent to 6.5 percent ($212–$312 billion), the creation of 2 million jobs, and consumer prices that would be 6 percent lower than otherwise.[24]

U.S. industry generally favored the move to completing the internal European market, largely because most U.S. multinational corporations with subsidiaries on the Continent had long emphasized a regional marketing approach and were therefore well positioned to take advantage of further internal European trade liberalization. However, U.S. business also expressed a number of concerns regarding discriminatory elements of the program, and the U.S. government promptly responded by creating interagency groups to monitor proposed changes. In several cases, the U.S. government agreed that U.S. commercial interests were threatened and immediately intervened with the EU Commission in an effort to secure changes in draft directives before they were finalized and sent to member countries for ratification. For the most part, as the USTR noted, the EU "responded positively to U.S. concerns and modified or removed the offending provisions" before adopting the directives.[25]

For example, U.S. businesses were initially concerned with the EU's demand for full reciprocity in several sectors, most notably in banking. Arguing that the single European market would provide new benefits to foreign companies doing business there, the EU demanded that its companies in these sectors operating overseas should receive the same treatment from host governments that foreign companies would receive within the newly liberalized European market.[26] In mid-1989 the U.S. government successfully lobbied the EU to apply instead the principle of national treatment, in which foreign firms are subjected to the same regulations and benefits as are domestic firms.

Less amenable to resolution were U.S. concerns about uncertainties in standards, testing, and certification activities. At issue were the details and simplicity of new European product standards in general, and whether the EU would authorize U.S. test labs and quality control boards to certify that U.S. exports meet EU legal requirements.[27]

Conclusions and Outlook

Debates about the appropriate course for U.S. trade policy toward the EU are still dominated by a consensus preference for continued efforts at mutual accommodation and conflict resolution. The underlying assumption is that the U.S. and EU common heritage and interdependent economies make nonsensical any course of action other than maximized efforts to keep bilateral economic relations on a steady, cooperative course. Implicit in U.S. advocacy of preserving harmony is the assumption that an enlightened but firm U.S. approach is the best strategy for preventing the EU's retreat into the dreaded "Fortress Europe." The possibility of a radical upgrade in the distant future of U.S.-EU economic cooperation was suggested by positive responses in 1995 to initial trial balloons advocating negotiation of a Trans-Atlantic Free Trade Area between the two sides.

The number one threat to preservation of the U.S.-EU policy status quo over the long term is less an impending incompatibility of economic interests than the new global political situation. The strong centripetal force exerted by the mutually perceived need to preserve at all costs the political-military alliance is dissipating commensurate with declining fears of Russian expansionism. The marginalization of NATO (compared to its cold war preeminence) likely will lead to a diminished tolerance by both the United States and the EU of each other's injurious trade practices, perhaps encouraging the ascendancy of hard-liners on both sides.

Ironically, Asia may become one of two major variables determining the tone of future U.S. trade relations with Western Europe. Increased mutual fear of rising economic competition from Japan, China, and the newly industrialized countries (e.g., South Korea and Taiwan) should provide the Atlantic alliance with a common external economic threat that at least partially picks up the slack left by the cold war's conclusion.

It is possible that the EU may increasingly adopt what could be termed regional economic nationalism, no matter what the United States does. Intensified discrimination against nonmembers of the EU could develop under either or both of two scenarios. The first consists of EU institutional strains that could result from the burden of accommodating a large number of new members or from nationalistic second-guessing about final movement into full monetary union. The second scenario is a further, rapid diminution of European global competitiveness induced by relatively high labor costs, expensive governmental social programs, and so on. In either of these two cases, EU member countries would be loathe to improve nonmembers' access to their single market and might well reduce it. In either case, the result would be increasing numbers of Americans becoming convinced that the economic costs of discrimination against nonmembers of the EU had grown larger than the political benefits of European integration.

Increased frustration with an inward turn by the European Union would add credibility to the vocal minority of U.S. trade critics who would prefer to relegate the Atlantic orientation of U.S. international economic policy to a completed chapter in history. The proposed new focus is Asia and the Pacific Community. This region is now the locus of the majority of U.S. trade flows, the site of the world's most dynamic, fastest-growing economies, and presumably a fertile ground for regional trade liberalization and integration.

For Further Reading

Archer, Clive, and Fiona Butler. *The European Community: Structure and Process.* New York: St. Martin's Press, 1992.

European Community. "The European Community in the Nineties." 1992.

Gianaris, Nicholas V. *The European Community and the United States: Economic Relations.* New York: Praeger, 1991.

House Foreign Affairs Committee. *Europe and the United States: Competition and Cooperation in the 1990s.* Washington, D.C.: U.S. Government Printing Office, June 1992.

Hufbauer, Gary Clyde, ed. *Europe 1992: An American Perspective.* Washington, D.C.: Brookings Institution, 1990.

Pinder, John. *The European Community: The Building of a Union.* New York: Oxford University Press, 1991.

Swann, Dennis. *The Economics of the Common Market.* 6th ed. London: Penguin Books, 1988.

Tsoukalis, Loukas. *The New European Economy.* New York: Oxford University Press, 1993.

U.S. International Trade Commission. *The Effects of Greater European Integration Within the European Community on the United States.* (An initial report and five follow-up reports have been issued, 1989–1993.)

Notes

1. European Community, "European Unification: The Origins and Growth of the European Community," 3rd ed., 1990, p. 21.

2. The European Union accounts for a greater flow of trade than the NAFTA area when both intra-EU trade ($927 billion in imports in 1992) and trade with nonmember countries ($632 billion of imports in 1992) are included. Data from EU Information Office, Washington, D.C.

3. "U.S.-European Economic Relations," U.S. Department of State press release, December 16, 1981, p. 5.

4. Glennon J. Harrison, "The European Union: The World's Largest Trading Bloc," Congressional Research Service report, December 22, 1994, p. 5.

5. European Community, "E.C.-U.S. Relations, Progress Report," no. 1, July 1993, p. 2.

6. Glennon J. Harrison, "U.S.–European Union Trade and Investment," Congressional Research Service report, December 20, 1994, p. 6.

7. U.S. Department of Commerce, *Survey of Current Business,* July 1993, p. 52.

8. European Community Information Office, Washington, D.C.

9. U.S. Department of State, "U.S. Trade with the European Community, 1958–1980," special report no. 84, June 28, 1981, p. 4.

10. Commission of the European Communities, "General Overview of EC/US Relations," July 3, 1992, p. 1.

11. Office of the U.S. Trade Representative, "Trade Policy Review Mechanism: The European Communities, Statement by the United States, May 18–19, 1993," p. 1.

12. *New York Times,* April 8, 1986, p. D1.

13. *Washington Post,* January 15, 1984, p. A19.

14. Data from U.S. Department of Commerce, *Survey of Current Business,* various issues.

15. Robert E. Hudec, "Legal Issues in US-EC Trade Policy: GATT Litigation 1960–1985," in R. Baldwin, C. Hamilton, and A. Sapir, eds., *Issues in US-EC Trade Relations* (Chicago: University of Chicago Press, 1988), p. 18.

16. Stephen Woolcock, "US-European Trade Relations," *International Affairs,* Autumn 1982, p. 611.

17. International sales of aircraft are denominated in dollars, and in 1988 the dollar was depreciating relative to European currencies, thus forcing profit-shaving price adjustments by Airbus to stay competitive with Boeing.

18. John W. Fischer, "The Airbus Controversy: Revisited?" Congressional Research Service report, April 19, 1993, pp. 3–4.

19. As quoted in Donna Vogt and Jasper Womach, "The Common Agricultural Policy of the European Community and Implications for U.S. Agricultural Trade," Congressional Research Service report, May 1986, p. 16.

20. Charles Hanrahan, "The U.S.–European Community Oilseeds Dispute," Congressional Research Service memorandum, November 13, 1992, pp. 1–3.

21. Charles Hanrahan, Penelope Cate, and Donna Vogt, "Agriculture in the GATT: Toward the Next Round of Multilateral Trade Negotiations," Congressional Research Service report, April 1986, pp. 17–18.

22. *Ibid.,* pp. 22–27.

23. As quoted by Dennis Swann, "The Single Market and Beyond: An Overview," in Swann, ed., *The Single European Market and Beyond* (London: Routledge, 1992), p. 13.

24. Paolo Cecchini, *The European Challenge, 1992: The Benefits of a Single Market* (Brookfield, Vt.: Gower Press, 1988), pp. 98–102.

25. U.S. Trade Representative, *1991 Trade Policy Agenda and 1990 Annual Report,* p. 62.

26. In the original Second Banking Directive, the EU stated that mirror-image reciprocity would become a precondition for foreign banking entry. Thus for U.S. banks to operate there, European banks would have to be given the same freedom to operate in the United States as U.S. banks enjoyed in the EU (e.g., the right to operate in any member state). This raised alarms in the United States, where banking laws are far more stringent and banks are also subject to state laws. For example, U.S. commercial banks at that time could not operate on a nationwide basis, and they are strictly limited in their investment banking activities, a practice allowed in Europe.

27. Another major source of bilateral conflict was certain provisions of the EU's Utilities Directive, an edict that regulates governmental telecommunications, water, transport, and energy procurement contracts. The directive permits discrimination against bids from nonmember countries that do not contain a minimum of 50 percent local content and requires that non-EU tenders must be 3 percent lower than the lowest EU bid to be given consideration. In response, U.S. Trade Representative Mickey Kantor announced in February 1993 that trade sanctions would be applied to the EU if the discriminatory provisions of the Utilities Directive were not liberalized. In a partial compromise, the Europeans secured a slight easing in discriminatory U.S. procurement rules and in turn agreed to open their public purchases of power generating equipment to non-EU firms in a nondiscriminatory fashion. However, the EU refused to end discriminatory treatment in the awarding of governmental contracts for telecommunications equipment. The U.S. government retaliated as promised, albeit on a more limited basis than originally threatened, prohibiting most EU countries from bidding on several kinds of federal contracts.

11   Trade Relations with the Nonindustrialized Countries

The less developed countries (LDCs) and countries in transition from communism account for the vast majority of both the world's population and number of sovereign countries in the world today. Nearly 150 nation-states belong to this group—if all the the former Soviet republics, China, and the least developed East European countries are included. Most of the LDCs of the so-called Third World (also referred to as the South) share a certain alienation from the global trading order through their belief that the rich developed countries have dominated the system in a manner that assures that the interests of the North are served first and foremost and that relegates the special needs and problems of the LDCs to secondary importance.

Beyond this common grievance, the LDCs collectively share little in common. They consist of an extremely disparate group of national economies encompassing oil-rich, high per capita income countries (Saudi Arabia, United Arab Emirates), technologically advanced countries (South Korea, Singapore), "upper level" moderately developed countries (Thailand, Chile), "lower level" moderately developed countries (Indonesia, India), and the desperately poor (Somalia, Chad). LDCs include not only countries with stagnant economies, like Afghanistan, but also the fastest-growing economy in the world today—China.

Sheer numbers as well as the economic and geographical diversity of the LDCs preclude the possibility of a single, all-purpose U.S. trade policy toward them. Some LDCs, such as those in sub-Saharan Africa, account for minimal trade with the United States and are not of major national security interest to U.S. foreign policy. But some advanced LDCs, such as Mexico, Saudi Arabia, South Korea, and Brazil, are economically and politically important and thus rank just slightly below the major industrial countries on the list of U.S. trade priorities. Russia is of extraordinary national security importance.

U.S. trade policies toward the nonindustrialized countries therefore need to be considered on a disaggregated basis. Thus U.S. trade relations with these countries are discussed here from several different angles. On a functional basis, the unique aspects of U.S. economic relations with LDCs are examined. This is followed by a survey of (1) the legislatively approved programs designed to assist them, and (2) the protectionist U.S. policies that respond to domestic needs but at the LDCs' expense. Finally, the three major geographic segments of U.S. trade relations are examined—

those involving Latin America, the newly industrialized economies of East Asia, and the countries in transition: China, the former Soviet Union, and Eastern Europe.

Unique Aspects of U.S.-LDC Trade Relations

Aside from their heterogeneous national economies and diverse trade performances, the LDCs pose extraordinary considerations for U.S. trade policy that transcend traditional commercial considerations. Since the 1950s, the United States has been committed to help alleviate poverty and promote economic development among LDCs for both moral reasons and national security reasons. Originally, foreign aid outlays were justified as cold war–related efforts "to win the hearts and minds" of LDCs so as to dissuade them from entering the Soviet orbit. U.S. belief in the magic of the marketplace as well as limited budgetary resources by the 1980s produced a policy emphasis on the desirability of "trade, not aid." This concept proclaims that economic self-help, not charity, is the best means of fostering economic development in the South. Global economic efficiency is maximized to the extent that industrial countries purchase goods competitively produced in the LDCs. A "win-win-win" situation develops because (1) domestic consumers in the industrialized North benefit from low-cost imports; (2) market-oriented economic development in the South is promoted; and (3) exports by industrialized countries to LDCs eventually are boosted (by enhanced LDC earnings of hard currency).

Nevertheless, like all other industrial countries, the United States has practiced a degree of hypocrisy in its trade relations with the countries of the South. In doing so, it has restricted the ability of its own citizens to import goods made more cheaply in LDCs, many of which are sufficiently poor or strategic to be foreign aid recipients. This book's now-familiar thesis of the government's need to balance domestic against international priorities is the reason for the propensity of import restraints to get in the way of import encouragement from the LDCs. More specifically, many citizens in the industrialized countries view the relatively cheap, nonunionized, often exploited labor in the LDCs as a particularly dangerous threat to domestic jobs. Part of this fear is fully justified: The LDCs' comparative advantage in the production by low-skilled workers of labor-intensive goods (e.g., low-priced apparel, radios, umbrellas, and baseball gloves) is empirically demonstrable. The abstract argument that it is an economically justifiable trend for the United States (or any other country) to be constantly upgrading its labor force and production patterns is lost on low-skilled, low-paid U.S. workers who lose their jobs to imports and who are unable to find better ones. Furthermore, the tolerance of the United States for unrestricted imports from LDCs is undermined by the potentially serious competitive effects of combining cheap labor in LDCs with manufacturing technology and equipment shipped in by multinational corporations.

Industrialized countries' limits on imports from the LDCs notwithstanding, the relative importance of trade over foreign aid as a source of precious foreign exchange to the LDCs is an economic fact of life. The $667 billion of total imports by industrialized countries from the LDCs in 1992 was more than ten times the amount ($61 billion) of estimated official development assistance given in that year by the North.[1] The impact of this import total on the LDCs as a whole is somewhat exaggerated because it includes oil purchases of about $135 billion and imports from the four newly industrialized countries of about $150 billion. The United States provided a total of $11.7 billion in official development assistance in 1992 (much of which went to just two countries, Egypt and Israel) at the same time that its imports from the LDCs totaled $191.5 billion, of which about $40 billion consisted of oil imports.[2] To state the result another way, annual U.S. imports from the LDCs are now more than triple the amount of total foreign aid from all the OECD (Organization for Economic Cooperation and Development) countries. (It would be to the LDCs' maximum economic benefit to earn more foreign exchange from grant aid than from exporting, since the latter involves the shipment overseas of real economic resources in exchange for hard currency.)

Trade relations with LDCs as a whole do not receive the same top priority accorded by the U.S. government to the European Union, Japan, or multilateral trade negotiations. The gap is narrowing, however. Increased attention to LDC trade policy is necessitated by the growing number of developing countries in Asia and Latin America (e.g., Indonesia and Brazil) that are large and rapidly growing overseas markets for U.S. companies or that are major suppliers of manufactured goods and primary products. Of total U.S. exports in 1993, 41 percent, or $191 billion, went to developing countries; 41 percent of total imports, or $240.3 billion, arrived from these countries. Of the top twenty U.S. trading partners (imports and exports combined) in 1993, eleven were classified as LDCs (except for Saudi Arabia, they were all in East Asia and Latin America).[3] LDCs also account for the fastest-growing overseas markets for U.S. goods: Between 1990 and 1992, U.S. exports to developing countries increased on average 12.7 percent per year, but those to industrialized countries grew only 3.5 percent.[4] Between 1987 and 1993, U.S. exports to developing countries increased by 119 percent, whereas exports to developed countries increased by only 65 percent; exports to the former were 70 percent as large as exports to the latter in 1993, up from 53 percent in 1987.[5]

LDCs, especially in the Middle East and parts of Africa, are also of critical importance as a source of imports of raw materials either not produced in the United States or produced in amounts inadequate to meet domestic demand. The most important example of the latter is petroleum; imports in 1994 were heading toward a 50 percent share of total U.S. oil consumption. Nearly 80 percent of U.S. petroleum imports is provided by nonindustrialized countries (see Table 11.1).

TABLE 11.1   Top Ten Suppliers of Petroleum Products to the United States in 1993 (imports in millions of dollars)

Total U.S. oil imports	49,685
Total U.S. oil imports from OPEC countries	24,624
Saudi Arabia	7,345
Venezuela	7,050
Canada	6,761
Nigeria	5,222
Mexico	4,808
United Kingdom	2,431
Angola	2,082
Kuwait	1,759
Algeria	1,330
Colombia	1,197

Source: U.S. Department of Commerce, *U.S. Foreign Trade Highlights, 1993.*

If Russia and the former Soviet republics are included, LDCs also account for a disproportionate amount of the major industrial raw materials on which the United States is heavily import-dependent (see Figure 11.1).

Virtually absent in the ensuing discussion of U.S. trade relations with the LDCs is any mention of U.S. trade policies designed specifically to deal with Africa. The reason is that there are no significant policies to speak of. The U.S. trade incentives and trade barriers discussed in the next section have relatively little impact on Africa, a continent that continues to account for a minuscule portion of U.S. trade flows. Exclusive of Egypt (a major recipient of U.S. foreign aid), U.S. exports to Africa were valued at $6.7 billion in 1993, a little more than 1 percent of total shipments. Nonoil U.S. imports from African countries (excluding South Africa, a major supplier of industrial raw materials) in 1993 amounted to about $2.5 billion, a mere 0.004 percent of total U.S. imports.[6]

U.S. LDC Trade Policy Giveth and Taketh

U.S. trade policy toward the LDCs is yet another example of the relevance and utility of the integrating thesis of this book: U.S. trade policy is ultimately a trade-off between contrasting priorities, a reconciliation of a search for a reasonably balanced position somewhere between the opposite poles of completely free trade and pervasive protectionism. U.S. trade policies in general and toward the LDCs in particular are always calibrated in a manner to keep them from going too far in any one direction. On the one hand, there is a benevolent strain in U.S. trade policy. The ethical desire and foreign policy motivation to help LDCs dovetail with a basic predilection to keep the U.S. market relatively open to imports. The United States is one of the

FIGURE 11.1 *U.S. Net Import Reliance for Selected Raw Materials, 1993*
(percent of estimated U.S. consumption)

Material	Percent	Major Sources (1989-92)
Arsenic	100	Chile, China, Mexico, France
Bauxite and alumina	100	Australia, Jamaica, Guinea, Brazil, Guyana
Columbium (niobium)	100	Brazil, Canada, Fed. Rep. of Germany
Graphite	100	Mexico, China, Canada, Madagascar, Brazil
Manganese	100	Rep. of South Africa, France, Australia, Brazil
Mica (sheet)	100	India, Belgium, Brazil, China
Strontium (celestite)	100	Mexico, Fed. Rep. of Germany
Thallium	100	Belgium, Canada, United Kingdom (U.K.)
Diamond (industrial stones)	98	Ireland, U.K., Zaire, Rep. of South Africa
Gemstones (natural and synthetic)	98	Israel, Belgium, India, U.K.
Asbestos	95	Canada, Rep. of South Africa
Fluorspar	89	Mexico, China, Rep. of South Africa, Canada, Morocco
Platinum-group metals	88	Rep. of South Africa, U.K., former U.S.S.R.
Tantalum	86	Fed. Rep. of Germany, Australia, Canada, Brazil
Tungsten	84	China, Bolivia, Peru, Fed. Rep. of Germany
Chromium	82	Rep. of South Africa, Turkey, Zimbabwe, Yugoslavia
Tin	81	Brazil, Bolivia, China, Indonesia, Malaysia
Cobalt	75	Zambia, Zaire, Canada, Norway
Potash	71	Canada, Israel, former U.S.S.R., Fed. Rep. of Germany
Cadmium	66	Canada, Mexico, Australia, France
Nickel	64	Canada, Norway, Australia, Dominican Republic
Barite	58	China, India, Mexico
Antimony	57	China, Mexico, Rep. of South Africa, Hong Kong
Peat	56	Canada
Iodine	51	Japan, Chile

Source: U.S. Department of the Interior, *Mineral Commodity Summaries, 1994,* p. 3.

most outspoken advocates of an international economic order in which the LDCs enlarge and strengthen their economies primarily through reliance on the private sector and an emphasis on market-oriented, nonprotectionist trade policies. As discussed later, Congress has enacted into law a number of programs, some unique to the United States, to alleviate the special trade problems of LDCs.

Furthermore, market access in the United States for goods produced in the LDCs, especially manufactures, compares favorably with that of the other industrialized countries. According to GATT figures, in the early 1980s about 40 percent of all LDC exports to developed countries went to the United States, double the level to Japan and significantly more than to all of the EU countries.[7] In the late 1980s, the United States was taking over 50 percent of the LDCs' manufactured exports, compared to less than 30 percent by the EU and 8 percent by Japan.[8] Just how receptive the U.S. market is to exports of manufactured goods from the advanced LDCs is further demonstrated by the fact that of the countries accounting for the largest bilateral U.S. deficits in manufactured goods, three of the top five and thirteen of the top eighteen in 1992 were Asian LDCs (none was in Latin America or Africa).[9]

On the other hand, a number of (mostly legislated) safety switches installed to constrain U.S. generosity take the form of limitations on increased flows of imports from the South that compete with domestic production. Included in these measures is the occasional unseemly demand by the big and rich that the relatively small and poor voluntarily restrain their exports to limit dislocations in import-sensitive sectors. Political necessity precludes the United States—as well as all other industrialized countries—from allowing labor-intensive manufacturing sectors, such as apparel, and relatively inefficient agricultural sectors, such as sugar, to face the full force of competition from low-wage countries that have a comparative advantage in such goods. The industrialized countries differ only in style and intensity in terms of manifesting inconsistencies between intent and application in their LDC trade policies.

It is an economic fact of life that LDCs are better able to pay for the imports needed to accelerate their economic growth and to repay their international debts if they are able to increase export earnings. Consequently, the United States, like all other industrialized countries, accepts in principle the obligation to increase imports, especially of manufactured goods, from developing countries. As noted in the USTR's annual report for 1992, "The creation of trade opportunities for developing countries is an effective, cost-efficient way of encouraging broad-based economic development, and a key means of sustaining the momentum behind economic reform and liberalization."[10]

The United States has been at the forefront of efforts to urge LDCs to practice liberal, export-oriented trade policies. Data consistently demonstrate that since the 1970s, the LDCs following this trade strategy have been more successful in promoting both economic and export growth than those countries employing protectionist, import-substitution policies.[11] In addition to providing this valuable advice, the United States (and other industrialized countries) consciously practices a differentiated trade policy designed to give a boost to the economies of LDCs. At the heart of this trade posture are specially designed import programs, all based on congressionally passed statutes, that specifically discriminate in favor of LDC-produced goods. Such a strategy was officially endorsed by the Tokyo Round agreement to legitimize "special and differential" trade treatment on behalf of LDCs. Approval was necessary because this approach violates the all-important GATT principle of nondiscrimination in which identical import barriers are supposed to be applied to all countries.

The most widely administered discriminatory program on behalf of the LDCs is the Generalized System of Preferences (GSP). In the early 1970s, the LDCs' demands for better market access in the North led to variants of this program being implemented by all industrialized countries. GSP provides tariff-free incentives—on a nonreciprocal basis—to exports of most (not all) manufactured goods from LDCs. A competitive edge is given to LDC goods exempted from tariffs to the extent that importing countries impose tariffs on comparable goods produced in and exported by industrialized countries.

The U.S. program of GSP allows imports of most manufactured goods of eligible countries and territories—numbering more than 140 in the mid-1990s—to enter the United States duty-free, up to certain proscribed amounts. Invariably, a relatively few advanced LDCs garner a disproportionate amount of GSP benefits—because only a few LDCs have efficient, sizable industrial sectors that are competitive. Prior to 1989, at which time they were involuntarily "graduated"—that is, removed—from the program, South Korea, Hong Kong, Singapore, and Taiwan were the major beneficiaries of tariff preferences. In 1988 they shipped more than half of all imports receiving U.S. GSP tariff-free treatment; if Brazil and Mexico were included, this figure would exceed two-thirds of total GSP benefits.[12] Since then, the same pattern of concentrated benefits has prevailed, except with different countries. In 1993 the top five beneficiaries—Mexico (graduated in 1994), Malaysia, Thailand, Brazil, and the Philippines—accounted for approximately $13.7 billion, or 70 percent, of the $19.5 billion of goods receiving duty-free treatment under GSP (Mexico alone accounted for 28 percent of the total).[13] The GSP program remains highly valued among the developing countries that can take advantage of it—so much so that U.S. trade officials have been able to use the program as a lever to get recipients to modify their trade behavior (e.g., enforcing workers' rights and intellectual property rights protection) in accordance with U.S. demands.

It is easy to look at the U.S. GSP program and complain that the glass is half empty. Critics of U.S. trade largesse can point to the program's quantitative limitations, multiple loopholes, the list of products periodically removed from duty-free eligibility, and the graduation of the four Asian NICs and Mexico. On a larger scale, critics categorize the program as a miniature version of the broader schizophrenia by which the U.S. government simultaneously seeks to support low-wage LDCs and to protect import-impacted domestic producers. Even when viewed in the best light, GSP provides benefits to only a handful of relatively advanced developing countries with competitive manufacturing sectors: The top fifteen national beneficiaries of the program regularly account for more than 90 percent of total GSP imports every year. In addition, only $19.5 billion in goods, a mere 3 percent of total U.S. imports in 1993, entered duty-free under GSP. Since total U.S. imports from GSP-eligible countries in 1993 were $123 billion, only 16 percent of their exports to the United States actually received duty-free treatment. This small share is partly explained by the exclusion from GSP of important labor-intensive goods (textiles, apparel, and most kinds of footwear) and partly by various technical factors such as quantitative "competitive need" ceilings that limit the market share of any one country for U.S. imports of specific GSP-eligible goods.[14]

In sum, the GSP program has acted as a meaningful stimulus to the manufacturing sectors of a few LDCs. Yet it is a small factor in relation to total U.S. imports and an even smaller factor in relation to total U.S. consumption.

The same qualified endorsement can be applied to the effects of two subheadings of Section 9802 of the Harmonized Tariff Schedule of the United States.[15] Goods assembled in other countries using U.S. parts and components are permitted under these provisions to be imported back into the United States with tariffs applied only on the value added in assembly—that is, the dollar value of the foreign processing. The resulting ability of U.S. companies to rationalize production and maximize cost controls by shifting labor-intensive assembly operations to low-wage countries has led to an extensive array of foreign assembly plants in some Latin American and Asian countries but most extensively in Mexico (where they are called *maquiladoras*).

Given the added attraction for foreign firms to use U.S. parts in goods they ship to the U.S. market, Section 9802 can be viewed as a mutually beneficial program. The provision is open to all countries, yet LDCs accounted for 86 percent of the $15.3 billion of U.S.-origin content imported duty-free in 1992 under the two subheadings of Section 9802. Although these duty-free imports are only a small part of all U.S. imports, goods entering under Section 9802.00.80 accounted for 48 percent of Mexico's and 54 percent of the Dominican Republic's overall shipments to the United States in 1992.[16]

Although at first glance the de facto import restraints imposed by the United States on textile and apparel products appear to be a glaring symbol of rampant protectionism, a close look at import data suggests a slightly less dramatic situation. Initiated on a multilateral basis in 1974 and extended five times since, the Multifiber Arrangement (MFA) constitutes a de facto international cartel regulating the South-North flow of textile and apparel products. It does so by providing regulatory guidelines for a series of bilateral voluntary export restraint agreements that set quantitative ceilings on allowable LDC shipments of these products to individual industrialized countries. In return for these restraints, LDC signatories get guaranteed market access and automatic annual increases in their allowable shipments. The U.S. government has negotiated bilateral agreements under the MFA that cover more than 100 specific types of textile products and apparel with some forty-five LDCs (almost all of which are in Asia, Latin America, and Eastern Europe) accounting for almost 80 percent of its import volume of these two product categories. By one estimate, clothing prices in the United States are 53 percent higher than they would be in a free trade situation; by another estimate, the MFA on a global basis is depriving LDCs of exports of about $8 billion annually (in 1986 dollars).[17] Negotiating the permanent phaseout of the MFA was understandably a priority Uruguay Round agenda item for the South.

Nevertheless, the U.S. textile and clothing industries have empirical evidence to bolster their complaints that the import restraints imposed on their products are at least as porous as they are protectionist. Inherent loopholes (new kinds of products are constantly being introduced, new fabrics are devised, new countries begin exporting, and so on) and outright cheating in the form of illegal transshipments by some countries have been responsible for a steady growth in U.S. imports of these products. (The U.S. government in 1993 alleged that China was illegally shipping textiles via third countries worth as much as $2 billion annually.)

Official U.S. trade statistics show that imports of products subjected to MFA limitations (mainly apparel) increased on average by about 11 percent annually in the 1980s. U.S. imports of textiles and apparel in 1992 (about 2.8 million kilograms) were more than four times greater than their 1980 levels. The U.S. domestic market share taken by imports increased from 12 percent in 1980 to just over one-third of total 1992 consumption.[18]

The proximity of Central American, Caribbean, and South American countries to the United States has given these countries a special status in U.S. efforts to liberalize trade. Negotiations to create a free trade area with Canada and Mexico can be viewed as merely an important first step in achieving the expressed long-term U.S. government goal of creating a Western Hemisphere free trade area "from Anchorage to Tierra del Fuego." In June 1990, President Bush stated that the United States "stands ready to enter into free trade agreements with other markets in Latin America and the Caribbean, particularly with groups of countries that have associated for purposes of trade liberalization," because free trade is a "prescription for greater growth and a higher standard of living in Latin America" and the United States.[19]

In the meantime, the United States has initiated a number of unilateral market-opening measures to provide improved access on a nonreciprocal basis for its hemispheric neighbors. Some call these efforts "too little, too late," but others see evidence of the start of a transition toward a regional trade bloc:

- The Caribbean Basin Initiative (CBI) was implemented in 1984 by the Caribbean Basin Economic Recovery Act to expand the exports of and foreign investment in twenty-four designated countries in the region, mainly by extending duty-free entry into the United States for a wide range of products. Although there is considerable overlap between the benefits extended by this program and the GSP, there are some incremental benefits. For example, the CBI has no statutory expiration date, is slightly more flexible in terms of product coverage and levels of ceilings on duty-free entry, and provides special trade benefits for imports of leather products and footwear. In addition, some U.S. officials have advocated that all free trade benefits provided to Mexico under the North American Free Trade Agreement should be extended to the Caribbean countries participating in the CBI.
- The Andean Trade Preference Act, initiated in 1992, is designed to extend approximately the equivalent of the CBI's duty-free market access benefits to Andean countries of South America (especially those engaged in the struggle against narcotics production).[20] Colombia and Bolivia have been designated as beneficiary countries with Ecuador and Peru named as potential beneficiaries.
- The Bush administration's Enterprise for the Americas Initiative is a vaguely defined economic initiative containing consultative mechanisms to promote debt relief and investment promotion efforts as well as trade liberalization programs. Attracting the most interest among South American and Caribbean countries was the provision articulating the goal of hemispheric free trade and the invitation to all interested countries to negotiate "framework agreements" to establish "principles" and a "process" for further negotiations on hemispheric trade liberalization. (Such agreements were subsequently signed with the vast majority of Latin American and Caribbean countries.) In connection with this initiative, Chile and the United States agreed in 1992 to initiate negotiations on a bilateral free trade agreement following ratification of the North American Free Trade

Agreement. The U.S. policy goal of hemispheric free trade took a giant step forward when the December 1994 Western Hemisphere summit meeting called for the initiation of negotiations to create a Free Trade Area of the Americas early in the next century.

The CBI is an apt metaphor for U.S. trade policy inconsistencies vis-à-vis the LDCs. Inconsistencies in this case are caused by the U.S. government's desire to temper its international efforts to bolster the export sectors of the Caribbean countries because of the domestic political need to protect import-sensitive constituencies. On the one hand, almost two-thirds of all U.S. imports from the CBI-eligible countries (about $6 billion) entered free of tariff duties in 1992 because of the CBI and GSP programs and because the United States imposes no duties on a limited number of goods shipped by any country receiving MFN treatment. Thanks mainly to significant, sustained growth in what are dubbed nontraditional exports (most of which are manufactured goods) from Caribbean-area countries, U.S. duty-free imports in 1992 designated as entering under the CBI initiative amounted to $1.5 billion, nearly triple the value in 1984, the initial year of the program.[21]

On the downside, U.S. trade policy toward the Caribbean countries has excluded certain key manufactured goods (e.g., apparel) from duty-free treatment, and it has failed to halt the steady lowering of the ceiling on annual U.S. sugar import quotas, an action necessitated by domestic price support considerations. Protectionist U.S. sugar policies forced a sufficiently severe decline in the traditional exports of some Caribbean countries to the United States during the 1980s so as to offset much of the recorded increase in nontraditional exports, some of which would have occurred even in the absence of the CBI (e.g., via the GSP program).[22]

Two final arguments need to be cited as part of the seemingly inconclusive debate about the true balance between generosity and protectionism in U.S. trade policies toward the LDCs. The first is the allegation by LDCs of excessive harassment of their exports. One form of this perceived harassment is repeated requests for voluntary export restraints, which effectively are negotiated export quotas. Another form is the allegedly excessive application of U.S. statutes designed to neutralize trade practices judged to be unfair and injurious—namely, dumping, governmental subsidies, and violation of intellectual property rights. In response to the latter complaint, the U.S. government can say that it is obligated to protect local producers from injury inflicted by what are internationally recognized dirty trade tricks—no matter whether the home country of the offending companies is rich or poor.

The second argument deals with the limited, unenthusiastic U.S. participation in international commodity agreements designed to stabilize the prices of key primary products exported mostly by LDCs. After a number of years of limited global demand for commodities and of declining or flat prices, LDCs' earnings of foreign exchange from commodities sales were stagnant. Throughout the early 1990s, virtually none of the few surviving commodity agreements was able to effectively reduce global oversupply of the commodity sought to be price-stabilized (the one possible exception being the natural rubber agreement). Tolerance for this situation is largely a function of one's attitude toward trusting the market mechanism to ultimately send the right message on prices as opposed to belief in the efficacy of governmental interference in the marketplace in the pursuit of fairness.

The Advanced Developing Countries of East Asia

In addition to the major oil exporters, a few countries have grown out of poverty and backwardness by building a thriving and increasingly sophisticated manufacturing sector that has been extraordinarily successful when selling in the international marketplace. The relatively sudden emergence during the 1970s of an unprecedented breed of competitor in the world economy gave rise to such new terms as *newly industrialized countries*,[23] *Little Dragons*, the *Gang of Four*, and *export platforms*. The four original NICs—South Korea, Hong Kong, Singapore, and Taiwan—eventually will be joined by a second generation consisting of Malaysia, Thailand, Indonesia, possibly China (if it is not placed in a category of its own), and for the first time, two countries outside East Asia, Brazil and Mexico.

Thus far, there are only two common denominators of the NICs' economic policies. The first is their current embrace of outward-oriented, pro-export trade strategies. Except in the case of free trade Hong Kong, these trade policies were adopted only after unsuccessful experiments with the more protectionist, inward-oriented import-substitution strategy. The second economic commonality is enlightened industrial policies (except in free market Hong Kong) that guided the development of a privately owned and operated industrial sector. Also common to the industrial sector of the NICs has been a steady shift up-market. Their first wave of exports, concentrated in low-tech goods such as apparel, gradually progressed to more sophisticated, higher-value goods like televisions, stereo equipment, semiconductors, personal computers, machine tools, and automobiles. In 1993 the United States imported goods worth $64.6 billion from the four NICs, up eightyfold from $800 million in 1967. The reverse flow reflected the NICs' economic growth and relatively open markets; U.S. exports to these four countries over the same period jumped fiftyfold from $1.1 billion to $52.5 billion.[24]

U.S. trade policies toward the NICs have gone through three phases: virtual inattention, anxiety, and most recently, upgrading them to the status of mature competitors. Once in the latter category, they are no longer considered to be LDCs with regard to international trade relations. The most significant constant of U.S. trade policy toward the four NICs has been maintenance of a relatively open market to their exports. U.S. trade officials cite a number of statistics in defense of their claim that the United States accounts for a disproportionately large percentage of the NICs' manufactured goods exports:

- In the late 1980s, the United States took nearly 50 percent of Taiwan's exports, 40 percent of South Korea's, over one-fourth of Hong Kong's, and nearly one-fourth of Singapore's; for each country, the United States represented the single largest export market and was disproportionately important as a market for sophisticated manufactured goods.[25]
- The United States absorbed about 44 percent of the NICs' export growth between 1980 and 1987, in comparison to Japan's 9 percent share.[26]
- In the late 1980s, the United States accounted for nearly 40 percent of South Korea's exports, about twice as much as Japan, a country that geographically is much closer to South Korea.[27]

The export dynamism of the NICs plus shortcomings in U.S. export competitiveness has led to a major trade disequilibrium. Among the ten largest U.S. bilateral trade deficits in manufactured goods in 1992 were those with the four NICs plus three would-be NICs: China, Malaysia, and Thailand. With Japan added, the United States incurred a manufactured goods trade deficit with eight East Asian countries that was equivalent in size to 170 percent of the total multilateral U.S. trade deficit in manufactured goods in that year ($112 billion versus $66 billion).[28] Consequently, the United States in the late 1980s successfully applied to South Korea and Taiwan (and to a much lesser extent, Singapore) some of the initiatives used in bilateral relations with Japan, namely the demand for reciprocal market-opening measures and the demand that their apparently undervalued exchange rates be allowed to appreciate in line with market forces. (Hong Kong's free trade policies have exempted them from U.S. criticism.)

By the early 1990s, the thrust of U.S. trade policy toward the NICs was completely distinct from LDC trade policy as a whole. Rather than accommodating their development needs through favorably discriminatory import programs, current U.S. trade policy toward such countries as South Korea emphasizes the advantages they would accrue by extending the process of liberalizing their international trade and financial regulations to an extent that makes them eligible for membership in the OECD. In other words, after graduating the NICs out of its GSP program, the United States began seeking to graduate at least some of the NICs from Third World to First World economic status.

A second important contemporary innovation in U.S. trade policy toward the NICs is associated with the gradual but ongoing shift in the perceived center of gravity of U.S. trade flows from Europe to East Asia. Asia-Pacific trade by the United States exceeded its total European trade by about 50 percent in 1993 ($362 billion versus $240 billion), and East Asia is generally viewed as possessing the world's most dynamic regional economy. Possibilities of increased economic cooperation and regional trade liberalization among the so-called Pacific Rim countries have become extremely fashionable topics in U.S. trade policy. For some, the beginning of a new era of cooperation among the United States, Japan, and the developing countries of the Asia-Pacific region was symbolized by the convening of the Asia-Pacific Economic Cooperation forum's first heads-of-state meeting, hosted by President Clinton in November 1993, and by the unexpected agreement to draft a timetable for a regional free trade area concluded at the summit meeting held in the following year (see Chapter 14).

Countries in Economic Transition

As the cold war fades from memory and as China and countries of the former Soviet Union and of Eastern Europe continue their unprecedented mass transition from communist-style command economies to market-oriented capitalist systems, U.S. trade policy toward these countries has undergone a fundamental shift. National security concerns still dominate commercial concerns. However, today's national security priority of promoting political stability and economic growth in these countries, particularly the former Soviet republics possessing nuclear weapons, is a 180-degree turn from the priorities of the cold war.

From the 1950s until well into the 1980s, U.S. trade policy toward these countries was commandeered by the larger goal of containing Soviet and Chinese expansionism. Trade policy therefore sought to inflict the maximum degree of economic deprivation in the hopes of fomenting radical changes in the politics of countries dominated by "international communism." Trade flows were minimized by the U.S. government through a highly restrictive system of export controls designed to prevent shipment of all military-related goods, commercial technologies having potential for dual use in the military sector (e.g., computers), and state-of-the-art capital goods that would improve the communist bloc's industrial efficiency. Imports of nonessential goods from bloc countries were discouraged by virtue of the fact that the United States denied them MFN trade status, the legal result of which was to apply the onerous Smoot-Hawley tariff rates to most of their goods. The tendency for the communist countries to retaliate in kind by using the United States only as a market of last resort further discouraged the two-way flow of trade.

During the cold war era, U.S. trade policy toward the communist bloc employed national security criteria to distinguish three categories of countries. In the first of these, the U.S. government categorically banned all trade with countries whose foreign policies were deemed unacceptably aggressive. China was on this list for almost twenty-five years. A few countries, including Cuba and North Korea, were still so designated at the end of 1994. At the opposite extreme were countries for which U.S. foreign policy strategy dictated pursuit of closer trade relations; this was accomplished by extending MFN tariff status to their exports to the United States and by easing export controls on shipments to them. Poland and later Romania and Hungary received such treatment as a de facto reward for their efforts to exert independence from the Soviet Union. The middle category consisted of countries with a moderate number of goods under export control; the most significant member was the Soviet Union.

Trade relations between the communist countries and the United States were (and are) minimal for several economic and political reasons—some of which apply today, even as these countries move toward capitalism and democracy. First, there is the elementary statistical fact that, even including China, the formerly communist countries were and are relatively small factors in global trade; they collectively accounted for a mere 5 percent of total world trade in the early 1990s.[29] Most of the foreign trade of the Soviet republics and East European countries was conducted among themselves in conformity with regional economic planning imposed by the Soviets through the Council for Mutual Economic Assistance (popularly known as COMECON). Furthermore, the small amount of trade that the bloc countries did conduct with industrialized democracies was and is concentrated in Western Europe and Japan. This pattern reflects geographic proximity as well as the effects of these countries' more relaxed approach to trade sanctions as a means of modifying Soviet behavior and retarding the growth of Soviet military strength. In other words, the United States adopted considerably more restrictive trade policies than its allies in support of national security policies.

A final factor that limited U.S. trade with communist bloc countries involved the short-lived efforts to improve Soviet-U.S. trade relations following the Nixon administration's 1972 détente initiative. These overtures were soon short-circuited by two events illustrating linkages among trade policy, trade law, and national security concerns. The first occurred when the Soviets refused to accept the conditions necessary to qualify for MFN treatment under the Jackson-Vanik amendment to the Trade Act of 1974. This provision, imposed by Congress on a reluctant Nixon administration, specifically mandated that new MFN recipients must first provide the U.S. government with "assurances" that restrictions on emigration (mainly affecting Soviet Jews) would be eased. The Jackson-Vanik amendment is another vivid example of this book's broad thesis that laws can shape U.S. trade policy in accordance with congressionally mandated political imperatives. The second event occurred some four years later when the Soviet invasion of Afghanistan put both bilateral political détente and improved trade relations on hold.

The former communist countries' participation in the international trading system is still constrained by their very limited ability to produce manufactured goods that the West wants to purchase. In turn, the resultant shortage of convertible foreign exchange and, beginning in the 1980s, a sharply diminished ability to borrow from commercial banks have limited the ability of these countries to import relative to their needs. In generic economic terms, these are the same circumstances contributing to limited trade flows between North and South.

Since the end of the cold war, U.S. economic policy toward these countries has shifted from a strategy based on containment and denial to one based on cooperation and assistance as a means of expediting the long-term development of democracy and capitalism in these former adversaries. If this book had been written before 1990, there would have been a separate chapter on a subject then important but now defunct: U.S. East-West trade policy. The largely negative elements of a policy that specifically targeted the economic systems and foreign policy of the East have been replaced by a positive series of policy initiatives that essentially replicates the generic strategy and programs long extended to friendly noncommunist LDCs. MFN tariff treatment was extended to all of those East European countries not already receiving it and to most of the countries emerging from the breakup of the Soviet Union. The policy of accommodation more recently was expanded to include (1) direct foreign aid to help ease the wrenching adjustments inflicted by the transition to market economies; (2) approval of hundreds of millions of dollars worth of new U.S. government loans and loan guarantees to finance exports of industrial and agricultural goods to Russia and the former Soviet republics; and (3) certification of eligibility in the GSP program for several former Soviet republics (the three Baltic republics and Russia were the first so designated) and most of Eastern Europe.

Despite the recent shift to a more accommodating U.S. trade policy vis-à-vis the countries in economic transition, short-term economic reality has precluded significant increases in the volume of bilateral trade (except with China). The move away from central planning and total government control of production has resulted not only in widespread decreases (in the short term) in the real GDPs of these countries but in their total foreign trade as well. The former Soviet Union experienced a dramatic decline of 47 percent (in real terms) in the value of its total exports and imports between 1989 and 1992; Eastern Europe's trade in this period declined by 9 percent.[30] That there is a lag between a more positive, nurturing U.S. trade policy and commercial reality is demonstrated by U.S. trade statistics: U.S. exports to the transition countries (excluding China) were valued at $6.1 billion in 1993, little more than 1 percent of total exports in that year. U.S. imports from these same countries of $3.5 billion in 1993 represented a meager 0.6 percent of total U.S. imports.[31]

China is the major exception to the rule of minimal U.S. trade flows and trade disputes with countries in economic transition. It is thus far the most visible example (see Table 11.2) of the commercial boom that can result when a country adopts economic reforms to move away from a command economy and when the United States seeks normalization of political relations. In the late 1970s, a competitive con-

TABLE 11.2   U.S.-Chinese Trade (millions of dollars)

	U.S. Exports	U.S. Imports
1971	nil	5
1976	135	201
1981	3,599	1,895
1986	3,106	4,771
1991	6,278	18,969
1993	8,767	31,535
1994	9,300	39,200

Sources: Unpublished U.S. Department of Commerce statistics for 1971–1990 trade flows; "U.S. Merchandise Trade," U.S. Commerce Department press release, January 19, 1995.

sumer goods sector and aggressive export tactics began to emerge in China. At the same time, the U.S. trade sanctions imposed on China in the early 1950s after it entered the Korean War were progressively phased out in accordance with the favorable tilt of U.S. foreign policy toward that country.

The boom in U.S.-Chinese trade that began in the 1980s brought with it an unusual, nearly nonstop array of frictions and confrontations. Trade tensions arose because of several factors. The U.S. government was sensitive to a dramatically large increase in its bilateral trade deficit (see Figure 11.2). More important, frictions were all but inevitable between China's hybrid part-capitalist, part-planned economic system and the market-oriented global trading system. The ability of China's factories to expand exports seemed to far outpace the ability of China's nondemocratically elected government to do two things: (1) appreciate the importance of complying with long-established rules of international commerce and (2) comprehend that the

FIGURE 11.2 U.S.-Chinese Trade (in billions of dollars)

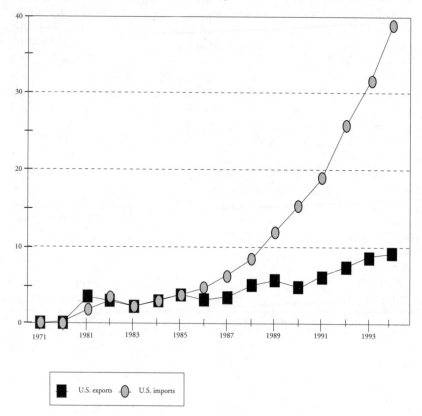

Source: Published and unpublished U.S. Department of Commerce data.

U.S. desire for "strategic engagement" with China did not give it a blank check to ignore those U.S. trade laws that it found inconvenient. Nevertheless, the major common denominator in Chinese-U.S. trade disputes, only some of which are outlined here, was the two countries' inability to interrupt significantly the larger trends of increased bilateral commerce and economic interdependence.

Since its imposition of trade sanctions following the Tiananmen Square massacre in 1989, the U.S. government has threatened or actually imposed additional sanctions for a number of alleged Chinese political and economic transgressions. On several occasions within just a few years, the United States was on the brink of a trade war with the world's most populous country and fastest-growing market. The threat of terminating MFN treatment to China and the latter's equally serious threat to retaliate against U.S. goods overshadowed a number of less publicized disputes that fell into two broad categories. The first consists of political actions taken by China and deemed unacceptable by the U.S. government. These included further allegations of continued human rights abuses, use of prison labor to make exported goods, and shipments of missiles and offensive weapons in violation of international treaty obligations. When the Clinton administration determined in 1993 that China was violating the Missile Technology Control Regime (by allegedly selling missile parts to Pakistan), it was bound by domestic law to retaliate with export sanctions. The result was imposition of restraints on exports of several categories of high-tech goods to China. Although this action was limited in scope, it was extraordinary in that no punitive trade measures were imposed by any of China's other trading partners in response to this alleged infraction.

The second category of Chinese behavior angering the United States consists of three areas of commercial improprieties deemed to be inconsistent with U.S. trade laws and practices: illegal shipments of textile goods to the United States; violations of U.S. intellectual property rights; and import barriers contributing to what in the early 1990s had become the second largest U.S. bilateral trade deficit. Reflecting the stressful overall state of bilateral economic relations was the fact that friendly, quick, and definitive settlement of any of these bilateral economic disputes was nonexistent through the first half of the 1990s.

In the first instance, the U.S. government accused the Chinese government of massive fraud in its efforts to circumvent the export quotas on textile and apparel shipments to the United States that were negotiated under the Multifiber Arrangement. Seeking to discourage continued illegal transshipments of textile products through third countries (country-of-origin documentation is altered to disguise their true source), the U.S. government unilaterally reduced China's 1991 textile and apparel export allotment to the United States. At the beginning of 1994, the Clinton administration was on the verge of a massive (25 percent) retaliatory cutback in textile imports from China for the same reason. This move was averted at the last minute when the two governments signed a new agreement that dealt mainly with suppressing illegal textile transshipments, the existence of which had never been denied by the Chinese government.

The amended Section 301 provision (Special 301) requires the executive branch to identify "priority" countries that violate U.S. intellectual rights and then either to secure agreements to end such violations or to impose economic retaliation. Overwhelming evidence of massive Chinese violations of U.S. companies' patents, trademarks, and copyrights led the Bush administration to demand that the Chinese government put an end to these large-scale rip-offs. After an extended period of re-fusal by China to provide such assurances, temporary resolution of the problem was achieved by a bilateral agreement signed in January 1992—just in time to avoid im-plementation of promised U.S. retaliation and threatened Chinese counterretalia-tion. However, the U.S. government dismissed as insufficient the level of Chinese enforcement of subsequently enacted laws and regulations to curb piracy of American goods such as software, movies, books, and recorded music. Bilateral trade tensions once again escalated.

The Clinton administration decided that the need to respect U.S. trade laws out-weighed any other commercial or foreign policy consideration. Accordingly, on February 4, 1995, it announced imminent imposition of 100 percent tariffs on $1 billion worth of imports from China—potentially the largest commercial trade retal-iation in U.S. history. The Chinese government immediately responded with the sentiment that it was ready for a fight and announced its plans for counterretalia-tion.[32] Once again, the existence of a hard deadline induced a last-minute settlement. In this case, a political phenomenon within the United States was a critical factor in settling the ensuing eyeball-to-eyeball encounter on terms mainly favorable to American demands. When the vast majority of trade-oriented American companies held firm in their support of the administration's hard-line determination to enforce U.S. law, China's resolve withered. Agreement on a multifaceted Chinese govern-ment commitment to crack down on piracy of U.S. intellectual property rights was reached just in time to beat the scheduled late February imposition of U.S. sanctions.

The third commercial dispute referred to previously—U.S. dissatisfaction with market access—seemingly was resolved when the two countries reached agreement on Chinese market-opening measures in October 1992. Following a familiar pat-tern, the two sides had struck a last-minute deal in order to avoid imminent trade hostilities; the U.S. government had threatened to impose higher duties on $3.9 bil-lion worth of imports in retaliation for identified trade barriers, and China threat-ened retaliation against a comparable level of U.S. exports.[33] In an equally familiar second phase, the U.S. government was strongly dissatisfied with the extent of Chinese compliance with its promised trade concessions. In this case, dissatisfaction was converted mainly into outspoken and successful U.S. opposition in late 1994 to China's being admitted as one of the founding members of the World Trade Organization. The United States adamantly insisted that China's eagerly sought after accession to the new organization had to be delayed until that country liberalized its trade regime sufficiently to bring it to a minimum level of compatibility with mar-ket-oriented economies.

Conclusions and Outlook

The diversity that characterizes U.S. trade policies toward the so-called less developed countries is inevitable. It is a direct outgrowth of our familiar theme that trade policy is a series of compromises between domestic and external economics and politics. Superimposed on the basic U.S. ideological predilection for liberal trade are conflicting objectives in dealing with the LDCs. These include the ethical imperatives of helping less fortunate human beings and protecting human rights throughout the world; the national security objectives of promoting stability and friendship with such key countries as Russia, Mexico, and Saudi Arabia; the need to cope with and occasionally restrain unusually rapid increases in import competition from the advanced LDCs; and the need to reduce or eliminate unjustifiable LDC barriers to U.S. exports.

Furthermore, the inevitability of ambivalence and inconsistencies in U.S. trade laws and dealings with developing countries reflects the heterogeneity of the LDCs' economies. Some developing countries have adopted successful domestic economic policies that have spilled over into dynamic international trade performances. Some have enjoyed neither internal nor external economic success. Still others are former communist countries burdened with the unprecedented problem of navigating the uncharted waters of a transition from a command, state-owned economic system to a market-oriented, entrepreneurial system never experienced by the people living in these countries.

U.S. trade relations with LDCs in the late 1990s and at the turn of the century are important in their own right, but they should be viewed in the larger context of two broader themes. The first is the favorable outlook in many of the advanced developing countries for rapid, sustained growth in both their internal economies and their foreign trade sectors—successes associated with their recent embrace of market-oriented, low-inflation policies. These countries, most of them Latin American and East Asian, will provide U.S. producers of goods and services with most of their fastest-growing overseas markets. Conversely, their increasingly competitive export sector, stimulated by an inflow of state-of-the-art capital equipment and management techniques associated with accelerating inflows of foreign direct investment, suggests the possibility of a degree of competition of unprecedented intensity for U.S. corporations and labor. In addition to increasing sensitivity to internal dislocations caused by skilled but cheap foreign labor, U.S. trade policy toward the LDCs is likely to emphasize efforts to nudge the import policies of these countries to a degree of openness equal to that of the First World industrialized countries.

The second trend is the unfavorable economic outlook for the LDCs whose minimal growth prospects and primitive production capabilities suggest a limited ability for the foreseeable future to pay for needed imports by means of increased exports. For these countries, U.S. trade policy is of limited relevance, and in the short term it will be overshadowed by U.S. foreign aid programs.

For Further Reading

Bradford, Colin I., Jr., and William Branson, eds. *Trade and Structural Change in Pacific Asia.* Chicago: University of Chicago Press, 1987.

Chan, Steve. *East Asian Dynamism.* Boulder: Westview Press, 1993.

Krueger, Anne O. *Economic Policies at Cross-Purposes.* Washington, D.C.: Brookings Institution, 1993.

————. *Trade Policies and Developing Nations.* Washington, D.C.: Brookings Institution, 1995.

Lardy, Nicholas R. *China in the World Economy.* Washington, D.C.: Institute for International Economics, 1994.

Preeg, Ernest H., ed. *Hard Bargaining Ahead: U.S. Trade Policy and Developing Countries.* New Brunswick, N.J.: Transaction Books, 1985.

U.S. International Trade Commission. *The Year in Trade* (annual reports on the operation of the Trade Agreements Program).

Whalley, John, ed. *Developing Countries and the Global Trading System.* 2 vols. Ann Arbor: University of Michigan Press, 1989.

Notes

1. International Monetary Fund, *Direction of Trade Statistics Yearbook, 1993*; and OECD Development Assistance Committee data as reproduced in the Japan Economic Institute's Report 32B, dated August 27, 1993.

2. Japan Economic Institute Report, *op. cit.*; and U.S. Department of Commerce, *U.S. Foreign Trade Highlights 1992,* June 1993.

3. U.S. Department of Commerce, *U.S. Foreign Trade Highlights 1993,* July 1994, p. 29.

4. Federal Reserve Bank of New York, *Quarterly Review,* Winter 1992–93, p. 66.

5. *U.S. Foreign Trade Highlights 1993,* p. 20.

6. Calculated from data in *U.S. Foreign Trade Highlights 1993.*

7. USTR press release of the testimony of Michael Kantor to the Senate Finance Committee, May 20, 1993, p. 4.

8. USTR press release of the statement of Rufus Yerxa to the GATT Trade Policy Review Mechanism, December 14, 1989, p. 4.

9. *U.S. Foreign Trade Highlights 1992,* p. 44.

10. USTR, *1992 Annual Report,* p. 111.

11. For data on the benefits of export-oriented over import-substitution trade policies, see World Bank, *World Development Report 1987,* chap. 5. Also see the text of the October 29, 1993, speech in Monterrey, Mexico, of IMF Executive Director Michel Camdessus.

12. U.S. International Trade Commission, Annual Report, *Operation of the Trade Agreements Program,* 1988, p. 153.

13. U.S. International Trade Commission, *The Year in Trade, 1993,* June 1994, p. 131.

14. *Ibid.*

15. The two subheadings were previously designated 806.3 and 807.

16. U.S. International Trade Commission, *Production Sharing: U.S. Imports Under Harmonized Tariff Schedule Subheadings 9802.00.60 and 9802.00.80, 1981–1992,* February 1994, pp. xi, 1-1, and 1-2.

17. Anne O. Krueger, *Economic Policies at Cross-Purposes* (Washington, D.C.: Brookings Institution, 1993), p. 126.

18. U.S. International Trade Commission, *U.S. Imports of Textiles and Apparel Under the Multifiber Arrangement: Annual Report for 1991*, p. A-3; and unpublished U.S. Department of Agriculture data.

19. *Weekly Compilation of Presidential Documents* (Washington, D.C.: U.S. Government Printing Office), vol. 26, July 2, 1990, p. 1011.

20. U.S. International Trade Commission, *The Year in Trade, 1993*, p. 133.

21. U.S. International Trade Commission, *Impact of the Caribbean Basin Economic Recovery Act on U.S. Industries and Consumers*, annual report for 1992, September 1993, pp. 2-11, 2-12.

22. Krueger, *op. cit.*, pp. 144, 145, and 151.

23. Some prefer to call them "newly industrialized economies" because of lack of recognition of Taiwan and Hong Kong as sovereign countries.

24. *U.S. Foreign Trade Highlights 1993*; and U.S. Department of Commerce, *Overseas Business Reports*, April 1974.

25. USTR, "U.S. Trade Policy Toward Newly Industrializing Countries in Asia," internal fact sheet, April 20, 1988, p. 1.

26. *Ibid.*, p. 2.

27. USTR press release of the speech of Clayton Yeutter, March 2, 1988, p. 2.

28. Calculated from data in *U.S. Foreign Trade Highlights 1992*. This apparent mathematical paradox is simply explained by the fact that the United States has some bilateral *surpluses* in manufactured goods. The multilateral trade balance is a *net* figure for U.S. trade with *all* countries.

29. International Monetary Fund, *Directions of Trade Yearbook, 1993*.

30. European Bank for Reconstruction and Development, *Annual Economic Outlook*, September 1993, p. 68.

31. "U.S. Merchandise Trade: December 1993," U.S. Department of Commerce press release, February 17, 1994.

32. Despite the escalation in U.S.-Chinese commercial frictions on the issue of intellectual property rights (IPRs) during February 1995, elsewhere an otherwise business-as-usual atmosphere prevailed. For example, three days after threatening to impose massive sanctions, the Clinton administration offered China $20 million in wheat subsidies lest a major export deal be lost to lower-priced foreign competitors. Simultaneously with the less than friendly negotiations on IPRs, U.S. Energy Secretary Hazel O'Leary arrived in China, as scheduled, leading a high-level delegation of U.S. executives from energy and power-generating companies. Undaunted by the rising tension, participants in these talks soon produced a number of government-to-government and private joint venture deals potentially worth in excess of $6 billion.

33. The facts of the cited bilateral commercial disputes are summarized in Wayne M. Morrison, "China-U.S. Trade Issues," Congressional Research Service issue brief, March 7, 1994.

12 Regional Trade Liberalization: The North American Free Trade Agreement

The three-year effort to negotiate and implement the U.S.-Mexican portion of the North American Free Trade Agreement (NAFTA) is an extraordinary case study in U.S. foreign trade policy that engendered an uncommon amount of controversy.

On the one hand, *traditional* fundamentals of trade politics and economics dominated the decisionmaking process. Reduced to bottom-line simplicity, the process involved a series of complex decisions that had to be made—with limited, ambiguous data—as to how far trade liberalization could proceed before it became unacceptably costly. The steps leading to passage of the legislation ratifying NAFTA in November 1993 demonstrated all of the domestic and foreign political and economic crosscurrents repeatedly cited in this book as constituting the underlying forces shaping U.S. foreign trade policy. These factors included the inevitable designation of winners and losers, minimal economic forecasting certainties, a plethora of unknown medium- and long-term economic results, a Congress unsure of how to respond in the face of ambiguous public sentiment, and firm presidential commitment to further trade liberalization.

Dominating all of these traditional issues was the core reality that no matter how great the perceived economic merits of this trade agreement, it would never have become operational had Congress not passed legislation authorizing U.S. participation in it. In the final analysis, this complex trade policy controversy was decided by the simple question of whether Congress would provide such authorization. Legislative approval was assured only because of a number of political compromises, some involving domestic constituents, others the Mexican government.

On the other hand, a sufficient number of *unique* circumstances were present to cause public debates about the nature and significance of the agreement to produce levels of public scrutiny and political emotion unknown in the modern history of U.S. trade agreements. Despite the preponderance of traditional trade liberalization issues, the debate about NAFTA's passage or defeat was imbued with a level of nearly metaphysical importance seldom seen in foreign trade policy debates. Some viewed creation of a free trade agreement with a low-wage country anxious to attract U.S. foreign direct investment as a dangerous precedent. Many others viewed it as nothing less than a critical indicator of future directions in the U.S. way of life and the U.S. role in the international community.

The political economy of efforts to phase out U.S.-Mexican trade barriers produced a situation very different from past experience, thereby endowing this episode with unique characteristics. However, many of the major issues surrounding the NAFTA debate will surface in the future to the extent that the United States pursues additional trade liberalization agreements with low-wage countries in East Asia and South America. In an era of high international mobility of capital and technology, the potential impact of such agreements on trade and employment patterns can be far-reaching.

History, Content, and Objectives

In the broadest sense, the creation of a free trade area in North America can be viewed as the logical culmination of a pattern of increasing commercial integration among the private sectors of the three countries constituting the region. The specific and immediate catalyst was the emergence in the early 1980s of economic problems in Canada and Mexico. Although these problems were different in nature, both governments deemed their successful resolution to require a common solution: negotiating a free trade agreement with the United States.

In the mid-1980s, Canada's political leaders had become seriously worried about market access to what is by far Canada's largest overseas market; exports of goods and services to the United States account for almost 20 percent of Canada's GDP. Specifically, there was a perception of a dangerous upsurge in U.S. measures to counter what U.S. government officials and affected industry executives alleged were unfair Canadian trade practices. The Canadian government's concerns also were intensifying about the ability of the country's industries to achieve economies of scale—and thereby stay competitive—while producing within a market vastly smaller than that of any of the major industrial markets, the United States, the European Union, and Japan. Comforted by the fact that the vast majority of bilateral trade already had evolved to the status of zero or nominal tariff duties, the government of Prime Minister Brian Mulroney overcame generations of Canadian anxieties about economic domination by their larger neighbor to the south. The result was the request in late 1985 to the Reagan administration to initiate the negotiations that would lead to the implementation of the U.S.-Canada Free Trade Agreement in 1989. Canada subsequently opted to expand this agreement into a trilateral arrangement after the United States and Mexico commenced negotiations to create their own bilateral free trade agreement.

The Mexican government's similar decision to overcome generations of fears of economic domination by Mexico's larger neighbor to the north was an outgrowth of a 1990 decision by President Carlos Salinas de Gortari. He was determined to reinforce and perpetuate through an international agreement the economic reforms that had been introduced in the late 1980s to rescue Mexico from its deteriorating domestic economic situation. By the early 1980s, Mexico's state-dominated economy was performing very poorly. A growing number of money-losing state-owned enterprises and import-substitution policies were important contributors to an economic policy syndrome that produced slow growth, high inflation (caused mainly by large federal budget deficits), massive capital flight, and unproductive investments.

Conditions deteriorated in part because corrective measures were postponed, thanks to the government's ability to leverage the country's potential oil wealth and borrow tens of billions of dollars from commercial banks. This phenomenon continued until Mexico was forced to announce to an unsuspecting world in summer 1982 that it would be unable to service its existing debts without a massive bailout. The resulting refusal of commercial banks to increase their exposure in Mexico as well as the decline in oil prices quickly produced a state of economic austerity and malaise.

The remedy chosen was to move quickly in the direction of a market-based economy. Prominent in the shock therapy applied by the Salinas administration immediately after its inauguration in late 1988 were accelerated reductions in trade barriers and initiation of measures to encourage new foreign direct investment, policies designed to enhance domestic efficiency and to improve the ability of Mexico to repay its foreign debts, respectively. Within the space of a few years, Mexico shifted from being "one of the world's most protected economies into one of the most open systems."[1] But further initiatives were deemed necessary to induce a greater long-term stimulus to Mexican economic growth.

President Salinas (like Canadian Prime Minister Mulroney) decided that Mexico needed assured, permanent access to its largest foreign market, and it needed to take steps that would prevent a return to the discarded emphasis on state-interventionist policies. Establishment of a free trade area with the United States would accomplish both objectives. With no need to worry about opposition from another Mexican political party, all that remained was for Salinas to convince the Bush administration to agree to negotiate a free trade agreement. This was not a difficult task when the assertions were advanced that the agreement would help Mexico reinforce its commitment to a market-based economy and in so doing would strengthen its economy and social fabric and gradually reduce the flow of illegal immigration to the United States. A positive Bush administration response was further encouraged by the fact that most large U.S. industrial corporations supported the idea. The administration's enthusiasm for the agreement was quickly evident as President Bush proudly pointed to it as a major accomplishment and another reason that he should be reelected. Unlike his Canadian and Mexican counterparts, however, Bush could not assume that legislative ratification was merely a formality.

On August 12, 1992, the United States, Mexico, and Canada successfully concluded a quick series of negotiations on an agreement to establish what was billed as the world's largest free trade zone.[2] Specifically, the accord called for the gradual phaseout within a maximum of fifteen years of all tariffs and all traditional nontariff barriers to trade among the three countries in both goods and services. Eliminating trade barriers is simple in concept but incredibly complex in execution. The NAFTA accord consists of a five-volume, approximately 2,000-page text plus three side agreements. It lays out detailed rules on the achievement and practice of hemispheric free trade—for example, rules of origin to qualify for free trade, emergency restraints in cases of import surges, protection of intellectual property rights, and dispute settlement procedures. The agreement also contains detailed provisions on how liberalization measures are to be applied to such key economic sectors (most of which are of major importance to the United States) as agriculture, automobiles and automotive parts, energy, financial services, telecommunications, and textiles and apparel. (The three governments maintain significant intervention or regulated trade flows in all of these sectors.)

The agreement moved beyond the usual parameters of a free trade area in several respects. It contains a number of measures to liberalize treatment of, and to provide protection for, incoming foreign direct investment. These provisions include nondiscriminatory treatment by requiring all signatories to treat foreign investors identically to any other investor and by mandating guarantees of free transfers of funds, expropriation protection, and elimination of performance requirements. Liberalization in the trade of services was assured (except where specific exemptions have been listed) by inclusion in the agreement of several guarantees. The latter include ease of entry into each country for specified categories of businesspersons who are citizens of the other member countries, national treatment of foreign-owned service companies (government regulation of domestic and foreign-owned corporations is identical), the right to sell services across borders, and so on.

In addition, the Clinton administration fulfilled a campaign promise and negotiated two side agreements to meet major complaints (above and beyond trade liberalization) about the NAFTA proposal by U.S. environmental interest groups and organized labor. The first supplementary agreement encourages high environmental standards in principle, creates a cumbersome trinational bureaucracy to oversee enforcement of domestic environmental laws, and promises funding for environmental cleanup projects. Hence, overall supporters could praise the NAFTA as the first "green" free trade agreement, but at the same time most overall opponents criticized the enforcement power of these provisions as being woefully inadequate. The second side agreement establishes forums—as opposed to binding enforcement mechanisms—for intergovernment cooperation to encourage enforcement of most existing labor protection laws, to promote improved labor conditions, and to provide a system for resolving labor-related problems between member countries. Although the U.S. labor movement was virtually unanimous in its dismissal of this agreement, the environmental movement was of two minds on the merits of the first side agreement.

Economic theory states that a free trade area should be a positive-sum game for all parties (although to the extent that trade diversion to member countries rather than trade creation throughout the world results, nonmembers can be adversely affected). Consumers benefit from access to cheaper imports, and domestic resources released from making noncompetitive goods can be reallocated to more efficient production and product specialization. Efficient firms increase production to maximize export sales in an expanded market. In doing so, they probably will hire more workers who tend to be paid above-average wages because of their above-average productivity levels. The resultant increases in real income tend to create a virtuous cycle of faster domestic growth and expanded trade. The larger, more technologically advanced U.S. economy would seem to have fewer economic and political fears from a free trade arrangement than the smaller, less sophisticated Mexican and Canadian economies, each of which could more legitimately worry about becoming economic appendages of the United States within a free trade area.

Although very few Americans were distraught over the implications of concluding a free trade agreement with Canada, the prospects of free trade with the 85 million people living in Mexico, a country whose measured GDP was less than one-twentieth the size of that of the United States, generated deeply felt concerns and threats to a significant number of Americans. Much of this anxiety was linked to the fact that previous examples of successful free trade areas (or of the more advanced form of cooperation, customs unions) occurred between countries at comparable, advanced levels of economic development.[3] U.S. wage rates in the industrial sector in 1992 were about seven times as high as those of Mexican workers, who also do not enjoy the same legal rights to form unions, strike, bargain collectively, or receive minimum safety standards. Furthermore, Mexico at this time did not practice multiparty democracy and was not committed to the rule of law to the same extent as the United States. Critics of NAFTA viewed Mexico not as an equal trading partner but as a poorer country whose officials were bent on luring numerous U.S. companies to move south of the border to exploit lax environmental standards and cheap labor. It was also feared that NAFTA would lead to U.S. companies repeating a threat to their U.S. workers: If you do not accept wage and benefits restraints, we will be forced to shift production to lower-cost Mexico.

Proponents stressed the argument that the establishment of a free trade area in North America would be merely a de jure recognition of de facto economic trends and would serve the overall U.S. national interest in several ways. In their view, NAFTA was fully consistent with the strong and abiding interest of the United States in promoting economic growth, political stability, and a move toward democracy in a country with which it shares a long border and that just a few years ago was on the economic critical list.

On a more narrow, commercial basis, a majority of U.S. industries stand to reap greater benefits from a mutual elimination of trade barriers than do their Mexican counterparts. In the early 1990s, the average U.S. tariff level imposed on Mexican goods was low: approximately one-third of the average for tariffs imposed by Mexico on U.S. goods. In addition, a far greater share (45 percent) of Mexican goods entered the United States duty free in 1990 than the 18 percent of U.S. goods that entered Mexico duty-free[4] (in part because of the U.S. market access programs especially designed for LDCs, as described in Chapter 11). With Mexico buying about

70 percent of its imported goods from the United States, higher domestic growth in the former provides a disproportionate stimulus to the exports of the latter. Furthermore, in an exercise in which both countries phased out barriers to imports of services, Mexico had to give up much more than did the United States with its relatively low level of restrictions. Highly competitive U.S. service industries, like financial services and telecommunications, will gain access to a market that effectively had been closed to them.

The combination of Mexico's economic recovery and its unilateral trade liberalization had already contributed to generating such a boom in U.S. exports that Mexico in 1992 surpassed Japan to become the second largest overseas market (after Canada) for U.S. manufactured goods. As indicated in Table 12.1, the value of U.S. exports of manufactured goods to Mexico increased by 113 percent between 1988 and 1992, whereas the comparable rate of increase to all countries was only 52 percent. On the other hand, some of this growth can be attributed to two of the noncommercial factors discussed in Chapter 4. First, U.S. exports to Mexico in the late 1980s were coming off a low base because of the debt crisis in the middle of the decade. Second, the Mexican economy had suffered a decline in competitiveness when the peso appreciated by a considerable amount relative to the dollar during the 1988–1992 period. This sharp upturn in U.S. exports was used by NAFTA's proponents to challenge the opponents' argument that low levels of purchasing power in Mexico would preclude its ability to buy considerable amounts of U.S. goods. However, this upward trend could not by itself refute the assertion by some NAFTA critics that the U.S. export boom was strictly a one-time, short-term phenomenon that would reverse itself for a variety of reasons. When the peso suffered a sudden, dramatic drop in value in early 1995—thereby reducing Mexicans' ability to pay dollars for U.S. goods—the critics of NAFTA shouted, "We told you so."

A majority of the economic forecasts conducted to guide U.S. policymakers on NAFTA's likely long-term impact concluded that it would provide a net plus—albeit a small one—for the overall U.S. economy. Typical of these findings was a report by

TABLE 12.1   Comparison of U.S. Global Trade in Manufactured Goods with U.S.-Mexican Trade in Manufactured Goods (in billions of dollars)

	1980	1988	1989	1990	1991	1992
U.S. global trade in manufactured goods						
U.S. exports	144	217	245	283	309	329
U.S. trade balance	12	− 129	− 116	− 87	− 63	− 80
U.S.-Mexican trade in manufactured goods						
U.S. exports	11	15	18	22	26	32
U.S. bilateral trade balance	7	− 0.3	0.7	2	5	7

Sources: U.S. International Trade Commission, *Chartbook, Composition of U.S. Merchandise Trade 1988–92*, March 1993; and unpublished U.S. Department of Commerce trade statistics.

the U.S. International Trade Commission (an independent governmental agency with no constituency to protect) concluding that "it is likely that a United States–Mexico FTA would provide net economic benefits to the United States, but the benefits would be small in relation to the size of the U.S. economy at least in the near to medium term. The benefits of an FTA would probably increase in time, but remain fairly small in the foreseeable future."[5] Citing similar reasons, namely the small size of the Mexican economy and recent progress in both countries to lower trade barriers, the Congressional Budget Office (CBO) also estimated that small net benefits would accrue to the United States from free trade with Mexico: U.S. GDP would be increased but only "as much as one-quarter of one percentage point."[6]

There was also general agreement that the smaller, more backward Mexican economy would gain more from NAFTA in relative terms than the United States. Interestingly, the CBO suggested that the larger economic benefits accruing to Mexico would come not from increased trade but from increased foreign investment encouraged by NAFTA's removal of most barriers to investment flows among the three member countries. The key to Mexico's development strategy, said the CBO, is "to attract and productively absorb foreign capital." In addition to NAFTA's investment provisions making Mexico safer and "more attractive for U.S. investors," the agreement "would lock in Mexico's domestic reforms because it represents an international commitment to maintain them, which further reduces the riskiness of investment in Mexico."[7] NAFTA opponents and skeptics worried aloud that the already declining number of new U.S. manufacturing jobs would be at risk if the Mexican government planned to use the agreement primarily as a magnet for new foreign direct investment rather than as an engine of free trade.

The Importance of Symbolism in the NAFTA Debate

Negotiating NAFTA was the easy part of the U.S. decisionmaking process. Assuring congressional passage of the necessary implementing legislation under the fast-track statute was a far more difficult endeavor. Problems arose on two levels. One was the traditional disagreement (described in the next section) by potential winners and losers as to the likely economic consequences of the agreement. The prospect of tens of thousands of job losses was immediate and concrete, whereas promises of economic benefits were more abstract, further down the road, and not guaranteed to last on a permanent basis. Only time, not economic theory, can provide a definitive reading on the future effects of a sweeping elimination of foreign trade barriers.

The second level was an extraordinary, still not completely explicable event in U.S. trade policy: the emergence of unusually acrimonious political debate in which emotional heat frequently overshadowed intellectual light. NAFTA came to be portrayed in extreme terms as either a necessary good or an avoidable evil. In either case, the expected good or evil was usually portrayed as materializing in amounts significantly greater than anything suggested by the small size of the Mexican economy and the limited reduction in existing bilateral trade barriers. Congress's acceptance or rejection of NAFTA was considered a matter of major economic, political, and social importance. So public and pervasive was the debate that it was the first trade policy issue to become grist for network talk shows, comedy monologues of late-night comedians on television, and even comic strips.

Proponents and opponents effectively converted the polemic into a grandiose plebiscite. Since there was no unanimity as to what exactly the plebiscite was about, the NAFTA debate in the final analysis was about raw political power today and future changes in the distribution of income. Underneath the verbal hoopla, there was disagreement as to whether NAFTA's victory or its defeat would result in the metaphorical opening of a gigantic Pandora's box with the subsequent release of varying forms of uncontrollable demons, damage, and despair.

Some argued that NAFTA was really about industrial competitiveness and the upgrading and modernizing of the U.S. economy to flourish in a rapidly changing global economy. President Bill Clinton said that at the core of the NAFTA debate was a fundamental question: Was the United States "going to face the future with confidence that we can create tomorrow's jobs, or are we going to try against all the evidence of the last 20 years to hold on to yesterday's?"[8] Conversely, former presidential candidate Ross Perot warned of economic disaster. Alluding to a "big sucking sound," he claimed that as many as 5.9 million U.S. jobs were at risk of being lost to Mexico.

Foreign policy advocates looked beyond jobs and described what they saw as the global strategic implications of NAFTA. Henry Kissinger said, "About once in a generation, this country has an opportunity in foreign policy to do something defining, something that establishes the structure for decades to come. . . . A new architecture needs to be created [in the new world order], and NAFTA is the first and crucial step in that direction."[9] Representative Peter Hoagland (D., Neb.) was quoted as saying that he was not alone in likening a possible rejection of NAFTA to the retreat into isolationism that followed the U.S. rejection after World War I of membership in the League of Nations.[10] Conversely, presidential candidate Patrick Buchanan spoke for isolationists and those persons suspicious of the growing power of international economic organizations relative to national governments when he wrote that NAFTA was about much more than trade: "It is the chosen field upon which the defiant forces of a new patriotism have elected to fight America's foreign policy elite for control of the national destiny. . . . Contemptuous of states' rights, regional differences and national distinctions, NAFTA would supersede state laws and diminish U.S. sovereignty."[11]

In some cases, NAFTA symbolized not a pure economic issue but a force for either increased or reduced levels of toxic waste accumulation and other forms of land, air, and water pollution. On the one hand, some environmental groups believed that NAFTA would cause grievous incremental damage to the already serious cases of industrial-based pollution along the border. Much of this pollution originated from the clustering near the border of what had become a major factor in bilateral trade flows: hundreds of so-called *maquiladora* plants that import U.S. parts duty-free and then reexport them back to the United States with duties paid only on the value added in Mexico (usually assembly work by low-paid workers). The environmental groups opposed to NAFTA foresaw its creating a magnet whereby numerous U.S. factories would flock south of the border, attracted by relatively lax Mexican enforcement of its admittedly impressive array of environmental laws. Instead of reduced trade barriers, these groups demanded reduced pollution. On the other hand, other environmental groups cited the rule of thumb that economic development traditionally leads to stronger popular demands for improved environmental standards as well as increased governmental resources to enforce them. They also cited the agreement (as well as the separately negotiated environmental side agreement) as proof that both environmental conditions and enforcement of existing Mexican laws would improve at least slightly after NAFTA was implemented but that this would not occur if Mexico continued to manage its environmental policy on an independent, unilateral basis.

Another important symbolic dimension of the debate concerned the plight of those U.S. workers who would pay the personal price of losing their means of livelihood for the overall social good. Specifically, ethical questions arose from the consensus that job losses in the United States would fall disproportionately on unskilled and uneducated workers in the manufacturing sector—precisely those persons who would have the most difficulty in finding comparable or better-paying new jobs. In some respects, a kind of class politics issue was at work: Big business as a whole could look forward to greater profits, but some workers faced the prospect of losing their jobs. The Clinton administration sought to defuse this moral dilemma by promising increased funding for income maintenance, retraining, and job search assistance for workers who lost their jobs because of production shifts and increased imports. (Some members of the media wondered out loud if the intellectual class would be so pro-NAFTA if their jobs, too, were at stake.[12])

Many U.S. labor unions opposed the agreement by drawing verbal pictures of worker exploitation in Mexico. They told of abuses such as children being forced to work long hours, cited instances of unhealthy and unsafe factories, and accused the Mexican government of union-busting activities. U.S. workers, they argued, should not be asked to compete on such unequal terms. Given the apparently weak enforcement mechanisms of the side agreement on labor, these unequal terms were seen as enduring after NAFTA's implementation. Conversely, it was argued by some that NAFTA symbolized a coming upgrading of Mexican working conditions and salaries that would naturally follow an increase in Mexico's economic prosperity. As with the environmental issue, advocates of NAFTA pointed to the separately negotiated side agreement on labor laws and labor-related disputes among the three countries as leading to improved working conditions and stronger enforcement of existing laws in Mexico.

Some took a noncommittal position, believing that the debate had lost sight of the issues at hand and had become a metaphor for political confrontation:

> The NAFTA debate is no longer about the agreement itself, or about Mexico, but about competing domestic political agendas and irreconcilable world views. Appeals are made not to economic interest but to nationalistic fears. On one side, there are scare-mongering claims about Mexican instability; on the other, crude appeals to the most xenophobic strains of American populism. Critics exaggerate the risks of more rapid economic integration while minimizing its rewards; advocates, no more responsibly, do just the opposite. On both sides, the agreement's true purpose—and its likely effects—have been distorted and obscured.[13]

Economic Arguments and Counterarguments

Most of the technical economic arguments in the NAFTA debate revolved around four core themes:

1. Investment: Would NAFTA encourage significantly higher rates of new investment in Mexico that otherwise would have been made in the United States with its higher wages and tighter government regulations?
2. Net job changes: Would NAFTA have a positive or negative net effect on total jobs in the United States? Could those workers losing low-wage jobs move up to higher-skilled, higher-paying ones?
3. Wage impact: Would wages rise on balance as more capital-intensive goods were shipped to Mexico or drop as production was shifted south of the border?
4. Trade: To what extent would NAFTA affect the volume, product composition, and net balance of U.S.-Mexican trade?

Despite the appearance of many elaborate economic models designed to generate answers to these critical questions, virtually no definitive, universally accepted answers materialized. The models exhibited substantial differences in their quantitative findings. In large part, this was because of fundamental differences in methodology and assumptions made, often because analysts were predisposed to obtaining results either praising or condemning NAFTA. For example, in some pro-NAFTA models, the somewhat dubious assumption of full employment in the United States was made, with the not unexpected result that NAFTA-induced unemployment was nil; in another instance, job losses were predicted to be minimal by the simple act of assuming little or no diversion of new investment from the United States to Mexico. One of the anti-NAFTA models largely ignored U.S. potential export gains and focused on investment flowing into Mexico.[14]

A Joint Economic Committee study spoke for many nonpartisan observers when it concluded that the economic impact studies were "at best, only partially useful" in providing a broad range of possibilities. It found that none of the many models it had examined "represents a thorough and comprehensive approach to [the] full range of economic questions."[15] The study also quoted the congressional testimony of one of this book's coauthors who asserted that the "vast majority of existing studies are so strongly influenced by their authors' theoretical views and prior beliefs that they do little more than quantify those preconceptions."[16] Not surprisingly, models emanating from major governmental and private institutions indicated employment changes that fell in the very broad range of job gains of 1.5 million to job losses of 900,000 by 1999.[17] The majority of forecasts fell into the much narrower range of plus or minus 200,000 jobs (created or lost).

Even on broad issues, the debate rolled on inconclusively. One side of the argument liked to emphasize the small size (only 4 percent as measured by GDP) of the Mexican economy in comparison with the United States. The other side preferred to compare labor statistics, to wit, the millions of unemployed and underemployed Mexicans available to fill jobs taken from the United States. NAFTA advocates expressed delight at the well above average increase in U.S. exports to Mexico after it began unilaterally reducing its import barriers in the late 1980s. However, opponents warned that the upsurge in U.S. sales was short term and had already peaked by the early 1990s; hence, the complete elimination of Mexican trade barriers would have only marginal results. NAFTA-skeptics further argued that given the large component of capital goods in U.S. exports to Mexico, the result would be first increased Mexican industrial production and then increased exports back to the United States in the long run.

Proponents noted that the large net increase in U.S. exports to Mexico between 1986 and 1992 had created more than 400,000 new jobs.[18] Opponents countered with the argument that a longer time horizon was necessary for proper analysis. Their forecasts pointed to a large cumulative net job loss and a large gross number of job dislocations, mainly for unskilled workers who were likely to have greater than average difficulty in finding comparable new jobs. One side argued that NAFTA-induced job losses would represent a very small fraction of the turnover in the overall U.S. labor force. The other argued that, at the margin, any additional jobs lost in the manufacturing sector were worrisome because between 1973 and 1993 the United States had experienced an *absolute* decline in manufacturing jobs. Some claimed that newly created export-related jobs would pay better than the import-sensitive jobs lost to Mexico; others could point to preliminary calculations suggesting that on a weighted average, wages paid by new export jobs would be about the same as jobs displaced by imports.[19]

Symptomatic of the argument-counterargument-counter counterargument pirouette into intellectual gridlock was the issue of how to properly calculate Mexican wages. Opponents of NAFTA claimed that the Mexican government suppressed the already low local wage rates as a means of attracting foreign direct investment.

Proponents argued that the productivity of U.S. workers was higher than their Mexican counterparts by approximately the same multiple as the wage difference, thus virtually negating any effective differential in the cost of labor. The rejoinder to this assertion was that Mexican productivity in a number of key manufacturing sectors was rising more rapidly than wages, the result in such cases being reduced unit labor costs.[20] According to this argument, the proper comparison was not average productivity for the entire economy but rather sectors in which highly trained Mexican workers were joined with advanced state-of-the-art capital equipment and managerial know-how. In one study, the low-paid Mexican workers at an automobile engine plant were found to be 75 percent as productive as their U.S. counterparts in a comparable U.S. factory.[21]

Opponents argued that disregard for workers' rights in Mexico had caused real wages in the early 1990s to be well below levels prevailing ten years previously. The counterargument was that a different base period to compare real wage levels was necessary because soaring inflation and economic retrenchment caused by Mexico's debt crisis had indeed curbed wage increases in the mid-1980s but that they had resumed a steady growth after 1987. Some proponents simply downplayed the importance of wages by claiming they were a small factor in decisions about where to make investments relative to such factors as a country's infrastructure. According to this argument, the more crucial factors in deciding where to produce goods were the work force's level of education and skills, proximity to suppliers, and the like—an assertion supported by the fact that the preponderance of U.S. overseas investment in the manufacturing sector is located in other industrialized countries with high wages.

Many predictions on the flow of U.S. foreign direct investment to Mexico portrayed a massive outflow of companies in search of cheap labor and loosely enforced environmental regulations. Others, however, suggested that since U.S. import barriers were relatively low, most U.S. companies interested in Mexico had already established subsidiaries there. Proponents of NAFTA also pointed to the prospect of a number of existing U.S. subsidiaries being closed down in Mexico and their production facilities brought back to the United States because they would no longer be necessary to leapfrog that country's import barriers. A particularly effective investment-related argument by proponents was that to a large extent, new U.S. corporate ventures in Mexico would come mainly at the expense of potential U.S. investments in the low-wage countries of Southeast Asia. This would be a positive step because manufacturing and assembly plants located in Mexico would more likely use U.S.-made parts and production equipment and hire U.S. technicians and engineers.

NAFTA proponents argued that when low-wage, relatively less developed countries (Greece, Spain, and Portugal) became members of the European Union, they neither attracted massive numbers of runaway factories from the high-wage countries nor caused measurable downward pressure on their wage levels. The opposition sought to discredit the EU analogy on the grounds that the Mexican-U.S. income gap was wider than European income disparities and that the Europeans had a much more advanced social safety net and retraining program for displaced workers.

The Final Phase: Marketing NAFTA

After NAFTA was signed by the three heads of state in December 1992, the ensuing preparations for congressional ratification triggered the most dramatic, emotional, expensive, and mass-marketed public debate in U.S. trade policy history. Three factors were mainly responsible. The first was that a value judgment, not a scientific judgment, was mandated by the aforementioned lack of definitive economic proof as to NAFTA's net long-term consequences. This was a perfect example of the situation alluded to implicitly throughout this book: Trade policy decisions designed to enhance the U.S. "national interest" are invariably complicated by the twin dilemmas of how to define this term in specific circumstances and who should do it. Proponents and opponents spoke very different languages when articulating the rewards and hardships to be expected from adopting free trade with Mexico. What they shared was the belief that their opinion was correct, important, and worthy of carrying the day.

The second factor was the perception by dozens of important interest groups that they needed to wage an aggressive lobbying campaign because their collective welfare was about to be significantly impacted. They viewed NAFTA's enactment or rejection as unleashing some very good or bad political, economic, social, and environmental changes. Projections of the impact by economic sector are presented in Box 12.1.

The final cause of the long, anguished policy debate was the repetition of the divisiveness factor at the aggregate level of public opinion. Polls repeatedly showed the American public was about evenly divided on the overall desirability of NAFTA,[22] and most members of Congress therefore had no clear national mandate to guide their voting.

In plain terms, what ensued was an unprecedented, no-holds-barred, and sometimes shameless struggle to win the hearts and minds of enough members of Congress to assure passage or defeat of the NAFTA enabling legislation. Most of this effort was directed at the House of Representatives, where a large number of announced opponents and undecided members meant that passage was in real doubt, whereas passage seemed assured in the Senate. The main supporting players in the struggle on Capitol Hill were, first, governmental entities, most of which supported NAFTA: the Clinton administration and state and local U.S. governmental bodies as well as the Mexican government. In addition, there were countless private sector interest groups active on behalf of a full range of views, including the U.S. and Mexican business communities, U.S. labor unions, academic and think tank economists, environmentalists, consumer protection advocates, animal rights groups, lawyers, political pundits, and the media (see Box 12.2).

The only simple thing about the marketing of advice to Congress was that there were only two sides, each providing an unequivocal recommendation as to which way members should vote in order to avoid an economic calamity. At every turn, opponents and proponents sharply disagreed on how to interpret available data and on forecasts of the economic changes that would be unleashed by enacting the agreement. Some opponents denied that they were opposed to the principle of North American free trade and claimed they merely were demanding major changes in the text of the agreement. Hence opponents popularized the "Not *This* NAFTA" slogan, which supporters claimed was merely a ploy to kill the agreement by asking the U.S. government to make impossible demands on the Mexican government to renegotiate its terms.

To oversimplify slightly, the political debate about NAFTA was waged between the establishment and a variety of groups and individuals perceiving themselves as disenfranchised in terms of influencing policy. Many activists on the political right joined with many activists on the political left in an uncomfortable collaboration to galvanize opposition to the proponents of NAFTA—the White House, big business (the vast majority of business executives in the manufacturing, service, and agricultural sectors were in favor),[23] the political center, all of the living former U.S. presidents, and Nobel Prize–winning economists. Fearful of losing jobs on balance, several influential labor unions, such as the AFL-CIO confederation, joined with other single interest advocates, mainly environmental and animal rights groups, in urging a rejection of the implementing legislation. A *Washington Post* think piece tried to put the opposition of the economically threatened in broader context: "NAFTA is the target, but the anger encompasses much more: the sense of betrayal by the Clinton administration; the frustration of steadily declining wages for workers; [and] a fury at what is seen as a new and arrogant corporate, political, media, and academic elite."[24] A few industrial groups, mainly in the import-sensitive apparel sector, and a few farm groups were the limited opposition from the business sector.

The single most bizarre element of the political debate surely was the extreme to which NAFTA politics created strange bedfellows. Traditional alliances and political partisanship were replaced by a complex mosaic of disparate groups thrown together on the basis of how they perceived themselves to be net winners or losers of the Mexican free trade initiative. For example, right-wing isolationists found themselves aligned with radical environmentalists. Groups in the environmental lobby were split in half, roughly according to the militancy of their philosophy. The textile lobby was torn between the labor-intensive apparel segment opposed to NAFTA and the capital-intensive makers of yarns and fabrics who saw a great export potential in Mexico. (The U.S. apparel industry had been successful in getting a tough country-of-origin provision inserted into NAFTA; the so-called triple transformation test essentially allows Mexican apparel to be imported duty-free into the United States only if the finished goods are made mostly of yarns and fabrics produced within the three signatory countries.)

Political alliances on Capitol Hill were equally ad hoc. A majority of Republicans (including most of the party's leadership), who just a few weeks earlier had uniformly opposed President Clinton on his budget reduction package, now flocked to support him on NAFTA. At the same time, a majority of House Democrats (including two of its leaders, Majority Leader Richard Gephardt and Majority Whip David Bonior) resolutely opposed the president on NAFTA after having just supported him on the budget issue. Political ideology was no better guide than party affiliation

---

BOX 12.1 **Some Projected Industry Job Winners and Losers from NAFTA**

Winners

*Agriculture
  grains, oilseeds, corn, sorghum, soybeans, and livestock

Manufacturing
  food processing: alcoholic beverages, canned and processed beans and potatoes and similar items

  textiles and apparel: components for Mexican assembly plants

  chemicals: petrochemicals, chemical intermediates, pharmaceuticals

  stone and clay: cement

  primary and fabricated metals: high-tech steel, structured wire products, and high-value sheet metal products

Losers

*Agriculture
  sugar, fresh fruits and vegetables (especially citrus, winter, and manually harvested crops)

Construction
Manufacturing
  food processing: tuna canning

  textiles and apparel: knitting mills and some assembly operations

  chemicals: medicines

  *stone, clay, and glass: especially glassware

  primary and fabricrated metals: high-value specialty steel, plate, bar, rod, and tubular steel, and nonferrous metals

---

for predicting which members of Congress possessed deep commitment to fighting or supporting NAFTA. The closest thing to an accurate predictor of legislators' leanings was which geographical region they represented. The Sun Belt states on or near the Mexican border calculated that geographical proximity and a high rate of high-tech industry would allow them to be the source of a disproportionate increase in U.S. exports of goods and services to Mexico that everyone agreed would follow the dismantling of trade barriers. Their representatives in Washington clearly received their constituents' message that NAFTA was a good thing. On the other hand, most congressional representatives from the industrial states of the Midwest (often dubbed the Rust Belt) were ardently opposed to NAFTA. Their constituents had suffered more than most from the competitive problems encountered by basic manufacturing sectors such as steel and automobiles.

BOX 12.1 (continued)

*machinery: heavy machinery, machine tools, construction equipment	machinery: home appliances
*electronics: office equipment, high-tech electronics, TV components, semiconductors	*electronics: consumer electronics including radio and TV
*transportation equipment: autos, auto parts, and aerospace equipment	*transportation equipment: autos and auto parts
paper products	furniture
rubber and plastic products	
measuring instruments: medical devices	
Transportation and Communications	Transportation
transportation services and telecommunications	motor freight, especially trucking
Services	Services
banking and financial services, legal services, accounting services, insurance, and computer software engineering	hotels, motion pictures, amusesments

*Industries of projected greatest absolute or percentage employment change.

Source: "NAFTA: U.S. Employment and Wage Effects," Congressional Research Service report, April 27, 1993; data collated from several models and studies.

Members of Congress may have been divided, but there was no escaping being sensitized to the pros and cons of NAFTA. From 1991 through the final vote in November 1993, at least fifty different hearings were held by the many committees in the Senate and the House of Representatives with interests in various provisions of the agreement. Constituents' written and verbal communications bombarded Capitol Hill as part of a massive lobbying campaign. Special economic studies were issued by all of Congress's support agencies (the Congressional Budget Office, the Congressional Research Service, the General Accounting Office, and the Office of Technology Assessment).

In the private sector, the strange-bedfellows syndrome was epitomized by the unprecedented scene of togetherness among four ideologically dissimilar competitors in the shaping of public opinion and policy. Ross Perot, Patrick Buchanan, Jesse

---

BOX 12.2   Interest Group Attitudes Toward NAFTA

Groups Supporting NAFTA

Business groups supporting NAFTA include the National Association of Manufacturers, U.S. Chamber of Commerce, National Retail Federation, National Association of Insurance Brokers, American Electronics Association, American Petroleum Institute, National Electrical Manufacturers Association, American Apparel Manufacturers Association, American Fiber Manufacturers Association, American Textile Manufacturers Institute, National Engine Parts Manufacturers Association, National Confectioners Association, American Automobile Manufacturers Association, National Association of Beverage Importers, and National Foreign Trade Council.

Environmental groups supporting NAFTA include the National Audubon Society, National Wildlife Federation, World Wildlife Fund, Natural Resources Defense Council, Environmental Defense Fund, and Conservation International.

Agriculture groups supporting NAFTA include the American Farm Bureau Federation, Grocery Manufacturers of America, National Food Processors Association, National Grain and Feed Association, National Cattlemen's Association, American Meat Institute, National Corn Growers Association, National Grain Trade Council, and National Grange.

Other groups supporting NAFTA include Citizens for a Sound Economy, Consumer Alert, National Council of La Raza, Empower America, American Conservative Union, and Southwest Voter Conference.

Groups Opposing NAFTA

Labor groups opposing NAFTA include the AFL-CIO, UAW, ServiceEmployees Union International, Communications Workers of America, United Food and Commercial Workers, United Steelworkers, International Brother-

---

Jackson, and Ralph Nader found themselves in agreement—for different, sometimes conflicting reasons—that NAFTA should be rejected. One side feared too much power would be given to governments to enforce NAFTA's side agreements; the other side felt that the proposed enforcement authority was inadequate to solve environmental and labor standards problems.

Lobbying efforts took place on many fronts, and the push did not come cheap. U.S. companies and groups spent upward of $10 million trying to influence the Congress, and Mexican interests in the three-year period beginning in 1991 spent an estimated $30–$45 million on no fewer than twenty-four lobbying, public relations,

---

BOX 12.2 (continued)

hood of Teamsters, United Mineworkers. AFSCME, International Ladies Garment Workers' Union, International Association of Machinists and Aerospace Workers, and Amalgamated Clothing and Textile Workers Union.

Environmental groups opposing NAFTA include the Sierra Club, Friends of the Earth, Greenpeace-USA, Environmental Action, Clean Water Action, and International Wildlife Coalition.

Agriculture groups opposing NAFTA include the National Farmers Union, National Farmers Organization, and American Corn Growers Association.

Business groups opposing NAFTA include the U.S. Business and Industrial Council, National Knitwear and Sportswear Association, Atlantic Apparel Contractors Association, and American Apparel Contractors Association.

Consumer groups opposing NAFTA include Public Citizen, Citizen Action, and National Consumers League.

Other groups opposing NAFTA include United We Stand, National Rainbow Coalition, National Council of Senior Citizens, United Methodist Church, American Civil Liberties Union, Americans for Democratic Action, Humane Society, and American Society for Prevention of Cruelty to Animals.

Source: "NAFTA," fact sheet of the Democratic Study Group (a research facility serving Democratic members of Congress), November 12, 1993.

---

and law firms.[25] The elite of Washington lobbyists (some of them former trade policy officials) were retained to work Washington's corridors of power. Television and radio commercials collectively costing as much as $10 million appeared with increasing frequency as the critical House vote approached. Newspaper and magazine ads were equally plentiful. USA*NAFTA, the principal pro-NAFTA coalition established by the business sector, attracted over 1,400 members (some of whom did not provide any financial support) and spent an estimated $7 million to help guarantee passage of NAFTA.[26] Comparable amounts were spent by the major opponents: labor unions, coalitions (e.g., the Citizens Trade Campaign, the Alliance for Responsible Trade), and Ross Perot, who starred in self-sponsored television "infomercials."

As late as the month before the pivotal mid-November vote in the House, the votes for approval were not there. The message coming at the time from both sides was that "if the vote were held today, NAFTA would lose." The most critical force in assuring last-minute, come-from-behind victory for the NAFTA legislation was the late emergence of President Clinton as an indefatigable activist, fully committed to using the vast carrot-and-stick powers of the Oval Office. Pushing aside the effects of professional lobbyists and their sound bites, Clinton demonstrated the validity of the political maxim, "If you're 20 or 30 votes short, you can always win if you've got a president with the will to win."[27]

Indeed, the administration accepted the notion that passage of NAFTA was nothing short of a test of its ability to govern successfully. With deep commitment, it undertook a proactive, high-visibility, high-energy political strategy to achieve its goal. Ironically, President Clinton's objective involved finalizing an initiative of an administration that it had defeated just a few months earlier. One part of the successful Clinton strategy took the form of plain hard work: The president and his cabinet initiated a long series of personal contacts with reluctant or undecided House members by phone or at White House meals, and they gave uncountable speeches and interviews to extol NAFTA's benefits.

The second, more controversial and arguably more effective component of the administration's policy was to offer a wide range of deals, some directly related to the agreement's provisions and some not, to representatives in exchange for yes votes. NAFTA proponents viewed the ensuing exercise as hardheaded political pragmatism, the kind often exhibited throughout U.S. history in times of close legislative votes. Opponents viewed it as a costly, unseemly giveaway program whose total costs to the U.S. public could not be calculated, in part because some deals perhaps had not yet surfaced. The deals made public included creation of a North American Development Bank to lend to industries and workers affected (positively or negatively) by the agreement, special understandings made with Mexico that would limit increases in sugar and orange juice concentrate exports, and commitments to seek accelerated tariff reductions by Mexico on certain commodities.[28]

That dipping into the government "pork barrel" was a highly successful tactic is suggested by the unexpectedly large margin of victory: thirty-four votes. Not only was this arithmetically a big change from straw votes taken just a few weeks before, but it also upset the assumption that many undeclared representatives would vote against NAFTA (and thereby curry favor with constituents not tied to big business) once its passage was assured.

There were a number of exogenous variables, other than the simple lure of the pork barrel that attracted additional converts to a positive vote in the House. One was the perceived decisive victory of Vice President Al Gore in his much-discussed television debate with Ross Perot, who appeared unable to deal in factual specifics when attacking NAFTA. The debate came just days before the final House vote, and the results made it much easier for a number of uncommitted representatives publicly to endorse the administration's pro-NAFTA position.[29] Advocates of the bill had for some time vividly depicted the costs of a NAFTA defeat in terms of undermining confidence in President Clinton and of strained relations with Mexico. By fortuitous timing they could also make the unsettling suggestions that a mid-November 1993 rejection would make the House responsible for torpedoing the last-minute efforts to successfully conclude the Uruguay Round of multilateral trade negotiations and undermining the first heads-of-government meeting of the Asia-Pacific Economic Cooperation countries that Clinton would be hosting just one week after the vote.

Conclusions and Outlook

Despite many unique circumstances, the negotiation and implementation of NAFTA were ultimately consistent with the key underlying forces of U.S. trade policy identified in this book. In the absence either of conclusive economic proof that NAFTA was on net a bad deal or of crushing political opposition, the innate liberal trade instincts of policymakers dominated. The political system, bolstered by support from big business, gave the benefit of the doubt to further trade liberalization as is usually the case.

In keeping with this book's mandate to avoid value judgments, no evaluation is offered about the wisdom of creating NAFTA. One can only assume that the total number of net job losses or gains will be in amounts that are a very small proportion—well under 1 percent—of the U.S. labor force, and that neither massive trade diversion nor massive new environmental degradation will take place. One can also assume that things will not be noticeably worse than if the agreement had been rejected—if only because U.S.-Mexican economic interdependence most likely would have continued to solidify whether or not there was a negotiated framework for this process. In the words of a scholar of Latin American affairs:

> It is rather late in the game to debate whether the United States and Mexico should be closely connected, or to think that the United States unilaterally can stem the flow of capital and jobs across the border. . . . The central issue for the United States is whether the net benefits to this country of closer [bilateral] connections . . . are likely to be greater as a result of an unnegotiated and somewhat haphazard process of . . . accelerating functional integration . . . or whether the interest of the United States and of most of its citizens, on the whole, are more likely to be advanced within a thoughtfully negotiated framework.[30]

The question of whether negotiation of another, "better" agreement was possible is now a moot point. North America must make do with the NAFTA it has: an imperfect agreement that almost certainly will not be nearly as beneficial as its ardent advocates have claimed or nearly as damaging as its ardent opponents have warned.

Although it is doubtful that definitive data to measure the long-term results of NAFTA will emerge before the end of the century, a wide array of interim positive and negative evaluations inevitably will be offered without analysts admitting their dubious reliance on short-term phenomena. As early as mid-1994, some enthusiasts were pointing to what was only a few months of steady increases in U.S. exports to Mexico as empirical proof of the free trade area's net benefits. Conversely, in the early part of 1995, many opponents pointed to Mexico's economic troubles as "conclusive" proof that the free trade area would damage U.S. interests by contributing to an upsurge in imports from that country.

Any objective long-term forecast of NAFTA's impact must also be tempered with likelihood that it is still a work in progress. Additional countries, probably starting with Chile, will likely join in the not-too-distant future. Once completed, NAFTA probably will be a much larger free trade area, one encompassing most or all of the countries in the Western Hemisphere.

For Further Reading

Congressional Budget Office. *A Budgetary and Economic Analysis of the North American Free Trade Agreement.* July 1993.

Grinspun, Ricardo, and Maxwell Cameron, eds. *The Political Economy of North American Free Trade.* New York: St. Martin's Press, 1993.

Hufbauer, Gary Clyde, and Jeffrey J. Schott. *North American Free Trade: Issues and Recommendations.* Washington, D.C.: Institute for International Economics, 1993.

Joint Economic Committee. "Potential Economic Impacts of NAFTA: An Assessment of the Debate." October 1993.

Krugman, Paul. "The Uncomfortable Truth About NAFTA." *Foreign Affairs,* November-December 1993, pp. 13–19.

Lustig, Nora, Barry Bosworth, and Robert Z. Lawrence, eds. *North American Free Trade: Assessing the Impact.* Washington, D.C.: Brookings Institution, 1992.

Orme, William, Jr. *Continental Shift: Free Trade and the New North America.* Washington, D.C.: Washington Post Company, 1993.

Perot, Ross, and Pat Choate. *Save Your Job, Save Our Country: Why NAFTA Must Be Stopped—Now.* New York: Hyperion Books, 1993.

U.S. International Trade Commission. *The Likely Impact on the United States of a Free Trade Agreement with Mexico.* February 1991.

Notes

1. U.S. International Trade Commission, *The Likely Impact on the United States of a Free Trade Agreement with Mexico,* February 1991, p. 1-2.

2. In point of fact, the addition of Mexico's small GDP to the preexisting U.S.-Canada Free Trade Agreement did little to enlarge what technically was already the world's largest free trade area when measured by domestic economic size.

3. U.S. International Trade Commission, *op. cit.,* p. 2-1.

4. George Ingram, *NAFTA: Evaluating the Arguments* (Washington, D.C.: Foreign Policy Institute of the Johns Hopkins University School of Advanced International Studies, 1993), p. 5.

5. U.S. International Trade Commission, *op. cit.* p. 2-2.

6. Congressional Budget Office, *A Budgetary and Economic Analysis of the North American Free Trade Agreement* (Washington, D.C.: U.S. Government Printing Office, 1993), p. 23.

7. *Ibid.,* pp. xiii, 13.

8. *Weekly Compilation of Presidential Documents,* vol. 9, September 20, 1993, p. 1758.

9. As quoted in *New York Times,* November 17, 1993, p. 1.

10. *Wall Street Journal,* November 18, 1993, p. A1.

11. Patrick J. Buchanan, "America First, NAFTA Never," *Washington Post,* November 7, 1993, pp. C1,C2.

12. See, for example, A. M. Rosenthal, "NAFTA Hits Intellectuals," *New York Times,* November 16, 1993, p. A27.

13. William A. Orme, Jr., "The NAFTA Debate—Myths Versus Facts," *Foreign Affairs,* November-December 1993, p. 2.

14. See "Potential Economic Impacts of NAFTA: An Assessment of the Debate," Joint Economic Committee staff study, October 1993.

15. *Ibid.,* p. vi.

16. Robert A. Blecker, as quoted in *ibid.,* p. 34.

17. Arlene Wilson, "NAFTA: How Many Jobs Are at Risk?" Congressional Research Service report, May 19, 1993, p. 3.

18. "Administration Statement on the North American Free Trade Agreement," November 1993, p. 5.

19. See, for example, Gary Clyde Hufbauer and Jeffrey J. Schott, *NAFTA: An Assessment* (Washington, D.C.: Institute for International Economics, 1993), pp. 16–17.

20. Robert A. Blecker and William E. Spriggs, "On Beyond NAFTA: Employment, Growth, and Income Distribution Effects of a Western Hemisphere Free Trade Area," IDB-ECLAC Working Paper no. WP-TWH-28, March 1993, pp. 35–36.

21. Joint Economic Committee, *op. cit.,* p. 31.

22. See, for example, *New York Times,* November 16, 1993, p. A1; *Washington Post,* November 16, 1993, p. A23.

23. This assertion is demonstrated by the fact that when the public sector advisory groups submitted to the Bush administration their assessments of NAFTA, favorable findings came from the senior committee, the Advisory Committee for Trade Policy and Negotiations (ACTPAN), as well as the advisory committees on industry, services, and agricultural policies.

24. *Washington Post,* November 8, 1993, p. A10.

25. *Wall Street Journal,* May 20, 1993, p. A18, and November 15, 1993, p. A14.

26. *Wall Street Journal,* November 15, 1993, p. A14.

27. Quoted in *Wall Street Journal,* November 19, 1993, p. A7.

28. Some newspapers printed suggestions that some representatives from tobacco-growing states were promised that the administration would accept a lower increase in taxes on cigarettes in return for their favorable vote on NAFTA; although there was absolutely no proof to document this supposition, it sounded credible enough to warrant being reported. See, for example, "How a Sense of Clinton's Commitment and a Series of Deals Clinched the Vote," *Wall Street Journal,* November 19, p. A7.

29. Not-for-attribution interview with a Capitol Hill professional staff person, December 1993.

30. Abraham F. Lowenthal, "Recasting the NAFTA Debate," text of an address delivered at a conference on NAFTA held in Washington, D.C., June 28–29, 1993, p. 3.

13 Multilateral Trade Liberalization: The Uruguay Round Agreement

The pursuit of trade liberalization through a regional trading bloc in North America is only one corner of a larger policy picture. U.S. foreign trade objectives are pursued on several levels: unilateral imposition of trade barriers, export restrictions, export enhancements, and reductions of trade barriers. The progressive liberalization of trade, in turn, is pursued on several distinct tracks, including free trade agreements with select countries (Canada, Mexico, and Israel) that discriminate against outsiders; special arrangements with LDCs, such as the Enterprise for the Americas Initiative; and bilateral market-opening agreements with Japan. The preferred means to the end of trade liberalization used by the United States is still multilateral negotiations. However, according to an official statement, the United States "has decided to pursue trade liberalization opportunities wherever and whenever they exist, whether in a multilateral, plurilateral [best exemplified by the quadrilateral group: the United States, the EU, Japan, and Canada], or bilateral context."[1] Although critics can object to the multilevel approach of the U.S. pursuit of a more liberal international trading order as being somewhere between inconsistent and hypocritical, there is no inherent reason to assume this process is so finite that it must take only one form.

That U.S. trade policy is neither simple nor consistent was vividly demonstrated during the latter half of 1993. The U.S. government was ratifying its membership in the world's largest regional trade bloc created by NAFTA at the same time it was successfully leading the effort to conclude another round of global trade negotiations. Analyzed in this chapter are the results of the Uruguay Round agreement—the latest phase in the long-standing, deeply held U.S. commitment to creation of a more liberal trade regime governed by principles and practices applied on a multilateral basis.

As with the NAFTA process, the conclusion and implementation of this agreement embody the "two-level game" concept utilized by political economists. This concept denotes the executive branch's need to achieve certain international agreements by bargaining for the support of domestic forces—the Congress and the private sector—at the same time that it is conducting negotiations with foreign governments. Also as with NAFTA, the bottom line of the Uruguay agreement was the need to politically finesse a trade agreement in order to assure that Congress would approve implementing legislation.

Historical Precedents

Seven rounds of multilateral trade negotiations (MTNs)—also referred to as GATT rounds—were held prior to the Uruguay Round. All were designed to progressively reduce trade barriers on a global, nondiscriminatory scale, expand the list of trade rules, and facilitate dispute settlement procedures (see Table 13.1). Five minirounds were held between 1948 (when the GATT took effect) and 1962. The common catalyst in all five cases was the belief of the international economic hegemon, the United States, that trade liberalization efforts, slightly tilted in favor of the recovering economies of Western Europe and Japan, were important long-term investments in securing a stable international political order and a more open trading system. These negotiations dealt solely with tariff reductions, most of which applied to manufactured goods. The resulting reciprocal trade liberalization agreements in the first five rounds were mainly responsible for causing the average tariff paid on dutiable U.S. imports to drop from about 54 percent in 1930 to 12 percent in 1963.[2]

Intensifying commercial competition from Western Europe and Japan in the 1960s led to the erosion of U.S. international economic hegemony. Fearful of losing access to what was then called the European Community, the most important foreign market and most important political ally of the United States at the time, the Kennedy administration was the inspiration for an ambitious new trade round. Its major objective was to assure reciprocal tariff cuts sufficiently large to prevent the EU's common external tariff from becoming a major barrier to U.S. exports. In 1967, the Kennedy Round of MTNs produced the deepest—about 35 percent—and most numerous tariff reductions ever.

The next round of trade negotiations had a familiar origin: an initiative by the United States. U.S. efforts reflected both the old commitment to the multilateral liberalization process and a festering belief that the United States was being victimized by widespread, unjustifiable trade barriers that dwarfed U.S. protectionism. This belief translated into the specific position that the United States had more to gain than to give in negotiations. The other industrialized countries were responsive in part because of their common belief in the value of reciprocal reductions in trade barriers. But mainly they were conceding to the stratagem of the United States that as part of its terms for dropping the import surcharge imposed as part of the New Economic Policy in August 1971, they had to agree to begin informal talks about the working program of a new round.

Because average tariff levels in the industrialized countries had dipped below the 8 percent level by the start of the 1970s, the Tokyo Round was the first of the multilateral negotiations designed from the outset to concentrate on reducing and eliminating nontariff barriers (NTBs). Inasmuch as increasingly numerous NTBs had surged ahead of declining tariffs to become the larger obstruction to the free flow of international commerce, any new trade liberalization effort that ignored efforts to curb NTBs was doomed at the outset to produce, at best, marginal results. The Tokyo Round was also unique in that negotiators for the first time were charged with specifically addressing the special trade problems of less developed countries. This breakthrough reflected the LDCs' rising influence in the international trading order

TABLE 13.1   Multilateral Trade Negotiations in the GATT, 1947–1979

Years	Principal Results
1947	Held as part of the original GATT negotiations; twenty-three countries offered 45,000 individual tariff concessions.
1949	Held at Annecy, France; only 5,000 tariff cuts negotiated.
1950–1951	Held at Torquay, U.K.; produced 8,700 tariff reductions.
1956	Moderate tariff cuts covering $2.5 billion in trade.
1960–1962	Dillon Round: produced an additional 4,400 tariff reductions; marked first time European Union negotiated as an individual entity in place of individual member countries.
1963–1967	Kennedy Round: shifted from product-by-product approach to across-the-board tariff cuts with exceptions allowed on specific products; cut tariffs by about 35 percent affecting trade of $40 billion; first efforts made to liberalize NTBs and agriculture.
1973–1979	Tokyo Round: reduced worldwide tariffs by another one-third; established codes of conduct affecting NTBs and accorded preferential treatment to developing countries; modest reductions in agricultural trade barriers made for the first time

and the growing sensitivity of the industrial countries to the charge that the GATT was an insensitive "rich man's club."

The successful conclusion of the Tokyo Round talks in 1979 produced additional tariff cuts that brought average import duties in the industrialized countries down to the 5–6 percent range, very modest reductions in agricultural import barriers, and the enabling clause legitimizing "special and differential" treatment of LDCs (e.g., tariff preferences) by industrialized countries. In addition, the Tokyo Round produced the first systematic international agreement to curb NTBs by implementing codes of conduct establishing general guidelines for national behavior in such previously untouched areas as government procurement, import licensing, technical barriers (standards), export subsidies, and customs valuation.

More than a few trade analysts predicted that since the GATT process was becoming too cumbersome and because negotiators had reduced the vast majority of conventional barriers to trade, the Tokyo Round would be the last of the great rounds of multilateral trade liberalization exercises. They were wrong.

Almost exactly four years after the initial U.S. diplomatic push of November 1982 on behalf of launching yet another round of trade negotiations, agreement in principle was reached at Punta del Este, Uruguay, on the broad outlines of a work agenda. Consensus on the need for new talks in part reflected the international community's concern with containing a proliferation of unilateral protectionist measures; a number of observers around the world perceived them as threatening to erode confidence in the GATT system.[3] Most of these restrictions were taken in response to the increased export competitiveness of East Asian countries or the dislocations associated with the second OPEC oil shock of 1979–1980.

Acceptance of the new round of MTNs also was due in part to agreement by other countries with the U.S. government's contention that multilateral trade rules and liberalization measures needed to be applied to important new trade problems that had yet to be subjected to any international agreements. The U.S. initiative in demanding that international negotiations include such unprecedented topics as agriculture, services, and protection of intellectual property rights was the end product of domestic political interactions among the private sector, the Congress, and the executive branch. As discussed in Chapter 6, the U.S. business community took the lead in creating new trade issues by alerting U.S. government officials to the service sector's lost export opportunities and by claiming estimated losses to U.S. companies of as much as $60 billion annually from foreign violations of U.S. patents, trademarks, and copyrights. Before Congress provided trade negotiating authority for the executive branch, it inserted into the Omnibus Trade and Competitiveness Act of 1988 a long list of negotiating objectives to be fulfilled in the Uruguay Round, including progress in the new issues—agriculture, services, protection of intellectual property, workers' rights, and so on.

The Political Economy of Successful Negotiations

With negotiations stretching from September 1986 through December 1993, the Uruguay Round was by far the longest trade negotiation in history as well as the one with the greatest number of missed deadlines for completion. (The original ministerial declaration in 1986 called for the round to conclude by the end of 1990.) The primary reason for this prolonged delay was political: the nonnegotiable demand by the United States for an unprecedented agreement on major reductions in trade barriers on agricultural goods. Two trade giants, the United States and the European Union, found it excruciatingly difficult to achieve common ground on what arguably has been and still is the world's single most politically charged trade liberalization issue. When compared to concluding the agreement on agriculture, all of the other major issues on the negotiating agenda fell into place quickly and easily. Agricultural trade has always been a sacred cow, exempt from meaningful liberalization. There is a simple political reason for this: Farmers in all industrialized countries wield domestic political power far in excess of their proportion of the national population. The vast majority of the world's farmers demand that their government provide them with high support prices for their crops and keep out lower-priced import competition.

Unflinching U.S. insistence on significant liberalization of the agricultural sector could in theory have been categorically rejected by other countries intent on protecting their farmers from imports, even at the cost of a collapse in the trade talks. However, the U.S. demand presumably struck a responsive chord in EU country capitals, for such an agreement would both advance and preserve what was discreetly deemed a necessary domestic policy shift. Economic officials were becoming anxious to restrain soaring budget outlays for crop price supports and export subsidy programs, both of which had become serious drains on scarce governmental revenues. Various efforts to quantify the global bill for agricultural subsidies produced a wide range of estimates, but all involved staggering sums. By one calculation, direct payments and indirect government transfers in 1988 were $59 billion in the European Union, $34 billion in Japan, and $28 billion in the United States.[4] According to a GATT Secretariat estimate, the total costs in 1992 to consumers in the OECD countries of agricultural support programs through higher prices and governmental outlays totaled approximately $354 billion, or $360 per capita. For the United States, total costs were put at $91 billion in 1992, and for the EU and Japan, $156 billion and $74 billion, respectively.[5]

The second factor prolonging the conclusion of the Uruguay Round negotiations was procedural. Until December 1993, the traditional agreement-forcing mechanism was absent: imminent termination of the U.S. president's legal authority to implement trade liberalization commitments previously agreed to. Without a fixed deadline staring them in the face, trade negotiators stubbornly refused to compromise, presumably in the hope of wearing down fellow negotiators, obtaining the maximum extent of net concessions, and avoiding criticism at home that they yielded too much too soon.

In every trade bill Congress has passed since 1934, it has delegated trade liberalization authority to the president for a strictly limited period of time, typically three to five years. In the case of the Uruguay Round talks, the mutually accepted termination date was the last day (December 15, 1993) on which the president could notify Congress under the fast-track provision (see Chapter 7) that he intended to sign the Uruguay Round agreement and later submit it for formal congressional approval. If this deadline was not met, the ability of the United States to ratify the agreement would very much be at risk; without U.S. participation, implementation of the agreement would be postponed indefinitely. (Only the statutory language of the fast-track provision could guarantee that the bill authorizing U.S. implementation of the Uruguay Round pact would be immune from potentially crippling special interest amendments.)

To be sure, overnight results should not be expected when more than 100 participating governments have to weigh many complicated trade-offs of their national interests. No quick consensus was likely in view of the shifting alliances exhibited in the Uruguay Round's fifteen separate negotiating groups (see Table 13.2) handling a broad range of disparate trade issues. For example, the LDCs opposed both the industrialized countries' push for liberalization of trade in services and their desire for more restrictive rules to prevent violations of intellectual property rights. At the same time, the LDCs recognized that concessions would have to be made on these two issues if they were to have any hopes of achieving one of their negotiating priorities—cracking the industrialized countries' reluctance to liberalize import barriers on textiles and apparel. Food-exporting LDCs aligned with the United States and

TABLE 13.2   Uruguay Round Negotiating Structure

Group of Negotiations on Goods
  Tariffs
  Nontariff measures
  Natural resource–based products
  Textiles and clothing
  Agriculture
  Tropical products
  GATT articles
  MTN agreements and arrangements
  Safeguards
  Subsidies and countervailing measures
  Intellectual property rights
  Trade-related investment measures
  Dispute settlement
  Functioning of the GATT system

Group of Negotiations on Services

A surveillance body also was established to monitor the commitment (known as the "standstill" agreement) not to apply new trade barriers while the talks were in progress and to encourage prompt unilateral rollback of GATT-illegal trade barriers.

Source: Office of the U.S. Trade Representative.

Canada in demanding that the EU and Japan open their markets to more agricultural imports.

The need to reach closure on all these diverse trade issues reflects the fact that MTNs are a comprehensive undertaking. For good reason, no agreement is complete or final until consensus is reached on the entire package. Progress in one area effects—and affects—progress in all others. Assembling a multilateral trade agreement in discrete segments would restrict the willingness of negotiators to make concessions in some areas in order to gain them in others. Nevertheless, it is difficult to accept the notion that seven years of virtually nonstop effort was necessary to forge the requisite compromises. In fact, framework agreements (which establish broad principles to which technical details are appended) for eleven of the fifteen negotiating areas had been reached by what was termed the midterm review meeting held in December 1988.[6]

The critically important political will to continue negotiating in the Uruguay Round, year after year with no clear end in sight, was sustained by an old and simple formula: Countries felt there was far more to be gained from success than failure. Economic analysis consistently predicting major gains in global trade, output, and efficiency was a permanent force for sustaining the negotiating process. The economists of the GATT, the OECD, and the World Bank predicted increases in global economic welfare (lower prices, greater returns on investment, and so on) in the range of $213 billion to $274 billion (in 1992 dollars) by the early years of the next century, or upward of a 1 percent increase in estimated planetary income at that time. It was further estimated that a successful conclusion of the negotiations would increase world trade by about $270 billion by the year 2002.[7] The anticipated effects of trade liberalization measures led the Office of the U.S. Trade Representative to predict cumulative increases in world production ten years after a Uruguay Round agreement of more than $5 trillion and a cumulative increase in U.S. output of more than $1 trillion (the equivalent of an additional $17,000 per average American family of four).[8]

Every major participating government had a legion of powerful domestic business sectors pressing wish lists for foreign market-opening and rules-making agreements. For a government to be committed to a successful outcome, it was only necessary that the coalition of anticipated winners was perceived as being economically larger and more politically influential than the anticipated losers. Import-sensitive domestic groups naturally would unequivocally oppose any agreement calling for reductions in their existing levels of protection from foreign competition. Another factor was the apparent absence of any influential government official who was anxious to provide the world with its initial empirical test of the consequences of the first failed round of multilateral trade liberalization talks. For everyone, looming in the background more explicitly than ever was the untested, potentially divisive alternative to multilateralism: inward-looking regional trade blocs forming in Western Europe, the Pacific, and North America. By 1993, many of the advanced LDCs came to fear that a collapse of the MTNs would threaten the rising investor confidence in their markets that had caused their stock markets to boom and foreign investment inflows to increase.[9]

However, in the final analysis, the critical catalyst for bringing the Uruguay Round to a successful conclusion was the realpolitik decision of the United States and the European Union to "get over their hang-up of open and transparent negotiations and go into the back room and cut a final deal."[10] Given the facts that in the end, no other country—including Japan—wished to challenge the traditional U.S.-EU "deal maker" roles in MTNs and that most countries had come to fear the implications of a collapse of the talks, this initiative generated more sighs of relief than antagonism.[11]

The Substance of the Agreement

The breadth of the Uruguay Round agreement in reducing trade barriers and installing new rules of national behavior is unprecedented. Forty specific agreements are involved. No previous multilateral trade exercise produced as many first-time arrangements on previously unregulated trade issues. Although in virtually no instance were its negotiating objectives completely met, the U.S. government was largely successful in converting priority objectives into agreements on liberalization measures and in inaugurating sets of rules on newly emerging issues.

As is always the case at the conclusion of a multilateral trade negotiation, there were net winners within the U.S. economy: relatively competitive export-oriented sectors (e.g., capital goods, paper, semiconductors, medical equipment); industries previously victimized by unfair foreign trade practices that will now be constrained (e.g., aircraft makers and software producers); and consumers and retailers. On the losing end, as usual, were the relatively less competitive, import-sensitive sectors (mainly textiles and apparel), as well as industries unable to attain the overseas market access (e.g., motion pictures) or relief from unfair foreign practices (e.g., pharmaceuticals and steel) that they ardently sought. A third category would include those sectors with inconclusive, offsetting results (e.g. financial services) and the presence of both winners and losers because of highly differentiated products (e.g., agriculture).

Specific agreements in the 500-plus pages of the Uruguay Round's Final Act can be divided into five categories: improved market access, strengthened trade rules, new trade rules, agriculture, and improvement of the governance of the international trade regime.[12]

Improved Market Access

At the heart of any MTN agreement is movement toward a more liberal trading system through implementation of a series of measures reducing official barriers to the free flow of trade.

- When the agreement is fully phased in, the size of reductions in global tariffs will, on average, exceed one-third and thereby reduce the level of tariffs imposed by the major trading countries on industrial goods to an average of about 3 percent. In some manufacturing sectors, industrial countries will eliminate tariffs entirely; in other sectors, they will make deep tariff cuts of more than 50 percent. LDCs in most cases will cut their tariff rates by smaller amounts.
- Progress in reducing nontariff barriers came in the form of clarifying the provisions, broadening the coverage, and tightening the rules of the codes of conduct originally negotiated in the Tokyo Round. Improvements were made in codes covering government procurement, customs valuation, import-licensing procedures, and technical barriers to trade (health, safety, and environmental standards).
- Bilateral quotas on textiles and apparel negotiated under the Multifiber Arrangement between most industrialized countries and most LDC suppliers will be completely phased out over a ten-year period after the entry into force of the Uruguay Round agreement. At the conclusion of this transition period, textile and clothing will be subjected to the same GATT discipline as other sectors. The agreement provides that all signatory countries (developed and less developed) to the agreement provide improved market access in this sector, and it establishes improved safeguard mechanisms, mainly to prevent import surges during the phaseout period.

Strengthened Trade Rules

The agreement also sought to strengthen and clarify the rules of national behavior associated with three long-standing, controversial trade practices that some critics charge have proliferated and expanded beyond their original intent and have become disguised forms of protectionism.

- The antidumping agreement, among other things, provides new rules to assure greater transparency of investigations (public notice and written notice of governmental actions, for example), more detailed rules concerning standard procedures to be followed in investigations, standardized methods of determining the existence of dumping and injury, and time limits on the duration of antidumping duties once imposed. The U.S. government tenaciously fought off efforts to curtail the scope of its own antidumping laws in the face of foreign accusations that they are administered in a capricious manner and constitute a de facto protectionist device.
- The agreement on subsidies and countervailing measures clarifies both the definitions and the rules to be followed when governments investigate whether imports are unfairly priced because foreign producers have benefited from subsidies provided by their governments. The most important component of this agreement is the delineation of three categories of subsidies: those that are flatly

prohibited, those that are permissible but actionable if they have demonstrably adverse effects on importing countries, and those that are nonactionable (permissible) if they comply with stipulated restrictions, such as governmental assistance to private companies for support of basic research and precompetitive development.

- Safeguard measures protect domestic producers from injury induced by fair foreign competition, but the review procedures utilized and the criteria for curtailing imports have varied widely among countries. Key provisions of the safeguard agreement include clearer definitions of injury from fair competition, a phaseout within four years of "gray area" import-retarding measures like orderly marketing agreements and voluntary export restraints, more transparency for the process of determining injury, and a maximum duration period for a safeguard action to restrict imports.

New Trade Rules

The international trading system has evolved well beyond the simple exchange of merchandise. Among the most innovative parts of the Uruguay Round agreement was a major effort to update the GATT's provisions by applying worldwide behavioral standards to three heretofore unregulated trade-related activities.

- Services, now the fastest-growing segment of international trade, became subjected to trade liberalization measures and universal rules of conduct for the first time in history. International trade involving cross-border transactions in tourism, banking services, transport, telecommunications, insurance, engineering and construction, films and television programs, accounting and legal advice, and so on are conservatively estimated (statistics on most services are sketchy) to have surpassed $1 trillion in 1994.[13] Service companies account for more than $90 billion in U.S. exports, 60 percent of U.S. output, and more than 90 percent of new jobs created in the United States since 1980.[14]

  The agreement on trade in services imposes a number of basic obligations on countries adhering to it, including most-favored-nation treatment, market access, national treatment (in which a government treats all firms in an identical manner), and the free international financial flow of payments and transfers. Since these obligations are not immediately and unconditionally applicable to all services sectors, the agreement also specifically lays the basis for progressive liberalization of trade in services through successive rounds of negotiations in the future.

- Trade-related intellectual property rights (TRIPs) is another agreement fostered by a U.S. initiative to address a major trade grievance of American business. The agreement promulgates a series of understandings that collectively improves international standards for protecting intellectual property, strengthens provisions for enforcing those standards, and establishes procedures for dispute settlement between governments. Specifically, the protection of intellectual property rights applies to patents, copyrights, trademarks, industrial designs, trade secrets, integrated circuit designs, and geographical designations (such as those used for identifying wines).

- Trade-related investment measures (TRIMs) needed to be subjected to international commercial norms because of the increased linkage between trade flows and foreign direct investment (see Chapter 4). The agreement seeks to reduce the trade-distorting effects of domestic regulations affecting foreign investors by denying signatories to the agreement the right to impose investment regulations that are inconsistent with GATT principles. Specifically named in an illustrative list of such measures are demands for minimum local content in goods domestically produced by foreign investors and for trade-balancing requirements under which the foreign investor must export as much as it imports.

Agriculture

Disagreements about the appropriate extent of the liberalization of barriers and distortions to trade in agriculture were the greatest single threat—from start to finish—to undermine the Uruguay Round. On one side of the issue were steadfast advocates of maximum liberalization, all of which are relatively efficient agricultural producers, mainly the United States and the nine member countries of the so-called Cairns Group (including Canada, Australia, Argentina, and Brazil). The hard-line advocates of a go-slow approach were led by the European Union countries, which wished to protect the integrity of their Common Agricultural Policy (see Chapter 10), and Japan and Korea, which wanted to keep their domestic rice markets fully shielded from imports.

Inability to agree on a common formula for agricultural trade liberalization was not made easier by the fact that meaningful action had to encompass simultaneous curbing of three interrelated, politically sensitive market distortions: domestic crop subsidies, import quotas, and export subsidies. Ministerial-level meetings in 1988 and again in 1990 collapsed because of the inability of negotiators to find among the hundreds of agricultural proposals introduced into the talks a way to resolve differences and forge a consensus. The apparent compromise agreement reached in November 1992 by the EU and the United States, dubbed the Blair House Accords, produced short-lived jubilation. France accused the EU Commission of having exceeded its negotiating mandate and threatened to veto the agreement unless it was renegotiated to better accommodate the needs of French farmers. The United States initially refused to comply on the grounds that the accord was final, and once again the Uruguay Round appeared to be at risk. But the EU's staunch commitment to unity subsequently convinced the Clinton administration of the necessity to yield to the French demand for modification in the details of the agricultural liberalization formula already agreed upon. Last-minute bilateral talks privately convened led to a U.S.-EU agreement. Accepting a fait accompli, the more hard-line opponents of agricultural liberalization like Japan and Korea acquiesced and agreed to partial market-opening measures; they were unwilling to be held responsible for the collapse of the round. Finally, the first giant step was taken in reducing agricultural trade barriers.

The heart of the agreement is a six-year schedule calling for reductions of at least 36 percent in budgetary outlays for export subsidies, reductions of 21 percent in the quantities of agricultural goods exported with subsidies, and reductions of 20 percent in trade-distorting farm subsidies. All nontariff barriers on agricultural imports, most of which are quotas and outright bans, must be converted to tariffs; they, along with existing tariffs, are then due to be reduced by 36 percent on average (24 percent for LDCs) over six years. In addition, a formula was included to assure guaranteed minimum access (expressed as a percentage of domestic consumption) for imports of all protected agricultural goods. The scope of this agreement was considerably more modest than the original U.S. proposal in 1987 for a sweeping elimination of governmental subsidies and controls in the agricultural sector.

A separate but related agreement established rules and disciplines for sanitary and phytosanitary regulations on animal and plant life—measures adopted by countries to protect human health and the environment. The agreement specifically recognizes the sovereign right of countries to establish such laws and regulations at whatever levels of stringency they deem appropriate. But it also provides specific guidelines designed to prevent a contracting party from using them as disguised barriers to imports.

Changes in the International Trade Regime and Creation of the World Trade Organization

Ratification of the Uruguay Round agreement heralds two important operational changes in the international trade regime. The first consists of a number of amendments to provisions that already existed in the GATT Articles of Agreement (see Chapter 8). Perhaps the most significant revision is the new procedures agreed upon for strengthening and streamlining the GATT's facilities for settling trade disputes between contracting parties. A new Dispute Settlement Understanding mandates a speedier process and greatly increases the likelihood that more judgments by dispute resolution panels will be adopted and implemented. It will now be much more difficult for a contracting party to block panel decisions that favor the other party to the dispute. In addition, enhanced rules and standards affecting governmental trade actions were added in several relatively technical areas, such as the more explicit language dealing with the use of restrictive trade practices by a country experiencing serious balance of payments problems.

The second basic change in the governance of the international trade regime consists of institutional innovation. Agreement was reached on the structure and mandate of a new World Trade Organization (WTO). Unlike the GATT, it will be a permanent, formal international organization and have authority beyond regulation of merchandise trade. When it formally came into existence at the beginning of 1995, the WTO was in effect superimposed on top of the existing GATT machinery, as amended by the Uruguay Round. The new organization's broader power begins with authority over international rules covering merchandise trade, which technically will still be spelled out in the GATT's Articles of Agreement. The WTO also was given legal responsibility for administering the provisions of the Uruguay Round's path-breaking international trade agreements—principally trade in services and trade-related intellectual property rights—that were judged to be outside of the GATT's mandate. The WTO agreement requires that member countries adhere to GATT rules as well as to virtually all provisions of multilateral trade pacts negotiated under the GATT; in closing a major loophole in international trade rules, the WTO mini- mizes the "free rider" syndrome whereby some countries could avoid compliance with trade agreements they did not like, such as any or all of the codes of conduct agreed to in the Tokyo Round. Furthermore, the WTO will manage the Trade Policy Review Mechanism, a new system for reviewing members' trade policy performance. With a charter designed to be expansive and flexible enough to give it jurisdiction over new trade issues that emerge in the future (see Chapter 15), the WTO likely will evolve into an organizational equal of the International Monetary Fund (IMF) and the World Bank.

In the final phase of the legislative process to approve the statute implementing the Uruguay Round legislation, the most controversial issue in Washington was not the extent of trade liberalization but rather the WTO's alleged threat to U.S. sover- eignty. First, the general concern was voiced by some opponents that the United States might someday find itself being outvoted by smaller countries, should one- country-one-vote procedures supersede the initial plan to operate the WTO (like the GATT) by consensus. More important, several key members of Congress voiced sympathy for the more specific fear that the WTO's enhanced dispute settlement procedures would produce a "secret tribunal" whose binding legal decisions could force the United States into changing its laws and adopting trade measures against its will. Despite strenuously arguing that this was not the case[15] (e.g., a country that loses a dispute settlement decision may simply opt to accept retaliation from the winning country), the administration agreed to a last-minute compromise with in- coming Senate Majority Leader Robert Dole. The two sides agreed to draft supple- mental legislation designed to "protect" U.S. sovereignty by establishing a domestic review mechanism for dispute settlement decisions and procedures to facilitate a congressionally mandated withdrawal from the WTO under specified circum- stances. Articulation of concern for U.S. membership in the WTO was largely re- lated to Congress's long-standing concern that U.S. trade policy could tilt too far away from concern for domestic interests and too far in the direction of internation- alism.

Conclusions and Outlook

Parallel with the forces previously identified as contributing to the approval of NAFTA, U.S. acceptance of the Uruguay Round agreement ultimately reflected a domestic political consensus that the majority of U.S. companies, workers, and consumers would gain substantial economic benefits from the global market-opening measures that had been agreed upon. An intensifying national predisposition to the ideology of liberal trade re-created two key phenomena. First, the United States recorded yet another success in its forty-year record of global leadership in encouraging the initiation of new rounds of multilateral trade negotiations. Second, the administration ultimately was able to coax Congress into giving it full legal authorization to implement the agreements concluded in the Uruguay Round. Throughout the process, the legislative branch demanded minimum U.S. negotiating achievements and provided a credible "bad cop" to bolster the administration's negotiating leverage with foreign governments. However, Congress never disagreed with the majority of U.S. business in supporting a successful Uruguay Round outcome. Unable to halt the approval of implementing legislation, the minority of domestic producers that will be hurt (e.g., the apparel industry) by the further phaseout of trade barriers is left with only two options: quickly achieving improved efficiency or applying for long-established legislative remedies for import-induced injury.

The Uruguay Round agreement will probably be best remembered for its unprecedented scope in broadening the process of multilateral trade liberalization to include new areas of action, principally services and agriculture. Although this move was a major event, praise for the results of the round needs to be qualified. The sheer number of different agreements means that some are better articulated and constructed than others. Some will be better enforced than others. The first agreements on specific trade issues are seldom, if ever, definitive because the priority of compromise leaves many rough edges to be smoothed out. Loopholes have not yet been discovered and exploited. The private sectors in all countries will grumble for years that their government conceded too much and got too little. Furthermore, no matter how innovative, the Uruguay Round agreement cannot prevent the introduction and escalation of new trade disputes.

The agreement marks the start of another phase in the history of both the international trading system and U.S. trade policy. It is a temporary phase because future global negotiations, perhaps with more limited, less ambitious agendas, are inevitable. The task of liberalizing existing trade barriers is still far from being completed, and clever policymakers and businesspeople are sure to invent new barriers. Government officials and trade negotiators are still playing catch-up—and probably always will be—with the ever-evolving dynamics of the international marketplace.

For Further Reading

Bhagwati, Jagdish. *The World Trading System at Risk.* Princeton, N.J.: Princeton University Press, 1991.

Golt, Sidney. *The GATT Negotiations 1986–1990: Origins, Issues, and Prospects.* Washington, D.C.: National Planning Association, 1988.

Report to the Congress on the Extension of Fast-Track Procedures. Presidential submission (via the Office of the U.S. Trade Representative), March 1, 1991.

Schott, Jeffrey J. *The Uruguay Round: An Assessment.* Washington, D.C.: Institute for International Economics, 1994.

"Trade Agreements Resulting from the Uruguay Round of Multilateral Trade Negotiations." White House statement, December 15, 1993.

Notes

1. Office of the U.S. Trade Representative, *Annual Report of the President of the United States on the Trade Agreements Program, 1984–1985* (Washington, D.C.: U.S. Government Printing Office, 1986), p. 61.

2. Ernest Preeg, *Traders and Diplomats* (Washington, D.C.: Brookings Institution, 1970), p. 15.

3. Office of the U.S. Trade Representative, *op. cit.,* p. 59.

4. "The Uruguay Round of GATT Trade Negotiations," Federal Reserve Bank of New York research paper no. 9119, June 1991, p. 29.

5. General Agreement on Tariffs and Trade, "GATT Focus," August-September 1993, p. 5; and *Financial Times,* August 16, 1993, p. 3.

6. "Report to the Congress on the Extension of Fast-Track Procedures," presidential submission, March 1, 1991, p. 5.

7. *Financial Times,* December 16, 1993, p. 15; and *New York Times,* December 15, 1993, p. D18.

8. Office of the U.S. Trade Representative, *1993 Trade Policy Agenda and 1992 Annual Report,* p. 31.

9. Not-for-attribution interview with U.S. Trade Representative official, January 1994.

10. *Ibid.* A second factor helping to expedite the conclusion of the round was the so-called Dunkel draft. Arthur Dunkel, then director general of GATT, in late 1991 distributed for everyone's consideration the draft text of a complete Final Act. The GATT Secretariat added suggested compromise language for provisions on which no agreement had yet been reached.

11. *Ibid.*

12. Most of the data on the Uruguay Round's Final Act found in this section are based on the text of the information letter sent by the president to the Congress December 15, 1993; it provides an excellent summary of the terms of the agreement.

13. World Trade Organization, "Focus," March-April 1995, p. 5.

14. "Report to the Congress on the Extension of Fast-Track Procedures," p. 51.

15. See, for example, "Description of Agreement with Senator Dole," USTR press release, November 23, 1994; and the text of the letter to Senator Robert Dole from the USTR, Michael Kantor, November 23, 1994.

14 Trade Policy Options for the Future

During the initial post–World War II period, U.S. international economic hegemony contributed to an unusually broad-based consensus on U.S. import and export policies. The nearly universally accepted priorities included espousing liberal trade in general, opening the U.S. market wider to its new allies in the cold war, accepting the latter's limited ability to import U.S. goods, and restricting exports of military and high-technology goods to communist bloc countries. The consensus began fading in the late 1960s because of structural changes in international economic and political relations. Western Europe and Japan rose to the ranks of international commercial superpowers and challenged U.S. competitiveness in world markets. Then the Soviet empire suffered political and economic disintegration, ending the cold war and further eroding consensus.

In the mid-1990s, disagreement abounds on the quality of existing policies and on the nature and extent of needed changes in current trade tactics and strategy. The continuation of annual U.S. merchandise trade deficits in the $100 billion–plus range is a definite cause of domestic political alarm and a probable cause for economic concern (e.g., it could trigger a precipitous fall in the dollar's exchange rate). A solid majority of public opinion exists only on the assertion that change in the trade policy status quo is needed.

In this chapter we first assess contemporary trade policy and then outline the wide range of strategies available for immediate adoption. These options for the future course of trade policy will be offered in a nonjudgmental manner; we discuss the strengths and weaknesses of each but do not advocate one over another. There is no implication that U.S. trade policy needs to select just *one* of these options. The alternative courses of action described here are not always mutually exclusive. In many cases, ideas from several policy scenarios are sufficiently compatible that they could be stitched together to form additional variations of foreign trade objectives and strategies.

The First Task:
Identifying Economic Reality

An unusually high degree of ambiguity about the "proper" direction for U.S. trade policy in the twenty-first century is inevitable. In the first place, this ambiguity is an offshoot of the larger uncertainty concerning precise calculations of the degree of weakness (if any) of the U.S. trade position. Before trying to fix something, it is logical first to confirm that something is wrong and then determine its source and severity.

The answer to the question of the gravity of the problem cannot be properly measured in terms of the large mathematical size of the U.S. merchandise trade deficit. How big a deficit is too big? How relevant is this deficit when looked at in isolation? Should it be offset by factoring in the consistent surplus in the services account of the U.S. balance of payments? Should the trade deficit be tracked as a percentage of GDP? Is the size of the deficit a simple, inevitable derivative of the domestic saving-investment imbalance? If so, there is no foreign trade problem per se. Or is the deficit the result of a secular decline in U.S. industrial competitiveness? If so, the correction once again lies not primarily in traditional trade policy tools but in internal reforms such as greater capital formation, larger increases in productivity, and improved education. Should international monetary forces, namely additional dollar depreciation, be looked to as the primary means of reducing the trade deficit? There are no clear answers to any of these questions.

A second major factor complicating the debate on where to go from here is the blurring of the distinction between import and export policies. Support is growing for implementing U.S. import barriers as retaliation for other countries' refusal to reduce their barriers to U.S. exports. Another complication is that the growing acceptance of the limits of conventionally defined trade policy has meant a new emphasis on changes in related domestic policies—in macroeconomic issues, science and technology, education and worker training, regulatory practices, and so on—in the effort to improve the U.S. trade balance. There is also a growing appreciation of how other international economic issues, like exchange rate policy and patterns of foreign direct investment, are major variables in U.S. export and import performance.

Determining the proper direction for future U.S. trade policy presupposes clear answers to the unusually large number of critically important but virtually unanswerable dilemmas that had accumulated by the mid-1990s. For example, there is no clear answer about the extent to which the commercial priority of export maximization should displace the national security, foreign policy, and human rights considerations that repeatedly have spawned U.S. export restraints.

On the import side, there is widespread acceptance (outside of the environmental community) of the abstract notion that the ultimate guiding star of U.S. trade policy should be dogged pursuit of a more liberal trading system through a gradually phased-in dismantling of barriers to trade with all countries fully participating. However, the fundamental question of what policies to adopt in the short run still remains. Most economists argue that importing is the most important part of foreign trade, and that for the United States, as for all countries, the overall national welfare benefits from acquiring cheap imports. Hence, according to this argument, the U.S. government should emphasize liberal trade policies no matter what other countries do. Other policy advocates have argued that the way to protect free trade is to retaliate against those who do not practice it. Finally, there is no agreement on how much the U.S. trade deficit is an external trading problem and how much is a competitiveness problem of internal origin, which may or may not require additional government intervention to reverse.

A final crucial question has overtones of game theory: What is the best way to respond to trading partners' practices that are perceived to be injurious? Different philosophies present at least three possible courses of action: immediately replicate the practices in full (trade barriers, industrial policy, and so on), diplomatically request their termination, or unequivocally threaten and resort to retaliation if they do not cease.

Options for Pursuing an Optimal Import Policy

The debate about future U.S. trade strategy is no longer a black-and-white argument between pure free traders and ardent protectionists. Instead, the debate is mainly between advocates of government activism and advocates of reliance on market forces.

Most analysts have sifted through a mountain of often contradictory data and priorities to make a somewhat hedged argument that tacitly admits their advice is not perfect but is, at a minimum, less flawed than the alternatives. The order in which the major trade policy options are briefly reviewed here is not necessarily indicative of either their public popularity or the authors' (unstated) personal preferences. Space constraints have curtailed discussion of potential changes in domestic policy that could or should complement potential trade policy changes.

Economists are still in the vanguard of those persons committed to the proposition that an essentially *free trade* strategy makes the most sense. The liberal trade case accepts the notion that the core assumption of comparative advantage is still applicable: Any country maximizes its welfare by producing those goods that are relatively cheaper to produce domestically and exchanging them for goods that would be relatively expensive to produce at home. As the Nobel-winning economist Paul Samuelson has written, "Free trade promotes a mutually profitable division of labor, greatly enhances the potential real national product of all nations, and makes possible higher standards of living all over the globe."[1]

The recommended course of action in this case is rigid adherence to an open trading system with an emphasis on multilateral, regional, and bilateral negotiations aimed at a steady dismantling of remaining barriers and distortions to trade. Free trade advocates argue that to impose import barriers, even if other countries do so, is tantamount to shooting oneself in the foot. The advisability of turning the other cheek to other countries' trade barriers is compatible with an economic argument traceable to Adam Smith: Since consumption is the sole end of production, consumers' interests come before producers' interests, especially those of inefficient producers. Carried to its logical conclusion, this strategy recommends that the U.S. government take no action to offset the de facto subsidies provided to domestic consumers when imports are sold at prices below fair value.

A relatively free flow of imports is seen as an essential ingredient for assuring the degree of competition necessary to generate ongoing cost reductions and productivity gains in U.S. industry. It is hard to dispute the proposition that external competition is a critical variable in convincing corporate executives and production line workers that their future success and well-being depend on their ability to constantly innovate, increase efficiency, and produce quality goods.

The free trade option is also defended on the grounds that the alternatives are excessively costly. Adoption of protectionist measures is often criticized on the basis that efforts to protect some industries invariably harm related industries, even if the injury is inflicted unintentionally. For example, end users suffer reduced price competitiveness to the extent that they are denied access to the cheapest source of components. As Anne Krueger has further argued, "A look at the important sectors in which the United States has adopted protectionist policies over the past several decades does not reveal a single instance of major economic gains."[2] (This argument is dismissed out of hand by proponents of the next two policy options.)

A large number of real-world people in business and politics believe that the alleged benefits of free trade are based on anachronistic assumptions. Nevertheless, there is virtually no advocacy from major opinion-makers for the diametrically opposite policy option: *unilateral U.S. protectionism.* For many years, no responsible voices have tried to make the rather untenable case that U.S. trade problems would best be cured by reviving the draconian worldwide import restrictions of the early 1930s.

The only new policy option proposal that comes even close to resembling old-style protectionism is *managed trade,* an inexact term used to describe a more activist governmental role in seeking to control inward and outward trade flows. On the import-retarding side, advocates of managed trade seek to replace the existing practice of resorting to trade barriers on an ad hoc basis with what the French once called "organized free trade." The latter supposedly would prevent excessive import competition in a limited number of sensitive, specifically designated product sectors. Import barriers and export restraints by foreigners also have the alleged advantage of giving temporary breathing space to import-impacted industries to restructure themselves to achieve greater efficiency.

U.S. supporters of managed trade claim that the decline of U.S. international economic hegemony and the embrace of industrial policies and trade restrictions by other countries have rendered obsolete any continuation of the arguably misplaced U.S. commitment to a trade ideology based strictly on laissez-faire concepts. The futile effort by the United States to construct the elusive but admittedly first-best policy of a free market–based international trading system, Robert Kuttner has argued, "not only disadvantages U.S. industry, but also leaves the world trading system with a dishonest and inefficient blend of subsidy, suboptimal investment, and subterfuge."[3] U.S. acceptance of a system of managed trade, it is argued, would add coherence to the existing U.S. pattern of imposing import restraints in a manner that many consider to be hypocritical and ineffective. Past and current departures by the United States from its liberal trade stance are characterized as being implemented with guilt, poorly thought out, lacking in long-term strategic purpose, and "generally not helpful either to the trading system or to America's own economic self-interest."[4]

A different strain of managed trade is called *aggressive unilateralism* (some refer to it as "bilateralism"). The core intellectual concept underlying this trade option is the need for the United States to more forcefully demand "reciprocity"—achieving access to every foreign market comparable in scope to the presumably more open U.S. market. On the operational level, this policy option emphasizes bilateral negotiations to reduce barriers in foreign markets to U.S. exports. This strategy originated in the assumption that the most effective means of eliminating the unsustainably large U.S. trade deficit is by increasing exports, not reducing imports. Although it includes the genuine threat of retaliation in the form of U.S. import barriers if other countries refuse to reduce their barriers, the clearly stated priority of aggressive unilateralism is to achieve trade expansion, more open markets, and increased global competition.

Opposition to this strategy is based on the belief that it is an overly aggressive approach in which the less-than-free-trade United States takes it upon itself to act as plaintiff, judge, and jury to decide unilaterally which foreign trade barriers are unacceptable and must be phased out. Most committed liberal traders abhor the possibility that failed diplomacy—a refusal of the targeted country to offer concessions—will result in an escalating trade war. When the United States feels obliged to retaliate with its own barriers, it runs the risk of triggering a mutually injurious spiral of retaliation and counterretaliation. Advocates of protecting and promoting import-sensitive domestic industries do not embrace aggressive unilateralism because most of them consider it to be excessively concerned with promoting the welfare of export industries.

Results-oriented trade policy is a combination of bilateralism, aggressive unilateralism, and managed trade. All of these options share the common intellectual heritage of being primarily a response to the "Japanese challenge." The perception that the world's greatest contemporary industrial miracle—Japan—succeeded largely by combining a unique quasi-market variant of guided capitalism with a pursuit of adversarial, nonliberal trade practices is by far the single most important instigator of the many new U.S. trade strategies suggested since the mid-1980s.

Results-oriented trade strategy heretofore has been aimed solely at dealing with the still-unanswered question of why countless Japanese liberalization measures have collectively failed to produce either the desired ease of foreign access to that market or equilibrium in the U.S.-Japanese bilateral trade balance. In some cases, U.S. high-tech industries have noted that despite high market shares throughout the world for their goods, their market share in Japan is far below average—despite the absence of overt trade barriers and the relatively high prices in Japan for most locally produced manufactured goods. A results-oriented trade policy would seek to induce the Japanese to accept a specific numerical target, such as a reduction in the dollar size of their bilateral U.S. surplus, an increase in their imports of manufactured goods, or a minimum market share for imports of a specific product. At a minimum, a basket of indicators would be established by which to judge sufficient results of specific import liberalization measures. The underlying theory is that their market is sufficiently different that it makes the most sense to give the Japanese specific expectations of import increases and then to tell them to go about achieving the stipulated voluntary import expansion in any way they see fit.

The definitive example of U.S. implementation of results-oriented trade policy (as of early 1995) was the bilateral semiconductor agreement originally signed with Japan in 1986, a key provision of which informally established a 20 percent market share target in Japan for all foreign-made semiconductors. A more abstract version of the results-oriented trade approach can be seen in the U.S.-Japanese framework agreement of July 1993, which covered a number of structural and sectoral issues. A key provision establishes the use of "objective criteria, either qualitative or quantitative"—as opposed to counting the number or sincerity of Japanese market-opening measures—to measure progress made by either side in complying with future market-opening agreements.

Despite the self-described hard-nosed realism of this strategy, the emphasis on achieving results represents a potentially dangerous abandonment of the fundamental reliance on rules to guide state behavior in the international trade regime. Substituting quantitative targets for normative behavior is a policy strategy that has been criticized as being arbitrary, fostering creation of more foreign cartels to assign incremental import requirements, wrongly presupposing that the U.S. government knows exactly what the appropriate minimum market share for a given product should be in a specific foreign market, and arrogantly assuming that the United States need offer no quid pro quo. Furthermore, some worry that this approach is open to abuse and illogical extremes, namely an unending array of demands that the Japanese (or anyone else) buy a minimum amount of U.S.-made goods that simply are not attractive and competitive in that market.

A final major trade option advocated for the United States entails support for the U.S. high-tech sector through *an activist science and technology policy.* This option, a euphemism for "industrial policy," would encompass more interventionist domestic policies with a "strategic trade" component designed to be responsive to contemporary changes in global business conditions. These changes include the extraordinary economic characteristics of vanguard high-tech industries (e.g., risky, extremely high-cost product development and production efforts) as well as the strong competitive challenge imposed by the targeting efforts of foreign industrial programs, primarily Japan's. High-technology industries are viewed as being disproportionately important to the future strength of the U.S. economy because of their unrivaled contribution to private R&D spending, unusually high social returns from innovations and technological advances that inure to other sectors, the above-average wages they pay to their high-skilled workers, their above-average rate of return on capital, the growing national security importance of commercial technology in advancing defense technology, and so on.

Prior to becoming the Clinton administration's first chairperson of the Council of Economic Advisers, Laura D'Andrea Tyson summarized the case for the interventionist option in the following terms:

> Technology-intensive industries violate the assumptions of free trade theory and the static economic concepts that are the traditional basis for US trade policy. In such industries, costs fall and product quality improves as the scale of production increases, the returns to technological advance create beneficial spillovers for other economic activities, and barriers to entry generate market structures rife with first-mover advantages and strategic behavior. A nation's competitive position in industries with these characteristics is less a function of its national factor endowments and more a function of strategic interactions between its firms and government, and between them and the firms and governments of other nations.[5]

It is important to note that Tyson expresses a number of caveats in connection with the interventionist option. As a self-described "cautious activist," she has stated her preference for policies that encourage trade and competition while noting that strategic trade policies ultimately are a stopgap measure "to defend American economic interests in the absence of multilateral rules."[6]

Critics of the activist-government approach to enhanced U.S. industrial competitiveness dismiss the idea that the U.S. government can pick winners and losers among different economic sectors, a task allegedly best left to private markets. There are no unambiguous economic criteria for selecting genuinely strategic technologies and rejecting pleas of special interest groups for government nurturing. Opponents argue that an industry viewed as having a bright future can raise capital from private investors and is not in need of federal subsidies. Strategic trade policy was criticized by two Brookings Institution economists on the grounds that it replaces competition among firms with competition among bureaucrats. They warned that given the nature of the U.S. political system, "any attempt to divide the pie would be based not on strategic economic and trade criteria, but on political trade-offs that would reflect lobbying skills."[7]

In a more gentle vein, another U.S. trade strategy option involves a quantum leap in the reduction of U.S. import barriers. *Regionalism* involves participation in free trade agreements with a limited number of like-minded countries, a goal at least partially inconsistent with the traditional U.S. emphasis on multilateral trade liberalization. This strategy originates partly from a defensive reaction to the expanding economic integration in Europe; it also springs from the increasingly popular belief that regional trade liberalization is a mutually advantageous, relatively efficient means of reducing trade barriers. For example, free trade areas strive to totally dismantle trade restrictions among member counties, in contrast to the piecemeal liberalization approach that was utilized in GATT, the multilateral forum. Free trade areas can also incorporate agreements on issues, as best exemplified by environmental and labor standards, that have not yet been adopted at the multilateral level.

In the mid-1990s, U.S. interest in creating and joining free trade blocs suddenly jumped to an all-time high. Within a matter of weeks at the end of 1994, President Clinton participated in two regional summit meetings, both of which resulted in agreement on the construction of long-term timetables for establishing regional free trade. If all goes according to design, the United States (and a few other countries) could, by the second decade of the twenty-first century, find itself a member of two overlapping free trade blocs—one in the Asia-Pacific region and the other in the Western Hemisphere. Presumably, U.S. trade officials are about to expend at least a decade's worth of time and energy in simultaneously seeking to negotiate a free trade arrangement under the aegis of the Asia-Pacific Economic Cooperation forum and to create the Free Trade Area of the Americas.[8]

The option of a more *environmentally friendly* trade policy has achieved greater prominence because of the recent efforts of environmental groups that until the late 1980s paid little attention to foreign trade issues. As a result of their domestic political clout, a new set of concerns has been inserted in U.S. trade policy philosophy. These groups want the global trading system to be altered in a way that assures a heightened awareness of the impact of international commerce on the world's ecosystems and natural resources. Environmentalists urge that less emphasis be placed on policies seeking the maximization of economic growth and consumption; they also advocate downgrading the emphasis placed on a means of achieving these ends: progressive liberalization of trade barriers. Environmental organizations argue the merits of promoting sustainable development. They also advocate embracing a price structure that factors social costs to the world's land, air, and water into calculations of production costs—so that manufacturers are not drawn to countries with the least enforcement of environmental protection regulations. These groups do not want GATT or any other multilateral rules to supersede U.S. environmental protection laws. They oppose any international regime that would force the U.S. government to relax the enforcement of these laws in order to descend to a less vigorous, least-common-denominator global environmental protection standard. Although no one opposes the ultimate objectives of cleaner air, water, and land, the culture and operating style of many environmental groups differ so significantly from traditional players in the international trade community that achievement of consensus between these two groups has been precluded by an excess of polemics. The sudden emergence in the United States of politically significant, unequivocal opposition by several environmental groups to both NAFTA and the Uruguay Round agreement exemplifies the insertion of their concerns into the overall trade policy equation.

A final, somewhat specialized trade policy strategy proposes adoption of an alternative method of restricting sensitive imports. Several international economists have suggested that the U.S. government conduct *quota auctions* in lieu of orderly marketing agreements and voluntary export restraints; the latter often allow exporting countries to capture economic rents—large profit margins through price increases instituted after supply is constricted. Foreign producers would be invited to make cash bids for shares of import quotas when the U.S. government decided that import relief was required to protect an injured industry. Presumably, the lowest-cost exporters would submit the highest bids. Payments from such bids would have two benefits: They would limit price increases for exports placed under quantitative limits, and they would increase U.S. government revenues (at the expense of foreign exporters). At least some of the revenues collected could be used to finance restructuring programs for the protected industries. A simple alternative option for the U.S. government is to impose *higher tariffs* when the imposition of new trade barriers is deemed unavoidable. Although tariffs are unfashionable for historical reasons and require compensation under GATT rules to exporting countries affected by them, as a whole they tend to be less distorting to the market mechanism than absolute quantitative restrictions.

Options for Restructuring Export Policy

Inherent contradictions and dilemmas continue to bedevil U.S. export policy at a time when the need for change seems to be imperative. On economic grounds, there are compelling reasons to increase exports: This is the optimal means of reducing the structural U.S. trade deficit (as opposed to reducing imports), and this is an effective means of allowing U.S. companies to increase profits, reduce unit production costs, and hire additional workers. Tactics for expanding exports fall into two programmatic categories: increased positive support and decreased negative efforts.

A genuine upgrading of the importance accorded to the positive aspect—programs to promote and expand exports—is the first of several options that are available for changing U.S. policy in this sector. A new export promotion strategy could be formulated in connection with an upgraded dialogue between the White House and the business leaders on the president's export advisory council (known by different names under different administrations), which through the years has had a marginal impact on policy at best. Efforts also would be needed to enhance the effectiveness and, if necessary, the dollar amounts of official U.S. export promotion programs. For example, the executive branch could create a unified export promotion budget that for the first time would allocate limited governmental funds according to a carefully crafted set of export enhancement priorities.

Two diverse options exist for the negative dimension of export policy: export controls (on designated goods) and sanctions (on designated countries). The government could preserve the existing high propensity to utilize such measures, or it could virtually eliminate them. Consensus as to which option is the wiser course of action is unlikely to be reached anytime soon because of the inherent dilemmas of deciding the relative merits of restricting exports. For example, it is difficult to impossible to differentiate beforehand between sanctions that have excellent prospects for achieving their stated objectives and those sanctions that will be symbolic, ineffectual, not cost-effective, and unlikely to effect a change in the behavior of government in the targeted country. It is pure value judgment to justify export restraints imposed on a unilateral basis if they merely make the initiating country feel righteous and moral while simultaneously promoting the exports of countries that continue selling to the targeted country. The U.S. trade policymaking process will not (and perhaps should not) easily shed such American values as an innate sense of morality, a desire to lead by doing, or a relatively relaxed view of the need for export maximization.

Conversely, economic benefits would accrue to U.S. companies to the extent that the U.S. government moderated its relatively onerous system of export restraints and adopted the more relaxed approach of the other industrialized countries. Reasons for doing so begin with the fact that the United States is suffering from a declining ability to intimidate targeted countries by single-handedly restricting exports. This lessened power is attributable to four trends:

1. the further erosion of the role of the United States as the free world's ideological leader;
2. the accelerating global proliferation of high-technology production capabilities;
3. the declining number of technologies in which U.S. industry maintains undisputed world leadership;
4. the increased importance of exports to all countries' national economic performance.

At some point, the U.S. government might consider reimbursing private companies for the costs of lost export sales inflicted by aggressive export sanctions practices.

The option exists for radical change by adopting a no-holds-barred export expansion approach that restricts sales only of weapons and the most sensitive of dual-use technologies and then only for purely national security, not human rights reasons. Quiet diplomacy to modify repugnant foreign political behavior would replace trade sanctions. It would be accepted as fact that most export sanctions do not work (even as an act of first resort) and that they usually hurt ordinary citizens and reward the elites who can establish and frequent a black market. Under such a scenario, U.S. trade sanctions policy would shift to an emphasis on friendly and closer commercial relations. The latter strategy, some would argue, is a better method than a punitive, hard-line approach for encouraging indigenous forces to moderate behavior of renegade governments. Resort to export controls and sanctions would become an infrequent exception rather than the rule, and official export promotion efforts through the Export-Import Bank and the Commerce Department would expand geometrically. Jobs and overseas sales would undoubtedly increase as part of a "if you can't beat 'em, join 'em" strategy that could go as far as seeking the level of the most mercantilist of U.S. trading partners.

In addition to diminished use of export controls and sanctions, the effort to make U.S. policy export-friendly would require changes in (1) all legislation that discourages or inhibits exports, including the Foreign Corrupt Practices Act and antiboycott laws; (2) existing tax laws and all future tax proposals that directly or indirectly could affect U.S. international commerce; and (3) the availability of official concessional export financing at below commercial market rates.

Nevertheless, export sanctions as leverage on foreign countries will always make sense in certain circumstances. Despite the recent reconfiguration of the world order that has blurred the designation of real and permanent enemies, the United States and countries friendly to it still have the same fundamental rationale for imposing export controls: Some goods need to be prevented from reaching some countries under some circumstances. Weapons of mass destruction are simply too dangerous to ship to governments that cannot be fully trusted. Actions by some governments (e.g., Iraq and Serbia) are deemed so offensive to accepted international behavior that they must be penalized at least by economic sanctions, if not by a military response as well.

The most likely export policy option to be selected by the U.S. government is a middle-of-the-road cooperative approach. It conceivably would be one built around a new, updated international regime of export controls, one modeled on the efforts pursued by the United States and its allies in the former Coordinating Committee on Multilateral Export Controls (COCOM). Although common rules and multilateral cooperation would continue to be watchwords, a new export controls regime is an option that would address the post–cold war reality of more frequent but smaller-scale threats posed by Third World countries to the interests of the United States and its friends. A North-South axis needs to replace the old East-West axis of multinational export control efforts. In addition, it is probably inevitable that restraints on the international sale of dual-use technologies will have to be strictly limited in number—"higher walls around fewer goods," in the jargon of export control. A final new export policy option is creation of a new institution managing global efforts to control the proliferation of weapons and related technologies. To achieve maximum effectiveness, it would need to have a broader membership than did COCOM. This means expanding membership in a new group to include not only traditionally neutral countries like Switzerland and Sweden but the old targets of COCOM as well: the former Soviet Union and China.

Conclusions and Outlook

A dispassionate examination of the various trade policy options just discussed reveals none that can be categorically dismissed on either economic or political grounds as being totally logical or totally inappropriate. It is not necessarily the case that one option needs to be chosen to the exclusion of the others. There is enough intellectual overlap among them that in many cases, differences are more a matter of nuance than substance. U.S. trade policy, more likely than not, will evolve in a way that further incorporates pieces of many or all of these options. Total conformity to a narrowly defined norm has not been noticeable in decades.

As the United States prepares for the new millennium, the prospects for the nation to speak with one voice on trade matters are minuscule. Prospects for achieving a broader national consensus are merely unlikely. On one side, current U.S. trade policy is criticized as being afflicted by excessive free trade ambitions, disregard for the plight of workers dislocated by imports, and half-hearted efforts to defend U.S. commercial interests abroad. Elsewhere, this policy is chastised for abandoning the market mechanism whenever a politically powerful interest group demands import relief and for preaching arrogantly and hypocritically to other countries about their trade behavior. Still others warn that concentration on maximizing production, trade, and consumption is not sustainable because this approach will deplete resources and destroy the environment.

As the global economy becomes increasingly complicated and as the dividing line between the domestic economy and the trade sector becomes increasingly blurred, the trade policy debate will likely become more fractious. As the list of proposals and points of contention grows, it likely will move further away from the relatively black-and-white argument between free trade versus protection. With a seemingly diminished ability to pinpoint what is "first-best" policy, U.S. trade policies at the turn of the new century will most likely display even more shades of gray than they do today.

For Further Reading

Bayard, Thomas O., and Kimberly Ann Elliot. *Reciprocity and Retaliation in U.S. Trade Policy.* Washington, D.C.: Institute for International Economics, 1994.

Bhagwati, Jagdish *Protectionism.* Cambridge, Mass.: MIT Press, 1988.

Carter, Barry. *International Economic Sanctions: Improving the Haphazard U.S. Legal Regime.* Cambridge, U.K.: Cambridge University Press, 1988.

Krueger, Anne O. *American Trade Policy—A Tragedy in the Making.* Washington, D.C.: The American Enterprise Institute Press, 1995.

Krugman, Paul. "Is Free Trade Passé?" *Journal of Economic Perspectives,* Fall 1987, pp. 131–143.

———. *The Age of Diminished Expectations: U.S. Economic Policy in the 1990s.* Cambridge, Mass.: MIT Press, 1990.

Kuttner, Robert. *Managed Trade and Economic Sovereignty.* Washington, D.C.: Economic Policy Institute, 1989.

Lawrence, Robert Z., and Charles L. Schultze, eds. *An American Trade Strategy: Options for the 1990s.* Washington, D.C.: Brookings Institution, 1990.

Twentieth Century Fund Task Force on the Future of American Trade Policy. *The Free Trade Debate.* New York: Priority Press, 1989.

Tyson, Laura D'Andrea. *Who's Bashing Whom? Trade Conflict in High-Technology Industries.* Washington, D.C.: Institute for International Economics, 1992.

Notes

1. As quoted in John Jackson, *The World Trading System* (Cambridge: MIT Press, 1992), p. 8.

2. Anne O. Krueger, "Free Trade Is the Best Policy," in Robert Z. Lawrence and Charles L. Schultze, eds., *An American Trade Strategy: Options for the 1990s* (Washington, D.C.: Brookings Institution, 1990), p. 75.

3. Robert Kuttner, *Managed Trade and Economic Sovereignty* (Washington, D.C.: Economic Policy Institute, 1989), p. ii.

4. *Ibid.,* p. 2.

5. Laura D'Andrea Tyson, *Who's Bashing Whom? Trade Conflict in High-Technology Industries* (Washington, D.C.: Institute for International Economics, 1992), p. 3.

6. *Ibid.,* p. 255.

7. Lawrence and Schultze, *op. cit.,* p. 31.

8. The eighteen countries in the Western Hemisphere, the western Pacific, and mainland Asia (including such other economic giants as Japan and China) that committed themselves to a timetable for dismantling international trade and investment barriers among themselves by the year 2020 collectively represented slightly over half of the world's GNP and about 40 percent of global trade in 1994.

15 The Unfinished Agenda

The rush of events during 1993 in the international trading system, most notably the inauguration of the EU's single market and final approval of NAFTA and the Uruguay Round agreement, might well have been followed by a period of consolidation in global trade relations. Governmental priorities could have been expected to concentrate on efforts to fine-tune these new agreements. Instead, the pace of change accelerated in 1994. Additional initiatives dealing with new trade policy issues will likely continue at a fast-paced momentum well into the new millennium. Official efforts to expand and create new regional trade blocs are already at hand. Additional trade policy problems will continue to emerge at least as quickly as agreements are reached on disposing of existing issues. The pace of private sector innovation in the global marketplace will not abate. No plateau is in sight for the introduction of new technology, new business alliances, and new production and marketing techniques—all of which will have substantial implications for the flow of international commerce.

Presented in this chapter is a brief preview of the trends and events most likely to require new policy planning efforts and hard decisions for U.S. trade policy decisionmakers through the start of the new century.

Emerging Issues

A look into the future—the late 1990s and the early twenty-first century—suggests that immediate additions to the U.S. trade agenda will consist of efforts to flesh out the Uruguay Round agreements covering the new areas of services, intellectual property rights, and trade-related investment measures. These agreements will require a period of trial and error and of consultation before emergence of global consensus on their operational details and means of enforcement.

The U.S. trade policy agenda will soon be further expanded with the initiation of what will probably be two very lengthy negotiations to promulgate the terms and timetable for creating the free trade areas already agreed to in principle: one in the Asia-Pacific region and one in the Western Hemisphere. Efforts in the distant future to negotiate even more dramatic moves toward global free trade (e.g., establishment of open trade links among the European, Asia-Pacific, and Western Hemisphere free trade areas) are a likely scenario under a plausible assumption. Elimination of all

288

overt U.S. import barriers may have become a matter of "when, not if." Although not irreversible, a fundamental shift in the balance of power was gathering momentum in the 1990s in the domestic politics of U.S. trade policy, a trend (if it continues) that could produce unprecedented reductions in U.S. trade barriers. With a growing majority of large U.S. goods and services companies operating on a multinational basis and a growing number of manufacturing companies importing components, sentiment in the U.S. business community is tilting increasingly in favor of sweeping trade liberalization, both regionally and multilaterally.

Three emerging issues on the U.S. trade policy agenda exemplify the broadening definition of foreign trade relations. Specifically they illustrate how the focus of many new trade concerns has shifted from barriers imposed at national borders to purely internal economic practices that distort flows of imports and exports. In earlier years, such ostensibly domestic matters would have been branded as being in the realm in which sovereign countries could do as they pleased without second-guessing by outsiders.

The first issue is the *trade-environment* nexus. The "green" issue will seek to assure an economically logical, politically acceptable balance between the promotion of a larger and more efficient planetary economic output on the one hand and protection of animal, plant, land, air, and water resources on the other hand. The consensus that only controlled, or sustainable, development will protect ecosystems and preserve key natural resources is only a first step in the process of maximizing the complementarity between environmental and commercial objectives. Trade policy officials in the United States and elsewhere already are struggling with the dilemmas inherent in the mix between trade and environmental polices. One major problem has been how to determine the circumstances under which trade regulations can legitimately and appropriately be imposed to enforce a country's environmental policy. A related problem is determining if a country's need to be globally competitive and its prior international commitments to liberal trade practices should take precedence over enforcement of domestic environmental laws.

Eventually, specific international codes of behavior will need to be drafted to determine when imposition of import barriers in the name of environmental policy is a legitimate policy act and when imposition is merely a disguised form of protectionism. Viewed from a different perspective, guidelines need to be established to determine when foreign countries can and should challenge a country's environmental laws as being disguised trade protection. Yet another aspect of this new agenda item is the environmentalists' growing concern about the temptation to pursue a global "downward harmonization" of environmental protection in order to prevent the shift of production (and exports) to countries with relatively low standards of enforcement of antipollution legislation.

A second emerging U.S. trade policy concern, also gaining the public spotlight for the first time as a concern in the NAFTA debate, is the "blue" issue of *labor standards*. Past advocates of having the United States dismantle trade barriers did not envision the contemporary scenario of U.S. workers having to compete head-to-head in a free trade environment with relatively productive foreign workers who, by American values, are being exploited. Politically, the U.S. trade policymaking system cannot ignore a growing inflow of increasingly sophisticated manufactured goods from countries known to subject their labor force to long hours of toil for minuscule pay and no fringe benefits in unsafe factories, to deny workers the legal right to collective bargaining, and sometimes to utilize underage factory workers. U.S. government officials in the future almost certainly will seek to prevent "social dumping" by urging multilateral efforts (perhaps in the World Trade Organization) to refine and make more easily enforceable the obscure and largely ignored protective standards for workers promulgated in the past by the International Labor Organization, a United Nations specialized agency.

Two spin-offs of the labor standards issue seem destined to become major sources of future concern in U.S. trade policy. The first is the academic question of the extent (if any) to which rising import competition from LDCs is an explanation for the largely inexplicable, prolonged, and widespread downward drag on real wages in the U.S. manufacturing sector that has been experienced since the mid-1970s. Looming farther out on the horizon is a second important labor-related academic debating point: the possibility that a structural disadvantage is being inflicted on relatively high-paid labor in the industrialized countries by relatively cheap foreign labor becoming progressively more productive through help from foreign companies. Trade patterns are likely to be increasingly impacted by the cumulative success of multinational companies in integrating low-paid workers in countries like China and Mexico with advanced capital equipment, sophisticated manufacturing know-how and worker training programs, and managerial skills honed in the parent countries of these manufacturing companies—all of which are now easily transportable to distant lands.

Issues grouped under the rubric of domestic *competition policy* constitute a third candidate for prominent additions in the medium term to the U.S. trade policy agenda. In addition to use of antitrust laws to prevent price-fixing and market allocation schemes, competition policy deals with governmental tolerance within the home market of a number of anticompetitive business practices, including collusive efforts to discriminate against imports, rigged bidding practices, restricted access to distribution channels, and the procurement practices of private monopolies (e.g., telecommunications).

Longer-term Issues

On a longer-term basis, a *reconfiguration of the structure of the world economy* can be expected to set the stage for major changes in the world's trade agenda. A historic dispersal of global economic power is looming on the horizon. In addition to a gradual breakdown in the North-South economic divide, the world economy is in the first stage of digesting the long-term effects of the erosion of the East-West economic divide. The proliferating trend in Asia, Latin America, and parts of Africa of reduced state interventionism in favor of private sector–driven, market-directed policies and the virtual elimination of state-run command economies in the former Soviet Union, Eastern Europe, and China are likely to radically alter long-established international commercial relations.

As the North-South and East-West divisions that artificially obstructed trade and investment among regional neighbors continue to dissipate, geography should play an increasingly dominant role in determining foreign trade and direct investment flows.[1] U.S. membership in additional *regional trading blocs* would contribute to the larger trend of a gradual transformation in the long-entrenched, disproportionate concentration of commercial flows among the relatively few industrialized countries of the North. This concentration developed because of the latter's similar levels of domestic economic development, not their geographical proximity to one another. Preferential and free trade agreements will be based on overlapping categories of regional, subregional, and bilateral arrangements. Western and Eastern Europe will pursue expanded preferential trade relationships. Even the idea of negotiations leading to a preferential trade agreement in the Middle East among Israel and some nearby Arab countries cannot be dismissed as impractical.

Assuming U.S. participation in more regional trading blocs, it follows that regional economies within the United States eventually could experience greater increases in commercial activity with nearby overseas regions than with distant regions within the United States. For example, southern states are likely to concentrate more vigorously on enhancing commercial ties with Latin America and the Caribbean; Pacific Coast states would concentrate more vigorously on increased ties with the Asia-Pacific region; the industrial Midwest would focus on central Canada; and so on. The political dynamics holding together the liberal trade coalition in Congress will become even more complex if such geographical shifts in economic relations do in fact materialize.

Yet another candidate for eventual elevation to important status on the U.S. trade policy agenda is the *need to modernize basic trade rules and standards*. At some point early in the next century, it may become conventional wisdom that countries are "no longer the relevant economic units" in international commerce.[2] The first of two trends suggesting this outcome may occur is the likely growth of subregional trade relations. The second trend is the potentially dominant role of corporations in determining trade flows of manufactured goods. The continued move toward globalization of production by multinational companies suggests that at some point, a majority of sophisticated manufactured goods will become "amalgams"—products assembled with many components made in so many different points on the globe that a single country of origin will be nearly impossible to determine. The potential exists for the demise of a national identity for many goods (and, to a lesser extent, many companies) involved in international trade. A progressive decline is likely to occur in the probability that the value of local content of goods assembled by "domestic" companies necessarily exceeds the domestic content of imports bearing "foreign" labels. If this trend persists, governments may eventually decide that a new generation of trade policies designed to influence selection of the national origin of components used in the value-added process (in commercial aircraft and automobiles, for example) would be more beneficial than traditional import barriers.

By the start of the next century, the increasing linkage among international trade, investment, and monetary policies likely will lead to changes in the overall governance of the international economic order. The increasing overlap among the global trade, monetary, and financial systems likely will produce more systematized working relationships among the major international economic organizations. The annual joint meetings between the International Monetary Fund and the World Bank logically should be expanded to include the WTO. U.S. and other trade policymakers would then have a more formal voice in reviewing the fundamental forces and national policies affecting the course of the global economy.

A Concluding Outlook

An old French maxim is the theme for this concluding commentary: The more things change, the more they will remain basically the same. On the one hand, policymakers will continue to be confronted by transformations in the nature of international business. The further globalization of production will alter the economic forces that collectively determine which countries export or import which goods and services. Increased globalization also will further erode U.S. business support for official protectionist barriers to the flow of international trade and investment. In addition to these trends, foreign trade is sure to become more politicized as it becomes a bigger variable in most countries' domestic economic performance. Calculating optimal trade policy will become more problematic as interest groups affected by trade flows become more numerous and splintered.

On the other hand, most of the fundamental principles of the U.S. policy process will not change. No matter how different tomorrow's trade issues are, the decision-making process cannot escape its complex heritage of economics, politics, and the laws passed to finesse the differences between external and internal considerations. Trade policymaking simply cannot shed its traditional quixotic quest for accommodation among the differing needs of its four component sectors: domestic economics, domestic politics, international economics, and international politics. Reduced to its lowest common denominator, U.S. trade policy will always consist of an imperfect process of determining how best to serve these four separate components, an uphill task given that the objectives of these components seldom can be simultaneously maximized with a single policy or action. For the foreseeable future, the process of reconciling priorities will be administered by a partnership between an executive branch partial to external priorities and a legislative branch partial to domestic priorities.

No matter how rapid the pace of change in the world economy, however, U.S. government officials will always have to judiciously weigh the benefits of making further reductions in trade barriers against such factors as new economic theories, the injury (real or imagined) inflicted on import-sensitive sectors, and the ongoing political desire to avoid antagonizing powerful interest groups. The domestic economic advantages of minimizing U.S. export controls will still have to be measured against national security and foreign policy objectives. The desirability of using threats of retaliation to secure greater access to foreign markets for U.S. goods will still have to be balanced against the possibility of a foreign backlash and counterretaliation. In nearly every one of these cases, difficult choices will be made primarily on the basis of value judgments, not scientific truths.

Compromises will outnumber dramatic shifts in policy. U.S. trade policy will always represent the end product of selections among conflicting recommendations, each with limited degrees of wisdom and truth but not enough of either to attract universal support. The bottom-line result is that paradoxes, inconsistencies, strengths, and weaknesses will continue their uneasy coexistence in U.S. trade policies.

For Further Reading

Bergsten, C. Fred. "The Rationale for a Rosy View." *The Economist,* September 11, 1993, pp. 57–62 of special section.

Esty, Daniel C. *Greening the GATT: Trade, Environment, and the Future.* Washington, D.C.: Institute for International Economics, 1994.

Feketekuty, Geza. *The New Trade Agenda.* Group of Thirty Occasional Paper #40 (Washington, D.C.), 1992.

Hormats, Robert D. "Making Regionalism Safe." *Foreign Affairs,* March-April 1994, pp. 97–108.

Lawrence, Robert Z., Albert Bressand, and Takatoshi Ito. *A Vision for the World Economy: Openness, Diversity, and Cohesion.* Washington, D.C.: Brookings Institution, 1995.

Notes

1. Robert D. Hormats, "Making Regionalism Safe," *Foreign Affairs,* March-April 1994, p. 101.

2. C. Fred Bergsten, "The Rationale for a Rosy View," *The Economist,* September 11, 1993, p. 61 (of special section).

Appendixes

Appendix A   U.S. International Trade in Goods and Services: Balance of Payments (BOP) Basis (billions of dollars)

	Exports			Imports			Trade Balance		
	Total	*Goods*	*Services*	*Total*	*Goods*	*Services*	*Total*	*Goods*	*Services*
1970	56.6	42.5	14.2	54.4	39.9	14.5	2.3	2.6	(0.3)
1975	132.6	107.1	25.5	120.2	98.2	22.0	12.4	8.9	3.5
1980	271.8	224.3	47.6	291.2	249.8	41.5	(19.4)	(25.5)	6.1
1981	294.4	237.0	57.4	310.6	265.1	45.5	(16.2)	(28.0)	11.9
1982	275.2	211.2	64.1	299.4	247.6	51.7	(24.2)	(36.5)	12.3
1983	266.0	201.8	64.2	323.8	268.9	54.9	(57.8)	(67.1)	9.3
1984	290.9	219.9	71.0	400.1	332.4	67.7	(109.2)	(112.5)	3.3
1985	288.8	215.9	72.9	410.9	338.1	72.8	(122.1)	(122.2)	0.1
1986	309.5	223.3	86.1	448.3	368.4	79.8	(138.8)	(145.1)	6.3
1987	348.0	250.2	97.8	500.0	409.8	90.2	(152.0)	(159.6)	7.6
1988	430.2	320.2	110.0	545.0	447.2	97.9	(114.8)	(127.0)	12.1
1989	489.0	362.1	126.8	579.3	477.4	101.9	(90.3)	(115.2)	24.9
1990	537.6	389.3	148.3	616.0	498.3	117.7	(78.4)	(109.0)	30.7
1991	581.2	416.9	164.3	609.1	490.7	118.4	(27.9)	(73.8)	45.9
1992	616.9	440.4	176.6	657.3	536.5	120.9	(40.4)	(96.1)	55.7
1993	641.7	456.9	184.8	717.4	589.4	128.0	(75.7)	(132.6)	56.9

Parentheses indicate deficits.

Source: U.S. Department of Commerce, *U.S. Foreign Trade Highlights 1993.*

298

Appendix B U.S. International Trade in Goods: Balance of Payments Basis, 1980-1993

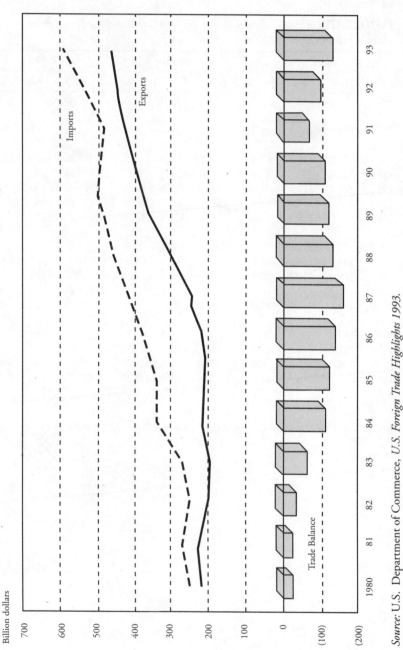

Source: U.S. Department of Commerce, *U.S. Foreign Trade Highlights 1993.*

Appendix C   Commodity Composition of U.S. Goods Trade with the World: Census Basis, 1993

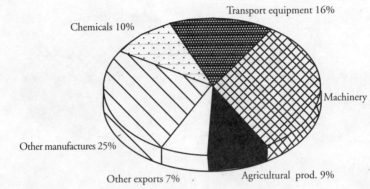

Exports: $465 Billion

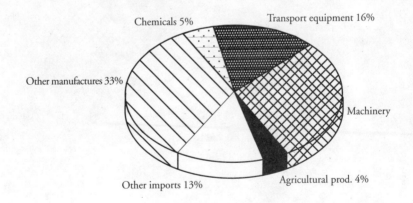

Imports: $581 Billion

Source: U.S. Department of Commerce, *U.S. Foreign Trade Highlights 1993.*

Appendix D Country Composition of U.S. Goods Trade with the World: Census Basis, 1993

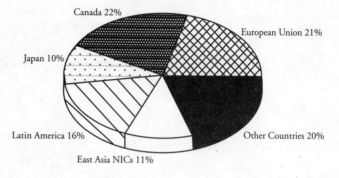

Exports: $465 Billion

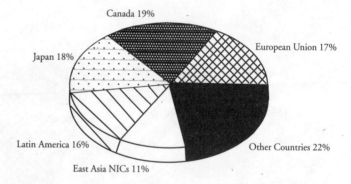

Imports: $581 Billion

Source: U.S. Department of Commerce, *U.S. Foreign Trade Highlights 1993.*

Appendix E   U.S. Manufactures Trade, 1987 and 1993. Top Ten Product
Exports, Imports, Balances; Sorted by 1993 Value Two-digit SITC Product Groups
(Census basis; millions of dollars)

SITC		1987	1993
	Exports		
77	Elec machinery & parts, nes	16,670	43,178
78	Road vehicles	21,370	41,178
79	Transport equipment, other	17,917	33,394
75	Office & ADP machines	19,945	31,348
89	Misc. manufactured articles, nes	10,303	24,282
74	Industrial machinery & parts	8,573	20,126
71	Power generating machinery	10,311	19,676
72	Special industrial machinery	9,676	18,338
87	Prof/scientf/control instruments	8,381	15,844
76	Telecomm. & sound reprod. equip	5,656	14,237
	Total Top 10 Exports	128,801	261,598
	Imports		
78	Road vehicles	72,585	83,332
77	Elec machinery & parts, nes	23,747	46,752
75	Office & ADP machines	18,318	43,182
84	Apparel/clothing/accessories	20,495	33,787
89	Misc. manufactured articles, nes	19,467	31,783
76	Telecomm. & sound reprod. equip.	20,797	27,302
71	Power generating machinery	10,650	17,163
74	Industrial machinery & parts	11,403	17,084
72	Special industrial machinery	11,233	13,546
66	Nonmetallic mineral mfrs.	8,853	11,558
	Total Top 10 Imports	217,548	325,489
	Surpluses		
79	Transport equipment, other	12,307	25,454
87	Prof/scientf/control instruments	3,546	7,392
72	Special industrial machinery	(1,557)	4,792
57	Plastics in primary form	2,944	4,683
59	Chemicals, nes	1,748	4,137
74	Industrial machinery & parts	(2,830)	3,042
71	Power generating machinery	(339)	2,513
51	Organic chemicals	2,287	1,922

(continues)

Appendix E (continued)

SITC		1987	1993
54	Medical & pharmaceutical prod.	1,241	1,708
55	Essential oils/perfumes/soaps etc	10	1,333
	Total Top 10 Surpluses	19,356	56,976
	Deficits		
78	Road vehicles	(51,215)	(42,154)
84	Apparel/clothing/accessories	(19,237)	(28,835)
76	Telecomm. & sound reprod. equip	(15,141)	(13,066)
75	Office & ADP machines	1,627	(11,834)
85	Footwear	(7,248)	(10,473)
89	Misc. manufactured articles	(9,164)	(7,502)
67	Iron and steel	(7,822)	(6,510)
66	Nonmetallic mineral mfrs.	(6,313)	(6,292)
88	Photo eq/opt. goods/watches	(2,868)	(4,221)
68	Nonferrous metals	(5,517)	(4,123)
	Total Top 10 Deficits	(122,899)	(135,009)

"Nes" = not elsewhere specified; parentheses indicate deficits.

Source: U.S. Department of Commerce, *U.S. Foreign Trade Highlights 1993.*

About the Book and Authors

This unique text integrates for the first time the three critical aspects of U.S. foreign trade policy formulation and implementation: economics, politics, and laws. In a comprehensive and nonjudgmental manner, a political scientist, an economist, and a legal scholar combine efforts to present a well-rounded view of the nature and impact of trade policy as well as how it is made. First, they give a quick review of the history of U.S. trade policy and follow this with an explication of key economic principles and theories. They outline political processes and actors, then examine the laws that emanate from the political arena as they apply to imports, exports, the GATT, and the World Trade Organization.

A final section combines the three perspectives in an analysis of key challenges to contemporary U.S. trade: Japan, the European Union, nonindustrialized countries, NAFTA, and the Uruguay Round of GATT trade negotiations. Looking toward the future, the authors conclude that given constant changes in the political, economic, and legal environments of trade, the import and export policies of the United States (and of most other countries) are subject to constant evolution—and occasional revolution.

Stephen D. Cohen is professor of international relations at The American University's School of International Service. Prior to joining the faculty in 1975, he served as a senior staff member on the White House–Congressional Commission on the Organization of the Government for the Conduct of Foreign Policy. Among Dr. Cohen's books are *The Making of United States International Economic Policy* (now in its fourth edition), *Cowboys and Samurai: Why the United States Is Losing the Battle with the Japanese, and Why It Matters,* and *International Monetary Reform, 1964–69: The Political Dimension.* **Joel R. Paul** is professor of law at the University of Connecticut School of Law and past chair of the International Economic Law Group for the American Society of International Law. He received his J.D. from Harvard University, and he was awarded an M.A. in law and diplomacy from Tufts University. Dr. Paul has also taught at the University of Leiden in Holland, Yale University Law School, and the Washington College of Law at The American University. His articles have appeared in such journals as *Harvard International Law Journal, Columbia Journal of European Law,* and *Wisconsin Journal of International Law.* **Robert A. Blecker** is associate professor of economics at The American University and a research associate at the Economic Policy Institute, both in Washington, D.C. He received his B.A. from Yale University and his M.A. and Ph.D. from Stanford University. He is the author of *Beyond the Twin Deficits: A Trade Strategy for the 1990s* and the editor of a collection of readings on *U.S. Trade Policy and Global Growth.* His articles have appeared in such journals as *Cambridge Journal of Economics, Journal of Post Keynesian Economics,* and *Weltwirtschaftliches Archiv.*

Index

Adjustment assistance, 66, 145
Advanced Technology Program, 112
Advisory committees, U.S. trade policy, 118, 180
Afghanistan, 48, 131, 155, 230
AFL-CIO. *See* American Federation of Labor and
    Congress of Industrial Organizations
Africa, 93, 219, 220
Aggressive unilateralism, 43
Agricultural imports, 112, 145, 203, 209–211.
    See also Uruguay Round of multilateral
    trade negotiations, agricultural issues
Agriculture, U.S. Department of, 134, 209
    trade policy responsibilities,112, 152
Airbus, 126, 133, 206, 208
American Federation of Labor and Congress of
    Industrial Organizations (AFL-CIO), 39,
    251
Andean Trade Preference Act, 225
Antidumping. *See* Dumping
Antitrust laws, 92
APEC. *See* Asia-Pacific Economic Cooperation
Apparel, 126, 223, 268. *See also* Textiles, trade in
Argentina, 49, 92
Arms Export Control Act, 157
Asia, 93, 219, 221, 228, 249
Asia-Pacific Economic Cooperation (APEC),
    228–229, 257, 282
AT&T Corporation, 22, 126
Atomic Energy Act, 157
Austria, 200
Autarky, 10
Automobiles, trade in, 129, 188, 191–192

Balance of payments, 12, 86–87, 111
  U.S. deficits, 16, 38
Bhagwati, Jagdish, 179
Blecker, Robert, 88
Boeing Corporation, 22, 138, 208
Boycotts, 92, 155–156
Brazil, 92, 219, 223, 227
Bretton Woods Agreement, 94, 96
Buchanan, Patrick, 245, 253
Budget deficits, U.S., 86–87

Bureaucratic politics model, 131–136
Bush, George, 19, 22, 135, 190, 225
Business cycle, 85

Cairns Group, 270
Canada, 138, 165–166, 260
    and North American Free Trade Agreement,
    239–240, 242
    See also U.S.-Canada Free Trade Agreement
CAP. *See* European Union, Common Agricultural
    Policy
Caribbean Basin Initiative, 142, 225–226
Carter, Jimmy, 48, 131, 155
CEA. *See* Council of Economic Advisers, U.S.
Cecchini, Paolo, 213
"Chicken war," 209
Chile, 225
China, 18, 43, 46, 75, 126, 217, 227, 228, 290
    MFN status, 19–23, 118, 131
    U.S. allegations of unfair trade practices, 20,
    224, 232–234
    U.S.-Chinese trade disputes. *See* China, U.S.
    allegations of unfair trade practices
    U.S.-Chinese trade imbalance, 231–232
    U.S. sanctions against, 233, 234
Citizens Trade Campaign, 255
Civil War, U.S., 29
Clinton, Bill, 127, 131, 154, 156, 190–191, 270,
    282
    and China, 19, 22–23, 234
    and NAFTA, 241, 245, 246, 255–256
COCOM. *See* Coordinating Committee on
    Multilateral Export Controls
Codes of conduct. *See* General Agreement on
    Tariffs and Trade, codes of conduct
Cold war, 34, 46–48
COMECON. *See* Council for Mutual Economic
    Assistance
Commerce, U.S. Department of, 23, 134, 135
    export control responsibilities, 47, 112,
    155–156, 284
    investigation of imports, 111, 134, 147–150,
    160 (nn 15, 16, 20)

trade policy responsibilities, 111, 145, 152
Commission on Industrial Competitiveness, 87
Commodity control list, 155
Commodity Credit Corporation, 152
Common market. *See* Customs union; European
    Union
Communist countries. *See* China; Europe,
    Eastern; Russia; Soviet Union
Comparative advantage, 28, 56–61, 79
Competition policy, 290
Competitiveness, U.S. international, 43, 85,
    87–89, 99, 136
Competitiveness Policy Council, 88
Computers, trade in, 126
Congress, U.S., 127–128, 132, 136–138, 263
    attitudes toward imports, 8, 116, 137, 162
    and International Trade Organization, 35
    and North American Free Trade Agreement,
        116, 251–253, 255–256, 264–265
    relations with executive branch, 4, 15, 20–23,
        27–33, 35–37, 40–41, 48, 106–107,
        108–109, 141–142, 292
    trade policymaking authority, 3, 15, 22,
        27–28, 40, 42, 46–48, 114–116, 264, 272
Congressional Budget Office, 115, 244
Congressional Research Service, 115
Connally, John, 136
Coordinating Committee on Multilateral Export
    Controls (COCOM), 47–48, 155, 285
Council for Mutual Economic Assistance
    (COMECOM), 230
Council of Economic Advisers, U.S. (CEA), 43,
    110, 111, 134
Countervailing duties, 40, 268
    U.S. laws, 128, 149–150
Court of International Trade, 144
Cuba, 18, 155, 229
Customs union, 77, 165, 198, 206

Debt crisis, 92–93
Decisionmaking, 106–108
    general guidelines, 121–123
    theories of, 124–136
Defense, U.S. Department of, 47, 110, 112, 133,
    135, 208
Democratic Party, 27, 30, 32
Depression, 31–32
Destler, I. M., 137
Dillon Round of multilateral trade negotiations,
    36, 205, 211, 262
Dispute settlement. *See* World Trade
    Organization, dispute settlement process

Division of labor, 56–57
Dole, Robert, 272
Dollar, U.S., 16, 84
    exchange rate, 16–17, 18 –19, 39, 41, 94–97
Dumping, 12, 126, 167–169, 268
    U.S. laws, 40, 43, 146–149
Dunkel Draft, 274 (n10)

East-West trade. *See* China; Europe, Eastern;
    Russia; Soviet Union
Economic summits, 190, 207
Economies of scale, 13, 70, 72
ECSC. *See* European Coal and Steel Community
EFTA. *See* European Free Trade Association
Egypt, 200
Eisenhower, Dwight D., 35, 36, 146
Elasticities, 86
Electronics, 126
Employment. *See* Foreign trade, and jobs
EMS. *See* European Union, European Monetary
    System
Enabling clause, 262
Energy, U.S. Department of, 112
England. *See* United Kingdom
Enterprise for the Americas Initiative, 225
Environmental issues, and foreign trade, 163,
    282, 289
    and North American Free Trade Agreement,
        241, 245–246, 251
Environmental Protection Agency, 113, 134
Escape clause, 40, 143–145, 165, 208, 269
EU. *See* European Union
Europe, Eastern, 197, 201, 205, 229–231
Europe, Western, 38, 200, 261
    relations with United States, 34, 35–36
European Coal and Steel Community (ECSC),
    199, 200
European Community. *See* European Union
European Free Trade Association (EFTA), 197
European Union (EU), 14, 36, 77–78, 221, 249
    Commission. *See* European Union, institutions
    Common Agricultural Policy (CAP), 203–204,
        209–211, 249
    common external tariff, 36
    Council of Ministers. *See* European Union,
        institutions
    EC 1992, 211–213
    European Monetary System (EMS), 202
    harmonization, 202–203
    institutions, 199–204
    and less developed countries, 200 –201
    Maastricht Treaty, 200

membership, 200
origins, 196, 199–200
role in world trade, 197
Single European Act (single market), 212, 288
U.S.-EU disagreements, 169, 199, 204–211, 216 (nn 26, 27). *See also* Airbus
U.S.-EU trade, 197–198, 261, 264, 267, 270
and Uruguay Round, 264
Exchange rates changes, 39, 41, 96–97
impact on trade flows, 16–17, 18–19, 97, 243
Executive branch, U.S., 108–113, 130–136
relations with Congress, 4, 15, 20–23, 27–33, 35–37, 40–41, 48, 106–107, 108–109, 141–142, 292
Executive Office of the President, 109–110
Export Administration Act, 48, 137, 155, 156
Export Control Act of 1949, 46–47, 138
Export controls. *See* Export policy, controls and sanctions
Export-Import Bank, 13, 45, 113, 152, 284
Export policy, U.S., 6, 13–14, 17–19, 34, 44–49, 137–138, 283 –285
controls and sanctions, 14, 18, 46–49, 51(n34), 90, 92, 155–157, 229, 283–285
voluntary export restraints. *See* Orderly marketing agreements
Export promotion policies, 13–14, 45, 112, 152–154, 227, 283, 284
Export Trading Company Act of 1982, 153
Externalities, 67, 69

Factor-price equalization theorem, 64
Fair trade, 137
Fast track provision, 40, 142, 264
Federal Communications Commission, 113
Finance Committee, Senate, 116
Finland, 200
First-best policies, 67
Flat panel display screens, 126
Footware imports, 135, 223
Ford, Gerry, 138
Foreign Agents Registration Act, 118
Foreign aid, 34, 218, 219
Foreign asset controls, 156, 157
Foreign Corrupt Practices Act, 92, 156, 157, 285
Foreign direct investment, 71, 97–99, 125, 197–198, 205, 244
impact on trade flows, 98
multinational corporation lobbying, 125
Foreign exchange market, 96
Foreign policy, U.S., 8–9, 12, 28, 108
Foreign trade

benefits of, 7, 57–61, 65
definition, 5–6
and domestic economy. *See* U.S. economy, domestic
and foreign policy. *See* Foreign policy, U.S.
free trade, 5, 61–64, 241–242, 277–278
import barriers. *See* Protectionism
inconsistencies, 4, 7, 79, 133, 293
and jobs, 37, 62–64, 66, 218
and political factors, 8–9, 26
See also Protectionism
France, 90, 270, 278
Free trade. *See* Foreign trade, free trade; Trade liberalization
Free Trade Area of the Americas, 226, 282
Free trade areas. *See* Regional free trade areas

GATS. *See* General agreement on trade in services
GATT. *See* General Agreement on Tariffs and Trade
General Accounting Office, United States, 45–46, 115
General Agreement on Tariffs and Trade (GATT), 11, 128, 150, 151, 206, 261–263, 266, 282
articles of agreement, 163–166, 272
codes of conduct, 41, 167, 169–170, 268, 272
dispute settlement. *See* World Trade Organization, dispute settlement process
obligations of participating countries, 164–165, 198, 206, 209
and U.S. laws, 162–163
See also Dillon Round of multilateral trade negotiations; Kennedy Round of multilateral trade negotiations; Tokyo Round of multilateral trade negotiations; Uruguay Round of multilateral trade negotiations; World Trade Organization
General agreement on trade in services (GATS), 170
Generalized System of Preferences (GSP), 222–223, 226, 228
"graduation," 223, 228
Gephardt, Richard, 251
Germany, 94, 203, 212
Gold, 39
Gore, Al, 131, 256
Government procurement, 169–170
Great Britain. *See* United Kingdom
Greece, 197, 200, 249
Group of Seven (G–7), 43, 189, 190
G–7. *See* Group of Seven
GSP. *See* Generalized System of Preference

Haiti, 18
Hamilton, Alexander, 27, 28

Heckscher-Ohlin theory, 60–61, 62–65, 69–73, 79

Hegemony, 30, 31, 34

High-tech industries, 131, 279–280

Hong Kong, 20, 227–228

Hoover, Herbert, 31–32

Hormats, Robert, 197

Hormones. *See* European Union, U.S.-EU disagreements

Hull, Cordell, 10, 32–33

Human rights, 18, 20 –21

IBM Corporation, 189

Ideology, 123, 276

IMF. *See* International Monetary Fund

Import policy, 5, 7, 15–19. *See also* Trade liberalization

    barriers to imports. *See* Protectionism

    import-induced injury, 11–12, 17, 26, 40, 62–65, 143–144, 149, 150

Import substitution policy, 227

Income elasticities. *See* Elasticities

Indonesia, 219, 227

Industrial policy, 71, 280–281

Infant industry argument, 60

Injury, import-induced. *See* Import policy, import-induced injury

Intellectual property rights, 12, 92, 125, 143, 151, 154–155, 234, 263, 265. *See also* Special 301

Interior, U.S. Department of, 112

International Emergency Economic Powers Act, 156–157

International Monetary Fund (IMF), 94, 272, 292

International monetary system, 93–97

International trade. *See* Foreign trade

International Trade Commission, 40, 113

    investigations, 143–145, 148–151, 159 (nn 6, 8), 244

International Trade Organization, 32, 162

Intraindustry trade, 70, 181

Investment, 88

Invisible hand, 57

Iran, 18, 126, 133, 155

Iraq, 18, 155, 157, 285

Israel, 155–156, 200

Italy, 135

Jackson-Vanik amendment, 230

Japan, 17, 36, 38, 43, 71, 90, 93, 94, 98, 221, 228, 261, 267, 271

    auto dispute of 1995 with United States, 154

    criticisms of, 176, 179–180

    domestic economy, 182–184

    export restraints, 187–188

    framework negotiations, 191–192

    import barriers, 179–180, 181, 188–190

    import liberalization, 124, 185, 187–188

    industrial policy, 183–184, 280

    keiretsu, 182

    manufacturing sector, 183

    market access. *See* Japan, import liberalization

    market-oriented sector-selective (MOSS), 189

    saving rates, 184

    social values, 182–183

    Structural Impediments Initiative, 154, 190

    trade disputes with United States, 185, 187, 192, 206

    trade surpluses, multilateral, 177, 181

    trade surpluses with United States, 177, 178, 279

    U.S. government attitude toward, 135

    U.S. strategy toward, 135, 138, 175, 184–192, 193, 207, 279–280

    See also Managed trade; Semiconductor agreement, U.S.-Japan

Jobs. *See* Foreign trade, and jobs

Johnson, Lyndon, 96

Joint Economic Committee, 116, 249

Judicial branch, 40, 106

Justice, U.S. Department of, 118

Kennedy, John F., 35, 36, 37

Kennedy Round of multilateral trade negotiations, 37, 38, 205, 211, 261, 262

Kindleberger, Charles, 31

Kissinger, Henry, 245

Korea, North, 22, 155, 157, 229

Korea, South, 76–77, 93, 227–228, 271

Krueger, Anne, 278

Krugman, Paul, 72–73

Kuttner, Robert, 279

Labor. *See* Foreign trade, and jobs

Labor costs, 75–77, 218

Labor, U.S. Department of, 112, 145

Labor standards, 241, 246, 289–290

Laissez-faire, 55

Latin America, 92–93, 219, 225–226. *See also* Debt crisis

LDCs. *See* Less developed countries

Legislative branch. *See* Congress, U.S.

Leontief Paradox, 69
Less developed countries (LDCs), 165, 201,
    217–220, 235, 265–266
Libya, 18, 155, 157
Lobbying, 26, 106, 116–118, 124–128, 263

Malaysia, 227, 228
Managed trade, 278–279
Maquiladoras, 224
Marine Mammal Protection Act, 163
Market failures, 66
Marshall Plan, 34
Mercantilism, 12–13, 56, 180
Mexico, 75, 84, 92, 223, 224, 227, 290
    dolphin-tuna dispute with United States, 163
    trade with United States, 242–243
    See also North American Free Trade Agreement
MFN. *See* Most Favored Nation policy
MIT Commission on Industrial Productivity, 88
MNCs. *See* Multinational corporations
Monopolistic competition, 72–73
Morita, Akio, 180
MOSS. *See* Japan, market-oriented sector-selective
Most Favored Nation policy (MFN), 40, 138,
    229, 231
    China. *See* China, MFN status
    Europe, Eastern, 229–231
    and General Agreement on Tariffs and Trade,
    163
MTNs. *See* Multilateral trade negotiations
Mulroney, Brian, 239, 240
Multifiber Arrangement, 127, 138, 224, 233, 268
Multilateral trade negotiations (MTNs), 39
Multinational corporations (MNCs). *See* Foreign
    direct investment

NAFTA. *See* North American Free Trade
    Agreement
Narcotics Control Act, 157
National Academy of Sciences, 47
National security, 165
National Security Council (NSC), 36, 110, 133
NATO. *See* North Atlantic Treaty Organization
New Economic Policy, 16, 39, 131, 136, 261
Newly industrialized countries (NICs), 41, 71,
    223, 227–228
New protectionism, 41
Nicaragua, 157
NICs. *See* Newly industrialized countries
Nixon, Richard, 16, 38, 39, 48, 131, 146, 230
Nonmarket economies, 229–230

Nontariff barriers (NTABs), 41, 90, 141, 142,
    143, 164, 212, 261
North American Development Bank, 256
North American Free Trade Agreement (NAFTA),
    77–78, 116, 118, 142, 145, 166, 225, 288
    benefits of, 242–244, 245, 247–249
    employment issues, 241, 246, 247, 248, 249,
    252(box)
    foreign direct investment issues, 244, 249
    lobbying, 250–255
    opposition to, 242, 245–246, 248–249, 252
    origins, 239–240
    provisions, 241
    side agreements, 241
North Atlantic Treaty Organization (NATO),
    135, 155
North-South trade. *See* Less developed countries
NSC. *See* National Security Council
NTABs. *See* Nontariff barriers

OECD. *See* Organization for Economic
    Cooperation and Development
Office of Management and Budget (OMB), 110,
    111, 134
Office of Technology Assessment, Congressional,
    115
Oil. *See* Organization of Petroleum Exporting
    Countries; Petroleum, trade in
Oligopolies, 73
OMAs. *See* Orderly marketing agreements
OMB. *See* Office of Management and Budget
Omnibus Trade and Competitiveness Act of 1988,
    42–43, 116, 136, 157, 189, 263
OPEC. *See* Organization of Petroleum Exporting
    Countries
Orderly marketing agreements (OMAs), 14–15,
    38, 41, 43, 90, 91, 135, 138, 164–165,
    187, 188, 207, 283
Organization for Economic Cooperation and
    Development (OECD), 219, 264, 266
Organization of Petroleum Exporting Countries
    (OPEC), 59, 188

Pacific Rim. *See* Asia
Panama, 18, 157
Pareto Improvement, 64
Perot, Ross, 245, 253, 255
Petroleum, trade in, 10, 146, 155, 219–220
Pipeline dispute, U.S.-European, 49, 207
Plaza Agreement, 41, 42, 189
Porter, Michael, 88 –89

Portugal, 200, 210, 249
Preferential trade arrangements. *See* Regional free trade areas
Prestowitz, Clyde, 185
Product cycle theory, 74–75
Productivity, 85, 88, 183
Protectionism, 5–6, 28–32, 61–62, 278
Public Law 480, 152

Quota auctions, 282–283
Quotas. *See* Nontariff barriers

R&D. *See* Research and development
Raymond, Vernon, 74
Reagan, Ronald, 18–19, 41, 42, 48–49, 138, 188–189, 208
Reagonomics, 41, 97
Reciprocal Trade Agreements Act of 1934, 33, 141
Reciprocity, 42, 213, 279
Regional free trade areas, 77–78, 165, 281–282, 288–289, 291
    Western Hemisphere free trade, 225, 226. *See also* North Atlantic Free Trade Agreement; U.S.-Canada Free Trade Agreement.
Republican Party, 27, 30
Research and development (R&D), 13, 88, 281
Results-oriented trade. *See* Managed trade
Ricardo, David, 57–59, 69
Roosevelt, Franklin D., 32
Russia, 155, 220, 231

Safeguard mechanism. *See* Escape clause
Salinas de Gortari, Carlos, 239
Samuelson, Paul, 64, 277
Sanctions. *See* Export policy, U.S.
Sanitary and phytosanitary measures, 170
Saving, 84, 86, 184
Saving-investment balance, 86–87, 97
Science and technology policy. *See* Industrial policy
Second-best policies, 67
Section 201 Provision. *See* Escape clause
Section 232 Provision, 146
Section 301 Provision, 18, 42, 153–154, 192, 234. *See also* Super 301 Provision
Section 337 Provision, 151. *See also* Intellectual property rights
Section 9802 Provision, 223–224
Semiconductor agreement, U.S.-Japan, 106, 136, 153, 189–190
Serbia, 18, 155, 157, 285
Services, trade in, 84–85, 125

and Uruguay Round, 265, 269. *See also* Uruguay Round of multilateral trade negotiations
Shoes. *See* Footware imports
Singapore, 227–228
Smith, Adam, 56, 278
Smithsonian Agreement, 39, 96
Smoot-Hawley Tariff, 32–33, 38, 141, 229
South Africa, 12, 18, 157
South America. *See* Latin America
Soviet Union, 18, 34, 46, 48–49, 146, 155, 229–231
    pipeline, 207
Soybeans, 48, 166, 210–211
Spain, 135, 200, 210, 249
Special 301, 234. *See also* Intellectual property rights
Special Trade Representative. *See* U.S. Trade Representative
Standards, 90, 167, 169, 291
State, U.S. Department of, 35, 36, 110, 133, 135–136
    trade policy responsibilities, 36–37, 110–111, 157
Steel, trade in, 126, 127, 135, 207–208
Stolper-Samuelson Theorem, 63
Strategic trade, theory of, 73–74, 281
Structural Impediments Initiative. *See* Japan
Subsidies, 12, 149–150, 167–168, 208, 264, 268–269, 271, 281. *See also* Countervailing duties
Sugar imports, 127, 226
Summits. *See* Economic summits
Super 301 Provision, 42, 43, 154, 190
Sweden, 200
Syria, 49, 155

Taiwan, 76–77, 227–228
Tariff acts, U.S., 27–28, 29, 31–33
Tariff cuts. *See* Dillon Round of multilateral trade negotiations; General Agreement on Tariffs and Trade; Kennedy Round of multilateral trade negotiations; Tokyo Round of multilateral trade negotiations; Uruguay Round of multilateral trade negotiations
Tariff of Abominations, 29
Tariffs, 89, 142, 164, 261, 283. *See also* Protectionism
Technology. *See* High-tech industries
Telecommunications, trade in, 89, 126, 191
Televisions, trade in, 188
Terms of trade, 59, 179

Textiles, trade in, 38, 127, 138, 223, 224, 233, 251, 268
Thailand, 227–228
Third World. *See* Less developed countries
Tokyo Round of multilateral trade negotiations, 40, 142, 145, 211, 261–263
    agriculture, 204
    codes of conduct. *See* General Agreement on Tariffs and Trade, codes of conduct
    and less developed countries, 222
Toshiba Corporation, 127
Trade. *See* Foreign trade
Trade Act of 1970, 39
Trade Act of 1974, 40–41, 142, 188
Trade Act of 1979, 142
Trade barriers. *See* Protectionism
Trade blocs, 77–78. *See also* Regional free trade areas
Trade deficits. *See* U.S. trade deficits
Trade diversion and trade creation, 78
Trade Expansion Act of 1962, 37, 142
Trade legislation. *See* specific trade bills
Trade liberalization, 2, 6, 11, 33, 36–37, 141–142, 273
    virtues of, 56–62, 198, 241, 266
Trade Policy Review Group, 113
Trade Policy Staff Committee, 113
Trade Promotion Coordinating Committee, 113
Trade-related intellectual property rights (TRIPs), 170, 269–270
Trade-related investment measures (TRIMs), 170, 270
Trade surpluses, 84, 177–181
Trading with the Enemy Act, 156–157
Transportation, U.S. Department of, 112
Treasury, U.S. Department of, 134
    trade policy responsibilities, 23, 111
TRIMs. *See* Trade-related investment measures
TRIPs. *See* Trade-related intellectual property rights
Turkey, 197
Tyson, Laura D'Andrea, 43, 281

Unfair foreign trade practices, 12, 40, 111, 135, 146–151, 165
United Kingdom, 16, 30, 35, 37, 129
United Nations, 12, 157
U.S.-Canada Free Trade Agreement, 142, 165–166, 239

U.S. economy, domestic, 41, 85–87
    impact of foreign trade, 7, 9, 15–16, 44
    saving-investment imbalance, 86–87, 97, 179
U.S. export policy. *See* Export policy
U.S. exports, 15–16, 44, 297–301. *See also* geographical designations and specific products
U.S. import policy. *See* Import policy
U.S. imports, 38–39, 42, 97, 220, 221, 228, 231, 297–302. *See also* geographical designations and specific products
U.S. trade deficits, 39, 42, 84, 96–97, 125
    significance, 83–85
    size, 41
U.S. trade policy. *See* Foreign trade
U.S. Trade Representative (USTR), 37, 92, 109, 133–134, 135, 213, 222, 266
    and Section 301, 153–154
Uruguay Round of multilateral trade negotiations, 89, 142, 166, 211, 256, 288
    agricultural issues, 264, 270–271
    benefits of, 266
    negotiating structure, 265
    origins of, 261–263
    provisions of agreement, 224, 267–272
USA*NAFTA, 255
USTR. *See* U.S. Trade Representative

Vietnam, 18, 157
Voluntary export restraints. *See* Orderly marketing agreements

War of 1812, 29
Ways and Means Committee, House, 116
Wheat, trade in, 48, 131, 155
Wilson, Woodrow, 31
World Bank, 266, 272, 292
World Trade Organization (WTO), 192, 234, 292
    articles of agreement. *See* General Agreement on Tariffs and Trade, articles of agreement
    codes of conduct. *See* General Agreement on Tariffs and Trade, codes of conduct
    creation of, 271–272
    dispute settlement process, 166–167, 206, 271, 272
    and General Agreement on Tariffs and Trade, 162
World War I, 27, 30, 245
World War II, 27, 33, 34
WTO. *See* World Trade Organization